Death is Different

Hugo Adam Bedau

Death is Different

Studies in the

Morality, Law,

and Politics of

Capital Punishment

Northeastern

University Press

Boston

Northeastern University Press

*Library of Congress Cataloging in
Publication Data*

Bedau, Hugo Adam.
  Death is different.

  Bibliography: p.
  Includes index.
   1. Capital punishment—United States.
  2. Capital punishment—United States—
  Moral and ethical aspects. 3. Capital punish-
  ment—Political aspects—United States.
  I. Title.
  HV8699.U5B39   1987   364.6′6′0973
  86-31266
  ISBN 1-55553-008-7 (alk. paper)

Designed by Jennie Ray Bush.
Composed in Sabon by Eastern Typesetting
Company, South Windsor, Connecticut.
Printed and bound by Halliday Lithograph,
Hanover, Massachusetts.
The paper is Warren's #66 Antique, an acid-
free sheet.

MANUFACTURED IN THE UNITED
STATES OF AMERICA
92 91 90 89   5 4 3 2

For Constance

Contents

Acknowledgments

Half the chapters of this book were written first as lectures, either for the classroom (as in the case of Chapter 3) or for special occasions (as was true of the second, fourth, fifth, and seventh chapters). I am grateful to these captive audiences for their patience in bearing with me as I worked out the early versions of my ideas. All the chapters are based on material originally published elsewhere; each has been thoroughly edited for republication in its present form here. In some cases this involved no more than rectifying minor errors, attempting to remove conspicuous blemishes in style and expression, and correcting dated information. In several cases, however, major revisions were undertaken, as anyone who wishes to compare the original versions of the second, fifth, ninth, and tenth chapters with what appears here will easily see.

Because each of the chapters originally had to stand on its own, bits and pieces of my thought reappear and overlap with one another from chapter to chapter. Not in all cases have I tried to excise these ostensibly redundant passages. Although I do not believe any argument is the sounder for being stated more than once, occasional repetition of central ideas or of important dates and facts can help to fix them more indelibly in the reader's mind.

Conspicuously missing here are dozens of footnotes that appeared in the originals. Half of the book's ten chapters were first published in law reviews, and law review editors impose a standard of citation that most readers—including most scholars—would regard as excessive. I have removed such needless references with no small satisfaction. Many of them have been obviated by the Table of Cases.

The provenance of the essays is as follows:

Chapter 1 originally appeared under the title "Capital Punishment," in *Matters of Life and Death*, ed. Tom Regan (New York, Random House, 1980, 2nd ed., 1986), pp. 175–212. © 1980, 1986, Random House, Inc.

Chapter 2 is an expanded and much-revised version of the main part of an essay, "The Death Penalty and the State's Right to Kill," originally written for presentation at a symposium on the death penalty held at the School of Criminal Justice, Rutgers University, Newark, New Jersey, in 1984.

Chapter 3 originally appeared under the title "Bentham's Utilitarian Critique of the Death Penalty," in *The Journal of Criminal Law and Criminology* 74, no. 3, fall 1983, pp. 1033–66.

Chapter 4 was previously published under the title "Thinking About the Death Penalty as a Cruel and Unusual Punishment," *U. C. Davis Law Review* 18, no. 4, summer 1985, pp. 873–925.

Chapter 5 is a much-revised, updated, and expanded version of an essay that appeared originally as "The Death Penalty in the United States: Imposed Law and the Role of Moral Elites," in *The Imposition of Law*, edited by Sandra B. Burnam and Barbara Harrell-Bond (New York, Academic Press, 1979), pp. 45–68. © 1979 by Academic Press, Inc.

Chapter 6 appeared originally as "The 1964 Death Penalty Referendum in Oregon: Some Notes from a Participant-Observer," *Crime & Delinquency* 26, no. 4, October 1980, pp. 528–36.

Chapter 7 was published originally under the title "*Gregg* v. *Georgia* and the 'New' Death Penalty," *Criminal Justice Ethics* 4, no. 2, summer/ fall 1985, pp. 3–17.

Chapter 8 is a revised version of an essay, "The Death Penalty and State Constitutional Rights in the United States of America," which appeared in a United Nations publication, *Crime Prevention and Criminal Justice Newsletter,* nos. 12 and 13, November 1986, pp. 19–24.

Chapter 9 is a revised version of an essay originally published as "Felony Murder Rape and the Mandatory Death Penalty: A Study in Discretionary Justice," *Suffolk University Law Review* 10, no. 3, spring 1976, pp. 493–520. The second section of that paper, reviewing the literature, has been omitted from the version published here.

Chapter 10 first appeared as "Witness to a Persecution: The Death

Penalty and the Dawson Five," *Black Law Journal* 8, no. 1, 1983, pp. 7–28. The version reprinted here omits the closing section of that article.

An earlier and much briefer version of the Conclusion was part of my prepared testimony on H.R. 2837 and other bills relating to the federal death penalty, presented in April 1986 to the Subcommittee on Criminal Justice, Committee on the Judiciary, House of Representatives. A version substantially identical with the one that appears here was published under the title "Reflections on the Morality of the Death Penalty: Exposing the Myths," in *The Defender,* published by the New York State Defenders' Association, 8, no. 2, July/August 1986, pp. 19–22.

It remains only to thank those who helped in various ways to bring this book to fruition. First and foremost is Constance Putnam. I cannot praise her enough for the intensity, patience, and skill with which she has worked with me to improve these essays for (re)publication. The reader, too, should be grateful for the many improvements she has made in my style, diction, and grammar, all of which help these essays to read more smoothly than they otherwise would. With gratitude and affection I dedicate the book to her.

Additional editorial assistance was provided at a critical stage by Karen Hohner. Deborah Kops, of Northeastern University Press, was a source of encouragement from the start and, as the book developed, more than once made helpful suggestions and talked me out of some of my more unworkable ideas.

Other debts, less encompassing but no less deserving of acknowledgment, were incurred in the course of producing several of the essays. My colleague Dan Dennett gave me the benefit of his experience in the classroom using an earlier version of Chapter 1, and this led to some useful revisions. In the preparation of Chapter 3, I was much stimulated by the invitation in 1977 to present a talk to the Thyssen Philosophical Group, all of whose members at that session, and especially the two other invited guests—Charles L. Black, Jr., and Henry Schwarzschild—gave me provocative responses. Watt Espy used the resources of his incomparable archives on death sentences and executions to answer a query. Stephen Nathanson's comments on an earlier draft of the chapter were quite helpful and encouraging. I first sketched out my ideas for Chapter 5 in conversation with my son, Mark Bedau, and I am grateful to him for his perceptive reactions. My colleagues in the Tufts Sociology Colloquium gave me some helpful criticism on the first draft, and I am grateful to Richard Moran for his comments on the version I presented to the Conference on The Social Consequences of Imposed Law, held at

Warwick University in April 1978. The initial version of Chapter 6 was much improved by criticism from two of my colleagues in the 1964 Oregon referendum campaign, Mike Katz and Janet McLennan. Conversations with Henry Schwarzschild—invariably stimulating, not least when they are the most diverting—helped set me straight on several matters germane to my theme in Chapters 7 and 8. The research reported in Chapter 9 could not have been done without grant support from the Ford Foundation and LEAA to the Center for Studies in Criminology and Criminal Justice, University of Pennsylvania, for its project on the Death Penalty and Discretion in the Criminal Justice System. I am indebted to Marvin E. Wolfgang, the Center's director, for having enough confidence in me—a philosopher, not a criminologist—to let me direct the Massachusetts portion of the research project. The six undergraduate students at Tufts without whose labors there would have been no data to analyze have my thanks here as well as at the beginning of Chapter 9. The events reported in Chapter 10 would never have happened, or at least would have happened without involving me, had it not been for Team Defense and its director, Millard Farmer, having invited me to serve as an expert witness in the Dawson Five case. The text of my essay would contain little of the exact language used by the principals in the case, inside or outside the courtroom colloquy, were it not for the generosity of attorney Roy Herron, who put his transcript of the trial at my disposal. Jan Stepan, vice-director of the Swiss Institute of Comparative Law, provided me with information—as he so often has—that I could obtain nowhere else. Stephen Nathanson asked me to read a draft of his forthcoming book on the death penalty, and some of his ideas, I am sure, helped to shape my thoughts in several places in Chapter 2 and the conclusion, though I fully absolve him of any fault for my errors in what I have written under his influence. To all these friends, colleagues, and former students, I am most grateful.

Authors also learn from their critics and from others who disagree with them, or at any rate they say they do; and I would not deny that the views of those who have disagreed with me in writing—notably Raoul Berger, Walter Berns, and Ernest van den Haag—have occasionally stimulated me to think again about this or that point. Accordingly, here and there in the following pages I have replied to their criticisms or commented on their views at variance with my own. In order to keep the text as free as possible from polemic, I have confined my rebuttals to the footnotes. The interested reader can locate these passages quickly enough by using the index entries under the names of the above writers.

Death is Different

Introduction

In 1976 the United States Supreme Court ruled that the death penalty is not unconstitutional: Although some of the laws imposing or regulating the administration of the death penalty might be in violation of the constitutional prohibition against "cruel and unusual punishment," or some other provision of the Bill of Rights, the death penalty per se is not a mode of punishment absolutely barred by the federal Constitution. Six months later, in January 1977, the first lawful execution under the "new" death penalty laws took place. In the decade since that execution, more than half a hundred other convicted murderers have been executed in a dozen states. The moratorium on the death penalty, which began in 1967 and seemed to many (including me) to have ushered in a new era, now appears to have been but a brief interlude. Today the death penalty looks reasonably secure to most observers.

"Reasonably"? The ardent defenders of capital punishment in our society think otherwise. For them, the nearly two thousand prisoners awaiting execution on the death rows of America are a constant irritant. Angered by the temporizing decisions of the state and federal appellate courts that delay these executions, furious with the largely volunteer defense attorneys whose persistence in postconviction litigation is unflagging, intolerant of elected or appointed officials who stand in the way of carrying out death warrants, complacent in the knowledge that the vast majority of the American public professes to favor the death penalty for murderers—these "hanghards" (as Arthur Koestler once called their counterparts in England) fear the death penalty is not secure at all, let alone "reasonably."

Those of us who oppose the death penalty also find little or nothing "reasonable" in the way in which killing as a punishment continues to exert its grip on the imagination of the public. Frustrated by our inability to persuade our elected representatives and governors to limit or abolish the death penalty, indignant with the way appellate courts often give no more than perfunctory review of the issues in capital cases and thereby abet the race to execute, disgusted by the capricious and arbitrary manner in which criminals are selected for a death sentence, mindful of the follies now enshrined in the laws that regulate the use of capital punishment—we find nothing "reasonable" in its current status, either.

The purpose of the essays in this book is to investigate and challenge any claim to reasonableness that this kind of punishment has. My theme, expressed in an epigram borrowed from one of the Supreme Court's death penalty opinions, is that *death is different* from other punishments practiced in our society—different in its morality, its politics, and its symbolism. My belief and hope is that once these differences are truly understood, support for punitive killing will lessen and eventually subside.

For nearly thirty years I have written, spoken, and—where opportunity allowed—worked actively with others to nullify death sentences and to repeal or oppose the enactment of capital statutes. From the beginning, I have been convinced that one should not oppose this (or any other) provision of the law without good reasons, and that the best reasons would be found only in a comprehensive study of the whole subject in its historical, political, legal, and moral dimensions. The essays that this book comprises, originally written independently of each other and for different audiences, constitute a series of investigations that examine different themes along each of these dimensions. They do not, I confess, discuss the death penalty from the standpoint of someone earnestly trying to find out whether to support or oppose it. For me that question was answered years before the first of these essays was written in 1976. Instead, what I do in this volume is develop, criticize, and explore a variety of arguments addressed to some of the specific questions that have figured in the ongoing debate over the death penalty.

Paramount among these questions is what *morality* has to say about the death penalty: What should we say for or against the death penalty from the moral point of view? Does the state have the right to kill as a punishment? Ought the state to exercise this right? Do even murderers have a right to life? How are such conflicting claims to be balanced against each other? Is the death penalty a "cruel and unusual punishment"? Are the laws that currently govern the death penalty defensible on moral grounds? Such questions have always seemed the most appropriate ones for me, as a philosopher, to explore in detail—lest they be ignored, left to brief comments by editorial writers, or dismissed out of hand as answerable only by appeal to personal moral convictions. In this book I try to set out my answers in enough detail so that one can see exactly what the issues are, and how, step by step, I propose to resolve them.

In addition to these normative and philosophical questions, I have also had occasion to address others of an empirical nature, and thus to think and write as a practicing social scientist might: Has opposition to the death penalty in the past generation been owing to nothing more than the persistent agitation of an intransigent elite, a self-appointed "Moral Minority"? What are the provisions of the "new" death penalty laws, and have they really improved on the laws they replaced? What can we learn from a careful study of how capital laws are applied in practice, such as the one statute in the nation that authorized a mandatory death penalty for the crime of felony-murder-rape? How did it happen, only two decades ago, that in one state the voters actually went to the polls and repealed the death penalty? These are among the many interesting and important questions that need to be answered in a thorough study of the death penalty.

The first essay, "A Matter of Life and Death," is an introductory yet comprehensive evaluation of the death penalty from the standpoint of some of the moral principles that a rational theory of punishment generally would include. I do not hold the view that there is some one moral principle or ethical ideal according to which we can settle the death penalty dispute, provided only we can identify the principle, get everyone to acknowledge it, and then apply it to get the correct result. Instead, I try first to identify a variety of plausible moral principles. Then I argue that these principles, taken together with the relevant facts of the matter, do lead to the conclusion that—on the balance of reasons—we ought to oppose capital punishment.

The next two chapters pursue in greater detail issues raised in the opening chapter. "The Right to Life and the Right to Kill" continues the discussion by addressing the two questions implied by the title. It explores whether the offender has a right to life, whether the state has the right to kill offenders as their punishment, and how the conflict between these two rights can be resolved. I argue that neither right is absolute, that the individual's is the more fundamental, and that—contrary to what philosophers such as John Locke argued long ago—*our* state ought not to claim or to act on this right.

The third essay, "A Utilitarian Critique of the Death Penalty," is a close examination of the most original and historically important criticism of the death penalty in the past two centuries, developed by the English philosopher and social reformer Jeremy Bentham. My purpose here is a double one: exploration in great detail of the nature of Bentham's argument, and evaluation of it in light of recent thinking about utilitarianism as well as current evidence on the nature of the death penalty in our society. I do not think that a purely utilitarian approach to social policy, especially with regard to the penal code, can suffice, and in this essay (as well as in those immediately preceding and following) I try to explain why.

The next essay, "Cruel and Unusual Punishment," is the longest and the most ambitious study in the book and therefore the centerpiece of the volume. More time and effort has gone into constructing it than all the other essays in the book combined, and I am still not wholly satisfied with the result. (The views expressed here also reflect a significant change in my thinking over what I originally wrote on this topic twenty years ago, reprinted as one of the chapters in my previous book of essays on this subject, *The Courts, The Constitution, and Capital Punishment.*) In this essay I try to show exactly what makes a punishment "cruel and unusual," and why we should judge that the death penalty in our society deserves that evaluative description. Throughout, my emphasis is not on what the Supreme Court says the Bill of Rights means by its clause prohibiting "cruel and unusual punishments," but on what such a constraint ought to mean to anyone concerned to limit the severity of punishments in a civilized society.

The fifth essay, "The Death Penalty, Imposed Law, and the Role of Moral Elites," moves the discussion away from a focus primarily on moral issues to empirical (historical and political) questions. The task here is to explore whether the de jure suspension of the death penalty for a decade (1967–1976), mainly as a consequence of skillful and sustained appellate litigation over federal constitutional issues, was a case of a self-appointed moral elite imposing its views on an unwilling but somnolent majority. I argue that such a view, plausible though it may be and attractive as it no doubt is to supporters of the death penalty, offers a far from adequate explanation. One critic of my argument in this essay thought that my alternative explanation was no more convincing than the one to which I objected.[1] In order to discourage other readers from reaching the same conclusion, I have used the present occasion to bolster my argument where I could.

In the next essay, "Abolishing the Death Penalty at the Polls," I have provided a detailed account of electoral political behavior in the 1964 public referendum campaign over the death penalty in Oregon. This short essay affords the opportunity to examine the death penalty controversy as a political issue in one of its most interesting settings, and gives some needed detail for the whole theme of abolishing or suspending the death penalty as a case of imposed law.

The seventh essay, "The 'New' Death Penalty Laws," brings the focus of discussion onto the current features of capital punishment as they stand after a decade of review and revision from the state legislatures and the federal appellate courts. Here I offer a critical evaluation of some of the main features of these current laws and of the leading Supreme Court rulings that produced them. The essay begins by reviewing the Court's reasoning in *Gregg v. Georgia,* the major 1976 case affirming the constitutionality of capital punishment. I explain why the statutes upheld by *Gregg* and subsequent cases have not significantly modified the way the death penalty is administered over what had been condemned in 1972 by the Supreme Court in its path-breaking ruling against the death penalty in *Furman v. Georgia.*

The next essay explores further details of the constitutional status of the death penalty. This chapter, "State Constitutional Law and the Death Penalty," shifts attention from the federal to the state appellate courts. Since the early 1970s, efforts have proved successful in several states to establish the unconstitutionality of capital punishment by reference to state constitutional law. In California, Oregon, and Washington, these rulings were overturned by the public at the polls. Not so in Massachusetts, New York, and Rhode Island. The story is largely untold; it deserves closer scrutiny.

The ninth essay, "Punishing Felony-Murder-Rape with a Mandatory Death Penalty," examines in detail the actual administration of an unusual and important capital statute in Massachusetts. When the Supreme Court in 1976 upheld the constitutionality of several capital statutes, it also decided in another case, *Woodson v. North Carolina,* that a *mandatory* death penalty for murder was unconstitutional. One of the few surviving mandatory death penalty laws in the United States relevant to the normal operation of the criminal justice system was the Massachusetts law that authorized a mandatory death penalty for anyone convicted of felony-murder-rape. The research reported in this essay, generously described by one criminologist as a "model of the kind of sociolegal research that needs to be conducted on a more extensive basis,"[2] shows the folly of thinking that, just because a legislature enacts a statute with mandatory punitive provisions, the criminal courts will in fact convict and sentence the guilty accordingly. Instead what we find is further evidence of discretionary justice, mocking the pretensions of those who think they can have both capital punishment and justice.

The final essay, "Witness to a Persecution," tells a personal story of events in a rural Georgia courtroom in 1977. Its larger purpose is to point out once again the arbitrary, and to that extent lawless, quality of the conduct of those empowered to prosecute capital cases. Because death is different and there is no effective way to limit or regulate the power to prosecute a criminal case, we have further reason to abolish the death penalty.

In the Conclusion, I make no attempt to review or summarize the arguments of the several essays preceding. Instead, I survey briefly the half-dozen major reasons why, in my view, people—or at least most Americans today—profess to support the death penalty. More than anything else, I believe, it is the symbolic role of this penalty that is paramount. The symbolism of power, rather than a sober desire for social defense and a reflective commitment to retributive justice, is what accounts for the death penalty's current level of popularity. Only when that symbolism is understood and discredited can we hope to live in a society that abandons the squalid practice of killing an arbitrary handful of criminals by electrocution, cyanide gas, or poisonous injection.

Chapter 1

A Matter of
Life and Death

I

When we confront the task of evaluating punishments from the moral
point of view, a host of questions immediately arises: Who should be punished? What offenses and harms should be made liable to punishment? What
is involved in making a punishment fit a crime? Are some punishments too
cruel or barbaric to be tolerated no matter how effective they may be in
preventing crime? Are some criminals so depraved or dangerous that no
punishment is too severe for them? What moral principles should govern
our thinking about crime and punishment?

In order to give reasonable answers to such questions, we need to appeal
to a wide variety of empirical facts. We will want to know, for example,
what would happen to the crime rate if no one were punished at all, or if
all convicted offenders were punished more leniently or more severely than
is now usual. We will want to know whether the system of criminal justice
operates with adequate efficiency and fairness when it metes out punishment,
or whether the severest punishments tend to fall mainly upon some social
or racial classes. We will also want to settle other things besides these matters
of fact. Social values, moral ideals, ethical principles are involved, and we
will want to know which values and which ideals they are and how to
evaluate them as well. Central among these ethical considerations are the

value, worth, and dignity of persons—the victims of crime, the offenders, and the rest of society. How, exactly, does our belief in the value of human life, the worth of each person, our common humanity, and our common dignity bear on the nature and methods of punishment as seen from the moral point of view?

No better setting in which to examine these questions exists than the one provided by the controversy over the morality of capital punishment. From a historical perspective, one of the most important relevant ethical values is the idea of *the sanctity of human life*. The idea derives from some of the earliest passages in the Old Testament. The central biblical text is Genesis 1:27, where we are told that "God created man in his own image." Other peoples of antiquity—the Homeric Greeks, the ancient Egyptians, Persians, and Babylonians—of course showed concern for the value of human life. The idea that human life is of transcendent worth, however, independent of the value that can be placed on a person by virtue of efforts, accomplishments, talents, or any other measure, and that this worth is equal for all, is an inescapably religious notion, and it is biblical in origin.

With the rise of rationalist thought in European culture during the Renaissance and the Enlightenment and the concurrent decline in an exclusively religious foundation for moral principles, philosophers increasingly gave their support to the doctrine of *the rights of man* as the basis for constitutional law and public morality. This doctrine took many forms; it is a prominent part of the moral, political, and legal thinking of the most influential European, British, and American writers of that era. Although these thinkers differed in their views about the nature of rights, all agreed that first and foremost among them was "the right to life."

Distinct as the sanctity of human life and the right to life are, they have a common bond. Each expresses the view that it is morally wrong to take a purely instrumental view of human life. By "instrumental view of human life" I mean any conception that makes it permissible to kill persons in order to protect some other value (e.g., property) or in order to advance some social or political goal (e.g., national liberation). If every human life is sacred or if every person has a right to life, then the murder of an insignificant peasant is just as heinous as the assassination of a king. Likewise, deliberately killing thousands in order to advance the welfare even of millions is forbidden. On an instrumental view of human life, however, when other things are assumed to be more "valuable" or "worthy" than the lives of some people, the deaths of many persons often can be justified as necessary to the accomplishment of various social goals. For example, in the eyes of the Nazis, the triumph of the "master race" justified the murder of millions of Jews and other "inferior" peoples. But if everyone has a right to life, or if everyone's life is sacred, then genocidal murder cannot be justified and stands condemned as a grave crime against humanity.

So far as the death penalty is concerned, it might seem that once it is granted that human life is sacred or that everyone has an equal right to life, the death penalty has to be morally indefensible. Such a punishment seems obviously inconsistent with ideals of human worth and value. The opposite, however, is true if we let history be our guide. Chief among the traditional defenders of capital punishment have been religious and secular thinkers who sincerely believed in these ideals. In fact, these thinkers usually invoked the sanctity of human life and the right to life as part of their defense and justification of death for murderers and other criminals. To see how such a seemingly paradoxical doctrine can be maintained, as well as to begin our examination of the major issues involved in the moral evaluation of the death penalty, we must scrutinize the traditional doctrine of the right to life.

II

The general idea shared by many philosophers, beginning in the seventeenth century, was that each person by nature—that is, apart from the laws of the state and simply by virtue of being born a human being—had the right to live. From this it followed that it was a violation of that right to kill another person, and that it was the responsibility of government to protect human rights, prohibit murder, and try to arrest, convict, and punish anyone guilty of this crime. Thus, the right to life can be thought of, first, as underlying the prohibition against murder common to the criminal law of all countries. On some versions of the theory, God was thought to be the source of this and other "natural rights," though few philosophers assumed a necessary connection between everyone's having the right to life and the existence of God as the creator. Hence, the right to life can be understood without significant distortion as a secular notion, free of any essentially religious overtones, and thus available to the moral philosophy of theist, atheist, and agnostic alike.

In addition to being *natural*, the right to life was traditionally understood to be *universal* and *inalienable*. A universal right is a right that everyone has, regardless of where one is born or lives and regardless of sex or race.

11

An inalienable right is a right that the possessor cannot transfer, sell, or give away to another person. Thus, killing one person is as much a violation of the right to life as killing any other person, and we cannot somehow give to others the right to kill us by giving up to them our right to life.

Any doctrine of rights that includes a right to life would seem to pose a problem for a policy of capital punishment.[1] Even if a person has committed murder (so the argument runs) and has therewith intentionally violated another's right to life, the criminal still has his or her own right to life. Would it not be a violation of the murderer's right for him or her to be put to death as punishment? If so, must not capital punishment be morally wrong? A few philosophers—notably Hobbes, Rousseau, and Beccaria—show signs of having been troubled by these questions, but they are the exceptions. Most philosophical proponents of the doctrine of a natural right to life were not troubled by them at all, because they adopted one or another variant of the position influentially expressed by Locke. It will suffice for our purposes to examine his views.

Locke argued that although a person's right to life is natural and inalienable, it can be "forfeited" and *is* forfeited whenever one person violates that right in another. A recent philosopher has made the point even more explicitly: "The offender, by violating the life, liberty, or property of another, has lost his own right to have his life, liberty, or property respected. . . ."[2] The idea is a familiar one, although there are troubling and unanswered questions: Can this right, once forfeited, ever be restored? If so, by whom? Under what conditions? Thanks to the doctrine of forfeiture, it was possible for Locke to assert without apparent contradiction both that everyone has a natural right to life and that the death penalty for a murderer does not violate that right.

Locke's actual reasoning was somewhat more complex and less plausible, but more revealing, than this makes it sound. According to Locke, a person forfeits his right to life whenever he or she commits a criminal act "that deserves death."[3] One obvious problem with this formulation is that it permits the use of capital punishment not only for murderers but for almost any crime whatever. Not only treason and the other traditional felonies (arson, rape, robbery, burglary) but relatively minor offenses against property and public order as well could be said to be properly punished by death. All that is required is some good argument to show that crime x "deserves" such punishment. It will then follow that anyone guilty of x has "forfeited" the natural right to life. Everything turns on the criterion used to decide whether a crime "deserves" death or some lesser penalty. Locke seems not to have given any thought to that issue. What he says is that in a "state of nature" we may punish "each transgression . . . to the degree, and with as much severity, as will suffice to make it an ill bargain to the offender, give him cause to repent, and terrify others from doing the like."[4] However rationally this may have been expressed, it does not give us much guidance for the use of capital punishment in a "state of civil society."

Locke's very sweeping doctrine of forfeiture was carried over intact a century later by the jurist Sir William Blackstone in his monumental *Commentary on the Laws of England*. Thus, the seeming inconsistency of English legal philosophy being founded on a doctrine of natural rights (including the right to life) and English criminal law authorizing capital punishment for dozens of minor offenses against property (by 1800, there were some two hundred capital offenses, ranging from arson in the dockyards to theft of goods from a bleaching ground) disappears. Locke's doctrine of forfeiture shows why the idea of a natural, universal, and inalienable right to life was not, historically, a rigid moral barrier to capital punishment. The right to life had never been seen as an *absolute* right.

Various objections to the classic theory of the right to life can be raised; two of them deserve to be mentioned here. First, underlying Locke's doctrine of natural rights and wholly independent of it are two important assumptions. One is that punishment under law is necessary for social defense. ("Social defense" refers to the prevention of crime by means of deterrence and incapacitation, as well as by the avoidance of incentives and opportunities for the commission of crimes. Thus prisons, police forces, controlling the sale of firearms, locks on doors, and threats of punishment can all be regarded as methods of social defense.) The other is that justice requires retribution: Criminals deserve to be punished, and the punishment must fit the crime. Such beliefs lead to the conclusion that the punishment for murder and other crimes should be death; they also force Locke to make some accommodation in his theory of natural rights. The device he hit upon, as we have seen—and one that subsequent generations of thinkers have also adopted—is to declare that the right to life could be forfeited under certain conditions.

Against Locke's doctrine of forfeiture several objections deserve to be considered. First of all, there are other alternatives. Suppose it is argued (as some of Locke's successors, notably Hegel, did) that one of the offender's natural rights is the right to be punished. If there is such a right, one that governs the appropriate responses of society to the offender, then it is an open question whether the offender's life is to be taken as his punishment.[5]

13

Alternatively, suppose it is argued that although punishments typically constitute harms or deprivations to the person who undergoes them, this is not necessary. What is necessary is that the punishment be imposed on the offender regardless of his preferences and choice. On this view, while it would be necessary for the offender to forfeit some rights in order to be punished, it would not be necessary to forfeit the right to life. Yet another possibility is to regard the right to life as an absolute right, one that cannot be forfeited and one that it is always wrong to violate. Whether any of these alternatives can be better supported than the doctrine of forfeiture need not be resolved here. They do show that forfeiture of rights as Locke presents it is not the only way to permit punishment under a theory of natural rights.

Another difficulty with Locke's doctrine is that it seems to collapse two distinct issues into one. Appealing to the forfeiture of rights in order to permit society to punish the guilty offender in the first place is one thing. Appealing to the forfeiture of rights in order to decide which among the available punishments is the appropriate one is quite another. Forfeiture is a plausible, even if (as we have seen above) not a necessary, solution to the first problem; but Locke uses it primarily in regard to the second. On his own assumptions, he is correct only if retributive justice and social defense in general require the death penalty for murderers. Otherwise, Locke's argument that a murderer (or any other criminal) forfeits the right to life collapses. This criticism is extremely important. There is no intrinsic feature of any natural right, including the right to life, that makes it subject to loss through forfeiture. The only basis for supposing that any right is forfeited rather than grossly violated by society when it punishes an offender by death is that just retribution and social defense together require the death penalty for offenders guilty of a crime of this sort. If this requirement turns out to be false, unsubstantiated, or doubtful, then the claim that a criminal's right to life has been forfeited turns out to be equally false, unsubstantiated, or doubtful. Since so much turns, therefore, on these questions of the necessity of the death penalty for just retribution and social defense, I shall return to examine them in more detail below.

Even if one concludes that a murderer or other felon does forfeit the natural right to life, however, it does not follow that a murderer *must* be put to death. The doctrine of forfeiture does not involve the idea that once a person forfeits a right to *x*, then those to whom it is forfeited have a *duty* to take *x* away from that person. Those who insist that the death penalty is justified because murderers forfeit their lives often overlook this point. Forfeiting one's *right* to life is not and should never be considered identical with forfeiting one's life. A person may in fact continue to possess something for which he or she has forfeited the right of possession (by, say, failing to renew the lease on a house he or she still occupies); just so, the government may decide to let a person live who under the doctrine of forfeiture "deserves" to die. Furthermore, it may be that nothing wrong is being done—to the criminal's victims, to the rest of society, or even to the criminal. Another way of putting it is this: Although a person may have forfeited the right to life, it is within *our* rights to let him or her live; in doing so we do not necessarily violate any duty. What is true is that a person who has forfeited the right to life but nevertheless continues to live cannot claim to do so on the ground of that right. Whether we do the wrong thing in not killing someone who has forfeited the right to life is, of course, a further question (and I shall return to it in the next chapter). But enough has been said to show that even if someone has forfeited the right to life, that does not morally *require* that he or she be put to death.

Finally, we should note that Locke's doctrine of forfeiture makes his theory of natural rights vulnerable to utilitarian reasoning, with devastating effect. The chief attraction of the idea of natural rights is that it purports to provide each of us with moral armor (our rights) to protect us against burdens and deprivations that might otherwise be imposed. But Locke's theory requires any offender to forfeit the right to life whenever that is "deserved" by virtue of the nature of the offense. Surely, the harm done in a crime is part of its nature. Hence, it can be argued that crimes other than murder (such as treason, espionage, arson, rape) also "deserve" the death penalty because no other punishment can provide comparable protection for society. One may well doubt whether a theory of natural rights not impervious to reasoning of this sort is worth defending.

III

Although Kant by no means repudiated the doctrine of natural rights, he elevated to primary importance a different idea, the supreme worth or dignity of each person. The most famous single passage in which this doctrine and Kant's views on the punishment of murder are brought together runs as follows:

> If . . . he has committed a murder, he must die. In this case, there is no substitute that will satisfy the requirements of legal justice. There is no sameness of kind between death and remaining alive even under the most miserable conditions, and consequently there is no equality between the crime and the retribution

15

unless the criminal is judicially condemned and put to death. But the death of the criminal must be kept entirely free of any maltreatment that would make an abomination of the humanity residing in the person suffering it. Even if a civil society were to dissolve itself by common agreement of all its members (for example, if the people inhabiting an island decided to separate and disperse themselves around the world), the last murderer remaining in prison must first be executed, so that everyone will duly receive what his actions are worth and so that the bloodguilt thereof will not be fixed on the people because they failed to insist on carrying out the punishment; for if they fail to do so, they may be regarded as accomplices in this public violation of legal justice.[6]

We may ignore Kant's appeal here to the idea of the "bloodguilt" incurred by murder. The notion that murder, unlike other crimes, is a pollution that deeply stains the social fabric has ancient origins; but it cannot be taken literally today and made part of the theory of punishment appropriate for a secular society. The idea of the dignity of man, however, is more promising. For Kant, that idea enters explicitly only to rule out any aggravations and brutality attendant upon the sentence of death and its execution. For Kant, the dignity of man underlies the whole idea of a society of free and rational persons choosing to submit themselves to a common rule of law that includes the punishment of crimes. Accordingly, in punishment, "a human being can never be manipulated merely as a means to the purposes of someone else. . . . His innate personality protects him against such treatment. . . ."[7] Kant must therefore also reject the idea that a murderer should be punished with death because by doing so we prevent him from killing again and also discourage others from murder. Kant's appeal to the dignity of man requires him to rule out any role for incapacitative or deterrent benefits in the justification of capital punishment.

As the passage above also shows, underlying Kant's belief in the appropriateness of punishing murder with death is a principle of just retribution. This is reminiscent of Locke's view (recall the weight he attached to the idea of crimes that "deserve" the punishment of death), and it is probably also an echo of the ancient law of retaliation, *lex talionis* ("a life for a life"). The chief difference between Kant and Locke is that Locke thinks it is proper to take into account not only just retribution but also social defense to determine proper punishments, whereas Kant unequivocally rules out the latter. What Kant has done is to present us with two moral ideas—the dignity or worth of each person as a rational creature, and the principle of just retribution—that he regards as inextricably tied together. The latter principle he explained in the following way:

What kind and what degree of punishment does public legal justice adopt as
its principle and standard? None other than the principle of equality . . . , that
is, the principle of not treating one side more favorably than the other. Accordingly, any undeserved evil that you inflict on someone else among the
people is one that you do to yourself. . . . Only the Law of retribution . . .
can determine exactly the kind and degree of punishment. . . . All other standards fluctuate back and forth and, because extraneous considerations are
mixed with them, they cannot be compatible with the principle of pure and
strict legal justice.[8]

Kant, as is obvious from his remarks, thought that retribution *required* the
death penalty for murder. His view has widespread appeal even today.

Although Kant does not stress the point in the passages I have quoted,
he must have realized that apportioning punishments to crimes is not so
simple in actual practice as his principle of retribution seems to imply. A
person deserves to be punished, by Kant's reasoning, only when no excuse
or justification for the killer's conduct exists. In other words, only "inner
viciousness," manifested by someone's having "rationally willed" to kill
another entirely innocent person undeserving of any harm, "deserves" punishment. But Kant gave no clues on how to judge or recognize true "inner
viciousness."

If modern criminologists and psychologists are correct, however, most
murders are not committed by persons whose state of mind can be described
as Kant implies.[9] Empirical (clinical, experimental) criminology requires us
to test and verify our assumptions regarding the psychology (motivation,
intention, state of mind) of each person who kills, whereas Kant's theory
is formulated from beginning to end without regard to any empirical considerations at all. He argues abstractly and theoretically that *if* anyone
rationally wills the death of an innocent party and acts on that decision,
then such a person deserves to be put to death. Because such an abstract
doctrine is quite consistent with the reality described by social and clinical
scientists (few who perpetrate violent crimes act in such a coolly deliberate
and rational fashion), it is theoretically possible to accept Kant's doctrine
of just punishment and the death penalty for murder while opposing the
actual execution of most (perhaps even all) convicted murderers. Kant seems
to have entirely overlooked this possibility, owing perhaps to his unfamil-
iarity with criminal psychopathology and to the primitive state of the social,
behavioral, and clinical sciences of his day. Whether today we should accept
a doctrine of just retribution even in the abstract remains to be seen. Later
in this chapter I shall examine some of the most important retributive
principles that bear on the death penalty controversy.

17

In the course of presenting Kant's views, I have already identified three respects in which his theory is vulnerable. One is that, like Locke's, it assumes that just retribution *requires* capital punishment for murder. This assumption may be unnecessary and is in any case not proved. Another difficulty is that, unlike Locke's theory, Kant's seems to make no room whatever for the role of social defense in the justification of punishment. Because Kant's theory excludes this, one cannot argue (as utilitarians would) that if social defense does not require capital punishment for murderers or other criminals, then it is to that extent morally wrong to inflict this punishment on them. But one should be able to argue against a mode of punishment in this way, even if one concedes to Kant that social defense cannot be the only consideration in a system of just punishment.

Finally, a third objection follows from the fact that Kant's theory is so obviously abstract and unempirical from beginning to end. If we really take seriously the idea of the dignity of man, we may well be led in case after case of actual crime to reject Kant's reasoning on the ground that it is inapplicable in light of the actual facts of the case. Kant's theory tells us what to do only with ideally rational killers; what we need is a theory that tells us how to cope with the actual persons who kill. We need also to know how to deal with murderers in a way that acknowledges our common humanity with both the victim and the offender. The injustices to which all social systems are prone and the wisdom of self-restraint in the exercise of violence, especially when it is undertaken deliberately and in the name of justice, must not be forgotten.

IV

In sharp contrast to Kant, for whom social benefits deriving from the death penalty played no role in its justification, utilitarian thinkers have always viewed the beneficial and harmful consequences of law or policy as the only factors to be taken into account in evaluating it from the moral point of view. (Locke's theory, as we can now see more clearly, uneasily straddles the middle ground between these two extremes.) Just as Kant disregarded considerations of consequences in evaluating the morality of capital punishment, so utilitarians disregard any appeals to natural rights or the dignity of man. For them, these ideas at best mask a reference to social benefits; more likely, they are moral standards independent of (and thus potentially in conflict with) the principle of utility. At worst, they are rhetorical phrases of dubious content. The utilitarian, therefore, regards the death penalty—like everything else—as justified by the degree to which it advances the general welfare. Accordingly, its justification proceeds in the following manner: (1) consider the practice of the death penalty and all its present and future consequences—for the executed offenders, for the victims of crime, their friends and families, and the rest of society; (2) consider each of the alternative modes of punishment that might be imposed and their consequences were they to be employed instead; (3) decide in favor of the death penalty rather than any alternative only if, in light of all the facts, its practice would have the greatest balance of benefit over harm for everyone affected by it.

Two things are noteworthy about such a pattern of reasoning. First, everything depends on the facts, and diverse and complex facts are always in question. Moreover, these facts are not likely to remain constant in a given society decade after decade, much less from one society to another. The result is that it may be very difficult to reach agreement on all of them; the unending debate over the deterrent efficacy of executions attests to this. When that happens, reasonable utilitarians will have to agree to disagree with each other over whether the death penalty should be retained, modified, or abolished for this or that crime. We have, in fact, a perfect illustration of precisely such a disagreement between the two most influential classic utilitarian philosophers. Jeremy Bentham strongly opposed the death penalty throughout his life and in one of his last essays argued forcefully for its complete abolition in England and France. John Stuart Mill, however, when he was a member of Parliament in the 1860s, argued with comparable firmness against abolition of the death penalty for murder in the England of his day. Thus, within the space of half a century, Bentham and Mill, both professing utilitarians, disagreed over the desirability of abolishing the death penalty. (I discuss Bentham's views at length in a later chapter.) What should we make of this spectacle? Principally, that since complex facts are subject to uncertain estimate and calculation at best, a moral outlook founded on nothing but considerations that a consistent utilitarian can acknowledge may be insufficient for resolving the question.

A second point of interest is that the general welfare is an extremely abstract, remote, and elusive end-state to serve as the good to be aimed at in choosing among alternative penal policies. Utilitarians have devoted much energy to trying to give shape and content to this idea, or to what they regard as better-defined alternative conceptions. Still, even the utilitarian may have to be content, as a practical compromise, to rely on some inter-mediate moral principles less comprehensive in their scope than the principle of utility and more directly applicable to the problem of punishment and the death penalty controversy. As Mill himself once urged, "Whatever we adopt as the fundamental principle of morality, we require subordinate principles to apply it by. . . ."[10] Below I shall propose a small set of such principles in the hope that, among other things, they will serve this need; they are not, however, principles that only a utilitarian could endorse.

So far, my investigation has been largely historical—and largely inconclusive. We have seen how natural rights thinkers have *not* attacked the death penalty on the ground that it violates inviolable human rights. On the contrary, both Locke and Kant argue that the death penalty, whether on retributive or other grounds, is justified as a punishment for murder and perhaps for other crimes as well. Among utilitarians it is possible to find arguments against the death penalty (witness Bentham) but equally possible to find the principle of utility used in connection with a different assessment of the facts to yield a defense of the death penalty (as in Mill). Of course, it is always possible that a more exact and complete statement of one of these theories would give us a fixed and definitive judgment, once and for all, on the morality of the death penalty. I leave that possibility to be explored by others. Instead, in what I believe is a more contemporary and more conclusive approach, I will strike out in a different direction and review the entire subject more systematically.

V

A general sketch of why it is rational for society to have a system of punishment at all, quite apart from whether or not the death penalty is used as one of the modes of punishment, will help provide a fresh setting for the rest of the discussion. We are not likely to assess the morality of capital punishment correctly unless we understand the morality of punishment in general. Such a conception must take into consideration the value of human life.

Punishment, by its very nature, is unpleasant, distressing, often painful, and in any case either a deprivation of something deemed to be of value or the imposition of something deemed to be a hardship. Freedom of bodily movement and assembly with others, disposing of one's money and property as one pleases, having one's body (and one's life) intact—all these it is good to have and to have without interference. Why, then, does society insist on a system of punishment when this means inflicting so much suffering and deprivation upon persons? Punishment is in need of justification because it is always the deliberate infliction of deprivation or hardship on a person and thus the sort of thing no one would freely consent to have imposed on oneself.

The justification of punishment must begin with the fact that we regard some kinds of human conduct as harmful to innocent persons. This leads any rational society to prohibit and condemn such conduct. Condemnation is achieved by, among other things, the imposition of punishment. The next step is to establish degrees of severity in the punishments as a function of such factors as the community's judgment of the gravity of the offense, the difficulty and cost in detecting offenders, and so forth. In a society such as ours, where individual freedom is so highly prized, there is a tendency to make punishments more rather than less severe. This is done in order to compensate for restricting the police and the courts in ways that hamper them in bringing offenders to justice, lest they invade what we regard as our justifiable privacy, autonomy, and dignity.

Society is organized by reference to common rules that forbid anyone and everyone to engage in certain sorts of harmful conduct. When someone does deliberately, willfully, and knowingly violate such rules, and therewith harms the innocent, the offender has violated the rights of others and immediately becomes liable to a punitive response. Since the rules were originally designed to provide protection to every person, and since (so we also assume) the culprit knew in advance that his or her conduct was prohibited because it would be injurious to others, and since he or she freely and knowingly chose nevertheless to violate the prohibition, society cannot simply ignore the violation and continue to treat the offender as if no wrong had been done. It must attempt to bring the offender to judgment.

The reason is twofold. First, it is inconsistent for society to establish a set of fair rules, with penalties for their violation, and then, when actual instances occur, to ignore the violations, the violators, and their victims. Second, it is unfair for the law-abiding to have to suffer both the undeserved harms inflicted on them by lawbreakers and the inconvenience of complying with laws that they, too, might like to violate, while criminals indulge their lawless inclinations and suffer nothing in return. Thus, bringing the offender to judgment is not mainly to give a lesson to the offender or to set an example for others who might be inclined to imitate such lawless conduct.

Crime, on the model being developed here, is viewed as an attempt to take more than one's fair share of something. Theft of material goods is an obvious example. Murder and other crimes of violence against the person can be seen in the same way as conduct in which the offender takes more than a fair share of liberty with the bodies of others and disregards the lack of the victim's consent. Punishment, therefore, serves the complex function of reinforcing individual compliance with a set of social rules deemed necessary to protect the rights of all the members of society. Once it has been determined that one of these rules has been deliberately violated, then there is no alternative but to set in motion the system of criminal justice that culminates in the punishment of the guilty offender.

Such a system is essentially retributive in at least two respects: Crime must be punished, and the punishment must fit the crime. The theory relied upon here certainly acknowledges the first of these contentions. Punishment by its nature pays back an offender who has inflicted suffering and indignity on an innocent victim by inflicting suffering and indignity on the offender. Justice, more than any other consideration (social defense, reform of the offender), dictates that all crimes be liable to punishment, and that a reasonable portion of social resources (public expenditures) be allocated to the arrest, conviction, and punishment of offenders. The retributive principle that punishments must fit crimes is more difficult to implement, and I shall discuss it in detail later.

What sorts of punishments are available to society to inflict on offenders? What are the sorts of things any person could be deprived of that would count as punishment? Obviously, one could lose one's money or property, or the right to future earnings or an inheritance. But because so much crime against property and against the person is committed by the poor and untalented, by persons with no property and no prospects of any, and because the stolen property is so often disposed of prior to the offender's arrest, it is often pointless to levy punishments in the form of fines or confiscations. Where the crime in question is not against property but against the person, a new difficulty arises. If society were to punish assault and battery by, say, a fine of $1,000, it would be impossible for the very poor to be punished for the crime, and it would be merely a modest tariff on the conduct of the very rich, like higher taxes on their yachts and private planes—an inconvenience, but not much more. In either case, the victim of the assault and battery would have suffered injury quite incommensurate with the punishment (especially if the $1,000 were to go to the state rather than to the victim).

For reasons such as these society has long preferred to take other things of intrinsic value from persons in the name of punishment—notably, their freedom and their bodily integrity. Everybody, rich and poor, young and old, male and female, has life and limb and some degree of liberty to lose.

Historically, the objection to making punishments mainly a deprivation of liberty was that considerable tax revenues were needed to build and staff prisons. Partly for just such economic reasons, the earliest punishments were neither pecuniary nor incarcerative, but corporal: flogging, branding, maiming, and killing. These punishments were inexpensive and quick to administer, and acutely painful for the offender—it is hardly any wonder that every society today is heir to punitive practices involving widespread and varied use of corporal punishments.

What this discussion shows is that there is an argument on grounds of fairness for a system of punishment in the first place (given the fact that not everyone will always abide by fair rules that prohibit injury to others, and that it is necessary to have such rules), and another argument on grounds of fairness for modes of punishment that all can pay and that impose similar deprivations on all concerned. It should also be clear from this sketch that a system of punishment does not *require* capital punishment. Even if in the case of murder the punishment of death is the punishment most like the injury the victim has suffered, and even if it is the one punishment that guarantees the offender will never again commit another crime, there are other deprivations that are available to society and that may be preferable as punishment.

VI

I noted earlier that there is an important tie between the religious idea of the sanctity of human life and the secular ideas of the right to life and the dignity of man. Their common factor is the way each of these ideas rules out as immoral the taking of a person's life on grounds of social usefulness and nothing more. From the standpoint of moral theory, this amounts to the claim that when the moral principle of overall social welfare conflicts with the moral principle of the individual's right to life, the latter shall prevail. We have also seen how the right to life and the dignity of man generate the requirement that society must forbid and punish severely the crime of murder. From the standpoint of moral theory, this is an instance where a moral ideal is the source of a social or legal rule.

With a little reflection it is possible to connect several other moral principles with the idea of the worth of human life. We may regard these principles as corollaries or theorems of that ideal taken as an axiom or first principle of morality. Each of these principles bears on the moral desirability or permissibility of the death penalty. Some of these subsidiary principles we have already encountered; others will emerge in the discussions that follow. The full set looks like this:

1. Deliberately taking the life of anyone is not justified unless it is necessary, that is, as long as there is a feasible alternative.

2. Unless there is a good reason to punish a crime severely, a less severe penalty is to be preferred.

3. The more severe a penalty is, the more important it is to inflict it fairly and equally, that is, on all and only those who deserve it.

4. If human lives are to be risked, risking the life of the guilty is morally preferable to risking the life of the innocent.

All of the above principles can be seen, in one way or another, as expressive of ideas that have their origin in the worth of human life. In addition, two other principles have emerged that express aspects of the idea of retribution, or justice in punishment. These are:

5. Crimes should be punished.

6. Punishments should be graded in their severity according to the gravity of the crimes for which they are imposed.

The task I have set is to determine the scope and application of these several principles in order to render a judgment on capital punishment from the moral point of view. These six principles are not, of course, of equal weight or scope. Whether utilitarianism or Kantianism, for example, would give the better defense of these principles is not immediately obvious. Nothing short of a full-scale moral theory could incorporate each of these principles to the extent that is proper, and this is not the place for the development of such a theory. Instead, I will attempt to show how each of these principles enters into a line of reasoning relevant to the morality of capital punishment and thus how each can be accorded something like its proper weight. By the time I am finished, a plausible role for each principle will have been found. None of these principles has any specific reference to the morality of capital punishment. That should not be surprising, and it is certainly no defect. In general, one prefers a moral principle of broader rather than narrower application, one that covers many different kinds of cases and situations. If such broad generalizations can withstand criticism and counterexamples that test their plausibility, then they are likely to be sound principles.

VII

Some critics of opposition to capital punishment have complained that such opposition involves an overestimation of the value of human life: It tends to ignore the fact that we are all bound to die eventually. According to these critics, all that capital punishment does is to schedule a person's death at a definite time and place, by a definite mode and for a definite reason. This raises a new question for us, namely, whether the ideas of the value, worth, dignity, or sanctity of human life can be made consistent with the fact of human mortality.

Even though death is a fact of life, emphasizing the worth of human life is a way of giving sense to the familiar notions of an "untimely" death and of an "undignified" death. These terms are admittedly vague, and have application in a wide variety of settings, but they also have a place where crime and punishment are concerned. Other things being equal, if a death is brought about by one person killing another, as in murder, then it is an untimely death. If a death is brought about in a way that causes terror during the dying and disfigurement of the body, then it is an undignified death. This, of course, is exactly what murder and capital punishment both typically do. (The French film "We Are All Murderers" [1956] rendered this theme vividly.)

Historically, however, the most brutal methods of execution have been practiced in public, despite any objection that might be brought on these grounds. Such brutality was thought necessary to enhance the deterrent effect of the execution and to pay back the guilty offender, with interest, for the crime that had been committed. Stoning, crucifixion, impalement, beheading, even hanging and shooting, have often been hideously painful and terrifying to anticipate and experience. They have also left the executed person in various degrees of bodily disfigurement. In principle, of course, there is no medical or technical barrier to the development of modes of inflicting the death penalty that do not conspicuously affront human dignity. The gas chamber was introduced in this country in the 1920s as just such an "improvement" on the electric chair, much as the electric chair itself had been introduced in the 1890s in the belief that electrocution was more humane than hanging. During the 1970s, several state legislatures enacted laws to impose the death penalty by painless lethal injection.[11]

Confronted by these considerations, what should be the reply of the defender of the death penalty? One could argue that (1) neither retribution nor social defense, each of which does require brutal methods or administering the death penalty, is part of the purpose or justification of capital punishment. Or one could argue that (2) neither retribution nor social defense really requires any of the brutalities still characteristic of capital punishment. Or one could even argue that (3) the idea that death should be neither untimely nor undignified is a moral consideration of little weight, easily outweighed by other moral principles favoring the death penalty. No defender of the death penalty is likely to rest content with the first alternative. The second alternative is more promising, but for reasons suggested above and to be examined below, it really will not withstand close scrutiny. More likely, the defender of capital punishment would prefer to stand on the third alternative. If so, the dispute between defenders and critics of the morality of capital punishment will turn on how that punishment fares when measured by the requirements of just retribution and social defense. Accordingly, most of the remaining discussion will need to be devoted to resolving this dispute.

The most common punishments can be plausibly graded into three categories of relative severity: Fining (loss of property) is the least severe, imprisonment (loss of liberty) is much more severe, and death (loss of life) is the most severe of all. Fines, as we noted earlier, are often like a mere tax on conduct, and relatively little social disgrace is attached to illegal conduct if the main consequence for the offender is incurring a fine. Loss of liberty, however, not only curtails freedom of association and movement; it is also a stigma, as well as a reminder hour by hour to the offender that he or she is undergoing punishment in a form that makes one (at least for the time being) literally a social outcast. As for the death penalty, most of those who oppose it as well as those who favor it believe it is far more severe than imprisonment. In what way it is more severe, however, is often in dispute. Because opposition to the death penalty rests largely on the belief that this unusual severity is unnecessary and unjustified, it is important to examine this issue with some care.

Prolonged imprisonment without hope of release except by natural death has figured in dozens of novels and stories as the ultimate horror. Especially if the incarceration is compounded by wretched living conditions and solitary confinement, this is hardly surprising. Thus life imprisonment without the possibility of parole can verge on the borderline that normally divides imprisonment from death as the lesser from the greater punishment. Occasionally, prisoners under life sentence will commit suicide rather than face a bleak future any longer. "Lifers" also occasionally report that if they had known what it would be like to serve thirty or forty years in prison, they would have made no effort at their trial to avoid a death sentence.[12] For those of us with just enough exposure to prison life to be appalled by the thought of being imprisoned, and with imaginations vivid enough to realize what we would be deprived of once we were locked behind bars, it is understandable that some reach the sober conclusion that they would rather die than be imprisoned for life.

But do these considerations really show that death is not the more severe punishment? Do they indicate that life imprisonment can be as great or even a greater affront to the dignity of a person than the death penalty? The answer has to be negative. Personal preference of one penalty over another does not show that the latter is more severe than the former. First of all, it is not really possible to tell which of two penalties one prefers, where the one is death and the other life, the way it is possible to tell whether one prefers a week at the seashore or a week in the mountains. One can try each of the vacations and then, on the basis of actual experience, decide which is the preferable. But where a future punishment of death or life imprisonment is concerned, at most one can hope to *imagine* which of the two would be liked least. Any comparative judgment, in the nature of the case, must be based on no experience of the one (death) and very incomplete experience of the other (life imprisonment). If the severity of these alternative punishments must be judged in this way, we will never be able to tell which is the more severe. Or we will have to conclude that severity of punishments is a matter not for objective evaluation, but only of individual preference or arbitrary decision.

Further reflection on the matter makes clear that the idea of the severity of a punishment is complex and contains identifiable factors that permit clear comparison between modes of punishment. Roughly, of two punishments, one is more severe than the other depending on its duration and on its interference with things a person so punished might otherwise do. Death is interminable, whereas it is always possible to revoke or interrupt a life sentence. Death also makes compensation impossible, whereas it is possible to compensate a prisoner in some way for wrongful confinement even if it is not possible to give back any of the liberty that was taken away. Of most importance, death permits of no concurrent experiences or activities, whereas even a life-term prisoner can read a book, watch television, perhaps even write a book or repair a television set, and experience social relations of some variety with other people. Death eliminates the presupposition of all experience and activity: life itself. For these reasons, the death penalty is unquestionably the more severe punishment, no matter what a few de-spondent life-term prisoners or sentimental observers may think they prefer, and no matter how painless and dignified the mode of execution might be.

Of course it is possible to make even short-term imprisonment a living hell for prisoners. No doubt methods of imprisonment have been designed that would make death a blessed relief. Opponents of the death penalty, however, need favor no such brutal alternatives. To be sure, Europe's first outspoken opponent of the death penalty, the young Italian nobleman Ces-are Beccaria, recommended imprisonment over the death penalty because of "the perpetual example" that life-term prisoners afforded the public of what could happen to those who committed a felony. Beccaria thought this would make long imprisonment a better deterrent than death because of the "much stronger impression" on the imagination of a whole life in prison as opposed to a few moments on the gallows.[13]

Today most opponents of the death penalty would favor as an alternative punishment a prison term of relatively brief duration (say, ten years) and then eligibility for parole release, with actual release depending upon the likelihood of further violent offenses and upon the public acceptability of the offender's release. Thus, a Charles Manson might never be released,[14] whereas an armed robber who shot a gas station attendant during a holdup might be released in fifteen years or less (as, in fact, happens today in some such cases). The day-to-day prison regimen, while it need not approximate a country club—as it is cynically said to do by some of those who have never been to prison—also need not involve mistreatment, neglect, and brutality of a sort to delight the Spanish Inquisition, either.

We should also not forget that, as history shows, it is possible to aggravate the severity of the death penalty by any of several well-known techniques. Burning at the stake, for instance, would do very nicely as a more severe mode of execution than the electric chair. However, even if it could be established that such severe methods accomplished a marvelous improve-ment in the deterrent effect over less brutal methods, or that they were superbly fitted to repay a particular criminal for the kind of murder he committed, the indignity of such cruelties should prohibit their use. They would be widely if not universally seen as a dangerous throwback to more savage times. Our understanding of and respect for our common humanity has grown, and so we see that even retribution and deterrence have their moral limits, limits imposed in the name of human dignity.

In addition to the severity of the death penalty, killing persons as pun-ishment shares certain important features with other modes of corporal punishment once widely practiced in our society—maiming, flogging, branding—but now abandoned. All these other methods of corporal punishment have been prohibited in part because they are now seen to violate the dignity of the person being punished. We accept today that it is undignified to have to carry for the rest of one's life the visible stigma of having been convicted of a crime. But this is exactly what branding and maiming (such as cutting off the hand of a thief) did. Since the Freudian revolution earlier in this century, informed and reflective persons have become uneasy whenever violent physical abuse is deliberately inflicted by one person upon another who is helpless to do anything about it. Yet this is exactly what flogging involves. (By "flogging" I do not mean the paddling a parent might administer to the bottom of a wayward child. I mean tying a person to a post or a railing and then beating him raw on the naked back so that bloody welts are raised that leave scars for life, a standard form of punishment only a few decades ago and still used within prisons until fairly recently.) Any attempt by the authorities to revive such modes of punishment would be denounced as an unacceptable return to primitive techniques, and as needless physical violence that only hardens both those who undergo it and those who inflict it.[15]

Why has death as a punishment escaped the nearly universal social and moral condemnation visited on all these other punishments with which it is historically and naturally associated? In part, it may be owing to a failure of imagination. Whereas we all know or can easily and vividly imagine the pain and humiliation involved in other corporal punishments, executions today are carried out away from public view, they are quickly over, and the person punished by death is no longer in our midst as a constant reminder. Other factors come into play, too. One is the belief that in some cases there is truly no alternative, because if the criminal were not killed there would be too much risk that he or she would repeat the crime. If so, then neither retribution nor deterrence, but rather prevention, turns out to be the last line of defense. I shall examine this line of reasoning more closely below.

VIII

Capital punishment, it is sometimes said, is to the body politic what self-defense is to the individual. If the latter is not morally wrong, how can the former be? In order to assess the strength of this analogy, I will first review the morality of self-defense.

Except for absolute pacifists, who believe it is morally wrong to use violence even to defend themselves or others from unprovoked and undeserved aggression, most of us believe that it is not morally wrong and may even be our moral duty to use violence to prevent aggression directed either against us or against innocent third parties. The law has long granted persons the right to defend themselves against the unjust aggressions of others, even to the extent of using lethal force to kill an assailant.[16] To think of any convincing argument that would show it is never rational to risk the death of another in order to prevent death or grave injury to oneself is very difficult. Certainly self-interest dictates the legitimacy of self-defense. So does concern for the well-being of others, in at least some circumstances. So also does justice. If it is unfair for one person to inflict undeserved violence on another, then it is hard to see how morality could require the victim to acquiesce in the attempt by another to do so, even if resistance risks or involves injury to the assailant.

The foregoing account assumes that the person acting in self-defense is innocent of any provocation of the assailant, and that there is no alternative to victimization except resistance. In actual life, both assumptions—especially the second—are often false, because there may be a third alternative: escape, or removing oneself from the scene of imminent aggression. Hence, the law imposes on us the "duty to retreat." Before we use violence to resist aggression, we must try to get out of the way, lest unnecessary violence be used. Now suppose that unjust aggression is imminent, and there is no path open for escape. How much violence may justifiably be used to ward off aggression? The answer is: No more violence than is necessary to prevent the aggressive assault. Violence beyond that is unnecessary and therefore unjustified. We may restate the principle governing the use of violence in self-defense by reference to the concept of "deadly force" by the police in the discharge of their duties. The rule is this: Use of deadly force is justified only to prevent loss of life in immediate jeopardy where a lesser use of force cannot reasonably be expected to save the life that is threatened.

In real life, violence in self-defense in excess of the minimum necessary to prevent aggression, even though it is not justifiable, is often excusable. One cannot always tell what will suffice to deter an aggressor or to avoid becoming a victim; thus the law looks with a certain tolerance on the frightened and innocent victim who in self-defense turns upon a vicious assailant and inflicts a fatal injury even though a lesser injury would have been sufficient. What is not justified is deliberately using far more violence than is necessary to avoid becoming a victim. It is the deliberate, not the impulsive or the unintentional, use of violence that is relevant to the death penalty controversy, since the death penalty is enacted into law and carried out in each case deliberately—with ample time to weigh alternatives. Notice that I am assuming that the act of self-defense is to protect one's person or that of a third party. The reasoning outlined here does not extend to the defense of one's property. Shooting a thief to prevent one's automobile from being stolen cannot be excused or justified in the way that shooting an assailant charging with a knife pointed at one's face can be. Our criterion must be that deadly force is never justified to prevent crimes against property or other violent crimes not immediately threatening the life of an innocent person.

The rationale for self-defense as set out above illustrates two moral principles of great importance to this discussion. One is that if a life is to be risked, then it is better that it be the life of someone who is guilty (in this context, the initial assailant) rather than the life of someone who is not (the innocent potential victim). To expect the innocent prospective victim to run the added risk of severe injury or death in order to avoid using violence in self-defense that might kill the assailant is not fair. Rather, fairness dictates that the guilty aggressor should be the one to run the risk.

The other principle is that taking life deliberately is not justified so long as there is any feasible alternative. One does not expect miracles, of course, but in theory, if shooting a burglar through the foot will stop the burglary and enable one to call the police for help, then there is no reason to shoot to kill. Likewise, if the burglar is unarmed, there is no reason to shoot at all. In actual life, of course, a burglar is likely to be shot at by an aroused householder who does not know whether the burglar is armed; prudence may seem to dictate the assumption that he is. Even so, although the burglar has no right to commit a felony against a person or a person's property, the attempt does not give the chosen victim the right to respond in whatever way he pleases, and then to excuse or justify such conduct on the ground that he was "acting only in self-defense." In these ways, the law shows a tacit regard for the life even of a felon and discourages the use of unnecessary violence even by the innocent. Morality can hardly do less.

IX

The analogy between capital punishment and self-defense requires us to face squarely the empirical questions surrounding the preventive and deterrent effects of the death penalty. Executing a murderer in the name of punishment can be seen as a crime-*preventive* measure just to the extent it is reasonable to believe that if the murderer had not been executed he or she would have committed other crimes (including, but not necessarily confined to, murder). Executing a murderer can be seen as a crime *deterrent* just to the extent it is reasonable to believe that by the example of the execution other persons would be frightened off from committing murder. Any punishment can be a crime preventive without being a crime deterrent, just as it can be a deterrent without being a preventive. It can also be both or neither. Prevention and deterrence are theoretically independent because they operate by different methods. Crimes can be prevented by taking guns out of the hands of criminals, by putting criminals behind bars, by alerting the public to be less careless and less prone to victimization, and so forth. Crimes can be deterred only by making would-be criminals so frightened of being arrested, convicted, and punished for crimes that they overcome any desire to commit crimes with a stronger desire to avoid the risk of being caught and punished.

Capital punishment is unusual among penalties because its preventive effects limit its deterrent effects. The death penalty can never deter an executed person from further crimes. At most, it prevents the executed person from committing them. (Popular discussions of the death penalty are frequently confused in that they often assume the death penalty is a perfect and infallible deterrent so far as the executed criminal is concerned.) Even more important, it is also wrong to think that in every execution the death penalty proves itself to be an infallible crime preventive. True, once an offender has been executed, it is physically impossible for that person to commit any further crimes, since the punishment is totally incapacitative. But incapacitation is not identical with prevention. Prevention by means of incapacitation occurs only if the executed criminal would have committed other crimes if he or she had not been executed and had been punished only in some less incapacitative way (e.g., by imprisonment).

What evidence is there that the incapacitative results of the death penalty are an effective crime preventive?[17] From the study of imprisonment, parole, release records, this much is clear: If the murderers and other criminals who have been executed are like the murderers who were convicted but *not* executed, then (1) executing all convicted murderers would have prevented many crimes, but not many murders (about one convicted murderer in five hundred commits another murder); and (2) convicted murderers, whether inside prison or outside after release, have at least as good a record of no further criminal activity as any other class of convicted felon.

These facts show that the general public tends to overrate the danger and threat to public safety constituted by the failure to execute every murderer who is caught and convicted. While it would be quite wrong to say that there is no risk such criminals will repeat their crimes—or similar ones—if they are not executed, it would be nearly as erroneous to say that executing every convicted murderer would prevent many horrible crimes. All we know is that such executions would prevent a few such crimes from being committed; we do not know how many or by whom they would have been committed. (Obviously, if we did know we would try to prevent them!) This is the nub of the problem. There is no way to know in advance which if any of the incarcerated or released murderers will kill again. In this connection it is useful to remember that the only way to guarantee that no horrible crimes ever occur is to execute *everyone* who might conceivably commit such a crime. Similarly, the only way to guarantee that no convicted murderer ever commits another murder is to execute them all. No modern society has ever done this, and for two hundred years ours has been moving steadily in the direction of a more civilized and individuated system of justice.

These considerations show that our society has implicitly adopted an attitude toward the risk of murder rather like the attitude it has adopted toward the risk of fatality from other sources, such as automobile accidents, lung cancer, or drowning. Since no one knows when or where or upon whom any of these lethal events will fall, it would be too great an invasion of freedom to undertake the severe restrictions that alone would suffice to prevent any such deaths from occurring. We agree it is better to take the risks and keep our freedom than to try to eliminate the risks altogether and lose our freedom in the process. Hence, we have lifeguards at the beach, but swimming is not totally prohibited; smokers are warned, but cigarettes are still legally sold; pedestrians may have the right of way in marked crosswalks, but marginally competent drivers are still allowed to operate motor vehicles. Some risk is thereby imposed on the innocent. In the name of our right to freedom, we do not insist on having society protect our rights at all costs.

Determining whether the death penalty is an effective deterrent is even more difficult than determining its effectiveness as a crime preventive. In general, our knowledge about how penalties deter crimes and whether in fact they do—whom they deter, from which crimes, and under what conditions—is distressingly inexact.[18] Most people nevertheless are convinced that punishments do deter, and that the more severe a punishment is the better it will deter. For half a century, social scientists have studied the questions whether the death penalty is a deterrent and whether it is a better deterrent than the alternative of imprisonment. Their verdict, while not unanimous, is nearly so. Whatever may be true about the deterrence of lesser crimes by other penalties, the deterrence achieved by the death penalty for murder is not measurably any greater than the deterrence achieved by long-term imprisonment. In the nature of the case, the evidence is quite indirect. No one can identify for certain any crimes that did not occur because the would-be offender was deterred by the threat of the death penalty and could not have been deterred by a less severe threat. Likewise, no one can identify any crimes that did occur because the offender was not deterred by the threat of prison even though he would have been deterred by the threat of death. Nevertheless, such evidence as we have fails to show that the more severe penalty (death) is really a better deterrent than the less severe penalty (imprisonment) for such crimes as murder.

If the death penalty and long-term imprisonment really are equally effective (or ineffective) as deterrents to murder, then the argument for the death penalty on grounds of deterrence is seriously weakened. One of the moral principles identified earlier now comes into play: Unless there is a good reason for choosing a more rather than a less severe punishment for a crime, the less severe penalty is to be preferred. This principle obviously commends itself to anyone who values human life and who concedes that, all other things being equal, less pain and suffering is always better than more. Human life is valued in part to the degree that it is free of pain, suffering, misery, and frustration, and in particular to the extent that it is free of such experiences when they serve no known purpose. If the death penalty is not a more effective deterrent than imprisonment, then its greater severity is gratuitous, purposeless suffering and deprivation. Accordingly, we must reject it in favor of some less severe alternative, unless we can identify some other and more weighty moral principle that the death penalty protects and that an alternative mode of punishment violates. Whether there is any such principle is unclear.

X

A full study of the costs and benefits involved in the practice of capital punishment would not be confined solely to the question of whether it is a better deterrent or preventive of murder than imprisonment. Any thorough-going utilitarian approach to the death penalty controversy would need to examine carefully other costs and benefits as well, because maximizing the balance of all the social benefits over all the social costs is the sole criterion of right and wrong according to utilitarianism. Let us consider, therefore, some of the other costs and benefits to be calculated. Clinical psychologists have presented evidence to suggest that the death penalty actually incites some persons of unstable mind to murder others, either because they are afraid to take their own lives and hope that society will punish them for murder by putting them to death, or because they fancy that they are also killing with justification analogously to the lawful and presumably justified killing involved in capital punishment.[19] If such evidence is sound, capital punishment can serve as a counterpreventive or even an incitement to murder; such incited murders become part of its social cost. Imprisonment, however, has not been known to incite any murders or other crimes of violence in a comparable fashion. (A possible exception might be found in the imprisonment of terrorists, which has inspired other terrorists to take hostages as part of a scheme to force the authorities to release their imprisoned comrades.)

The risks of executing the innocent are also part of the social cost. The historical record is replete with innocent persons arrested, indicted, convicted, sentenced, and occasionally legally executed for crimes they did not commit.[20] This is quite apart from the guilty persons unfairly convicted, sentenced to death, and executed on the strength of perjured testimony, fraudulent evidence, subornation of jurors, and other violations of the civil rights and liberties of the accused. Nor is this all. The high costs of a capital trial and of the inevitable appeals, the costly methods of custody most prisons adopt for convicts on death row, are among the straightforward economic costs that the death penalty incurs.[21] Conducting a valid cost/benefit analysis of capital punishment would be extremely difficult, and it is impossible to predict exactly what such a study would show. Nevertheless, given the evidence we do have, it is quite possible that a study of this sort would favor abolition of all death penalties rather than their retention.

From the moral point of view, it is quite important to determine what one should think about capital punishment if the evidence were clearly to show that the death penalty is a distinctly superior method of social defense by comparison with less severe alternatives. Kantian moralists, as we have seen, would have no use for such knowledge, because their entire case for the morality of the death penalty rests on the way it is thought to provide just retribution, not on the way it is thought to provide social defense. For a utilitarian, however, such knowledge would be conclusive. Those who follow Locke's reasoning would also be gratified, because they defend the morality of the death penalty both on the ground that it is retributively just and on the ground that it provides needed social defense.

What about the opponents of the death penalty, however? To oppose the death penalty in the face of incontestable evidence that it is an effective method of social defense violates the moral principle that where grave risks are to be run it is better that they be run by the guilty than by the innocent. Consider in this connection an imaginary world in which executing the murderer would invariably restore the murder victim to life, whole and intact, as though no homicide had occurred. In such a miraculous world, it is hard to see how anyone could oppose the death penalty, on moral or other grounds. Why shouldn't a murderer die if that will infallibly bring the victim back to life? What could possibly be wrong with taking the murderer's life under such conditions? The death penalty would be an instrument of perfect restitution, and it would give a new and better meaning to *lex talionis*. The whole idea is fanciful, of course, but it shows as nothing else can how opposition to the death penalty cannot be both moral and wholly unconditional. If opposition to the death penalty is to be morally responsible, then it must be conceded that there are conditions (however unlikely) under which that opposition should cease.

But even if the death penalty were known to be a uniquely effective social defense, we could still imagine conditions under which it would be reasonable to oppose it. Suppose that in addition to being a slightly better preventive and deterrent than imprisonment, executions also had a slight incitive effect (so that for every ten murders that an execution prevented or deterred, another murder was incited). Suppose also that the administration of criminal justice in capital cases were inefficient and unequal, and tended to secure convictions and death sentences only for murderers who least "deserved" to be sentenced to death (including some death sentences and a few executions of the innocent). Under such conditions, it would be reasonable to oppose the death penalty, because on the facts supposed more (or not fewer) innocent lives would be threatened and lost by using the death penalty than would be risked by abolishing it. It is important to remember throughout our evaluation of the deterrence controversy that we cannot ever apply the principle that advises us to risk the lives of the guilty in order to save the lives of the innocent. Instead, the most we can do is weigh the risk for the general public against the execution of those who are *found* guilty by an imperfect system of criminal justice. These hypothetical factual assumptions illustrate the contingencies upon which the morality of opposition to the death penalty rests. And not only the morality of opposition. The morality of any defense of the death penalty rests on the same contingencies. This should help us understand why, in resolving the morality of capital punishment one way or the other, it is so important to know as well as we can whether the death penalty really does deter, prevent, or incite crime; whether the innocent really are ever executed; and how likely the occurrence of these things in the future is.

The great unanswered question that utilitarians must face concerns the level of social defense that executions should be expected to achieve before it is justifiable to carry them out. Consider three possible situations: (1) At the level of a hundred executions per year, each additional execution of a convicted murderer reduces the number of murder victims by ten. (2) Executing every convicted murderer reduces the number of murders to 5,000 victims annually, whereas executing only one out of ten murderers reduces the number of victims to 5,001. (3) Executing every convicted murderer reduces the murder rate no more than does executing one in a hundred and no more than does a random pattern of executions.

Many people contemplating situation (1) would regard this as a reasonable trade-off: The execution of each additional guilty person saves the lives of ten innocent ones. In fact, situation (1) or something like it may be taken as a description of what most of those who defend the death penalty on grounds of social defense believe is true. But suppose that, instead of saving ten lives, the number dropped to 0.5, that is, one victim avoided for each two additional executions. Would that be a reasonable price to pay? We are on the road toward the situation described in (2), where a drastic 90 percent reduction in the number of persons executed causes the level of social defense to drop by only 0.0002 percent. Would it be worth it to execute so many more murderers to secure such a slight increase in social defense? How many guilty lives is one innocent life worth? (Only those who think that guilty lives are *worthless* can avoid facing this problem.) In situation (3), of course, there is no basis for executing all convicted murderers, since there is no gain in social defense to show for each additional execution after the first out of each hundred has been executed. How, then, should we determine which out of each hundred convicted murderers is the one to be put to death?

If a complete and thoroughgoing cost/benefit analysis of the death penalty were possible, we might be able to answer such questions. But an appeal merely to the moral principle that if lives are to be risked it should be the lives of the guilty rather than of the innocent will not suffice. (I noted above that this abstract principle is of little use in the actual administration of criminal justice, because the police and the courts do not deal with the guilty as such but only with those *judged* guilty.) Nor will it suffice to agree that society deserves all the crime prevention and deterrence it can get as a result of inflicting severe punishments. These principles are consistent with too many different policies. They are too vague by themselves to resolve the choice on grounds of social defense when confronted with hypothetical situations like those proposed above.

Since no adequate cost/benefit analysis of the death penalty exists, there is no way to resolve these questions from that standpoint at this time. Moreover, it can be argued that we cannot have such an analysis without already establishing in some way or other the relative value of innocent lives versus guilty lives. Far from being a product of cost/benefit analysis, a comparative evaluation of lives would have to be available to us before we undertook any such analysis. (And no one has yet come up with a satisfactory means of doing this.) Without it, no adequate cost/benefit analysis of this problem can get off the ground. Finally, it must be noted that our knowledge at present does not indicate that we are in anything like the situation described above in (1). On the contrary, from the evidence we do have it seems we achieve about the same deterrent and preventive effects whether we punish murder by death or by imprisonment. Something like the situation in (2) or in (3) may therefore be correct. If so, this shows that the choice between the two policies of capital punishment and life imprisonment for murder will probably have to be made on some basis other than social defense; on that basis alone, the two policies appear to be virtually equivalent and therefore equally acceptable.

XI

No discussion of the morality of punishment would be complete without taking into account the two leading principles of retributive justice relevant to the capital punishment controversy. I have made reference to them several times. One is the principle that crimes should be punished; the other is the principle that the severity of a punishment should be proportional to the gravity of the offense. These are moral principles of recognized weight. Leaving aside all questions of social defense, how strong a case for capital punishment can be made on their basis? How reliable and persuasive are these principles themselves?

Given the general rationale for punishment sketched earlier, there cannot be any dispute over the principle that crime must be punished. In embracing it, of course, we are not automatically making a fetish of "law and order," in the sense that we would be if we thought that the most important single thing to do with social resources is to punish crimes. In addition, the principle that crime must be punished need not be in dispute between proponents and opponents of the death penalty. Even defenders of the death penalty must admit that putting a convicted murderer in prison for years is a punishment of that criminal. The principle that crime must be punished is neutral to our controversy, because both sides acknowledge it.

The other principle of retributive justice is the one that seems to be decisive. Under *lex talionis,* it must always have seemed that murderers ought to be put to death. Proponents of the death penalty, with rare exceptions, have insisted on this point; and even opponents of the death penalty must give grudging assent to the logic of demanding capital punishment for murder. The strategy for opponents of the death penalty is to argue either that (1) this principle is not really a principle of justice after all, or that (2) to the extent it is, it does not require death for murderers, or that (3) in any case it is not the only principle of punitive justice. As we shall see, each of these objections has merit.

Let us recall, first, that not even the biblical world limited the death penalty to the punishment of murder. Many other nonhomicidal crimes also carried this penalty (e.g., kidnapping, witchcraft, cursing one's parents).[22] In our own nation's recent history, persons have been executed for aggravated assault, rape, kidnapping, armed robbery, sabotage, and espionage.[23] We cannot defend *any* of these executions (not to mention some of the more bizarre capital statutes, like the one in Georgia that not so long ago provided an optional death penalty for desecration of a grave[24]) on grounds of just retribution. This entails either that such executions are not justified or that they are justified on some ground other than retribution. In actual practice, few defenders of the death penalty have ever been willing to rest their case entirely on the moral principle of just retribution as formulated in terms of "a life for a life." (Kant was a conspicuous exception.) Most defenders of the death penalty have implied, by their willingness to use executions to defend not only life but limb and property as well, that they did not place much value on the lives of criminals when compared to the value of either lives or things belonging to innocent citizens.

European civilization for several centuries has tended to limit the criminal homicides punishable by death. Even Kant took a casual attitude toward a mother's killing of her illegitimate child. ("A child born into the world outside marriage is outside the law . . . , and consequently it is also outside the protection of the law."[25]) In our society, the development nearly two hundred years ago of the distinction between first- and second-degree murder was an attempt to narrow the class of criminal homicides deserving the death penalty.[26] Yet those dead owing to manslaughter, or to any kind of unintentional, accidental, unpremeditated, unavoidable, unmalicious killing, are just as dead as the victims of the most ghastly murder. Both moral reflection and the law in practice show how difficult it is to identify all and only the criminal homicides that are appropriately punished by death (assuming that any are). Individual judges and juries differ in the conclusions they reach. The history of capital punishment for homicides reveals continual efforts, uniformly unsuccessful, to specify the criteria defining those homicides for which the slayer should die. Sixty years ago, Justice Benjamin Cardozo of the Supreme Court said of the distinction between degrees of murder that it was

> ... so obscure that no jury hearing it for the first time can fairly be expected to assimilate and understand it. I am not at all sure that I understand it myself after trying to apply it for many years and after diligent study of what has been written in the books. Upon the basis of this fine distinction with its obscure and mystifying psychology, scores of men have gone to their death.[27]

Similar skepticism has been expressed on the reliability and rationality of death penalty statutes that give the trial court the discretion to sentence to prison or to death. As Justice John Marshall Harlan of the Supreme Court observed more than a decade ago,

> Those who have come to grips with the hard task of actually attempting to draft means of channeling capital sentencing discretion have confirmed the lesson taught by history. ... To identify before the fact those characteristics of criminal homicide and their perpetrators which call for the death penalty, and to express these characteristics in language which can be fairly understood and applied by the sentencing authority, appear to be tasks which are beyond present human ability.[28]

The abstract principle that the punishment of death best fits the crime of murder turns out to be extremely difficult to interpret and apply.

If we look at the matter from the standpoint of the actual practice of criminal justice, we can only conclude that "a life for a life" plays little or no role whatever. Plea bargaining, even where murder is concerned, is widespread. Studies of criminal justice (see Chapter 9) reveal that what trial or appellate courts in a given jurisdiction decide on a given day is first-degree murder suitably punished by death could just as well have been decided in a neighboring jurisdiction on another day either as second-degree murder or as first-degree murder but without the death penalty. The factors that influence prosecutors in determining the charge under which they will prosecute go far beyond the simple principle of "a life for a life." Cynics, of course, will say that these facts show that our society does not care about justice. I would reply that either justice in punishment does not consist of retribution, because there are other principles of justice; or there are other moral considerations besides justice that must be honored; or retributive justice is not adequately expressed in the idea of "a life for a life"; or justice in the criminal justice system is beyond our reach.

Those who advocate capital punishment for murder on retributive grounds must face the objection that, on their own principles, the death penalty in some cases is morally inadequate. How could death in the electric chair or the gas chamber or before a firing squad or on a gallows suffice as just retribution, given the savage, brutal, wanton character of so many murders? How can retributive justice be served by anything less than equally savage methods of execution? From a retributive point of view, the oft-heard exclamation, "Death is too good for him!" has a certain truth. Are defenders of the death penalty willing to embrace this consequence of their own doctrine?

If they were, they would be stooping to the squalor of the murderer and denying the very tenets of civilized behavior they claim to be defending. Where the quality of the crime sets the limits of just methods of punishment, as it will if we attempt to give exact and literal implementation to *lex talionis*, society as a whole will find itself descending to the cruelties and savagery that criminals employ. What is worse, society would be deliberately authorizing such acts, in the cool light of reason, and not (as is usually true of criminals) impulsively or in hatred and anger or with an insane or unbalanced mind. Well-established and universally recognized moral constraints, in short, prohibit us from trying to make executions perfectly retributive. Once we grant that such constraints are proper, it is unreasonable to insist that the principle of "a life for a life" nevertheless by itself justifies the execution of murderers.

Other considerations take us in a different direction. Few murders, outside television and movie scripts, involve anything like an execution. An execution, after all, begins with a solemn pronouncement of the death sentence from a judge, is followed by detention in maximum security awaiting the date of execution (during which various complex and protected appeals

41

will be pursued, followed by a clemency hearing before the governor), and culminates in the condemned prisoner walking "the last mile" to the execution chamber itself. As Albert Camus once remarked,

> For there to be an equivalence, the death penalty would have to punish a criminal who had warned his victim of the date at which he would inflict a horrible death on him and who, from that moment onward, had confined him at his mercy for months. Such a monster is not encountered in private life.[29]

What, then, emerges from our examination of retributive justice and the death penalty? If retributive justice is thought to consist in *lex talionis,* all one can say is that this principle has never exercised more than a crude and indirect effect on the actual punishments meted out by society. Other moral principles simply do interfere with a literal and single-minded application of this one. Some homicides seem improperly punished by death at all; others would require methods of execution too horrible to inflict. In any case, proponents of the death penalty rarely confine themselves to reliance on nothing but this principle of just retribution, since they rarely confine themselves to supporting the death penalty only for murder.

Retributive justice need not be identified with *lex talionis.* One may reject that principle as too crude and still embrace the retributive principle that the severity of punishments should be graded according to the gravity of the offense. Even though one need not claim that life imprisonment (or any kind of punishment other than death) "fits" the crime of murder, one can claim that this punishment is the proper one for murder. To do this, one must accept a schedule of punishments arranged so that this mode of imprisonment is the most severe penalty used. Opponents of the death penalty can embrace this principle of retributive justice, even though they must reject a literal *lex talionis.*

During the past generation, the strongest practical objection to the death penalty has been the inequity with which it has been applied.[30] As the late Supreme Court Justice William O. Douglas once observed, "One searches our chronicles in vain for the execution of any member of the affluent strata of this society."[31] One does not search our chronicles in vain for the crime of murder committed by the affluent. Every study of the death penalty for rape (unconstitutional only since 1977) has confirmed that black male rapists (especially where the victim is a white female) are far more likely to be sentenced to death and executed than white male rapists.[32] Convicted black murderers are more likely to end up on death row than are others, and the killers of whites (whether white or nonwhite) are more likely to be sentenced to death than are the killers of nonwhites.[33] All the sociological evidence points to the conclusion that the death penalty is the poor man's justice; hence the epigram "Those without the capital get the punishment."

Let us suppose that the factual basis for such a criticism is sound. What follows for the morality of capital punishment? Many defenders of the death penalty have been quick to point out that since there is nothing intrinsic about the crime of murder or rape dictating that only the poor or only racial-minority males will commit it, and since there is nothing overtly racist about the statutes that authorize the death penalty for murder or rape, capital punishment itself is hardly at fault if in practice it falls with unfair impact on the poor and the black. There is, in short, nothing in the death penalty that requires it to be applied unfairly and with arbitrary or discriminatory results. At worst, such results stem from a fault in the system of administering criminal justice. (Some, who dispute the facts cited above, would deny even this.) There is an adequate remedy—execute more whites, women, and affluent murderers.

Presumably both proponents and opponents of capital punishment would concede that it is a fundamental dictate of justice that a punishment should not be unfairly—inequitably or unevenly—enforced and applied. They should also be able to agree that when the punishment in question is the extremely severe one of death, then the requirement to be fair in using such a punishment becomes even more stringent. There should be no dispute in the death penalty controversy over these principles of justice. The dispute begins as soon as one attempts to connect these principles with the actual use of this punishment.

In this country, many critics of the death penalty have argued, we would long ago have got rid of capital punishment entirely if equal and fair application had been a condition of its use. In the words of the attorneys who argued against the death penalty in the Supreme Court during 1972, "It is a freakish aberration, a random extreme act of violence, visibly arbitrary and discriminatory—a penalty reserved for unusual application because, if it were usually used, it would affront universally shared standards of public decency."[34] It is difficult to dispute this judgment, when one considers that there have been in the United States during the past fifty years about half a million criminal homicides, about a third of a million persons arrested for these crimes, but fewer than four thousand executions (all but thirty-three of which were of men).[35]

We can look at these statistics in another way to illustrate the same point. If we could be assured that the nearly four thousand persons who have been executed were the worst of the bad, repeat offenders impossible to incarcerate safely (much less to rehabilitate), the most dangerous murderers in captivity—the ones who had killed more than once and were likely to kill again, and the least likely to be confined in prison without chronic danger to other inmates and the staff—then one might accept half a million murders and a few thousand executions with a sense that rough justice had been done. But the truth is otherwise. Persons are sentenced to death and executed not because they have been found to be uncontrollably violent or hopelessly poor confinement and release risks. Instead they are executed because at trial they have a poor defense (inexperienced or overworked counsel), they have no funds to bring witnesses to court, they are transients or strangers in the community where they are tried, the prosecuting attorney wants the publicity that goes with "sending a killer to the chair," there are no funds for an appeal or for a transcript of the trial record, they are members of a despised racial or political minority. In short, the actual study of why particular persons have been sentenced to death and executed does not show any careful winnowing of the worst from the bad; it shows that those executed were usually the unlucky victims of prejudice and discrimination, the losers in an arbitrary lottery that could just as well have spared them, the victims of the disadvantages that almost always go with poverty. A system like this does not enhance human life; it cheapens and degrades it. However heinous murder and other crimes are, the system of capital punishment does not compensate for or erase those crimes. It tends only to add new injuries of its own to the catalogue of human brutality.

XII

My discussion of the death penalty from the moral point of view shows that there is no one moral principle that has paramount validity and that decisively favors one side of the controversy. Rather, I have shown how it is possible to argue either for or against the death penalty, and in each case to be appealing to moral principles that derive from the worth, value, or dignity of human life. I have also shown how it is impossible to connect any of these abstract principles with the actual practice of capital punishment without a close study of sociological, psychological, and economic factors. By themselves, the moral principles that are relevant are too abstract and uncertain in application to be of much help. Without the guidance of such principles, of course, the facts (who gets executed, and why) are of little use, either.

My own view of the controversy is that, given the moral principles identified in the course of this discussion (including the overriding value of human life), and given all the facts about capital punishment, the balance of reasons favors abolition of the death penalty. The alternative to capital punishment that I favor, as things currently stand, is long-term imprisonment. Such a punishment is retributive and can be made more (or less) severe to reflect the gravity of the crime. Adequate (though hardly perfect) protection can be given to the public. It is free of the worst defect to which the death penalty is liable: execution of the innocent. It tacitly acknowledges that there is no way for a criminal, alive or dead, to make complete amends for murder or other grave crimes against the person. Last but not least, long-term imprisonment has symbolic significance. The death penalty, more than any other kind of killing, is done by officials in the name of society and on its behalf. Yet each of us has a hand in such killings. Unless they are absolutely necessary they cannot be justified. Thus abolishing the death penalty represents extending the hand of life even to those who by their crimes may have "forfeited" any right to live. A penal policy limiting the severity of punishment to long-term imprisonment is one way of admitting that we must abandon the folly and pretense of attempting to secure perfect justice in an imperfect world.

Searching for an epigram suitable for our times, in which governments have waged war and suppressed internal dissent by using methods that can be described only as savage and criminal, Camus was prompted to admonish: "Let us be neither victims nor executioners." Perhaps better than any other, this exhortation points the way between unacceptable extremes if we are to respect the humanity in each of us.

Chapter 2

The Right to Life and the Right to Kill

In evaluating the death penalty from the moral point of view, we can proceed in several different ways. For those whose moral thinking is inspired primarily by religious tradition, reflection may well begin with acknowledging the sacred quality of human life, affirmed in Genesis and elsewhere in the Bible. Secular moralists who prefer a utilitarian (or some other cost/benefit) orientation would begin with an attempt to calculate whether the death penalty for murder, or for any crime, is more likely to increase a community's overall well-being (taking into account the well-being of the criminal, too) than any of the alternatives, such as long-term imprisonment. I looked at this approach briefly in the previous chapter and will do so in much greater detail in the next. A third line of analysis concentrates on the *rights* involved—those of society and of the individual. Such an approach might naturally begin with the assumption that the state has the right to defend itself against domestic or internal enemies, and then inquire whether this implies the right to kill them under certain conditions. Aspects of this approach were raised in the previous chapter; the purpose here is to explore them more thoroughly.

I

A sense of "the state has the right" exists, of course, in which all we mean is that some presumptively valid law gives the government the legal right to do something. Let us call this the *legal* sense of "has the right." Whenever a legislature enacts a statute authorizing the death penalty for murder, it can be asserted in this sense that the state now has the right to kill convicts as their punishment. As soon as such a law is repealed by a subsequent legislature or nullified on constitutional grounds by an appellate court, however, the state no longer has such a right. Legal rights in this sense can be cancelled or revoked as easily as they can be created in the first place. Similarly, in this purely legal sense of "has the right," it will turn out that at one and the same time some jurisdictions do and others do not have the right to use death as a punishment. Likewise, a given jurisdiction will have this right at some times and not at other times, and it will have this right regarding the punishment of some crimes but not of others.

Whether the state has the right to use death as a punishment in this legal sense of "has the right" is not a matter for debate, because the answer rests on fairly straightforward questions of fact. In the United States today, most jurisdictions have at least one death penalty statute that has sustained constitutional challenges, a few have a death penalty statute whose constitutionality is unsettled, and a few other jurisdictions have no such statutes. Consequently, anyone who wants to argue over whether the state has the right to use death as a punishment must be thinking of some sense of the phrase "has the right" other than the legal sense. We can call this other sense the *moral* sense of "has the right." Only if we recognize that the phrase has a meaning of this sort can we make sense of such sensible claims as these: Although a state has a constitutionally valid death penalty statute, it still has no right to use death as a punishment; or even if a state has no death penalty laws, it has the right to enact and enforce them. Let us, then, put aside the idea of the state's legal right to kill and begin at the beginning in an attempt to understand the moral sense of "has the right." That is what really underlies the controversy.

We cannot get very far in thinking about rights and their normative force without distinguishing clearly the claim that (1) *the state has the right to use death as a punishment* from the very different claim to the effect that (2) *the state is right to use death as a punishment*. The difference between the two propositions can most readily be seen if we consider their contradictories. The negation of (1) is that *the state does not have the right to use death as a punishment*. The negation of (2) is quite different; we deny (2) when we assert that *it is not right* (i.e., *it is wrong*) *for the state to use death as a punishment*. Clearly there is an important difference between the right to kill (or to be a killer), as in (1), and what might be called the moral rectitude of killing (or doing the right thing when one kills), as in (2).

We can also see the difference between the two when we consider what arguments would establish these two propositions. Roughly, we establish that some agent—a person, a group, or the state—*has a right* when we establish one or more of three different things. One is that the agent is under no duty or obligation not to act in a certain way, in which case the agent has a right in the sense of being free or at liberty to do as he wishes. Another is that others are under a duty or obligation not to interfere with (or are even under a duty or obligation to facilitate) the action of the agent if the agent chooses to act in the way in question. A third is that the agent has been authorized to act in a certain manner by others who have the authority (i.e., the right) so to empower the agent. How we establish, in their turn, one or more of these conditions is a further problem that need not concern us for the moment.

But if the question is whether *it is right* for a person or group to act in a certain way, this can be answered in the affirmative only by much more comprehensive and diffuse considerations. Everything now turns on the content of our entire moral theory—or, if we don't have a moral theory, then on the set of moral principles we hold and their logical consequences, in particular cases, which justify the action in question from our moral point of view. Merely knowing who has the right to what does not always settle the morality of anyone's conduct. Important as our rights are, they are not always the last word in the moral evaluation of how to act. We can always ask, for example, whether persons or groups who act on their rights are really doing the best thing, all things considered. We can often give moral reasons for doing something even though someone's rights are thereby violated.

To put the distinction between (1) and (2) in yet a third way, the question of whether the state is right when it kills as punishment can be answered (in the affirmative or the negative) without any reference to a theory or doctrine of rights. In fact, a theory of morally right action might not recognize or acknowledge any fundamental rights at all—as was true of most moral and political theories prior to the seventeenth century. But when we ask whether the state has a right to use death as a punishment (and are not using the phrase "has a right" in the purely legal sense), we obviously cannot answer in the affirmative without such a theory. Indeed, any affirmative answer will require us to explain the scope and origin of the right, as well as how the right is related to other moral and empirical (political, social, economic) conditions. These reasons make manifest the gap—both conceptual and moral—between *having a right* to do a thing and *doing the right* thing.

Given the distinction between the state's right to use death as a punishment and the overall moral propriety of state-authorized killing as punishment, closer investigation might support any of four possible positions on the death penalty itself. At one extreme the state could have the right, and the state could be right when it exercises the right (consistent with due process of law). Presumably, this is what most contemporary defenders of the death penalty believe. At the other extreme is the possibility that the state does not have the right to use death as a punishment, and the state never does the right thing when it kills even a duly convicted offender. Many contemporary opponents of the death penalty believe this to be true. Advocates and opponents of the death penalty rarely take up positions openly defending the one extreme and attacking the other, however. If they did, then witnesses to debates on the issue would at least know exactly what is being asserted and what denied.

The other two possibilities lie in between. One is that the state has no moral right to kill, but that it is not always wrong when it does kill—a position that may initially sound somewhat bizarre, though it is not incoherent. The remaining possibility is that the state has the right to kill, although rarely if ever does the state do the right thing when it acts on this right.

Of these four possibilities, the one that most nearly accords with my views is the last one. Like most professing constitutional democratic liberals, I am neither a pacifist nor an anarchist. Consequently, I can conceive of conditions under which it is within the state's authority or power—and in that sense, within its rights—to decide whether to kill a person. Yet I do oppose the death penalty in all cases in our society, so I think whenever our government decides to kill someone as his punishment, the state on whose behalf it acts does the wrong thing. Let us defer for the moment the large question of whether it is ever right for the state to use death as a punishment, however, in order to elaborate further on the idea of the state's right to do so.

First, the right to kill persons as a punishment is unlike many rights in that *only* the state can have it. You and I can kill, and a person may even have the right (legal as well as moral) to kill another person in certain cases. But many rights (such as the right to declare war, the right to tax, the right to make a treaty) are such that no individual person has them, except as a function of some office he or she holds. The right to punish crimes is one of these rights; only the agents of a state—government officials suitably empowered and authorized to act on behalf of a society—have the right to impose the death penalty and carry it out. To think otherwise is to confuse the lethal acts of private individuals, such as murder, lynching, and killing in self-defense, with the lethal act of carrying out the death penalty. Nothing is gained by such confusion.

Second, the state's right to kill persons as a punishment (if there is such a right) is neither a "natural" nor a fundamental right. Rather, it is an artificial or highly contingent and derivative right, because states and their moral authority are derivative and to that extent artificial; they are the products of human social and political contrivance and their powers are justified solely by the extent to which they serve humane purposes, social and individual. When (as I point out in Chapter 4) John Locke defined political power as "a right of making laws with penalties of death," he viewed this right as derivative from the natural rights of individual persons in a "state of nature." In the spirit if not the letter of Locke's thinking, we might say that the right to use death as a punishment is indeed not fundamental but derivative. It is derived from the state's fundamental duty to enact and enforce just laws (i.e., laws that protect and permit the exercise of individual rights in a manner fair to all persons) and its right to use the means necessary and appropriate to secure this end. If, as in Locke's theory, the state is the repository of all and only such rights of individuals as are transferred to it, so that the government is always the fiduciary and trustee of individual rights, then we must be able to point to some such individual rights that are (or are reasonably believed to be) protected by every exercise of governmental power.

Finally, the state's right to use death as a punishment might turn out to conflict with other rights or with certain duties. The possibility of conflicts arises because the right to use death as a punishment is not an *absolute* right and it is not the *only* right of the state. Any appeal to a right, whether an individual's, a group's, or a state's, always invites challenge by reference to other rights and duties. In the event of a conflict, a choice must be made between exercising one of these rights and either violating some other right(s) or failing to perform (or frustrating the performance of) certain duties. Resolving conflicts (if they occur) in favor of the state's right to kill can be done only if it can be shown that this right is paramount, that it works like trumps in the games of Bridge and Hearts, because it always prevails over conflicting rights and duties. Whether the state's right to use death as a punishment can be exercised without infringement of other rights and without violation of any duties remains to be seen.

II

We get a clearer picture of the state's right to use death as a punishment if we look at two other rights, one that is in opposition to this one and another that is analogous to it. The former is the individual's *right to life* and the latter is the individual's *right of self-defense*. We will look at the latter first.

Except for pacifist anarchists, most people generally agree that in morals and in law each individual has the right of self-defense (and third parties the right to intervene to assist) in warding off unprovoked and undeserved harm at the hands of an intending felon. Does this right include the right to use lethal force? It does, but only under certain provisos—that retreat or escape is not possible, and that the would-be victim (or intervener) reasonably believes that no lesser degree of force will suffice to ward off the felonious harm. Legal niceties apart, that is the essence of the traditional idea of the right of self-defense and the use of lethal force in exercise of that right.

What kind of state's right is there, if any, parallel to the individual's right of self-defense? A few paragraphs earlier, I noted that the state has the duty to defend its laws insofar as they are just or fair (the duty to protect just institutions), and that in exercise of this duty the state may threaten punishment for those who are found guilty of intentionally violating just laws to the harm of individuals, groups, or the state itself. Thus I accept a kind of analogy between the individual's right of self-protection against undeserved and unprovoked invasions of personal liberties, and the state's duty to defend just institutions; the analogy is not perfect, because it holds between an individual's *right* and the state's *duty*. To the extent that a right is unlike a duty, there is no parallel at all. To put this another way, whereas an individual may choose *not* to defend himself (that is the nature of an individual's right—one violates no duty if one does not choose to act or stand on one's rights), the state *must* defend its laws and just institutions. The reason is that the state has a duty to defend the rights of its members, and this cannot be done unless on some occasions the state uses not only persuasion and threats but force to protect just laws and institutions against those who would violate or refuse to support them.[1]

Lethal force may be used by the individual in self-defense with considerably more freedom than by the state. I am, perforce, the judge of whether, in the course of self-defense, I should shoot to kill the intruder. I do not have days or hours to decide, much less months and years. (Of course, I must eventually answer to others for my use of lethal force; unlike the fictional James Bond, no ordinary private citizen has a "license to kill.") Consequently, moral judgment and legal tribunals tend to err in the direction of generous excuse of those who use excessive or lethal force in self-defense.

The state's use of the death penalty as an exercise of a right to kill (in contrast, say, to a policeman's use of lethal force against an escaping felon), however, can be employed only well after the crimes it punishes and before any crimes its use might be intended to prevent. Consequently, the circumstances of the use of lethal force in the course of exercising the two rights are completely different. Typically, the individual must act without due deliberation and may shoot to wound and disable, rather than to kill; the state, however, acts *only* after due deliberation and its officials *always* shoot, electrocute, gas, hang, or inject with the intention of causing death. Wrongful exercise of the right to kill as punishment is thus impossible to excuse in any ordinary sense. One does not properly *excuse* the deliberate and the intentional, but only the accidental, inadvertent, involuntary, and the like. Rather, one *justifies* the deliberate and the intentional actions of individuals and of governments acting on behalf of the state—or one justifies them if one can.

This exploration of the analogy between the individual's right of self-defense and the state's right to kill as punishment shows the analogy is far from perfect. The analogy is closest at the point where it suggests that when one person kills another, it must be as a last resort, because there is no feasible alternative. Constitutional lawyers will recognize this as the moral imperative parallel to the "least restrictive means to enforce a compelling state interest" test, a familiar principle of constitutional law but not one usually used to review legislatively authorized punishments (some further discussion of this test will be found below in Chapters 4 and 6).

We see now more clearly why the state's right to use death as a punishment is a derivative and contingent matter, rather than anything fundamental. Locke and others who think that it is fundamental are simply wrong. Not even the state's right to punish, much less the right to punish *in this or that particular manner*, is fundamental. The state's right to punish is

52

properly derived from its duty to protect just laws, which in turn is a means to protect the rights of individual persons. Punishment is justified in part by its necessity as a means to this end; insofar as it is not necessary to that end, it is unjustified and other responses to crime and the threat of crime are appropriate.[2] But the right to impose the punishment of death, rather than some lesser punishment, depends upon whether such a severe punishment is necessary to achieve public protection. No doubt the government is rightfully empowered to pursue whatever means are necessary to its proper ends, as long as doing so does not violate any important moral principle. The right to kill as punishment cannot be derived from this consideration alone, however. It depends also on the empirical claim that such an extreme penalty is a necessary means to a just end. This imposes a weighty burden of empirical proof upon any state that would choose a severe punishment over a less severe punishment in order to achieve a good end. The state— at least, a state that deserves our respect and allegiance—is not free to choose whatever means to its ends it may desire. Put less abstractly, a government is not justified in defending its preference for the death penalty by appealing to the state's right to punish violations of just laws. The government must also show that no lesser punishment suffices to reach this end. That a severe punishment *suffices* to reach this end is not enough; it must be *necessary* as well. And the government, as the duly authorized agent of the society, must provide some evidence of this necessity when challenged.

III

We turn now to examine the individual's "natural" right to life and the conflict, such as there is, between that right and the state's alleged right to use death as a punishment. In the previous chapter something of the history of the idea of individual rights as natural, fundamental, and inalienable was reviewed. Over the three centuries between Locke's day and ours, the right to life has yet to be articulated in a manner adequate for its reliable use in all the contexts in which it plays a role in our moral and political thinking. As I have noted elsewhere,[3] talk about the right to life shows that its advocates treat it as a portmanteau concept; protections concerning the termination and prevention of human life are found in it along with guarantees concerning the preservation and fulfillment of human ambitions and potentialities. The right to life has been applied to such different and disconnected questions as the morality of abortion, the duties of famine relief, and even the plight of third-world peoples seeking to develop the natural resources of their countries for their own (rather than the first-world's) benefit.[4] The scope of this right appears to be quite broad, or would be if one were to accept all that has been asserted by those who would invoke it. Unfortunately, such a broad use has not been accompanied by any increased understanding of the nature and status of the right.

No less problematic is the weight, or stringency, of the right. Opponents of abortion and the death penalty often speak and write in a manner that implies they accord *absolute* moral weight to the right to life. Yet it is difficult to see how this can be correct. If the right to (human) life is absolute, then it must always be morally wrong to kill another, whether by acting on one's own authority or under the orders of another, whether or not one is acting intentionally, whether the person killed is oneself or someone else, whether or not the victim-to-be has consented, and whether or not there is any less drastic alternative to protect the innocent. The result is that *all* forms of killing—suicide, euthanasia, murder, legal executions, killing in wartime, self-defense, and abortion (if that involves the killing of a human person)—violate this right and are therefore morally wrong. But this is not all. If the moral status of the distinction between *killing* and *letting die* is collapsed (as many contemporary philosophers have argued that it should be), deliberately failing to intervene to prevent a death would also violate this absolute right. Surely, these extreme consequences serve only to discredit the very idea of the right to life as an absolute right in the first place.

A more defensible position would hold that the right to life expresses the presumption of wrongness in causing anyone's death, and thus this right would provide the weightiest of moral reasons—but not an absolute prohibition—against, above all, the deliberate killing of any person by anyone else capable of forming and acting on that intention. The right to life conceived in this more modest fashion not only underlies the law against criminal homicide but also provides the justification for the use of lethal force in self-defense and by the police. This account, of course, does not tell the whole story about the right to life; but whatever the rest of the story involves, it would be folly to undermine or override this fundamental part.

Even if the right to life is understood not to be absolute, that does not suffice to avoid the possibility of a conflict of rights with the state, once it is granted that the state has a right to use death as a punishment. I think it is important for both sides in the death penalty controversy to grant that, as soon as one holds the view that individuals have a natural (albeit not absolute and perhaps not inalienable)[5] right to life and that the state has the right to use death as a punishment, then there is a conflict whenever the state undertakes to exercise its right. The conflict can be avoided in practice only by the state not exercising that right. It can be avoided in theory either by denying that one (or both) of these rights is genuine, or by establishing a fixed ranking in the relative weight of these two rights (so that one always prevails over the other), or by some other tactic.

I will put aside without further examination the first alternative (the outright denial that one or both of these rights is genuine), since it undermines the whole point of the present investigation. The second alternative (a fixed ranking in the moral weight of otherwise conflicting rights) is interesting, but it may also be ignored here because there is no settled version of this doctrine at our disposal. The third alternative is the only one in need of scrutiny.

IV

The classic version of this alternative is the one sketched by Locke three hundred years ago, popularized a century later by Blackstone, and widely adopted since: the doctrine of the *forfeiture* of natural rights (discussed at the beginning of the previous chapter). According to this doctrine, a person forfeits one or more of his rights by any act in which he violates the rights of another. Some such maneuver seems necessary, for at least two reasons. The first is that the usual things done by the state to punish a person, such as killing or incarcerating him, or imposing a fine, would be obvious violations of that person's rights if done without his consent by any agent other than the state. Capital punishment would be murder and thus a deprivation of life, imprisonment a deprivation of liberty, a fine a deprivation of property—in each case a violation of the individual's rights. Since these acts of punishment by the state are usually not regarded in principle as a violation of anyone's rights, the rights of individual offenders must somehow be put aside; this is precisely what their forfeiture accomplishes. The second reason for subscribing to the doctrine of forfeiture is that, on any plausible theory, the offender has by virtue of his criminal act put himself in the wrong both with respect to the state (whose laws he violated) and to whichever person(s) he victimized (whose rights he violated). In saying this, I assume, of course, that moral reflection would sustain the judgment that the criminal act in question really is a violation of the rights of the innocent, as murder surely is. Once this is granted, it seems morally unacceptable that the offender's rights should nevertheless remain intact, since if they did that would bar any response to his deed that takes the form of restricting his liberty or property or person without his consent.

The doctrine of the forfeiture of natural rights as a device to permit the state to kill as a punishment has its problems, however. First, exactly what right does a person supposedly forfeit where some crime other than murder has been committed? Our society currently imprisons many different kinds of offenders, including over 95 percent of all convicted murderers and many offenders convicted of property crimes. Apparently, so far as current law is concerned, either the offender can forfeit a given right of his without having violated that particular right of some victim; or the government's choice among modes of punishment does not rest on the idea of the forfeiture by the offender of some *particular* right.

Locke, as it happens, seems to have preferred the first alternative. He argued that a person forfeits his life by virtue of any criminal act that "deserves death," but he supplied no criterion to enable us to distinguish between those criminal acts that deserve death and those that do not. Like others of his day, he indicated no reservations about the death penalty for crimes against the state or for crimes against property and his notion of criminal acts deserving death went far beyond what a criterion such as *lex talionis* ("a life for a life") would yield. The obvious way to improve on Locke's silence is to adapt this very criterion to provide that a person forfeits, not his very life itself, but his *right* to life, always and only by the crime of murder.

If we adopt Locke's position as modified in the manner suggested, then we have established a basis for asserting that the state is authorized—and in this sense, has the right—to put a convicted murderer to death. Even so, we can still ask whether the state *must* put him to death, and whether it *ought* to do so. How should we answer these questions? Since (as we have seen earlier) acting on one's rights is not the same as doing the right thing, and since having the right to do something is not the same as having a duty to do it, even if the state has the right to take a convicted offender's life, it is still an open question whether that is what it *must* or even *ought* to do. Suppose—as does happen—the surviving friends and family of the murdered victim very much want the convicted offender put to death; or suppose the rest of society does; or suppose the offender himself wants to be put to death for his crime. Are these good reasons for the state to do what it has a right to do? Or, in the absence of such demands for the death of a murderer, should mercy prevail and the murderer, despite his forfeited right to life, nonetheless be allowed to live?

56

Fortunately, our society has long abandoned such populist decision-making policies, and no good reasons counsel a return to them either in general or solely where the punishment of murder is concerned. Nevertheless, the criminal justice system does provide for choosing to execute only some among those who (by hypothesis) have forfeited their lives. The system allows this choice to be made openly and deliberately at exactly two points: when the trial court (judge or jury), in the absence of any mandatory death penalty statute, decides how to sentence someone convicted of a capital crime; and when the chief executive (governor, president, or whoever it is that exercises the clemency power) decides whether to commute a death sentence rather than sign the death warrant. On what grounds are these decisions made? Are they rational, predictable, morally acceptable, or are they arbitrary, whimsical, or—worse than that—governed by discernible prejudices? Since executive clemency in recent years has become so rare,[6] and no empirical research has been conducted on its exercise, we cannot answer these questions. Trial court decisions over the past decade, however, have resulted in some two hundred or so death sentences per year,[7] and large numbers of these decisions have been studied with scrupulous care. I shall say more below about what these studies show.

Yet the doctrine that the murderer forfeits his right to live surely suggests that there is no room for such decisions as these. The doctrine entails that these decisions are the result not of justice but of mercy, or of some other moral consideration that is allowed to outweigh the requirements of justice in particular cases. What the doctrine of forfeiture seems to require is nothing less than a policy of mandatory death penalties, with an execution guaranteed once the accused has been convicted of murder. The practice of mandatory capital punishment, however, is complex and, it has proved, historically, virtually impossible to achieve. Understood in the strictest manner—no choice by the prosecutor whether to indict for capital murder or some lesser degree of homicide, no choice by the trial court in sentencing once the offender is convicted of murder, no choice by the chief executive to commute the sentence from death to life—mandatory capital punishment has never existed in our history.[8] Few really want it today, if we can trust public opinion polls and the policies implied by those who have defended the death penalty in recent years in the public forum.[9] The fact that such statutes would also certainly be unconstitutional (see Chapter 6) as the punishment for most kinds of murder is not without interest, though it hardly settles what morality requires.

I can conclude only that those who insist on the dictum that a murderer forfeits his right to life either do not mean what they seem to be saying, or that our society has never been able to muster the courage to do what justice requires where the punishment of murder and other grave crimes is concerned. The only death penalty system that our society knows is one in which convicted murderers (and other capital offenders) are executed only after others acting in their official capacities have made further decisions—and the outcome of these decisions is that very few are actually executed. There is, of course, a third possibility: The doctrine of forfeiture is simply too crude—too primitive and too muddled—to enable us to understand what justice and the recognition of our rights requires.

The standard response of those who defend the doctrine of forfeiture is that, since all those convicted of a capital crime deserve death (because by their own acts they forfeited the right to live), it cannot be unfair to execute only some rather than all. Whom would it be unfair to? Not those we choose to kill, since by hypothesis they deserve to die. Surely it is not unfair to those we don't kill; very few complain of being unfairly treated when spared the death penalty despite a conviction for murder. Left in this neat form, the rejoinder may look convincing. But what it omits, or attempts to conceal, is crucial: The fact that all the members of a class (viz., the class of persons convicted of a capital crime) have forfeited their rights, according to the argument, fails to explain *why only some* are executed, rather than all, and why *these some* and not some others are the ones who get what all deserve. Forfeiture, as we have seen, at most explains how the state gets the *right to execute* them all. Something else has to explain why the agents of the state in any given case do the right thing when they decide not to act on this right in the vast majority of the cases that come before them.[10]

The defender of the death penalty at this point must take one of two lines of reply. One reply concedes that the decision is not in fact based on justice, but insists that it is still based on considerations no less legitimate. (The analogy to selective law enforcement by overworked police forces is a favorite.) The other reply defends each of the decisions for death on grounds of justice—but not the justice of forfeited rights and desert. Neither reply is convincing. We can see this clearly, but only if we are willing to examine in detail exactly how those with the power of decision in particular cases actually make these decisions in our society. To tell this story in the detail needed to convince the skeptic would require a book twice the size of this one. Fortunately, a detailed account continues to unfold in the writings of other researchers. In this book, I content myself with examining in some detail the administration of one death penalty statute (Chapter 9) and telling the story of one particular capital case (Chapter 10). Suffice it to say here that I believe my rejection of the argument made by the defender of the death penalty is amply supported by the available evidence.

The attempt to nullify the relevance of an individual's right to life by claiming that a murderer forfeits this right is not, I conclude, successful. The idea of forfeiture simply does not fit either the right-to-life doctrine or our actual practice, historic or current.

V

With the doctrine of the forfeiture of rights behind us, we can now return to the most fundamental question. Assuming, then, that the state has the right to punish by death and that the individual's right to life raises no more than a strong presumption against such killing, on what ground if any should the state proceed to enact capital statutes in the first place? Earlier in this chapter I claimed that the state is right to enact such laws and then enforce them only if it has at its disposal no other alternative, no less severe or less final mode of punishment as the necessary means to reach the end or goal of public safety and respect for the equal rights of others. Although, as we have seen, the individual may very well not have, or reasonably not think he has, any less drastic method to protect himself short of killing, or trying to kill, the intending felon against whom he is defending himself or some innocent third party, the state is never reduced to such desperation.

Certainly a modern state such as ours, with its wealth of resources, has plenty of alternatives sufficient to protect just institutions and respond to the violation of its criminal laws without resorting to the use of death as a punishment. This is simply a statement of fact, even though its truth seems to be doubted in many quarters. What seems to put it in doubt is the fact that convicted murderers who are not executed sometimes live to murder again. I say "sometimes" because the records show that recidivist murders do occur about two times for every thousand murderers paroled or otherwise released.[11] Not a perfect record, to be sure, but certainly good enough to exempt release authorities from a criticism of gross incompetence.

Since prison authorities would not turn a convicted murderer loose inside prison, much less back on the streets, if they *knew* he would kill again, the only cure for the problem seems to be one of the following: (a) Execute all convicted murderers, not because they have forfeited their rights, but because an unknown few of them will otherwise kill again; or (b) release no convicted murderers, but keep each of them under lock and key in solitary confinement until their natural death; or (c) improve the information available to prison authorities regarding the postconviction behavior of every convicted murderer so that the few who are truly dangerous can be without exception segregated from the rest; or (d) content ourselves with current practice. Alternative (a) has never been and cannot now or in the future be put into practice. The same is true of alternative (b), as any study of the theory and practice of incarceration will confirm. Alternative (c) has much to be said for it, but it is not clear that it can be carried out; it may be no more than a utopian aspiration. This apart, it is really only a much-improved version of current policy, alternative (d). Since this alternative is obviously feasible, it is clear that society does have a less severe and final mode of punishment available. Thus it would be wrong for the state to kill in exercise of its right to punish.

The only way around this conclusion is to argue that there is at least one "compelling state purpose" that only the death penalty can accomplish. What might such a purpose be? Perhaps the best candidate is the purpose of retribution. (It is little short of remarkable the way that retribution, over the past decade or so, has emerged from the darkness as the least defensible doctrine of penal theory into the light as the most defensible among penologists, philosophers, and members of the Supreme Court.[12]) I do not dispute that retribution is a valid purpose of punishment. But much turns on what one means by the term. For me, it is not a euphemism for "revenge"; it is simply another term for "deserved punishment" or for "justice in punishment." I will not even discuss whether the state is right in seeking to achieve retributive purposes; I readily grant that it is. Having granted this, the only way to avoid granting as well that it is right for the state to kill as a punishment is to show either that (a) retribution, contrary to the moral intuitions of many, does not require death for murder, or that (b) some other equally or perhaps more compelling state purpose is incompatible with retribution and should prevail over it. I think that both (a) and (b) can be defended.

Retribution, in so far as we think of it as a rational goal that the theory of punishment can defend, does not require the death penalty for murder. (This point is made more than once elsewhere in this book, and it suffices here to repeat the conclusions on the topic reached in the previous chapter.) What a responsible theory of punitive or retributive justice requires, insofar as reason and theory can defend it, is only this: (1) Punishments must impose a deprivation on offenders, just as crimes do on their victims; (2) only convicted offenders—those whose guilt is established as reliably as human institutions permit—are eligible for punishment; and (3) the severity of the punishment must be graded according to the gravity of the crime. From these principles it obviously follows that murder, the gravest (or one of the gravest) of crimes, must be punished with the utmost permissible severity; and that society should bend considerable effort to arrest, try, convict, and sentence murderers. These principles, however, tell us nothing about *which* modes of punishment should be used. In particular, they are silent on the upper bound of permissible severity.

In this connection, it is worth noting that death penalty advocates who are unwilling to compromise with their own professed retributive intuitions face an uncomfortable dilemma. If justice in punishment requires punishments that imitate the crime ("a life for a life"), then retributivists should openly favor decapitation, say, for murderers who dismember the body of the victim, and other equally savage modes of inflicting the death penalty where the murder itself was unusually savage. If they are not willing to go this far, then it must be because they tacitly recognize some upper bound to the necessary brutality even of retributive punishments. In fixing this upper bound, either they rely on some moral principle or they do not. If they do not, then they obviously beg the question in their own favor—they simply want to punish murder (and other crimes?) with death, no matter what moral principles or a consistent theory of punishment requires. But admitting to this discredits their views from any further serious consideration. If they take the other alternative and rely on some principle limiting the degree of savagery and brutality permitted in lawful punishment, then they must defend their principle against competing principles that would draw the line of permissible severity elsewhere.

Are there any principles according to which the death penalty is too severe? My earlier discussion shows, I believe, that the right to life itself can be seen as the source of such principles. (Several such principles were mentioned in the previous chapter, and others will be examined in Chapter 4.) One important and relevant principle is this: As the severity of punishments goes up (severity being measured not primarily by the infliction of physical pain but by the extent and quality of the deprivation imposed and the degree to which it is not reversible or compensable), so does the burden on society to be consistent and fair, rather than arbitrary or inequitable.

The Supreme Court tacitly acknowledged this principle more than a decade ago in the important case of *Furman v. Georgia* (1972). Evidence then and subsequently showed that the principle was most flagrantly violated where the death penalty was used in the punishment of rape. The *only* way

61

to explain the relatively high frequency with which black males were sentenced to death for the rape of white females was the racial factor—the racial *prejudice* that permitted all-white juries to bring in death sentences as if a black man's life were less valuable than a white man's and a white woman's violated virtue more deserving of punitive vindication than a black woman's.[13] With the death penalty for rape now a thing of the past (see Chapter 7), attention properly focuses solely on the extent to which racist sentiments and institutional practices, both conscious and unconscious, as well as other arbitrary and irrelevant factors, play a role in determining how the death penalty for murder is actually imposed by the criminal justice system. Social scientists are currently in disagreement[14] over some aspects of this large topic, but as I read the cumulative results of two decades of empirical research into this complex matter, I see no way to deny the arbitrariness and discrimination in the system.

As I see it, defenders of the death penalty who would argue that the state has the right to use the death penalty and that the state ought to act on this right must show one of two things. They must demonstrate either that (a) there are no principles other than retributive ones governing the upper bound of the severity of punishment, and retributive principles require the death penalty, or that (b) although there are such non-retributive principles (for example, the one I advocated above concerning the requirement of fairness in the administration of very severe penalties), the evidence shows the death penalty is and will probably continue to be administered with the requisite degree of fairness. Retributivists would like to defend (a), but, as I have tried to show, they cannot do so with consistency; their own retributivism requires them to acknowledge the proper function of precisely such non-retributive principles. (We can safely ignore the question-begging appeal to "a life for a life" for reasons explained in the previous chapter.) The defense of (b) requires us to look carefully at all of the evidence and propose punitive policies in its light. Without all that empirical evidence before the reader, I cannot convincingly argue the point here. Experience living in our society nonetheless tells me that we cannot count on our sense of fairness to dominate the workings of the criminal justice system in the future, any more than it has in the past, in such a way that factors like socio-economic status, lack of firm roots in the community, gender, and especially race and color—which ought to be irrelevant to why some are punished more severely than others—have little or no effect on whether an accused killer is indicted, tried, convicted, sentenced to death, and executed. Defenders of the death penalty, whether in scholarly treatises or in letters to the newspaper, have yet to carry the burden of persuasion on this important point.

VI

I hazard the view that an awareness of the undeniably superior incapacitative effects of the death penalty, yoked to the illusion that retribution requires death for murder ("murderers forfeit their lives"), results in what passes for rational belief that society at present needs the death penalty. Add to this the further illusion that the more severe the threatened punishment the better a deterrent it is, and the nagging and annoying conviction that it costs the public treasury thousands of dollars each year to keep a convicted murderer in prison when that same money could be put to better social use, and you have the mind-set of the modern believer in capital punishment.

The state's alleged right to use death as a punishment, and all that this idea entails, is rarely considered very seriously or thoughtfully. Perhaps it would be a good thing if it were. If my argument is correct, then we have to conclude either that the state has no such right, or that it is right for the state to punish by death only under conditions that do not in fact prevail today in our society, that have not at any time in the past, and that almost certainly will not in the foreseeable future.

Chapter 3

A Utilitarian Critique of the Death Penalty

I

During a long and productive life, Jeremy Bentham (1748–1832) twice undertook to apply his general utilitarian principles of punishment to a critique of the death penalty. The earlier and by far the more thorough effort was in 1775. At the age of twenty-seven, Bentham provided an extensive discussion of capital punishment in two chapters of Book II of his *Rationale of Punishment,* which was later reprinted in the Bowring edition of Bentham's *Works.*[1] This 1775 essay (as I shall henceforth refer to these chapters) contains about eight thousand words and is divided into two parts of unequal length and importance. The first and briefer of the two (Chapter XI, "Capital Punishment") is devoted largely to explaining the distinction between "simple" and "afflictive" death penalties, and to a severe criticism of the latter.* The second and more important part (Chapter XII, "Capital

---

*By "afflictive" death penalties, Bentham means a death preceded by aggravations and tortures, as for instance was provided by law in England for the punishment of "high treason." Here is how he described the "afflictive" punishment of death for "high treason": "1. Dragging at a horse's tail along the streets from the prison to the place of execution; 2. Hanging by the neck, yet not so as entirely to destroy life; 3. Plucking out and burning of the entrails while the patient is yet alive; 4. Beheading; 5. Quartering; and 6. Exposure of the head and quarters in such places as the king directs." (443,ii) (For all quotations from Bentham's *Rationale,* I henceforth indicate page and column numbers by arabic and roman numerals, respectively. Also, italics in quotations from Bentham in this chapter are in the original.)

Punishment Examined") is about two thirds of the whole; here Bentham argues his case against the death penalty on utilitarian grounds. I propose in this chapter to concentrate on his remarks in what follows.

Bentham's second and distinctly less instructive discussion of the same subject was written in the last year or so of his life. Entitled "On Death Punishment" and styled as an essay by "Jeremy Bentham to His Fellow Citizens of France," it was published in mid–1831.[2] First published as a pamphlet of a dozen pages, the essay would quite probably be unavailable today had it not been conveniently reprinted by Bowring.[3] The 1831 essay (as I shall henceforth call it) is about as long as the second and larger part of the 1775 essay. The style, however, is distinctly inferior, marked with frequent use of the somewhat telegraphic and elliptical nonsentences in which Bentham increasingly wrote toward the end of his life. Whereas the 1775 discussion is written in a manner suitable to what it is, a special application of the general principles argued in the earlier chapters of the *Rationale,* the later essay reads almost like an extended piece of correspondence,[4] with an informality and relative lack of structure that sharply contrasts with the style of Bentham's major treatises. Moreover, as we shall see, the argument against the death penalty itself is unbalanced, even warped, by a peculiar emphasis on what must be judged to be a quite ancillary consideration.

Despite these shortcomings, the 1831 essay does mark a development in Bentham's settled thoughts on the subject in at least one important respect. In his 1775 essay, a few paragraphs from the end, Bentham verges on making a concession to those who favor the death penalty. He writes that if a society

---

He adds, "This mode of punishment is not now in use." His strongest criticism, however, is directed at the "afflictive" death penalty then in use in the British West Indies, "by far the most severe punishment ever yet devised by the ingenuity of man." Here is his description:

> The delinquent is suspended from a post by means of a hook inserted under his shoulder, or under his breast bone. In this manner, the sufferer is prevented from doing anything to assist himself, and all persons are prohibited, under severe penalties, from relieving him. He remains in this situation, exposed to the scorching heat of the day, where the sun is almost vertical, and the atmosphere almost without a cloud, and to the chilling dews of the night; his lacerated flesh attracts a multitude of insects, which increase his torments, and under the fever produced by these complicated sufferings, joined to hunger and thirst, all raging in the most intense degree, he gradually expires.

Bentham adds that this punishment is reserved for "negro slaves" guilty of "rebellion."

Those who think of Bentham as a rationalistic eccentric and of utilitarian ethics as coldly calculating should read the next two paragraphs, in which Bentham excoriates his fellow countrymen for tolerating such "atrocious" penalties (444,i). He ends with this challenge: "Let the colonists reflect upon this: if such a [penal] code be necessary, the colonies are a disgrace and an outrage on humanity: if not necessary, these laws are a disgrace to the colonists themselves" (id.).

or its legislature is "determined to preserve the punishment of death, in consideration of the effects it produces *in terrorum,* then it should use this penalty only for those "offenses which in the highest degree shock the public feeling—for murders, accompanied with circumstances of aggravation, and particularly when their effect may be the destruction of numbers . . ." (450,ii). Although one cannot read this passage in context and view it as more than a concession made with some reluctance, it is also true that Bentham's overall argument in 1775 against the death penalty (whatever he may have believed about it) failed to provide adequate utilitarian grounds for complete abolition. At the end of his life, however, he seems to have thought that he had at last constructed an argument so strong and comprehensive that it no longer required him to have any reservations. In his 1831 essay, written at a time English criminal law had begun to move in the direction Bentham had long advocated, he confronted the policy issue at the very outset and answered categorically: "The punishment of death— shall it be abolished? I answer—*Yes.* Shall there be any exception to this rule? I answer, so far as regards *subsequential* offenses, *No* . . ." (525,ii–526,i).

Taken together, Bentham's 1775 and 1831 essays constitute a critique of the death penalty unique among leading philosophers. Since Socrates (who, as is well known, died a convict's death at his own hand from a cup of hemlock[5]), philosophers have examined the morality and policy of the death penalty; but Bentham devoted more space to the topic than any of his predecessors did. Hobbes, Locke, Montesquieu, and Rousseau, for example, all find reason to mention the topic in one way or another; yet they do so without ever using it as a set-piece for the application of general theory. Beccaria, to whom Bentham elsewhere readily acknowledges his indebtedness,[6] comes nearest to devoting comparable space and emphasis to the topic in his enormously influential little treatise, *Dei Delitti e delle Pene,*[7] published in 1764, a decade before Bentham began work on his own *Rationale of Punishment.* However, Beccaria had no clear and uniform theory of punishment; his arguments combine appeals both to utilitarian principles and to natural rights contractarianism. Nor is Beccaria a philosopher of Bentham's stature. Kant, who certainly is, and whose antiutilitarian views on the death penalty were published in 1797,[8] wrote only briefly on the subject, although, like Bentham, he used this topic as a convenient application of general theory.

Bentham's great utilitarian successor, John Stuart Mill, who might have been expected to carry on Bentham's attack on the death penalty, apparently never discussed it in his books or essays. When he did finally address it, it was not until late in life (1868), in a speech during debate in Parliament on a bill to abolish public hangings. Speaking against an amendment to abolish the death penalty outright, Mill defended this punishment for murder.[9] He employed that mix of reasons characteristic of his later semipopular writings that made his professed utilitarianism somewhat doubtfully the genuine article. Whether Bentham, who by that time had been dead for over three decades, would have been convinced by Mill's argument, we will of course never know. In any case, Bentham's critique is unswerving and shows him as one, perhaps the only, leading philosopher who, throughout his adult life, steadily and soberly opposed "Death Punishment" (as he called it) and expressed that opposition in writings that are still instructive.

In my examination of Bentham's argument, I shall emphasize exposition and internal criticism on the one hand, and evaluation of the argument's strengths and weaknesses from a modern vantage point in the United States on the other. The risk of distortion in appraising his views anachronistically is, I think, outweighed by the benefit of showing what we should think about his views in light of current knowledge.

II

In order to appreciate Bentham's critique, we need to place it within his general "rationale of punishment." As commentators on utilitarianism have made clear,[10] all versions of utilitarianism involve some combination of two things. One is a doctrine of the end-state to be realized, that is, a condition or state of affairs deemed to have intrinsic value toward which rational action is aimed. The other is the set of means to that end, that is, various possible actions open to the agent (person, legislature, society), the value of which is purely instrumental, because choice among these alternative actions is determined by how efficiently each leads (or would lead) to the end-state. According to Bentham, a punishment, like any other legal practice, must be morally justified by its conduciveness to the appropriate end. That end can be variously stated, and Bentham's own account of it varies depending on whether he has a proximate or the ultimate end in mind. In his best-known work, *An Introduction to the Principles of Morals and Legislation,* published in 1789, he writes: "The immediate principle end of punishment" is to "control action" (158, note a), the "action" of those who are liable to a punishment if they violate the law as well as the conduct of those who are undergoing punishment after having been sentenced for a violation. Bentham also declares that "the chief end of punishment" ought to be "general prevention" (396,ii), an end that will be achieved if and only if adequate "control" is attained. But both these ends are penultimate. The ultimate end of penal laws is one shared with all legislation, and Bentham describes it as follows: "The general object which all laws have, or ought to have, in common, is to augment the total happiness of the community. . ." (158). Precisely how this end-state is to be measured and in what it really consists are notorious problems, and we will return to these points later. Suffice it to say here that Bentham believes alternative social policies can be evaluated by reference to their efficiency in reaching various ends, but the only end-state that ultimately matters is that of the greatest happiness. Thus, in his theory, the only rational or justifiable punishments for a society to adopt are punishments that most efficiently produce the greatest happiness.

Since a utilitarian necessarily views any punishment as an "evil" (390,ii) such a harm can be justified only by being the necessary condition of some greater good, benefit, or happiness that exceeds the evil of punishment. The ideal punishment, therefore, achieves the maximum in social benefit at the cost of the minimum in social harm. Bentham believes that the capacity of any mode of punishment to approach this ideal can be evaluated by reference to a fairly small number of (not altogether independent) factors. These factors are relevant not solely because of their effect on reducing the crime rate through prevention and deterrence; what ultimately matters is the over-all effect of punishment on the general happiness. Such happiness includes not only a lower crime rate but much else, including the well-being of the persons being punished, as Bentham makes abundantly clear. "It ought not to be forgotten," he writes, ". . . that the delinquent is a member of the community, as well as any other individual—. . . and that there is just as much reason for consulting his interest as that of any other. His welfare is proportionably the welfare of the community—his suffering the suffering of the community" (398,ii). He calls these properties of punishment "Variability," "Equability," "Commensurability," "Characteristicalness," "Exemplarity," "Frugality," "Subserviency to Reformation," "Efficacy with respect to Disablement," "Subserviency to Compensation," "Popularity," and "Remissibility."[11] This list is common to the *Rationale* and to the *Introduction to the Principles of Morals and Legislation.*[12] As I shall explain below, the chief difference between his two critiques of the death penalty arises from his shift in judgment about the relevance and relative weights of these factors.

Since variations in the quality and severity of a punishment are easily under the control of the rational legislator, Bentham's general theory of punishment proposes multiple criteria for the proper apportionment of punishments to crimes. He formulates these criteria by giving a baker's dozen of "Rules,"[13] each of which is asserted with all the imperative force Bentham can muster. His language thus somewhat disguises the fact that the sole warrant for these rules is that compliance with them in the long run maximizes the general happiness. Thus, Rule 7 states: "To enable that the value of the punishment may outweigh the profit of the offence, it must be increased in point of magnitude, in proportion as it falls short in point of certainty" (401,ii). The reason such rules must be followed, Bentham implies, is that they enable the rational legislator to attach just the right quantum of pain in punishment to discourage the commission of the offense through deterrence and prevention, calibrated so that any increase in the severity of the penalty would in fact cause society distress greater than the good that would be achieved by any further reduction in crime.

Oddly enough, however, Bentham's two discussions of the death penalty make no explicit reference to these "Rules," even though it might seem that they would have provided the most direct way to evaluate the merits of the death penalty. This failure may be the one prima facie shortcoming in Bentham's utilitarian critique of the death penalty. Yet there is a reason for this omission, which Bentham (though he never mentions it) may well have had in mind. His discussions of the death penalty are intended to be completely general. That is, he undertakes to evaluate the death penalty as such, as a mode of punishment whose suitability for *any* crime is in question. Consequently, it would have been virtually impossible for him to try to evaluate its relative suitability by means of his "Rules" for each of the many capital crimes in the penal code of his day. This gain in scope and brevity for his discussions is not without a price, however. Where punishing murder is concerned—the crime whose punishment by death is likely to arouse the most controversy—Bentham's discussion is inconclusive. He fails to concentrate on showing that the death penalty for murder, when compared to the alternative punishments, is second best overall under the relevant "Rules" for apportioning punishment to crime.

This defect points to a consideration of general importance in Bentham's discussions of the death penalty. A utilitarian critique of any law or social policy cannot proceed except by reference to alternatives. What alternatives to the death penalty does Bentham consider? In each of his death penalty essays he considers only one, and it is essentially the same one. In 1831 he describes it as "prison discipline" (531,ii), thereby leaving open to speculation whether he meant natural life imprisonment, imprisonment for a fixed term or under an indeterminate sentence, imprisonment in solitary confinement, imprisonment during which labor would be exacted from the convict, or some combination of these. In 1775 he was more precise: "Perpetual imprisonment, accompanied with hard labour and occasional solitary confinement . . ." (450,i). Whether the vagueness of Bentham's language on the point in 1831 indicates some softening of his views on the preferred alternative is doubtful. Apparently Bentham never gave serious thought to less rigorous forms of incarceration for capital felons than what he recommended in 1775.[14]

The evaluation of a mode of punishment on utilitarian grounds, then, proceeds as follows. First, one must pick out the several factors by virtue of which any punishment may be said to yield effects upon the general happiness. Second, one must compare alternative punitive policies with respect to each of these factors. The identification and comparison may both be said to be part of what, following Bentham and his younger admirer, John Austin, came to be called "analytical jurisprudence."[15] These two steps by themselves, however, cannot suffice. One must also couple each factor in each alternative punishment with some empirical observations, evidence, or data based on the study of the actual effects of these punishments, so that the rational legislator can truly calculate the relative impact of the alternatives upon the general happiness. Without such evidence, not even an ordinal ranking of the two alternatives is possible except as a conjecture. Nevertheless, as we shall see, Bentham adduces *no* evidence for most of the many empirical claims on which his objections to the death penalty rest. To be sure, arguments over penal policies based on empirical evidence were hardly an established practice in 1775 or even in 1831. Still, Bentham nowhere shows the slightest concern over the fact that he offers virtually no evidence drawn from actual human experience relevant to the choice of punishments. He may have deceived himself into thinking that his conjectures were as good as genuine data. Or perhaps he thoughtlessly collapsed the analytic exercise of isolating relevant factors into the empirical enterprise of gathering data to show how different punishments actually function. Possibly the task of gathering relevant empirical evidence simply struck him as too boring to undertake, as it does most philosophers. In any case, a utilitarian defender of a the death penalty confronted with Bentham's critique need not back down before the onslaught of Bentham's evidence; during the course of his argument Bentham offers virtually none.

III

The structure of Bentham's 1775 critique of the death penalty could hardly be simpler: In favor of capital punishment there are four factors; against it there are also four; taken all together, the latter outweigh the former. Thus, given a choice between the death penalty and the alternative of "prison discipline," a utilitarian must favor the alternative. We need to look closely at each of the three steps in Bentham's argument.

The four relevant considerations that favor the death penalty, according to Bentham, are these: It is "analogous" to the crime, it is "popular," it is "exemplary"—that is, "an execution makes a deep and lasting impression" on all who witness it (444,ii),—and above all, it is wholly incapacitative, or "efficacious in the highest degree in preventing further mischief from the same source" (449,ii). To the exposition and support of the first two considerations, Bentham devotes only a few lines; the latter two he treats more amply. Even so, a reader not inclined in advance to agree with Bentham might well complain that the force of several factors (even on utilitarian assumptions) is underestimated, and that in any case he disposes of the argument for the death penalty far too briskly.

Analogy   The factor of "analogy" does not appear as such in Bentham's general catalogue of the dozen "properties" of any punishment. It is, however, identical with the property that does appear on that list under the heading of "Characteristicalness."[16] This factor favors the death penalty, as Bentham rightly points out, but only for the crime of murder. Since in 1775 English law authorized the death penalty for dozens of nonhomicidal crimes against the person, property, public order, and the state,[17] Bentham could as well have cited this factor to argue *against* the death penalty, except for the punishment of murder. Whatever the reason, he did not choose to adopt this tactic. As a factor favoring the death penalty even for murder, Bentham regards "analogy" as singularly weak and disposes of it with no more than an epigram: "Analogy is a very good recommendation, but not a good justification" (449,ii).

As a utilitarian, surely he is right. That a punishment is analogous to the crime for which it is meted out is at best a contingent, not a final, consideration in its favor. Analogies of this sort, by themselves, have little if any impact on the general happiness. The possibility that underlying the factor of analogy is a principle of reciprocity—it will be done to you as you have done to others—and thus of rough justice, seems not to have occurred to

Bentham. Or, rather, while it clearly does occur to him earlier in the *Rationale* in his general discussion of "Characteristicalness," this awareness deserts him when he shifts to the particular case of the death penalty. No doubt, as he implies, it is possible on utilitarian grounds to argue against *lex talionis* in general, but it is a regrettable oversight that Bentham fails even to comment on this powerfully attractive and perennial source of defense of the death penalty for murder.

Popularity Bentham dismisses the factor of "popularity" virtually out of hand, because he believes the then-current attitudes in favor of the death penalty were all based on ignorance and misinformation. The same explanation has been advanced in our own time from the Supreme Court by Justice Thurgood Marshall, who argued that if the general public were better acquainted with the actual facts surrounding crime and the death penalty in contemporary society, support for executions would wither away.[18] Once it is understood that the death penalty is not the deterrent or preventive that it is reputed to be, Bentham thinks, its popularity will wane. Today, we must regard this optimism as somewhat naive. Survey research and its scientific analysis strongly suggest that by no means all of the popular support for the death penalty can be traced to the (perhaps misguided) belief that it is a uniquely effective deterrent and preventive of crime. Rather, a considerable fraction of the support for this punishment seems to rest on other grounds, retributive or perhaps even vindictive.

Exemplarity Bentham's discussion of the deterrent effect of the death penalty is diffuse and indirect. He devotes as much space to this one theme as he does to the other three factors favoring the death penalty combined, but in such an oblique, incomplete, and disconnected manner that his exposition and criticism are distinctly inferior to what we would have expected him to provide. After all, he states early in the *Rationale,* just as we would expect of a good utilitarian, that "general prevention ought to be the chief end of punishment, as it is its real justification";[19] and that "general prevention" is a synonym for "deterrence." I diagnose the unsatisfactory character of his disucssion as the result of an attempt to bring most of the considerations affecting deterrence under his rubric of "Exemplarity." Unfortunately, it cannot be done. On the one hand, deterrence involves several considerations that do not conveniently fit here, as his discussion of the death penalty for "rebellion" under the heading of "Efficacy" makes abundantly clear. On the other hand, exemplarity provokes Bentham into speculations about the psychology of the would-be criminal and the effects of witnessing executions, which only obscures the more central issues. Accordingly, in my account of his views here, I shall make no attempt to convey the exact pattern of his discussion. Instead, I will reshape it in the interest of clarity and brevity.

First, Bentham argues that Beccaria was wrong in thinking that "the impression made by any particular punishment was in proportion to its duration, and not to its intensity" (444,ii). "For the generality of men," he observes, "among those who are attached to life by the ties of reputation, affection, enjoyment, hope, capital punishment appears to be more exemplary than any other" (445,i). Not, mind you, that it *is* more severe; here Bentham quite agrees with Beccaria, who believed that life imprisonment is by far the more severe of the two punishments.[20] But the death penalty *seems* more severe, and that is what matters to its "exemplary" role. As Bentham observes earlier in the *Rationale:* "The apparent value [i.e., severity of a punishment] influences the conduct of individuals. It is the real punishment that is the expense—the apparent punishment that gives the profit" (398,ii). Not surprisingly, therefore, he says that of the four reasons for the death penalty, this one "is the strongest" (450,i). Still, it is not strong enough.

Bentham's central counterargument is this: Perpetual imprisonment, with suitable aggravations of labor and solitary confinement, can be made to have a more terrifying impact on prospective criminals than it currently does and more than the threat of death does. After all, the criminally inclined classes are by temperament "brutal," "independent," and "wandering," all traits that render them "hostile to steady [confinement] and laborious industry . . ." (450,i). Make it clear that this, and not a quick and relatively painless death, is what awaits them, and they will shrink from crime the more. The law-abiding members of the middle class, who have long ago learned to chain themselves to factories, desks, and careers, overrate the finality of death and underrate the dreadful prospect of a lifetime confined behind bars. If, in short, prospective criminals were as rational as legislators ought to be, they would see that the prospect of life imprisonment ought to have a greater deterrent effect on their behavior than the death penalty.

How does this argument strike us today? Of primary relevance is the fact that very few opponents of the death penalty today favor natural life imprisonment at hard labor as the alternative.[21] It is not an attractive alternative, least of all to the rational legislator once he understands what it will cost the community in taxes for prison construction, custodial services, and so on. Even more to the point is the counterproductiveness, on utilitarian grounds, of making prisons so dreadful as to inspire the terror Bentham's argument requires. If virtually everyone in prison today is eventually going to be released (excepting only a few Charles Mansons or Richard Specks), then what is the point of ruining prisoners' lives behind bars, thereby adding injury to harm, with the result that the convict emerges in due course worse than when he went in? In sum, I doubt whether there really are utilitarian grounds for defending the alternative of prison over that of execution if this requires society to increase the horrors of imprisonment in order to make the threat of prison an even better deterrent than the death penalty.

Efficacy   Although Bentham opens the case for the death penalty by citing what in his *Introduction* he calls "Efficacy with respect to disablement" as the first of the four factors, it is doubtful whether he thinks it favors the death penalty more strongly than does "exemplarity" or deterrence. In any case, he confines his criticism to two points. The first and major criticism is that society already uses "confinement" as a sufficient mode of incapacitation for the criminally insane (449,ii). If such "confinement" suffices to prevent these dangerous offenders from recidivism, there is no reason why it cannot do the same for convicts who are not criminally insane. His second point is an arguable concession to those who favor the death penalty. He admits that in "the case of rebellion" (or, as we might say today, terrorist violence in the service of a revolutionary political ideology), an exception to total abolition may be "necessary" on grounds of incapacitation (id.). Even here, Bentham shrewdly counsels caution on the ound that executing terrorist rebels is more likely to turn them into martyrs who inspire rather than discourage their followers. In a prescient anecdote (whether genuine or fictitious, the context does not indicate), Bentham writes: " 'Look,' said the executioner to an aged Irishman, showing him the bleeding head of a man just executed for rebellion—'look at the head of your son.' 'My son,' replied he, 'has more than one head.' " As Bentham wisely advises, "It would be well for the legislator, before he appoints capital punishment, even in this case, to reflect on this instructive lesson" (450,i).

Bentham's discussion of incapacitation prompts some skeptical observations in light of current knowledge. First, as a purely logical point, Bentham comes close to committing the fallacy of inferring that if a convicted offender has been incapacitated, then crimes will thereby have been prevented. To be able to infer that, we would have to *know* that the offender (were he not effectively incapacitated) was certain to commit another crime in the future. Of course, we rarely if ever know that; at most, we can construct a certain probability of such recidivism given either the convict's past criminal record or his membership in some convict class whose recidivist characteristics have already been measured. This criticism is particularly relevant where the incapacitative powers of the death penalty are concerned. That the death penalty incapacitates is necessarily true. It is at best empirically true that this incapacitation prevents much recidivism.

Incapacitation by way of death, it is true, prevents a measurably greater number of recidivist murders than does imprisonment. Evidence at our disposal today shows that recidivist murder, rare though it is, does occur—also in prisons, a possibility Bentham overlooked. No doubt such recidivist murders could be prevented by execution of *all* convicted murderers. As any latter-day Benthamite would be quick to point out, however, it is also true that most of these crimes could have been prevented by other means as well, e.g., better parole review procedures. Nevertheless, a contemporary utilitarian who wants to evaluate the relative incapacitative effects of execution versus incarceration must realize that current policies governing imprisonment do not and probably cannot prevent *all* the crimes that full-scale use of executions could prevent. Of course it would be folly on utilitarian grounds to try to isolate this consideration from all others and elevate it into a decisive factor in favor of the death penalty. Even so, this factor does emerge from a critique with a slight margin still in favor of the death penalty—if not in Bentham's day, then in ours.

Finally, the punishment of terrorism and rebellion (an issue as relevant to deterrence as to incapacitation) has not been studied with sufficient care by empirically minded investigators. The general logic of Bentham's argument, however, remains as valid in our day as in his. Thoughtful students of contemporary terrorism have relied upon this argument perhaps without realizing that they were anticipated by Bentham two centuries ago.[22]

Evaluation   Has Bentham made out the strongest possible case for the death penalty on utilitarian grounds? The issue divides into four parts because we have to distinguish between (a) the argument for the death penalty as a mode of punishment for many or all of the major felonies—Bentham's primary target, and (b) the argument for the death penalty confined to the punishment of murder. We must also scrutinize (i) the adequacy of his argument under the four rubrics he has chosen, in contrast to (ii) the adequacy of an argument for the death penalty based upon all twelve of his "properties" of punishment (as well as upon others he may have overlooked). As these two sets of distinctions fully intersect, the evaluation of the adequacy of Bentham's argument has four separate stages. We have, however, already disposed of half of this task, viz., (i)(a) and (i)(b). I think Bentham is correct in concluding that it is difficult to defend the death penalty on utilitarian grounds as the proper punishment for many felonies, if utilitarian grounds are confined to the four that he identifies. I think he is also right with regard to the death penalty for murder, although here the case for the death penalty is a bit stronger than even Bentham himself realizes.

Could the utilitarian argument for the death penalty, whether confined to murder or extended to the punishment of other crimes, be enhanced by taking into account factors that Bentham identifies but ignores? Or by appeal to factors of which he is unaware but that a truly thoroughgoing utilitarian defense of the death penalty would uncover? Answering these questions may look like a much larger task than it really is. As an illustration, consider the general factor Bentham identifies as "Simplicity of Description." His failure to mention this as a factor favoring the death penalty seems surprising.[23] Surely, the fact that the death penalty, whether for murder or for other crimes, is easily understood "not only to the enlightened, but to the most unenlightened and ignorant" (405,ii), must seem to be a factor in its favor. Or, upon reflection, should we say that it is a factor that counts equally for the death penalty and for the alternative of imprisonment, because each is equally easily grasped by the multitude? Perhaps on balance we should say that this deterrence-relevant factor favors the death penalty over imprisonment but not by very much, and perhaps in the end it is of no more significance than the factor of "analogy."

The chief reason Bentham, during his discussion of the case for the death penalty, ignores so many of the "properties" of punishment that he elsewhere mentions is that he thinks all these other "properties" unambiguously favor the alternative of imprisonment. Let us, therefore, turn to this part of his overall argument and see whether we should agree.

IV

In 1775, the four characteristics of punishment that Bentham invokes against the death penalty relative to imprisonment are that it is "not convertible to profit," it lacks "frugality" as well as "equability," and it is "not remissible" (445,ii). If the space he devotes to developing his argument under each of these factors is any indication of his judgment of their relative weight, then clearly the third and fourth have the greater importance.

Profitability Bentham does not linger over the obvious point that a dead convict cannot provide "compensation" (445,ii). It does not matter whether the compensation is devoted to repairing the loss suffered by the victim of the crime or to the loss suffered by society in bringing the offender to justice. A regimen of capital punishment prevents both sorts of compensation.

The defender of the death penalty, of course, might well reply that it is in fact economically cheaper to execute convicts than to imprison them for life, so that the loss caused by their death and resulting incapacity to pay any compensation is more than offset by the gain produced by not having to expend public resources for their permanent custody. Bentham's failure to anticipate this objection is easily explained. In his day, prison enthusiasts shared the optimistic belief that prisons could be run as profitable "capitalistic enterprises."[24] In our time, the economic costs of long-term imprisonment have become a popular consideration in support of the death penalty. In truth, however, the actual additional cost of life imprisonment for persons currently sentenced to death would add little to the total annual cost of operating a maximum security prison. If anything, the costs of a criminal justice system in which the death penalty is authorized appear to be considerably greater, given present state and federal laws, than the costs of the same system without the death penalty.[25]

Frugality In order to clarify what Bentham would have regarded as a "frugal" punishment, consider this example: Fine a very wealthy convicted offender $10,000 and use the money to distribute $100 to each of a hundred destitute but law-abiding citizens. Thanks to the differing marginal utility of money, such a fine would inconvenience one wealthy person only slightly but would no doubt benefit many poor a great deal. The death penalty, however, Bentham argues, is "pre-eminently defective . . . in point of frugality" (445,ii). He seems to think that its infliction fails to produce a desirable quantum of pleasure coordinate with the pain produced for the person being punished, whereas imprisonment can do this effectively. (As one can see, this argument rather overlaps with his previous argument concerning the impossibility of using the death penalty for the purpose of "compensation.") Here, his reasoning runs as follows: The only way that a convicted criminal can profit or please society is by means of the good works he can do during punishment or afterwards. Both are possible with imprisonment, neither with death. Thus, through this back door Bentham introduces the idea of the utility of reform, perhaps even including post-punitive release; he says that under the punishment of "confinement and hard labour . . . there is a chance of . . . [the convict's] being reformed, and rendered of some use to society" (id.).

Equability   Under the heading of equability, Bentham has two quite distinct points to make; they are best discussed separately. Their relative importance in his mind is difficult to judge, however, partly because he fails to keep the two points completely separate.

The first aspect of inequability is the absence of what Bentham elsewhere calls "Variability,"[26] or that general property of punishment by means of which it admits of more or less (as do lashes of a whip or years in prison). The second property is that by virtue of which, when punishment is inflicted, everyone who undergoes it experiences the same amount of pain. Elsewhere, Bentham calls this second aspect "Equability."[27] Bentham argues that the death penalty fails the first, or variability, requirement because it is an all-or-nothing matter, an act that of itself admits of no degrees or room for variation. Of course, as he had already explained in his 1775 chapter on "afflictive death penalties," the death penalty can be preceded with tortures and followed by indignities visited upon the dead man's corpse. Bentham ignores these possibilities and, strictly, he is correct to do so: Neither torture nor desecration of a corpse is a way of varying *death*.

Bentham boldly insists that "*Variability* is a point of excellence in which the punishment of death is more deficient than in any other" (447,i). Does he mean "more deficient than in any other of its many defects," or "more deficient than in any other penalty"? It does not really matter, since on either interpretation he is wrong. First, the same deficiency can be found in many mutilative corporal punishments, e.g., castration. Second, as he himself soon points out, the death penalty is totally "irremissible," and surely this is as grave a defect as is its invariability—indeed, it is graver. Finally, it is hard to see why invariability is much of a defect if we are concerned with the punishment of only one type of crime narrowly defined, e.g., first-degree murder. Again, Bentham's failure to distinguish explicitly between assessing the death penalty as a general mode of punishment for a wide variety of crimes (where variability is surely an important factor) and assessing it as a mode of punishment specifically for the crime of murder (where variability is of little or no importance) undermines the persuasiveness and clarity of his criticism.

Bentham devotes his attention mainly to the second point, concerning "equability" strictly so called. For some offenders, Bentham allows that death constitutes "a very heavy punishment"; but for a person who is "a first-rate delinquent," long hardened to grim circumstances of life, it may be "next to nothing" (445,ii). Bentham thus repudiates the seeming egalitarianism of the death penalty, which holds that each of us has only one life to lose and that this life is as valuable for the rich as for the poor, for the talented as for the ungifted, and so on. Bentham chooses to try to establish the inequability of the death penalty by means of an indirect argument that is of some interest in its own right and that has been and still is used in quite a different way. He argues to the conclusion that the death penalty cannot serve as an effective deterrent from the fact that the prospect of death has such a differential impact on the imagination and motivation of prospective criminals. No doubt inspired by Beccaria,[28] Bentham reasons that the death penalty is for the prospective criminal at the threshold of the criminal act "an event by no means certain" (446,i), "at any rate distant" (446,ii), and not vividly imagined by most of those inclined to commit a capital crime in the first place. He infers from this that the impact of capital punishment must be uneven and so is "peculiarly defective in the case of the greater part of the most malignant and formidible species of malefactors . . ." (447,i). Its inequability, in short, means it is ill fitted for influencing persons of limited imagination and lack of involvement in a broad and complex network of human relations, or personal and family projects that stretch into the future. Thus he concludes there is no reason to hope that hardened criminals, or anyone else calloused and bruised by life, "ought . . . to be deterred from their profession [by the threat of the hangman any more] than [are] soldiers or sailors are from theirs, by the apprehension of bullets or of shipwreck" (id.).

As an argument against the death penalty, Bentham's reasoning survives as a standard part of every abolitionist's argumentarium. As an attempt by Bentham to prove the inequability of the death penalty relative to its alternative, however, it is confusingly presented and a failure. It is confusing because it needs to be linked directly to the reasoning he earlier advanced in criticism of the death penalty under the rubric of "Exemplarity." It is a failure, first, because Bentham gives no reason (much less any evidence) to cause one to think that the death penalty is any worse in the respects in question than is imprisonment. He may have overlooked his failure in this regard because, as noted above, he uses the rubric of "Equability" in his discussion to cover two different points, the other of which is "Variability"—a respect in which imprisonment does have an obvious edge over executions. But the superiority of prison over death with respect to variability is completely independent of whether prison is more, less, or the same in equability (narrowly defined) as death. Finally, for all Bentham knows or shows, many persons executed for their crimes have suffered *exactly* the same degree of loss, deprivation and pain. To be sure, such a possibility is best viewed, in Bentham's time as well as in ours, as an unverifiable empirical hypothesis. Bentham seems to think, erroneously, that we can reject it merely because *some* persons show different reactions to the experience of their execution, including its prospect. No doubt they do, but no argument of this form can suffice to show that *all* do.

Remissibility   As for many abolitionists, so for Bentham the winning ace is this: "for death there is no remedy" (447,ii). First, as he recognizes, there is no way to *correct* the erroneous infliction of the death penalty; imprisonment, however, can be abruptly ended as soon as there is reason to conclude that an innocent person is being punished. Second, there is no way to *compensate* the wrongly executed person; the wrongly imprisoned person can be (and sometimes actually is) awarded a compensatory sum. Bentham is also rightly skeptical of any prospect for ever perfecting the system of criminal justice so that such errors cannot occur. One might well say today what he wrote two centuries ago: "Judges will continue fallible; witnesses to depose falsehood; . . . circumstantial evidence . . . may be the effect of chance . . ." (id.). The proneness of the system to "caprice and mistake," as a leading contemporary abolitionist has neatly phrased it,[29] Bentham fully appreciated.

When one pauses to ask for evidence of the system's failures, however, Bentham does not have very much to offer. He does little more than assure the reader that "the criminal records of every country afford various instances of these melancholy errors," and so "though unknown, many other innocent victims may have perished." This will be far too vague to convince the skeptical. Bentham's only concession to our desire to know about actual cases is to cite without any elaboration "the melancholy affair of *Calas*" (448,i). The reference is to an international *cause célèbre,* the Dreyfus case of its day. In 1762, in Toulouse, France, an elderly Huguenot merchant, Jean Calas, was executed for murdering one of his sons for converting to Catholicism. Three years of dogged work by hundreds, led by the aging Voltaire, were needed to secure an official acknowledgment of Calas's innocence.[30] The entire affair was momentous and widely celebrated in the annals of eighteenth-century liberalism. One commentator has even cited the struggle to exonerate Calas as "the beginning of the abolition movement. . . ."[31]

The Calas case is instructive for our purposes because it points directly to a criticism that has been made especially in recent decades by defenders of the death penalty, to the effect that abolitionists cannot point to erroneous *executions,* but only to erroneous death sentences, convictions, indictments, and so forth—in short, only to cases where a wrongly convicted person was *not* executed. Bentham's example is invulnerable to this criticism. Can the same be said of a similar attack on the death penalty in the United States today? Between the end of the moratorium on executions (which began in 1967 and ended in 1977) and May 1986, fifty-six persons were executed.[32] It may well be that one of these persons was innocent. Some executions earlier this century were without doubt miscarriages of justice; the same can be said with even greater confidence regarding many whose death sentences were never carried out owing to timely intervention, newly discovered evidence, and so on. Since I have discussed the general topic at considerable length elsewhere,[33] I shall not pursue it further here.

During the course of his discussion of irremissibility, Bentham introduces two further objections to the death penalty that are strictly irrelevant to his theme but not irrelevant to the demerits of the death penalty. One, which he mentions in a footnote only, is to the effect that executing a convicted criminal *"destroys one source of testimonial proof"* (447,i) concerning other crimes, committed by the offender or by other criminals. That same criminal, however, if confined to prison, may well be persuaded to divulge such information and thereby aid the cause of justice. In utilitarian terms, the usefulness of the convict to the administration of criminal justice is frustrated by the death penalty, at least by comparison with prolonged imprisonment. Again, however, Bentham fails to cite any instances where evidence was forthcoming from prisoners after incarceration that would have been lost to the authorities if these convicts had been executed.

His other point is of considerable contemporary interest. It amounts to anticipation of one rationale for the current opposition to the death penalty by Amnesty International, the international human rights organization. Since 1977, Amnesty has stressed the connection between the death penalty, torture, "unexplained disappearances, extrajudicial executions and political murders."[34] As Bentham points out:

> If we reflect on those very unfrequent occurrences, but which may at any time recur—those periods at which the government degenerates into anarchy and tyranny, we shall find that the punishment of death, established by law, is a weapon ready prepared, which is more susceptible of abuse than any other mode of punishment. A tyrannical government, it is true, may always

re-establish this mode of punishment after it has been abolished by the legislature. But the introducing what would then become an innovation, would
not be unattended with difficulty. . . . Tyranny is much more at its ease when
exercised under the sanction of law, when there is no appearance of any
departure from the ordinary course of justice, and when it finds the minds of
people already reconciled and accustomed to this mode of punishment. (448,ii)

In effect, therefore, Bentham has introduced two other categories or
factors according to which punishments may be comparatively evaluated.
We might call them, respectively, and in imitation of Bentham's style, Ancillary Administrative Advantage and Corruptibility. He is right, I believe,
in concluding that on both points the death penalty scores lower than the
alternative of imprisonment.

Evaluation In principle, an evaluation of Bentham's argument against
the death penalty must proceed by means of the same distinctions introduced
earlier in order to evaluate his argument for it. However, there is really no
need to undertake the evaluative task here. One reason is that this task,
insofar as it is merely the inverse of its predecessor, is implicitly completed.
Whatever is a weakness (or strength, respectively) in Bentham's argument
for the death penalty is so because it is an overlooked or underestimated
strength (or weakness, respectively) in his argument *against* the death penalty. Another reason is that whereas Bentham adds nothing in his 1831
essay to the reasons he adduced in 1775 in favor of the death penalty, he
does revise and supplement his argument against it; hence it will be convenient to defer further evaluation of his case against the death penalty until
we have these revisions and additions before us.

V

Bentham's critique of the death penalty in 1831 differs both in structure
and in rhetoric from his essay of 1775. As was noted earlier, he opens the
1831 essay by expressing his categorical opposition to the death penalty, a
symptom of many changes (not all for the better), including an all-but-total
neglect of reasons that seem to favor retaining executions. Instead of making
the rather strict factor-by-factor critique that was so prominent a feature
in the earlier essay (with roughly an equal number of factors to be weighed
for and against the death penalty), Bentham in 1831 builds his argument
entirely around four "bad properties" of the death penalty. Considerations
"in favour of this punishment" he confines to one small paragraph. He

delays rebutting that paragraph until the sixth and penultimate section of his essay, which he turns into a relatively lengthy examination of why the death penalty remains so popular. He concludes that its popularity is owing entirely to a series of "prejudices" based on error, misunderstandings, tradition, and the like, which blind the people and their rulers to the superior merits of imprisonment. The public especially should banish these prejudices, Bentham argues, because (in anticipation of a theme widely echoed in our time)[35] "wherever death has place, the lower are sure to stand more exposed to it than the higher orders" (531,i). Thus, what in 1775 had seemed to Bentham the not entirely implausible sources of the death penalty's popularity, viz., belief in its superior deterrent and incapacitative power, turned out in 1831 to be irrational ignorance in the extreme. No doubt he was influenced in this harsh judgment by some unprecedented evidence relevant to deterrence, to be discussed shortly.

Of the reasons against the death penalty common to the two essays, the most obvious is its irremissibility. In the 1831 essay, however, the greater scope given to this factor did not result from the discovery of new miscarriages of justice. Rather, it is owing entirely to the inclusion under this rubric of the impossibility of "compensation" under death penalties, a point that had been treated in his 1775 essay as a separate factor. Also, in the 1831 essay irremissibility is no longer the chief objection to the death penalty; that role now seems to be assigned to "Bad property the first—inefficiency" (526,ii). This property was not even mentioned as such in the 1775 essay; nor should it have been, since if taken strictly, a punishment's inefficiency is both a composite of several of the other factors and also virtually indistinguishable from its overall inutility. In the earlier essay, it will be recalled, a property that might seem to be the opposite of inefficiency, viz., "Efficacy," was cited by Bentham as one of the chief virtues of the death penalty. In that essay, efficacy was in effect equated with incapacitation. In 1831, however, the incapacitative effect is merely one aspect of overall efficiency. Moreover, Bentham discounts efficacy to such an extent that he is ready to claim that his alternative (the "succedaneum," he calls it) is "preferable to it [the death penalty] in every imaginable particular . . ." (526,i), a claim that goes well beyond anything he advanced in 1775.

Bentham is also now confident that the death penalty falls short in every other aspect of efficiency, because of a "counteracting force" (526,ii), the increasing hostility to the death penalty among the accused, witnesses, prosecutors, judges, and juries. All of these parties to the administration of justice act to withhold the death penalty, so that "this punishment fails of being productive of the preventive effect looked for and endeavored to be produced" in a manner unlike what happens with "any other mode" of punishment (id.). What Bentham is complaining of is the problem of administrative and judicial nullification, a phenomenon that played a conspicuous part in the movement toward abolition of the death penalty both in England[36] and in the United States.[37] Interestingly, Bentham takes no notice of two developments in the criminal law of the United States that were directly responsive to this problem, growing as it did out of the practice in England of mandatory death penalties. I refer to the introduction of degrees of murder, with the death penalty confined to first-degree murder (introduced in Pennsylvania in 1794),[38] and to the statutory authority for the trial court to impose a sentence of life rather than of death even after the offender had been convicted of a capital crime (a practice sporadically present in American criminal law since colonial days).[39]

Three other changes distinguish the 1831 argument from its predecessor. Bentham's readers in 1831 were presented with an objection to the death penalty apparently unlike anything to be found in the 1775 essay, something he called its "Bad property the third—Tendency to produce Crimes" (528,i). Under this heading he does not have in mind, as we might today, the alleged generally brutalizing effect of executions upon the public, notably if not originally stressed by Karl Marx two decades after Bentham's death.[40] Nor was it pathological criminal behavior attested to both in anecdote and in clinical analysis, such as "suicide by murder."[41] Bentham seems to be unaware of all such counterdeterrence factors. Instead, his point here is merely an amplification of his 1775 footnote to the effect that the death penalty silences a source of testimonial evidence. "Death-punishment puts it in the power of any ill-disposed person, by extinction put upon true evidence, to produce any evil, producible by him by means of false evidence" (528,ii). Thus although the point is the old one, it has now assumed larger proportions in his mind. Once again, however, he cites no evidence from actual cases to confirm his objection that it "produces crimes" of the sort alleged.

The most peculiar addition to Bentham's argument against the death penalty in the 1831 essay is "Bad property the fourth—Enhancing the evil effects of undue Pardon" (528,ii). He dilates on this theme at length, giving to it as much space as he does to the other three "bad properties" combined. That he should do so to this extent cannot be explained by his utilitarianism or by any other relevant consideration. As a utilitarian, he would of course oppose executive meddling into the application of general laws to particular cases—but only so long as there was good reason to believe that strict enforcement of those laws would maximize utility. (Of course if it would not, then, he would insist, the laws should be changed until they would.) Pardon, as Bentham rightly says, is an act of "mercy" and as such is a "mischievous" (529,i) eruption of godlike attributes that have no place in a society governed by a penal code that takes "for its first principle the greatest-happiness principle" (529,ii). Even though there is no evidence that by 1830 royal pardon of capital offenders in England had reached alarming frequency,[42] Bentham may have formed an impression of the facts (though he alludes to none) that provided him with cause for worry in the vein of his argument here, addressed as it ostensibly was to his "fellow citizens of France." What he overlooks is that the suspension of those laws by executive acts of mercy cannot be so easily attacked on utilitarian grounds. On his own account of the matter, capital punishment statutes cannot be penal laws of maximal utility, in France or any country like it. To think otherwise is to attach an excessive belief in the utility of obedience to law, in recent years attacked by utilitarians as mere "rule worship,"[43] and rightly so. In any case, Bentham's preoccupation with the whole theme is bound to strike even the sympathetic observer today as tedious, eccentric, and unmotivated.

By far the most important improvement in the 1831 essay over its predecessor, the one crucial respect in which Bentham's later argument is conspicuously superior on utilitarian grounds to what he offered in 1775, is in regard to the deterrent efficacy of executions. It will be recalled that in 1775 Bentham evaluated most (but not all) of the considerations relevant to deterrence under the rubric of "Exemplarity," a factor he held tended to favor the death penalty over the alternative (though not as much as its supporters believed). In 1831, he ignores this factor entirely, perhaps because he was by then aware that "Exemplarity" was not an adequate rubric for his purposes. Instead, he argues that the death penalty in addition to its four "bad properties" also suffers from another, viz., "needlessness."[44] We reach this conclusion, he says, "by experiments actually made, and the experience thereby obtained" (526,i). What he has in mind he saves to the very end of his essay, where he reports the following:

In *Tuscany*, in the whole interval between the abolition of death-punishment, in that Grand Duchy, by the Emperor Leopold, while Grand Duke [beginning in 1765]—and the re-establishment of it [under Bonaparte in 1795]—the average number of crimes was considerably less than those after that same re-establishment: length of the interval many years: and, in that same interval, *assassinations* no more than *six:* while, in the Roman States, not much larger than Tuscany, the number, in a quarter of a year, was no less than *sixty.* (531,ii)

Bentham cites John Howard, the English prison reformer, as his source for the information about Tuscany under Leopold, and the French penologist Charles Lucas for his information about the Roman States. The Tuscany experiment was a favorite among abolitionists during the late eighteenth and early nineteenth centuries; it is cited in various forms by such leading American abolitionists as Benjamin Rush, William Livingston, John L. O'Sullivan, Robert J. Rantoul, and Charles Spear.[45]

These data, primitive though they are by today's standards, would seem to be typical of those available at that time and perhaps among the first ever used to establish that the death penalty is a less effective deterrent than imprisonment.[46] In the 1775 essay, there is nothing remotely like this attempt to marshal empirical data to support the general argument; it represents in principle the most salient improvement in Bentham's 1831 essay over his earlier critique, but only in principle. Although it is true that the form of Bentham's argument is precisely the sort that sociologists used until a decade ago, when the jurisdiction-matching techniques pioneered by Karl Schuessler[47] and Thorsten Sellin[48] were challenged by multiple regression analysis using aggregate national data,[49] the particular data on which Bentham relies can easily be explained away by anyone who believes that the death penalty really is a deterrent-cum-incapacitator *par excellence*. For example, perhaps detection and enforcement in Tuscany were much more efficient than in the Roman States (Bentham seems to assume that they were equally effective or ineffective); perhaps the size of the populations in the two districts makes the murder rates (which Bentham neither reports nor calculates) more nearly the same. Until one's mind is set at ease by answers to these and other questions, the gross disparity in volume of murder, on which Bentham relies, cannot plausibly be regarded as persuasive evidence that imprisonment is a more effective deterrent than the death penalty.

As a summary and convenient display of Bentham's 1775 and 1831

TABLE 1   Summary of Bentham's 1775 and 1831 Arguments

Factors Relevant to Assessing the Utility of a Mode of Punishment[a]	Relevance to the Death Penalty as Viewed by Bentham			
	Favors	*Opposes*	*Divided*	*Ignored*
Variability[b]		1775		1831
Equability		1775		1831
Commensurability	✓			1775 1831
Characteristicalness[c]	1775[d]	✓[e]		1831
Exemplarity	1775			1831
Frugality		1775 (1831)[f]		
Subserviency to Reformation		(1775)		1831
Efficacy with respect to Disablement	1775 (1831)			
Subserviency to Compensation[g]	(1831)	1775	✓	
Popularity	1775 (1831)			
Simplicity of Description[h]	✓[i]			1775 1831
Remissibility[i]		1775 1831		

[a] Bentham, *Rationale of Punishment*, in *Works*, vol. I, 402–6 (Bowring, ed.); *Introduction to the Principles of Morals and Legislation*, 175–86 (J. H. Burns and H. L. A. Hart, eds.).
[b] Discussed in 1775 under "Equability."
[c] In 1775 called "Analogy."
[d] Not cited as a factor in *Introduction*.
[e] As applied to all crimes other than murder.
[f] Discussed in 1831 under "Needlessness."
[g] In 1775 called "Unprofitability"; in 1831 included under "Remissibility."
[h] Not cited as a factor in *Introduction*.
[i] Indicates what Bentham could have concluded, but did not.
[j] In 1775 includes also destruction of testimonial evidence; in 1831 includes as well liability to judicial abuse (nullification) and executive abuse ("Undue Pardon").

Of the four properties of punishment that appear in Table 1 and are not mentioned as such in either of Bentham's two examinations of the death penalty, a word of explanation is needed here in regard to two of them. "Commensurability" is that property of punishments by virtue of which, given any two crimes that a would-be criminal might commit, the heavier punishment is attached to the graver offense.[50] In the case of the punishment of any single crime, such as murder, this factor is irrelevant; but given any two crimes of different gravity, their punishment would be incommensurable with their gravity if both are punishable with death. "Subserviency to Compensation" involves the idea of "profit" or gain from the offender's undergoing the punishment itself.[51] Assuming that the friends of the victim, and perhaps society generally, are vindictively inclined, no matter what the crime or who the criminal, then the death penalty presumably provides more compensation than any less severe alternative. However, since the death of the offender under this penalty also prevents any other "gain" from the punishment, whereas imprisonment does not, the factor admits of no uniform application to the issue at hand.

This attempt at tabular summary of Bentham's argument has its limitations, notably in failing to capture the quality of his argument in either essay on the deterrence question. But that, as I suggested earlier, is owing primarily to his own method of organizing his argument, especially in the 1775 essay.

VI

In his *Rationale of Punishment*, Bentham made great strides in identifying factors relevant to any possible utilitarian evaluation of the death penalty versus the alternatives. The dozen factors produced by his analysis are an enormous improvement over anything contributed by his predecessors toward constructing a general theory of punishment. This enables him to lay out a form of argument, particularly in his 1775 essay, that surpasses in scope and clarity anything achieved by others before him. Henceforth, utilitarian arguments could in principle (even if they did not always in fact) proceed to focus upon details and subsidiary matters, because the general form of the argument had been settled once and for all in a way neutral to the outcome. Bentham's analysis enables a utilitarian to defend or attack the death penalty in a way that any other utilitarian could immediately grasp and either reinforce or undermine, depending upon empirical considerations independent of the form of the argument itself.

This acknowledgment brings us face to face with the two great weaknesses of Bentham's argument, defects so substantial that no utilitarian could possibly have adequate grounds for believing that Bentham had proved his case on his own premises. The first defect is that Bentham does not adequately explain why the dozen factors he identifies have the relative importance he thinks they do. For example, he believes the "Remissibility" of a punishment is of greater weight in its effect on the general happiness than either "Simplicity of Description" or "Characteristicalness." Why is this so, if it is? Similarly, Bentham seems to believe that "Remissibility" is the gravest defect of the death penalty relative to imprisonment, whereas "Efficacy" (incapacitation) is its greatest advantage. Which effect is the greater upon the general happiness, and why? In neither case does Bentham tell us. Nor does he even tell us his own convictions about the factors he mentions, so that we are left to guess what he thinks their relative weights are. He also fails to provide any way in which we might make these judgments rationally. These omissions lead directly to the second objection.

Except for the data from the experience during abolition in Italy, Bentham's entire argument proceeds without any empirical evidence. As was noted earlier, it is impossible to give an adequate utilitarian argument for any law, policy, or act without some (preferably substantial) empirical evidence to back up each of the empirical premises in the argument. In addition to having the correct variables in the correct form of an equation, one must also be able to introduce real numbers, whether as approximations, estimates, or actual measurements, in order to use the equation to calculate a result. Laying out the correct form of an argument, by itself, can never suffice to prove its conclusion. To be sure, the social sciences were at best in their infancy when Bentham wrote, hardly less so in 1831 than in 1775. Still, no thoroughgoing utilitarian can overlook this striking insufficiency about Bentham's argument, even if the scholarly critic of today can excuse it.

Finally, an even more fundamental problem with Bentham's argument remains, one that plagues at least his form of utilitarianism if not every other: the impossibility of measuring the end-state and effects on it from various alternative acts. What, after all, does "the greatest happiness" or maximizing the general happiness really refer to? How, in actual practice, are we to tell which of two alternative penalty schemes has the more favorable (or the less unfavorable) effect on the desired end-state? Bentham seems to think either that there is no problem or that it is easily solved. Neither is true. For one thing, if maximizing the general happiness requires us to have a measure of interpersonal cardinal utility, then it is impossible to tell which of two alternatives tends toward this maximum, because we have no method for measuring interpersonal cardinal utility.[52] Even if we can get by with some ordinal method that will suffice to rank alternatives, as almost all contemporary utilitarians do,[53] it is still far from clear whether we can do anything more than conjecture which of two alternatives is the more likely to increase (or less likely to decrease) the general happiness.

Even this is not the chief problem. The very idea of "the greatest happiness" is itself so vague, abstract, unstructured, and all-encompassing that it is virtually impossible to have a grasp of how it is affected by one rather than another small-scale social policy. The choice between the death penalty and long-term imprisonment for a specific statutory offense in a given society at a given time is a choice of precisely this nature. What in fact tends to happen is that talk about rational choice between alternatives in such a case reduces (and some utilitarians have proposed that it should reduce) to a question of individual preference: Which do *you* prefer? A world in which there is a death penalty for murder (with all the empirical consequences thereof) or a world in which there is long-term imprisonment for murder (ditto)? Bentham's preferences are clear, and clearer in 1831 than in 1775. Whether there were objective reasons for others to share his preferences is less evident.

This difficulty about measuring effects upon the elusive and amorphous general happiness is what leads a utilitarian to content himself with measuring something more manageable. In the present context, choosing between alternative modes of punishment and sentences for grave crimes tends to rest largely upon the effect these alternatives have on the crime rate. For all practical purposes, this is as far as contemporary utilitarians seem willing to go, and it accounts for the prominence in their death penalty discussions of the relative impact on deterrence and incapacitation that executions and imprisonment have.[54] There is, however, no simple analytic or empirical connection between the concept of the greatest happiness and the crime rate. About all one can say is that, *ceteris paribus*, the lower the crime rate the greater the general happiness. But even this is a gross oversimplification. In any case other things are never equal, so the generalization does not take us very far.

Utilitarian arguments over the death penalty have not disappeared from the contemporary scene, but I know of none that attempts to improve upon Bentham's, much less any that succeeds in doing so.[55] Actual arguments, whether for or against the death penalty, usually turn out to be a mixture of utilitarian and nonutilitarian considerations (where they are not openly antiutilitarian[56])—and for good reason, if my criticisms above are in the main correct.[57] Moreover, whereas one might expect utilitarian considerations to dominate in legislative chambers, much of the debate over the death penalty in this country during the past two decades has been influenced by constitutional considerations. The key ideas—"due process," "equal protection of the laws," "cruel and unusual punishment"—take us in directions where purely utilitarian arguments cannot reach, or reach only with diffi-culty and obscurity (as I have explained at length in Chapter 4). As things stand at present, therefore, despite the impressive amount of information that has been collected relevant to the many empirical questions concerning the way the death penalty functions in our society, we cannot say with any precision whether the death penalty or its alternative is to be preferred on the kinds of grounds Bentham identified. Whether a utilitarian argument today could be constructed that would accomplish all Bentham believed his argument did, and whether if it could its conclusion on the policy question would be the same as Bentham's in favor of recommending complete ab-olition of all death penalties, has yet to be decided. This much does seem likely, however: If executions are to be brought to an end, as Bentham hoped they would be, it may well be without our having first carried out his utilitarian project to its proper conclusion.

Chapter 4

Cruel and Unusual Punishment

Beginning with its 1976 decision in *Gregg v. Georgia* and allied cases (*Jurek v. Texas* and *Proffitt v. Florida*)—in which it upheld several capital statutes and refused to rule that the death penalty is per se a "cruel and unusual punishment"—the Supreme Court has managed to make the entire subject *uninteresting*. Beginning in the late 1950s and through the next decade or so, scholarly debate and appellate court rulings showed problems with the death penalty in the neglected arena defined by the eighth amendment's prohibition of "cruel and unusual punishments." The controversy reached an apex with the 1972 decision in *Furman v. Georgia,* when the Court held that the death penalty—as then administered—violated the eighth and fourteenth amendments. The disarray in the opinions of the *Furman* majority[1] and the political opposition to the Court's ruling that quickly spread across the land[2] sowed ample seeds of discontent. They reached full flower in *Gregg, Jurek,* and *Proffitt.* The Court's refusal to invalidate the death penalty per se was perfectly suited to the national mood of developing and sustained approval of the death penalty, whether measured by public opinion polls, capital sentences meted out by criminal trial courts, infrequency of commutations, or actual executions. As a result, the jurisprudence of "cruel and unusual punishment" has noticeably languished.

Not, to be sure, for want of effort by the minority of the Court itself that still favors total abolition of the death penalty on eighth amendment grounds,[3] by scholarly commentators on the Court's opinions and decisions,[4] and by sundry other critics of the renewed national embrace of the death penalty.[5] Still, none of this criticism has breathed any life into the primary issue—our understanding of whether the death penalty as historically and currently practiced is a "cruel and unusual punishment."[6] Virtually all of the published discussion during the past two decades has been preoccupied with details of constitutional law, history, interpretation, and litigation. In order to reinvigorate the discussion it may be necessary to step somewhat outside the narrow confines of that debate.

The prohibition against "cruel and unusual punishments" is the only severity-limiting constitutional constraint on otherwise permissible punishments.* Accordingly, this provision has figured prominently in the Supreme Court's evaluation of the constitutional status of criminal penalties generally[7] and, since 1972, of the death penalty. When the eighth amendment became part of the Constitution in 1789, the prohibition against "cruel and unusual punishments" was already more than a century old. By now it has figured in the Anglo-American constitutional tradition for three centuries.[8] During this time English-speaking philosophers have had much to say about punishment (its justification, function, and limits)—and nothing to say about "cruel and unusual punishments."[9] John Locke set the pattern followed unwittingly by all his successors. At the very time when the prohibition against "cruel and unusual punishments" became part of the English Bill of Rights, in the late 1680s, Locke was putting the finishing touches on his *Two Treatises of Government*. There he took the extraordinary and virtually unprecedented step of *defining* the concept of political power as "a right of making laws with penalties of death."[10] The idea that some forms of administering this penalty might be morally or constitutionally unacceptable in his own society or under his own theory of political authority because they are "cruel and unusual," or that the death penalty itself might be so judged, never remotely figures in any of his discussions in the *Two Treatises*. Locke's British successors from David Hume to John Stuart Mill, and his spiritual heirs in this country from Jonathan Edwards to John

---

* The phrase has various formulations, including "cruel and unusual punishments," in the California Constitution, Art. I § 6, and in the Massachusetts Declaration of Rights and Liberties, Art. 26; and "cruel, inhuman, or degrading punishments," in the U.N. Declaration of Human Rights, Art. 5, and in the U.N. International Covenant on Civil and Political Rights, Art. 7.

Rawls, have all left the concept of cruel and unusual punishment entirely out of their published reflections on punishment.[11]

I

In attempting to remedy this neglect, we may begin with a pair of generalizations commended to us by common sense and sustained by critical reflection: Not all punishments can be reasonably judged to be cruel and unusual, and not only punishments can be so described. Not everything that hurts, nor even everything that one person deliberately does to another in order to cause hurt, is a punishment. Punishment is an *institution,* an act within a certain context of norms and understandings, a practice. Some religious rites and initiation ceremonies, some methods of warfare and techniques of medical treatment, even some insults and jokes, as well as some nonpunitive conduct toward animals and children, are cruel and unusual in any ordinary sense of those words. And to be sure, the very things done as a method of warfare or as a religious initiation, for example, could also be done as punishment, even by the same persons to the same persons. If they were cruel and unusual in the first context, they might well be so judged in the second. But this is not to say, nor would it show, that such a method of warfare is or ought to be regarded as a cruel and unusual punishment. Whatever else one may wish to say about warfare or religion, neither can be said to be the same institution or practice as punishment. However closely tied together the history and nature of punishment may be with the history of cruel practices generally,[12] the two must be distinguished and kept distinct. We cannot look to punishments indiscriminately for examples of acts or practices that are cruel and unusual, and we cannot be sure that in seizing on acts or practices that are cruel and unusual we will always find ... hment.

cases the punishment would not necessarily be unjustified, impermissible, excessive, or improper *because* of being cruel and unusual. Those who condemn all punishments, no matter what the offense or the offender,[13] go too far when they try to bolster their position by condemning punishment itself as a "crime." They would certainly go even further astray were they to argue that all punishment is morally wrong because it is, by its very nature, cruel. It is possible that every punishment actually imposed under law at the present time in our society is unjustified, though that is a judgment I would not make; it may also be that in most cases the severe punishments actually imposed on persons do them and the rest of society more harm than good, a view I am inclined to defend. But if either of these generalizations is true, it is not because the punishment itself is always and without exception cruel and unusual. The particular kind of condemnation of a punishment that is expressed by calling it "cruel and unusual" is simply inappropriate as the condemnation for *all* punishments without qualification and without any reference to their severity, effects, or rationale.

The reason for stressing this point at the outset, even at the risk of belaboring the obvious, is to show the reasonableness of looking for evidence concerning what "cruelty" means to acts and practices having nothing intrinsically to do with punishment at all. I wish further to show it is wrong to assume that *all* punishment is likely to prove to be cruel, provided only that one scratches a bit below the surface.

Some modes of punishment do not seem promising candidates for the epithets of cruelty and unusualness. Fines are an example. We can easily imagine excessive fines: $10,000 for overparking, or $50,000 for falsifying a federal income tax return for concealment of any amount of taxable income over $5.00. Consider, however, a crushingly burdensome fine, imposed on someone neither rich nor capable of large earnings, so that paying it off takes a lifetime's labor. Would it not be arguable that such a fine is cruel? Or suppose a judge sentenced a juvenile to five years of collecting rubbish on the weekends along roadsides. Under some circumstances this might be excessive. Or suppose the punishment were twenty years on a treadmill for eight hours each day—stupefyingly exhausting drudgery seemingly without end. One may still want to reply, nonetheless, that paying money or doing menial labor is not properly judged to be cruel even when carried to unfair, unusual, or senseless excess. Is this because these punishments lack certain qualities *required* of cruelty in punishment that are found only in physical torture or other acutely painful acts? Or is it instead because they lack features merely *typical* of the paradigms of cruel and unusual punishment? Perhaps, on sober consideration, a crushingly burdensome fine and years of labor on a treadmill really are cruel, and thus prove that even punitive fines and menial tasks can embody the excessive severity that is the hallmark of cruel and unusual punishments.

II

Grammatically, the phrase "cruel and unusual punishment" resembles "cruel and unusual ritual" or "cruel and unusual insult." The compound adjective appears to suggest something (a punishment, ritual, or insult) that simultaneously has two distinct properties: cruelty *and* unusualness. Such properties ought to be able to vary independently of each other, each having its own implicit standards, evidence, and methods of verification. There seems no reason to doubt that "cruel and unusual punishment" can be and sometimes is used in precisely this way; if the phrase has any ordinary or nontechnical meaning, this is probably an aspect of it. However, the Supreme Court apparently does not interpret the eighth amendment use of "cruel and unusual" in this manner; "and" in "cruel and unusual punishment" does not appear to be regarded as a true conjunction.[14] The Court also does not seem to interpret "cruel and unusual" as though it were equivalent to the adverbial phrase "unusually cruel."[15] If that were the preferred reading, it might appear that there are other, tolerably cruel, or cruel but not too cruel, punishments. But because judging a punishment to be cruel is already condemning it strongly, the idea of a "tolerably cruel punishment" verges on an oxymoron. (The converse possibility, that "cruel and unusual" means "cruelly unusual," can also be rejected. There is no evidence the Court ever considered such an interpretation; it would in any case place too much emphasis on the moral justifiability of punitive practices for no other reason than their familiarity or usualness.[16]) Instead, the Court seems to write as if this phrase were to be written as a ligature, "cruel-and-unusual punishments," designating a complex of intertwined and insepar-able properties rather than one set of properties correlated with "cruel" and another with "unusual." Philosophical analysis and moral argument can, of course, side with common speech and surface grammar, and against the Supreme Court's preferred usage, here as elsewhere. But because the phrase has no standard use in philosophical discourse and because of its importance in our constitutional tradition, there is no good reason for quarreling with the Court's usage. (Consequently, we can ignore here the question of whether a given punishment might be objectionable because it is cruel even though it is not unusual, or objectionable because it is unusual even though not cruel; similarly, such questions as whether a given punishment is more (or less) cruel than it is unusual, becoming unusual more rapidly than it is ceasing to be cruel, etc.)

Were we to try to isolate the unusualness of a punishment from its cruelty, we would focus on a property of punishments that has little or nothing to do with moral condemnation. No moral theory short of the crudest traditionalism would hold that a mode of punishment, *ceteris paribus*, is morally or legally unjustified merely because it is unusual. Novelty, lack of precedent, deviation from prevailing historic or current practice—none of these marks a property that is morally objectionable in a punishment. They do, however, signal caution to any legislators, administrators, or reformers who favor departures from usual punitive practice. Nevertheless, a morally sensitive and imaginative society needs to consider seriously *any* novel mode of punishment that might be a humane improvement on such well-known methods of punishment as imprisonment,[17] through which hundreds of thousands are deprived daily of their liberty, security, and property. Finally, a mode of punishment may be unusual today even though it was common in an earlier, less civilized, age. In such cases describing the punishment as "unusual" may well imply not only that it is no longer widely used, but that its use is now intolerable. What makes it morally unjustifiable now, however, is not the mere fact that it is an anachronism.

We should note that there is another way to read the term "unusual," a reading on which it is relevant to moral judgment. Suppose that although two punishments, P_1 and P_2, are traditionally available under law to the sentencer for a given offense, usually (although not invariably) sentencers choose to impose the less severe of the two, P_1. They reserve P_2 for special occasions. However, close scrutiny shows that the use of P_2 on these special occasions does not achieve any rational objective relevant to a system of punishment under law. Instead, these uses are prompted by nothing other than the sentencer's hostile attitude (anger, fear, contempt, disgust) toward the offender. The offenders on whom the sentencer imposes P_2 do not actually *deserve* the more severe punishment. Rather, the sentencer simply *wants* to punish them more severely than would be achieved by imposing P_1. Given such circumstances, an offender sentenced to undergo P_2 might well claim that such a severe punishment was morally objectionable and unfair because it is so unusual: It is not the usual punishment meted out for the crimes in question, or if—on the contrary—it *is* the usual punishment, this is because sentencers habitually rely on the unfair, objectionable, and irrelevant fact of the sentencer's own dislike for certain kinds of offenders.[18]

This reading of "unusual" renders it nearly independent of any reference to cruelty. In the foregoing example, P_2 need not be cruel or cruelly excessive relative to the crime for which it is imposed. P_2 need be only both more severe than P_1, and arbitrarily, irrationally, or randomly meted out instead of P_1. Such a reading of "unusual" is worth mentioning because it helps restore balance and symmetry in the sense of the phrase "cruel and unusual punishment" by taking some of the stress off the idea of cruelty.

In the context of the Constitution, this reading of "unusual" seems to coincide with at least part of what is prohibited by the equal protection clause of the fourteenth amendment: "[N]or shall any State . . . deny to any person within its jurisdiction the equal protection of the laws." Any punishment that is objectionably *unusual* in the manner indicated above is probably also objectionably *unequal,* and thus violates the constitutional requirement of "equal protection of the laws." Each of the five justices in the *Furman* majority wrote an opinion in which he made precisely this connection between the unusual quality of the death penalty and the unequal manner of its administration under law.[19] In a parallel maneuver, the dissenting Justices in *Furman* avoided, or played down, this reading of "unusual" in the eighth amendment in favor of a reading that allowed them to stress the traditional, familiar, not unusual character of the death penalty.[20]

My remarks in the foregoing do not constitute an argument in favor of one rather than another way of reading the term "unusual" in the eighth amendment. Rather, I have wanted only to show that there is a possible, even natural, interpretation of this term that gives it some weight in a moral judgment, which cannot be done if "unusual" is taken to mean merely atypical or novel or no longer practiced.

III

As noted earlier, the concept of cruel and unusual punishment has played no special role in theories of punishment or in the discussions of punishment by philosophers in the Anglo-American tradition. Only constitutional courts, scholars, and commentators, and the social critics and moralists on their fringes, have challenged punishments by evaluating them as cruel and unusual. Yet from the time of Socrates, philosophers have discussed the conditions under which punishment is morally justified. So it is natural to merge these lines of unconnected investigation and inquire directly how morally unjustified punishments are related to cruel and unusual punishments.

By hypothesis, at one extreme there is the possibility that these two concepts are completely independent of each other; at the other extreme there is the possibility that the two are identical, notwithstanding their apparent linguistic diversity. The first possibility is preposterous. To take it seriously would be like concluding that although someone's conduct is an act of murder, it is still entirely an open question whether the killing is morally objectionable. This is bizarre or unintelligible because "murder" usually is defined as either "inexcusable and unjustified criminal homicide" or "willful, deliberate and malicious killing of another." Under such definitions, there is no room to doubt whether an act, having been judged to be murder, is under a severe cloud of moral disapproval.[21]

The other extreme possibility is more plausible. Taken strictly, there are at least two different ways to conceive of the identity of morally unjustified punishments and of punishments that are cruel and unusual. One is to regard the *class* of cruel and unusual punishments as identical with the class of morally unjustified punishments. The other is to hold not only that the two classes are identical, but that the *concepts* of a cruel and unusual punishment and of a morally unjustified punishment are also identical. Each alternative is, of course, incompatible with a third possibility, that there is only some overlap between the two concepts and their coordinate classes. (This possibility also leaves open for further discussion whether the overlap is partial—because some morally unjustified punishments are cruel and unusual, but others are not—or whether it is complete, because one of the two classes is a subclass of the other.)

The argument against identity goes as follows. Assume for the sake of discussion any system of punishment you please so long as it is not uniformly draconian. Under this system there are certain to be lenient or mild punishments in some cases. The system will also have to decree the appropriate standards of punishment for especially grave offenses, and for unrepentant, recidivist, or dangerous offenders. Suppose that a sentencer in this system imposed a mild punishment on a person convicted of an extremely grave offense. Advocates of the penal system in question would probably conclude (as we would) that the punishment in a case of this sort was too lenient, and for that reason morally unjustified. The objection in this case would not be that such a punishment was cruel and unusual, excessive, too severe, or unduly harsh. But the idea of a cruel and unusual punishment—even prior to any analysis of that idea—assures us that the only basis for judging a punishment to be cruel and unusual is that it must be excessive, or too severe, or unreasonably harsh. Thus, we have in this example a punishment that is morally unjustified because it mocks the demand for justice and justification in punishment, quite apart from whether the punishment is cruel, unusual, or excessive. It follows from this that the two classes of punishments—those that are cruel and unusual, and those that are morally unjustified—are not coextensive. If the two *classes* are not coextensive, then the two *concepts* cannot be identical, since coextensiveness of the classes is a necessary (although not sufficient) condition for identity of the coordinate concepts.

In this context, it is appropriate to notice that an appeal to the eighth amendment prohibition of "cruel and unusual punishments" is not the only way to mount an argument against a punishment that is morally and constitutionally objectionable. Suppose that an American state legislature in the 1890s had enacted a penal statute for the crime of aggravated rape of a female by a male, and that the statute provided a *mandatory* death penalty if the convicted offender was nonwhite and the victim white, but a *discretionary* death penalty in all other cases. The Supreme Court unquestionably would have condemned this statute long before its 1972 ruling in *Furman*. Rather than rely on the eighth amendment prohibition against "cruel and unusual punishments," the Court could have applied the equal protection clause of the fourteenth amendment.[22] Such a statute would not be morally unjustified merely because the eighth amendment did not condemn it. We have what amounts to a moral condemnation of the punishment (or of the procedure whereby it is meted out), because we assume that whatever the Bill of Rights prohibits is *ceteris paribus* morally unjustified, whether or not the activity directly violates the eighth amendment prohibition of "cruel and unusual punishments." The point, of course, is not that moral condemnation of a punishment obtains its force from the provisions of a constitution: A constitution may be fundamentally unjust. Rather, certain provisions of our Constitution, quite apart from the eighth amendment, have a moral weight that allows us to condemn otherwise lawful practices inconsistent with them.

The argument so far comes to this: Morally unjustified punishments are not the same as cruel and unusual punishments. However, cruel and unusual punishments are morally unjustified because they are excessively severe. In other words, it appears that cruel and unusual punishments are a proper subclass of morally unjustified punishments. Alas, things are not quite so neat.

IV

To decide whether cruel and unusual punishments are a subclass of morally unjustified punishments, we must consider the remaining possibility—that the two classes partially overlap. Let us examine the unsettling possibility that some cruel and unusual punishments are morally justified.

I will first take up the most extreme position. Could it make sense to assert that under certain circumstances a given punishment for a given offender is morally justified just because it is cruel and unusual? Of course no Anglo-American appellate court would say this, because to do so would obviously be to flout the constitutional prohibition against "cruel and unusual punishments." But someone else might think a horrifying punishment justifiable when an offender commits a particularly horrible crime, and such a punishment might well be described as cruel and unusual—unusual in the sense of rare or even never before heard of, and cruel in the sense of inflicting exquisite agonies on the offender. For example, many talk as though the only morally justified punishments for the Adolph Eichmanns, Josef Mengeles, and Klaus Barbies of the world would be some especially cruel and unusual punishment.[23] The issue here is not whether such a position is persuasive. The point is only that it could make sense to formulate a position in support of a punishment that is judged to be both cruel and unusual and nevertheless morally justifiable. In some cases, given the nature and quality of the criminal act, it certainly does seem to make sense to insist that the offender deserves a cruel and unusual punishment.

Nevertheless, there is something troubling and slightly perverse in this reasoning. It is as though one were to say: "Since this crime is particularly heinous, society must impose what would ordinarily and quite properly be regarded as a morally unjustified punishment. The kind of punishment suitable on this occasion is precisely the kind normally regarded as cruel and unusual, and for that reason forsworn." Insofar as this makes sense to us, it shows that the usual morally condemnatory use of the phrase "cruel and unusual punishment" need not invariably be the use to which the phrase is put.

The careers of some of the most notoriously cruel tyrants in history may shed further light on this theme. Attila the Hun, Vlad the Impaler, and Ivan the Terrible are all reputed to have been responsible for some remarkably severe and ingenious punishments, not to mention other crimes and horrors they authorized to be inflicted on the innocent. We may find it instructive to try for a moment to stand in their shoes and consider their punitive acts and policies as they might have viewed them. Suppose they were imbued with the same sensibilities as other political leaders, but faced (or believed they faced) agonizing choices that most political leaders are spared. Perhaps these tyrants believed they could resolve these choices only, as Machiavelli coolly advised, by learning to be "cruel."[24] Perhaps the judgment of history vindicates them, by showing that they suffered no squeamishness, which would have been the undoing of lesser leaders, and that they thereby averted much greater calamities than those they caused.

Whether such an interpretation is historically correct, it cannot be ruled out as absurd in principle. We see from this perspective that a punishment may be cruel and unusual without also being morally unjustified. If this is true, then there is a partial overlap between "cruel and unusual punishments" and morally unjustified punishments. The earlier and initially more plausible hypothesis, that the former class is a subclass of the latter, would turn out to be false.

This conclusion has an impact on the paradigms of cruel and unusual punishment to be discussed below. The moral status of punishments is not free of social context, a priori justified or not by the very nature of a punishment in all times and climes, independent of socio-historical milieu. Even if we assume that the human body and human nature have not changed over the course of recorded civilization, and believe, for example, that death by stoning in 1500 B.C. was no less painful than such a death would be today, we must grant that the place of cruelty, terror, and violent death in our society is not the same as it was in societies centuries ago. Even if a painful death is what it always was, cruelty in human life is not.[25] Cruelty, and hence any cruel and unusual punishment, and the excessiveness (by whatever standard and in whatever manner) it implies take their moral discoloration from a context that is not fixed for all time. The concept of cruelty is social, moral, and cultural, rather than physiological, organic, or in some other manner essentially unhistorical. The moral condemnation that cruel and unusual punishments deserve depends on tacit reference to standards that are subject to revision because they are influenced and shaped by changing socio-historical and cultural factors. As others have rightly pointed out, "Cruelty . . . is a social phenomenon which can be understood only in terms of the social relationships prevailing in any given period."[26]

One way to express this is to say that our conception of cruel and unusual punishment is not static, or rigidly fixed over time. The moral status of the class of acts and practices to which the term applies therefore also changes, even if the concept of cruel and unusual punishment is relatively fixed.[27] The Supreme Court's own views may be understood in this manner. In a 1910 opinion, the Court observed that "cruel and unusual punishment . . . is not fastened to the obsolete but may acquire meaning as public opinion becomes enlightened by humane justice."[28] Four decades later, the Court advised that the "cruel and unusual punishments" clause "must draw its meaning from the evolving standards of decency that mark the progress of a maturing society."[29] Thus, as history will attest, some awful punishments may have been justifiable because they were (or were reasonably believed to be) the best thing to do in the circumstances. To concede this is not to imply that it would be morally justifiable or constitutionally permissible for a legislature to do such things today. The implication is rather that the assignment of a given punishment to the class of cruel and unusual punishments is a sensitive issue because the class is inescapably defined by reference to standards of fair, just, and justified punishment that are not fixed and rigid across culture and history.

<h1 style="text-align:center">V</h1>

Some punishments seem clearly and incontestably cruel and unusual. Boiling in oil, death by a thousand cuts, impalement, and burying alive are all acts that have been authorized by governments in the past as punishment. Unquestionably, imposing any of them in our society today would be cruel and unusual, no matter who the offender or what the crime. The Supreme Court's favorite examples of cruel and unusual punishments (torture, disembowelment, beheading, and dissection)[30] reflect an awareness of history and invite the inference that these modes of punishment have served and continue to serve the Court as paradigms of cruel and unusual punishments, just as they do for the rest of us.

Such paradigms (or, more cautiously, their possibility) prompt several questions. What do they tell us about the meaning of the constitutional phrase "cruel and unusual punishments"? Do they explain that clause's reference, the class of things each member of which can be said to be a cruel and unusual punishment? Do they provide the basis for how the term is or should be correctly used?

A paradigm of a term or phrase is an example of the reference of that term or phrase, an instance of the reference to which anyone who understands the term or phrase would unhesitatingly assent. Hence, a paradigm is suitable for citation as an uncontroversial case of the thing under discussion and serves as a benchmark for comparing and contrasting contested cases. Specification of one or more paradigm cases is also useful as a way of focusing attention and fixing ideas, so that analysis and argument can proceed from an agreed base line presumably neutral to the borderline cases over which controversy arises. The typical borderline case of cruel and unusual punishment has some, even many, but not all of the traits that a paradigm case has. Insofar as the meaning of a phrase involves certain standards or principles (as the meaning of "cruel and unusual punishments" does), a paradigm case of the reference of such a phrase would manifest those standards in a particularly conspicuous manner. A paradigm case of cruel and unusual punishment, therefore, would be an example that would force anyone who understands the term to acknowledge the example as a punitive act or practice to which that term applies. Consequently, one can discover the meaning of the phrase "cruel and unusual punishments" by a careful scrutiny of the paradigm cases, since they (and they alone) exhibit all the requisite properties. Of course, each may also exhibit some superfluous or adventitious properties. For example, crucifixion typically occurred on a cross of *wood*, but that is not part of the meaning of "cruel and unusual punishment," and so one does not refer to this property when one judges that crucifixion is a paradigm cruel and unusual punishment. The question of the pertinent properties of cruel and unusual punishment needs to be understood now that the death penalty is inflicted by lethal injection: Is painful-to-undergo an essential or an adventitious property of cruel and unusual punishments? If adventitious, is it yet enough to make death penalties administered in this way borderline cases of cruel and unusual punishments?

Some of the foregoing comments about paradigm cases can be recast in terms of the semantics of the phrase "cruel and unusual punishment," in particular its meaning and its reference. The *reference* of the phrase is the class of punitive acts and practices that are cruel and unusual. Included in this class are the paradigm cases, but they do not exhaust the reference. Indeed, the reference of this term is inexhaustible; we cannot write out a finite list mentioning each and every cruel and unusual punishment. The possibility always exists that some punishment never before practiced or never thought about turns out, under analysis, to qualify for membership in the class of cruel and unusual punishments. The term "cruel and unusual punishment" is not the name of any one punitive act or practice or even of several; it is a general term, and like all general terms, its reference is in principle inexhaustible. The most we can hope to do, therefore, is to exemplify the reference of this term, cite representative (paradigm) cases, or provide an illustrative partial list.

Thus, the logical relation between the paradigm cases of cruel and unusual punishment and the reference of the term is that of indefinite subclass to infinite class. The logical relation between the paradigm cases of this term and the *meaning* of the term is much more complex and subtle. A paradigm case of any general term is an instance of the term's reference, such that once one sees why it is a member of the class in question, one has grasped what the term means. One has some inkling of the meaning (or sense) of the term "cruel and unusual punishment," and so one may correctly apply or withhold that term from other cases. Error, of course, is possible; there is no guarantee of infallibility. One can grasp the sense of a term and employ it by and large correctly, that is, according to the criterion of its use shared by the linguistic community that understands it, without being immune from error.

Quite apart from error, there is no reason to assume that the sense of the term is and will remain fixed. Such a semantic theory is only one among several options. "Cruel and unusual punishment" is also not a rigidly designative term, in the way it has been argued that names of naturally occurring species (for example, "tiger") or inert natural kinds (for example, "diamond") are.[31] The sense of "cruel and unusual punishment" has to be taken from the properties of those punitive acts and practices that have been judged to be morally unacceptable in a particular historic time and culture. Thus by contrast with the relative simplicities in the sense-formation factors in proper names and rigidly designative general terms, the sense-formation factors in a term like "cruel and unusual punishment" are many, complex, and subject to change over time.

VI

Constitutional fundamentalists typically link the role of paradigm cases of "cruel and unusual punishments" to the "original intentions" of the several framers, founders, and ratifiers of the Constitution and the Bill of Rights. The point of this linkage is to force all contemporary interpretations of the "cruel and unusual punishments" clause into inferences by strict analogy with a very short list of paradigm cruel and unusual punishments taken from English and American history of the sixteenth and seventeenth centuries.[32]

Presumably, those who make such an appeal do not do so as a surreptitious ad hoc strategy to win debates. Rather, they propose a generally applicable consideration whenever constitutional interpretation is at issue. This approach has two purposes: It provides a neutral ground on which all can stand and debate the substantive issue, for example, whether the death penalty for rape is a "cruel and unusual punishment." It also constrains interpretation of the written Constitution by reference to an objective criterion for what is meant by the words being construed. This guarantees that any alternative and incompatible meanings, even if shared by all members of the Court at a given time, are irrelevant. But these purposes, however admirable, provide no evidence for the underlying semantic theory on which this approach rests. That theory involves at least two controversial claims, rarely formulated and never defended: (i) the meaning or sense of constitutional words and phrases, such as the "cruel and unusual punishments" clause, derives from the original intention with which it was used by those who introduced it into the Constitution, and (ii) the sense of the term "cruel and unusual punishment," insofar as this clause applies to the death penalty, is entirely provided by the paradigm cases that the framers intended the clause to prohibit.

However, we face substantial obstacles to ascertaining the original intention in this instance: (a) we have no text or document in which the framers stated their shared intention (if they had one) in including the clause in the eighth amendment; (b) the framers left no statement telling us what they understood the language of this clause to mean; (c) we have no list prepared by the framers specifying the properties a punishment must have to be prohibited under the clause; (d) the framers provided no exhaustive catalogue of the punishments they regarded as prohibited under this clause. Since we have no explicit indication in any of these four ways of what the framers understood by the clause, any knowledge that we claim of their intention in using it must be based on very indirect evidence. This predicament in trying to establish the framers' intentions is not, of course, unusual in interpreting central clauses in the Constitution and the Bill of Rights; in fact, it is typical. Unfortunately, those who appeal to the original intention to reach a correct interpretation of what the clause originally meant or means today fail to alert those who are neutral to substantive controversies over what is and is not an unconstitutionally "cruel and unusual punishment" to the awkward evidentiary predicament we are in.

When confronted with these facts about our ignorance, some will respond that it is probably hopeless to attempt to establish the original intention because the indirect evidence is too inconclusive. Although an original intention exists (so these critics would insist), thus far we have not discovered it, and so we cannot use it in contemporary disputes over the proper interpretation of the clause. Radical skeptics will argue that the very idea of an original intention is a myth. The inconsistencies in policy making, in public reasoning regarding the adoption of the clause, and in the behavior of the framers and their immediate predecessors and successors, all demonstrate the absence of any such original intention. Still other critics (among whom I would include myself) will argue more cautiously and elaborately that even if it is reasonable to assume or postulate an original intention, and even if there were evidence sufficient to tell us with reasonable clarity what the original intention was, we cannot appeal to it today to settle what the clause means or should mean. The essential subjectivity of mere intentions, even a shared intention such as the original postulated intention, makes them the wrong sort of thing on which to rest construction of the governing clauses in the fundamental charter of a free and rational society.[33]

There are, then, several different kinds of objections to appealing to the original intention that underlies the "cruel and unusual punishments" clause. As for the scholarly debate itself, I am convinced it is impossible to decide, on the evidence presently available, whether there was any such intention, and if so, what it was. Nor am I convinced by any argument that the very assumption of an original constitutional intention is a necessary condition of correct constitutional interpretation. Future scholarship, of course, may eventually shed further light on these issues and enable us to decide more rationally among alternative possibilities than we can at present. If, however, I am right and the underlying assumptions of the controversy are wrong, then nothing of importance turns on what future scholarship reveals. On do this in the absence of other evidence (of all the sort alluded to in (a) through (d) above) is to identify the cases (the paradigm cases) to which these utterers referred in the course of their use of these expressions.

Some scholars insist the evidence is at least clear enough to show it was not part of the original intention of the framers that the death penalty would ever be found to violate the clause.[34] They point to passages elsewhere in the Bill of Rights in which the death penalty is mentioned[35] in a manner that seems to presuppose its consistency with the eighth amendment. Pointing to capital statutes enacted by the First Congress,[36] they imply this legislature must have believed it was acting in accord with the clause. They could also point to prosecutions, convictions, and executions of capital offenders at the end of the eighteenth century[37] as further evidence of general belief two centuries ago that the death penalty and the clause were not inconsistent. All this must be granted, but it fails to prove the central point—that it was part of the original intention that the death penalty as such could *never* be incompatible with the eighth amendment.[38] Even more to the point, it fails to prove the underlying semantic thesis that really motivates the appeal to the original intention, namely, that the meaning of the clause is essentially connected with the intention with which its framers first used it. The reason it fails is that, until we know the standards and criteria, principles and assumptions that are built into the general language of the clause, no one knows what the clause means and therefore what it truly permits and prohibits. Since all interpreters of the scholarly record agree that the framers left no account of what they thought these standards and principles were, we cannot infer straightaway that all their actions and their intentions (as well as their beliefs and their expectations) were in fact consistent with those principles; it is possible that they were not.

Quite apart from these considerations there is another, more fundamental, objection to any purely historical account of what makes a punishment violate the clause. Suppose we knew that three modes of punishment, or three modes of inflicting a given punishment—P_1, P_2, P_3—exhausted the list of punishments in 1790 that were deemed to violate the clause. That is, we assume these three punishments are the only "cruel and unusual punishments," according to the explicit original intention. What rationale or justification might there be for the framers having such an original intention and proposing the clause to express and preserve it? Either their intention included no such rationale at all—the prohibition of P_1, P_2, and P_3 was completely whimsical, utterly arbitrary—or their intention did include such a rationale. The first alternative is simply too irrational to be taken seriously.

There must be a rational explanation for the conclusion that P_1, P_2, and P_3 are "cruel and unusual punishments," and that no other punishments are. That explanation is bound to have two features: (a) It will refer to certain properties, traits, or characteristics shared by P_1, P_2, and P_3, and lacking in all other punishments; and (b) it will refer also to certain standards and principles that show why punishments with these properties are morally wrong and should be barred by constitutional law. However, once these two features constituting the rationale have been acknowledged, the way is open for a later argument that some other punishment, P_4, also shares these properties. No matter that in the initial survey of punishments canvassed for their compatibility with the clause P_4 was judged consistent with it. Any of us can err in deciding whether a given punishment violates the principles implicit in the clause, just as we may err in the classification of anything else. This is necessarily part of what it means to recognize that the term "cruel and unusual" is a general term, that its typical use in evaluation of punishments is to express moral condemnation, and that at least one standard or principle is implicit in its meaning.

Disagreement may well arise about the properties common to P_1, P_2, and P_3 that put them in violation of the clause, and whether some other punishment, such as P_4, has enough of these properties to warrant being added to the list. Borderline cases will be difficult to resolve even under conditions of ideal observation. The principles that connect the abstract language of the clause with the concrete features of the several punishments deemed prohibited by it will also be controversial.[39] What is needed to resolve such disagreements is not armchair archeology into the unarticulated and elusive intentions of the framers. We need instead a rational reconstruction of the values to be protected by the clause in light of the history, conditions, and aspirations of the society whose Constitution contains the clause. This task cannot be carried out primarily by history and social science; it requires moral theory pre-eminently.[40]

History, however, does have its contribution to make, and any attempt to characterize the original intention would be bereft of context and thus incomplete without attention to that history. A study of the views of the eighteenth-century liberal penal reformers (whether Continental or English), jurists (such as Beccaria and Montesquieu), and philosophers (such as Voltaire and Bentham) shows that they believed there was neither necessity nor justice in the time-honored practices of aggravated physical torture, maiming, and savage bodily abuse commonly part of the infliction of the death penalty.[41] They concluded and persuasively advocated that these practices, cruel by the appropriate standards in their own time, must be stopped. This was the ideological context in which the clause barring "cruel and unusual punishments" was introduced into our Bill of Rights.[42] The counterpart to their reasoning, applicable to us today, goes like this: There is neither necessity nor justice in the time-honored practice of putting criminals to death; therefore, this practice, severe in any case by the standards appropriate for our time, is excessive and cruel and must be stopped. Just as the eighteenth century concluded that hanging is sufficient punishment, so our century must conclude that imprisonment is enough.

VII

One might argue that a given punishment is cruel and unusual (excessively severe) while conceding that there is no feasible alternative to it. Under such circumstances, society would have to choose between continuing to use a punishment condemned as excessive and refusing to use any punishment at all for the particular offense. What is a responsible government to do? Does it not verge on the pointless to mount an argument aimed at showing a given punishment is cruel and unusual, all the while knowing that society has no alternative? We can trivialize the problem by pointing out that there is *always* some feasible alternative punishment available to any society, whatever the offense and whoever the offender. "Feasible" does not mean "preferable" or "adequate," much less "effective." But this diverts our attention from the role played by feasible alternative punishments in judgments that condemn a given punishment as cruel and unusual, even as it invites us to ignore the serious task of identifying some criteria for feasibility in this context. Several different approaches warrant brief exploration.

The first and least plausible is that the availability of a feasible alternative punishment is part of the *meaning* of any judgment that a given punishment is cruel and unusual. This seems plainly false, if one contemplates the paradigms of cruel and unusual punishment discussed earlier. It seemed quite possible to regard crucifixion, for example, as a cruel and unusual punishment without also having in mind either a general idea of an alternative punishment or some particular alternative punishment that is not cruel and unusual. I see no good reason to insist on any semantic connection between judging something to be cruel and unusual punishment, and prior or concurrent tacit judgments about an alternative feasible punishment.[43]

A second possibility makes the existence of a feasible alternative punishment a *necessary condition* for the truth of a judgment condemning a given punishment as cruel and unusual. This is also incorrect. The reasons given earlier, which suggest what is required to support the claim that a given practice is a paradigm of cruel and unusual punishment, do not also show that the truth of such a claim depends on the truth of some further judgment affirming the availability of a feasible alternative. More precisely, it is not true that a given punishment, P_1, is cruel and unusual only if some other punishment, P_2, is a feasible alternative to P_1. Someone may conclude that P_1 is cruel and unusual without first or concurrently believing or knowing that another punishment, P_2, is not cruel and unusual and that it is a feasible alternative to P_1. There is simply no logical connection between the truth of "P_1 is cruel and unusual" and the truth of "P_2 is a feasible alternative to P_1." Thus, there is no epistemological connection between judgments of cruel and unusual punishment and judgments about feasible alternatives.

Nevertheless, a typical feature of arguments that the death penalty is a cruel and unusual punishment is that society does have a feasible alternative—a functioning system of penitentiaries, which administer long-term incarceration for persons not sentenced to death and executed. Thus, it is plausible to insist on the following constraint: No punishment, P_1, is cruel and unusual in a given society at a given time unless there is at least one feasible alternative punishment, P_2. If this constraint is neither semantic nor epistemological, then what is its nature?

The best answer may be that it is *forensic*. Crucial to the persuasive political effect that judging punishments to be cruel and unusual is normally intended to have is the availability of a feasible alternative. It would be unreasonable to expect a society to cease to use a given mode of punishment, just because it is cruel and unusual, when everyone concedes that there is no feasible alternative. Thus any complete argument—at least any likely to have political effect—against a given punishment on grounds of its excessive severity must include reference to an alternative punishment; and the alternative itself must be specified with sufficient detail to explain what is involved in institutionalizing it as a practice. Of course this alternative punishment must not itself have the traits that make a punishment cruel and unusual. If this, or something like it, is correct, then feasible alternative punishments play a central role in judgments condemning other punishments as cruel and unusual.

VIII

Let us now consider what "feasible" means in the present context and identify, if we can, appropriate criteria for reasonable alternatives in punishment. The easiest way to proceed is to consider what is generally regarded as the only feasible alternative to the death penalty in our society today: long-term incarceration.

As a constraint, "feasibility" means only that it is possible to make the practice work, given enough time, money, patience, and cooperation. Somewhat more narrowly, a feasible alternative must also be possible to put into practice given the actual resources in money, personnel, and physical plant, available at a given time in a given social situation. No punishment is a feasible punishment, many would argue, unless it meets this latter condition. It is also possible to narrow further the concept of feasible alternative punishments by reference to the adequacy of the alternative, as though to say: A punishment, P_2, is not a feasible alternative to another punishment, P_1, unless P_2 satisfies the goals or purposes of P_1 as well as P_1 does. Once "feasible alternative punishments" is understood in the latter manner, a dispute over whether a given punishment is a feasible alternative to another punishment turns on three considerations: what these goals or purposes are (or ought to be), the degree to which each of the punishments achieves them, and how to weigh the relative success of each of the punishments in satisfying these goals.

If we ask whether long-term incarceration is a feasible alternative to the death penalty, the answer is that it is indisputably feasible under the first two of the three criteria above. Feasibility in these respects is demonstrated by the decades of experience in those jurisdictions with no punishment more severe than imprisonment, beginning with such states as Michigan (death penalty abolished in 1847) and including the entire nation between 1967 and 1977 (executions suspended), not to mention foreign countries that long ago abolished the death penalty. Dispute plausibly arises today only under the third criterion. This is more controversial because of the normative and factual questions that must be resolved in order to establish whether a given alternative punishment really is feasible.

The arguments on both sides proceed down familiar paths. Defenders of the death penalty can argue their position in either or both of two ways. Their first argument holds that (1) protection of society is the central goal or purpose of punishment; (2) the deterrent and incapacitative efficacy of a punishment is the dominant factor in its capacity to protect society; (3)

the more severe a punishment is, *ceteris paribus,* the better it provides deterrence and incapacitation; therefore (4) the death penalty provides better protection to society than long-term imprisonment, a less severe punishment; and so (5) long-term imprisonment is not a feasible alternative to the death penalty. Opponents of the death penalty have typically conceded the first premise, ignored the second, and attacked the third and fourth propositions. In earlier chapters of this book, I have commented on the state of the evidence as it bears on (3) and (4). Suffice it to add here that, whereas the third proposition verges on triviality, there is no adequate reason to believe the fourth proposition on the evidence available. (The third proposition is true only because of the *ceteris paribus* clause. When other things are not equal, the proposition will clearly be false.) Even if the third proposition were nontrivially true, the conclusion in the fifth proposition would not be established by this argument.

The second argument has the same outcome but caters to a completely different outlook on the purpose and goals (perhaps even the nature) of punishment. It holds that (1) vindication of just laws and political authority are the central goals or purposes of punishment; (2) imposing punishments that are appropriate to the nature of the offense is the controlling factor in achieving these goals; (3) for the gravest crimes, notably murder, the death penalty achieves these goals markedly better than long-term imprisonment; therefore (4) long-term imprisonment is not a feasible alternative to the death penalty. Opponents of the death penalty have challenged all three premises to this argument and in effect have conceded that even if the argument is valid, it fails to prove its claim because one or more of the premises are false. Again, we need not review here the well-worn lines of criticism against these premises, because they have been discussed adequately in earlier chapters.

In the present context what is primarily at stake is not whether each of these arguments establishes the common conclusion. Rather, it is whether the stringent criterion of feasibility on which both rely is appropriate. The criterion permits one to consider the purposes of punishment in deciding whether a given punishment (long-term incarceration) is a feasible alternative to another punishment (the death penalty). My own view is that nothing crucial to the fundamental question of a punishment's cruelty and unusualness turns on whether feasibility is defined so as to exclude or include this criterion. It is reasonable, however, to try to keep separate the concepts of *feasible* alternative punishments and *desirable* alternative punishments. Since adding such a stringent criterion to the other criteria of feasibility obviously makes this impossible, "feasibility" should be defined solely in terms of the other criteria.[44]

IX

So far in this discussion I have noted more than once that cruel and unusual punishments are typically *excessively severe* punishments. Now it is appropriate to examine the several possible dimensions in which one can judge the excessive severity of a given punishment. Each uses a legitimate application of the concept of cruel and unusual punishment but does so by means of a different argument. Indeed, not only the arguments but the points of the arguments differ, even though the conclusion in each case—that the punishment in question is judged to be cruel and unusual—remains the same. Agreement that a given punishment is to be condemned as cruel and unusual almost certainly cannot be reached unless there is prior agreement over the dimension in which the punishment is to be assessed, and thus over the relevant argument and the appropriate standard.

First, we might argue that a punishment is cruel and unusual in relation to the offender because it is excessively severe to impose it, for example, on a juvenile or a first offender. This may be called an *offender-relative* argument. Alternatively, we might argue that the punishment is cruel and unusual in relation to the offense because it is an excessively severe punishment given the gravity of the particular crime. This is an *offense-relative* argument. Instead of either of these, we might argue that the punishment is cruel and unusual because it is more severe than the way such offenses are punished in the vast majority of similar cases with similar offenders. This argument is *frequency-relative*.

All three of these arguments rely on comparisons to punitive practices for other offenses or offenders. Thus, any conclusion that rests on one of these arguments tacitly refers to a class of other punishments and other offenders, which serve as a morally acceptable base line. Interesting differences among the arguments emerge when we examine possible lines of attack on each. Judgments condemning a punishment on offender- or offense-relative grounds must rely on standards of appropriate punitive severity that refer to the nature of the offender or the nature of the offense, respectively. Such arguments are vulnerable to rebuttal based on standards deemed more appropriate than those relied on in the argument itself. If these other standards are indeed more appropriate, then the punishment in question cannot be excessively severe. But frequency-relative arguments are virtually free of such necessary appeal to standards. Any conclusion that a punishment is cruel and unusual based on its rarity or infrequency is properly supported by evidence about current punitive practices whose moral acceptability is not in question. Consequently, the way to rebut a frequency-relative argument is to refer to evidence showing that the alleged deviations from normal practice are either nonexistent or defensible. For example, it may turn out that the usual punishment for the offenses or offenders in question really is not very different from the punishment meted out in the case under attack, because there are special features about the offense or the offender that have been overlooked, but that—when recognized—make the seemingly excessive punishment suitable after all. Frequency-relative arguments can also be defeated in another way. One may concede that, under current conditions, the punishment under attack is indeed unusually severe—and then go on to argue that it is equally feasible and rational to increase the severity of the normal practice instead of abolishing the unusually severe punishment in dispute.[45]

In addition to the above three dimensions in which to assess punishments as cruel and unusual, there are at least two others. We might argue that the punishment is cruel and unusual in relation to the purpose for its imposition because it is excessively severe when measured by the requirements of retribution or of prevention. This may be called a *purpose-relative* argument. Finally, we might argue that the punishment is cruel and unusual by virtue of its very nature because it is excessively severe when measured by its impact on the person of the offender, quite apart from any other consideration. An argument of this kind is *essence-relative*.

These two arguments are not like the first three, because they do not require comparative judgments to other offenses and other offenders; there is no tacit reference class of morally acceptable punishments on which these arguments rely. Purpose-relative arguments require specification of some purpose or purposes that the practice of punishment is fairly judged to serve, are more speculative and less readily verifiable than the factors at the center of the other arguments.[46]

X

Given these five types of argument to establish that a punishment is cruel and unusual, which are the most important and why? I want to suggest two convergent answers to this question, one purely conceptual or logical and the other constitutional and forensic.

A full exploration of the logical relations among the five types of arguments is tempting, but three comments will suffice for the present discussion. First, these five arguments are clearly not mutually exclusive. For instance, if a given punishment is judged to be cruel and unusual according to an offender-relative argument, the same judgment can also be reached by relying on an offense-relative argument. Second, the five arguments are somewhat independent. Thus, a given punishment may be cruel and unusual when imposed on juveniles or for crimes against property, and thus be condemned both on offender-relative and on offense-relative grounds. But it does not follow that this punishment can therefore also be condemned on frequency-relative or purpose-relative grounds.

The third and most important point is that the five arguments are noticeably different in their logical power or scope. If the logical power of an argument can be measured by the number of nontrivial conclusions it entails, then purpose- and essence-relative arguments are considerably more powerful than the others. If a punishment is cruel and unusual by virtue of the appropriate purpose(s) of punishment, then the punishment is cruel and unusual for *all* offenders and for *all* offenses, even if it is not also excessively severe on any frequency- or essence-relative ground. Likewise, if a punishment is excessively severe by virtue of its very nature and the nature of persons, then it also must be cruel and unusual for all offenders and all offenses, no matter what the purpose or frequency of application of the punishment.

Considerations of this sort seem to underlie some of the Supreme Court's own responses to criticisms of the death penalty as a "cruel and unusual punishment."[47] Consider first a criticism based on an offender-relative argument. Such a judgment must focus on one or both of two sorts of properties: (a) natural properties such as sex, age, or race of the offender; and (b) social properties such as the offender's vocation, class, or wealth. Of all such possibilities, the most attractively relevant is the property of *age*. A strong natural inverse correlation exists between youth and both criminal culpability and ordinary responsibility for the conditions of the life lived up to the age of sixteen or eighteen, at least by comparison with those over eighteen. No such strong correlation obtains between any of the other properties (natural or social) and culpability-cum-responsibility. Accordingly, it seems quite appropriate to reason that a certain mode of punishment (for example, strict solitary confinement for one week) may be morally permissible for an adult but cruelly excessive for a child or other juvenile. As a type of argument directed against the death penalty, however, this is largely futile, since jurisdiction over juveniles is pre-empted by courts not empowered to invoke this penalty.[48] Nevertheless, on those rare occasions when someone under eighteen at the time of the crime has been convicted of a capital offense and sentenced to death and appellate courts have intervened, it is not clear that they have done so solely on the ground that the death penalty for such an offender would be a "cruel and unusual punishment" in violation of the Constitution.[49]

What is unsatisfactory about offender-relative arguments can be brought out by a dilemma: All such arguments must proceed by assuming either that death for all others convicted of the same offense is a "cruel and unusual punishment" or that it is not. If the argument takes the latter route, then it forecloses or jeopardizes important possibilities raised by other kinds of arguments (such as frequency- or purpose-relative arguments) that might attack the same punishment when applied to any person, regardless of age, sex, or other characteristics. If the argument takes the former route, it must take for granted the soundness of some such additional arguments. Inevitably, therefore, arguments attacking the death penalty by reference solely to some special characteristic of the offender, such as age, are importantly incomplete and to that extent unsatisfactory.

The Court's rulings in *Woodson v. North Carolina* and related cases,[50] in which the Court held that certain mandatory capital statutes violate the eighth and fourteenth amendments because they prevent the sentencer from "individualizing"[51] the punishment, illustrate and confirm this reasoning. Individualizing in this way is an implicit requirement of *Furman v. Georgia*[52] and thus perhaps of all capital sentencing. Seen in the present context, the requirement of individualization in capital sentencing is simply the recognition that offender-relative factors must not be excluded by statute from the sentencer's consideration and that, once they are taken into account in particular cases, they may well provide an adequate ground for a noncapital sentence. *Woodson* and its progeny, which overturned many death sentences,[53] were understandably greeted with acclaim by opponents of the death penalty. Yet the Court found no difficulty in ruling against the death penalty in *Woodson* and in refusing on the very same day to rule against it in *Gregg, Jurek,* and *Proffitt,* as though to say: The death penalty may well be a "cruel and unusual punishment" insofar as it is imposed by a sentencer precluded by statute from considering offender-relative factors, but it is not a "cruel and unusual punishment" insofar as the nature of the person or the nature and purpose of punishment are concerned.

Much the same sort of problem arises with judgments that focus only on issues of disproportionality or arbitrariness and discrimination and thus rely on offense-relative and frequency-relative arguments. The Supreme Court has viewed these two sorts of arguments against the death penalty with cautious favor. In *Furman,* insofar as there was any common ground among the five Justices constituting the majority, the Court ruled against all nonmandatory capital statutes because their actual execution was "freakishly rare" and thus in any given case unusually severe.[54] This amounted to acceptance of an argument that the death penalty can be a frequency-relative "cruel and unusual punishment." As *Gregg, Proffitt,* and *Jurek* showed four years later, however, there was no logical inconsistency between such frequency-relative reasoning and subsequent decisions that found the death penalty not to be a purpose-relative or an essence-relative "cruel and unusual punishment." Furthermore, as events have shown, judicial and legislative friends of the death penalty can always argue that administrative defects in application of this penalty (the source of the "freakish" or "racially sensitive" use condemned in *Furman*) can be remedied administratively; the defects are not inherent in the mode of punishment or in capital statutes themselves.[55] This continuing debate has raised complex questions of fact that must be faced; it is easy to argue that during the past decade the Supreme Court has been insufficiently sensitive to the evidence that casts grave doubt on the possibility of a death penalty system in this country free of racial and class bias. Nevertheless, the limitations inherent in the logic of this type of argument require us to look elsewhere for the most fundamental objections to the death penalty on the ground that it is a "cruel and unusual punishment."

In other post-*Gregg* death penalty cases, the Court has ruled that a death sentence, even if imposed by a sentencer under an optional capital statute fully permitting an "individualized" determination of sentence, is still a "cruel and unusual punishment" if the crime for which it is imposed is nonhomicidal, such as rape[56] or kidnapping.[57] The death penalty is always "disproportionate" in its severity for such offenses, however grave they may be. This is, in effect, acceptance of an argument that the death penalty can be an offense-relative "cruel and unusual punishment" without retracting the prior conclusion that it is not "cruel and unusual" on purpose- or essence-relative grounds. How broadly the Court is prepared to extend this offense-relative argument against the death penalty will be known in part only when it rules whether the death penalty for treason and other non-homicidal offenses is a "cruel and unusual punishment"; this is not likely to happen soon.[58]

Thus the Court continues to resist the most powerful arguments against the death penalty (that is, those that are purpose- or essence-relative) even as it has granted, in one form or another, that the death penalty may well be a "cruel and unusual punishment" on offense-, offender-, or frequency-relative grounds. From both a constitutional and a philosophical point of view, therefore, by far the most interesting types of judgments that a punishment is cruel and unusual are those relating to the proper purposes of punishment and to the real nature of persons. Let us turn to a closer scrutiny of these types of arguments.

XI

The punishment of one person by another has as few or as many purposes as the punisher can sincerely claim. But insofar as the practice of punishment is morally defensible, its purposes must be more strictly limited.[59] Punishments must be controlled by the assumption that society imposes penalties only upon guilty offenders in the pursuit of protecting and vindicating justice as defined in part by compliance with the criminal law. Thus forward-looking purposes—rehabilitation, incapacitation, deterrence, and the prevention of crime generally—as well as backward-looking purposes—vindication, condemnation, and desert—have a place in any rational understanding of the practice of punishment. A punishment can be judged cruel and unusual, or excessively severe, if it imposes more pain, suffering, loss of rights, or other deprivation than is necessary to serve these purposes. Thus one way to conclude that the death penalty is excessively severe is to conclude that no matter what the offense or the offender, and no matter what its pattern or frequency of administration, it imposes more deprivation than is needed to secure the appropriate punitive purposes.

Note that if punitive purposes are narrowly specified, it is possible to settle the substantive question before us with dispatch. If one believes that utilitarian purposes in punishment should generally prevail over all non-utilitarian purposes, and that the best way to achieve them is to provide rehabilitation for all convicted offenders (regardless of the crime or the criminal), then the death penalty so thoroughly frustrates this purpose that it must be judged excessive without further ado. (It is, of course, possible to defend rehabilitation on grounds other than as a means to the end of crime prevention. It can be defended also as an end in itself, on the ground that society ought to undertake the moral regeneration of convicted offenders for their own good. Even more than when rehabilitation is placed within an utilitarian framework, this view eliminates any possible recourse to the death penalty.[60]) However, this argument has its dual: If one believes that retributive purposes should generally prevail over all nonretributive purposes, and that the criterion for appropriate punitive severity is a strict *lex talionis*—making the punishment "fit" the crime by ensuring that it imitates or reproduces that crime's characteristic feature—then the death penalty cannot be cruelly excessive for murder. The distinctive premises of these two arguments obviously lead to the contradictory conclusion that the death penalty for the offense of murder both is and is not cruelly excessive; at least one of these premises must be rejected.

Actually, we should reject them both. *Lex talionis* is a notoriously unacceptable principle of proportionate severity, and few if any—even among the serious defenders of retribution (and there are many)[61]—today incorporate it into their theory. As for rehabilitation, even if it is false (as it is) that "nothing works,"[62] there is no empirical or moral basis for supposing that rehabilitation could or ought to supplant all competing utilitarian considerations in the pursuit of crime prevention and law compliance. Thus the easy repudiation of the death penalty as a cruel and unusual punishment, or its equally facile vindication, comes to nothing.

Yet another possibility with comparably sweeping effect should be noticed, not least because it has proved somewhat attractive in the past. Some thinkers might argue that one (although not both) of the two purposes of punishment so far identified—roughly, the retributive and the utilitarian—is entirely illegitimate. This position, in conjunction with other considerations, could yield a decisive judgment on the death penalty as an excessively severe punishment. If it could be shown both that it is morally unjustified to let retributive purposes play any role in the practice of punishment in a just society (a view Bentham probably held—recall Chapter 3), and that the only defense of the death penalty (even without appeal to *lex talionis*) were to be found within these purposes, then repudiating them would pave the way for showing that the death penalty is excessively severe. Parallel considerations apply to the utilitarian purposes of punishment: If it could be shown that it is morally unjustified to let these purposes play any role (a view Kant seems to have held[63]), and that only they provide a basis for attack on the death penalty, then we must conclude that the death penalty is not excessively severe. However, I see no way to advance the major premise of either of these arguments (quite apart from the implausibility that also attaches to the secondary premises). Any theory that shows punishment to be legitimate by reference to its role in securing general compliance with roughly just laws cannot be formulated entirely free of retributive and utilitarian considerations. Moreover, the best way to integrate these backward- and forward-looking considerations does not materially advantage either side in the death penalty controversy.[64] Supporters and opponents of the death penalty are thus engaged in a debate whose rational resolution turns less on the particular role allotted to each of these punitive purposes than on the various factual considerations enlisted on behalf of the relevant retributive principles and utilitarian generalizations. In sum, no argument that the death penalty is a cruel and unusual punishment and no argument designed to prevent that conclusion can succeed if it repudiates outright either all utilitarian or all retributive purposes in the practice of punishment in a just society.

Once arguments of the above two sorts are put aside, it immediately becomes doubtful whether there is any legitimate purpose of punishment that, by itself, either requires or forbids the death penalty. At most, it appears, the purposes of punishment are consistent with this penalty, and accepting or rejecting it will turn on other considerations. Thus in regard to retributivism, once we drop *lex talionis* in favor of a more sophisticated alternative principle, the death penalty may turn out to be consistent with this principle. Whether it is nonetheless excessive in its severity would then turn on other considerations, either internal to the theory of retribution itself (such as the considerations that govern the general construction of the penalty scale) or external to it.[65]

Parallel considerations apply if we start instead with any of several utilitarian purposes. Once it is conceded, as it must be, that crime prevention and law compliance are always probably better secured by relatively severe penalties (rather than mild penalties or none at all), then it is not inconsistent in principle to adopt the death penalty. Whether the penalty is nonetheless excessively severe would then depend either on internal factors, all of which involve questions of fact, or on external factors that rely on nonutilitarian

121

considerations. In the nature of the case, there is no guarantee that the facts in question remain constant over time and under varied conditions. Thus holding constant the retributive or utilitarian purposes of punishment (trimmed of their talionic and rehabilitative features, respectively, and each prevented from ousting the other on grounds of general illegitimacy), one might easily conclude that, given the facts as they currently are and as they have been for some decades, the death penalty in this nation for all crimes and all offenders has become excessively severe, even if at an earlier time this was not true. In fact, the briefest possible characterization of the argument against the death penalty during the past quarter century in this country is precisely of this nature: Neither utilitarian nor retributive purposes *require* us to use the death penalty, and thus no rational purpose of punishment in a just society is more effectively served by the death penalty than by the less severe punishment of long-term imprisonment. To continue to use the death penalty is to persevere in using an excessively severe punishment.

One can readily see this argument at work, not only in the brief initially presented to the Supreme Court in *Furman*,[66] and in the concurring opinions in that case by Justice Brennan[67] and Justice Marshall,[68] but also in the writings of several previous[69] and subsequent[70] commentators. In none of these sources, to be sure, is the present purpose-relative argument kept distinct from other arguments, notably those discussed previously that rely primarily on frequency-relative considerations. Rather, these logically distinguishable arguments are usually found inseparably intertwined. Whether isolating these different types of argument would add to their separate or joint persuasiveness in any judicial or legislative forum is open to question; in any case, it is desirable to keep them distinct in the present discussion.

Distinguishable though they are, they share a certain difficulty. Both the frequency-relative and purpose-relative arguments rely heavily on several factual claims about social behavior. These behaviors and their best description and explanation are subject to change and are vulnerable to controversy over their verification—as the struggle by social scientists to settle issues of racial discrimination and deterrent efficacy convincingly shows. Thus, even though purpose-relative arguments have a greater logical power than do frequency-relative arguments, the former are no more immune from the vagaries of empirical data than are the latter. Even though the rational policy planner (as distinct from politically vulnerable legislators) would be guided by arguments as plainly empirical as these, many constitutional interpreters would not. The factual support required by these arguments runs counter to the reasoning relied upon by those strict reconstructionists who would explain the "cruel and unusual punishments" clause by reference and deference to the original intention of the framers.

XII

The strongest argument against the death penalty as an excessively severe punishment must take its direction from two main cues: It must subordinate wherever possible local or transitory empirical considerations, which frequency- and purpose-relative arguments cannot do; it must elevate to primary importance the more timeless and universal aspects of the nature of the death penalty on the one hand, and of the person on the other. In addition, these factors must be deployed against the proper background of a system of just laws in a society of persons, with rights, who recognize and respect the rights of others equally with their own. Without this setting, violation of the law cannot be morally condemned, and force cannot be morally defended when used to secure compliance with the law. And, of course, a feasible alternative punishment to the death penalty must be available.

We begin this final stage of our inquiry by examining a recent account of cruelty inspired by the great eighteenth-century French opponents of the cruelties of their day.[71] According to this account, cruelty is "the willful infliction of physical pain on a weaker being in order to cause anguish and fear."[72] The very ambiguity of this definition may enhance its attractiveness: In whom are the "anguish and fear" of "cruelty" willfully caused—the victim, or the witnesses, or both? When this concept of cruelty is used to judge the death penalty, it certainly fits classic paradigms of cruel execution: Roman crucifixion, Tudor disembowelments, tearing asunder by *l'ancien régime*. Even the fusillade of rifle bullets used in Utah[73] or the repeated jolts of high-voltage electric current used recently in Georgia[74] might fall under the scope of cruelty as defined above. But capital punishment as such? Never. Where the death inflicted is not "physically" painful, it apparently cannot be cruel. Where the intention is not to cause anyone "anguish and fear"— not the condemned offender or the official witnesses or the general public— but merely to blot out the criminal once and for all, cruelty evaporates. What emerges from this plausible definition is exactly what modern friends of the death penalty have always insisted: Capital punishment is not, per se, an excessively severe or "cruel and unusual punishment," even if (as all sensible persons agree) some of its historic modes of infliction were.[75]

123

But cruelty as defined above is only the first, not the last, word on the subject. Another thoughtful recent writer, steeped equally in the seminal eighteenth-century thinking about cruelty and in the widespread horrors of our own time, invites us to think about the subject in a more imaginative, thematic fashion,[76] and thus to go beyond what any typical dictionary will tell us about human cruelty. If we do this, we will see that the very "heart of cruelty" is best described as "total activity smashing total passivity."[77] Cruelty, on this view, consists of "subordination, subjection to a superior power whose will becomes the victim's law."[78] Where cruelty reigns there is a "power-relationship between two parties," one of whom is "active, comparatively powerful," and the other of whom is "passive, comparatively powerless."[79] These penetrating observations, proposed originally without any explicit or tacit reference to punishment under law, much less the death penalty, nonetheless are appropriate to it. They reveal the very essence of capital punishment to be cruelty. Whether carried out by impalement or electrocution, crucifixion or lethal injection, the "iron maiden" or the gas chamber, firing squad or hanging, with or without "due process" and "equal protection" of the law, there is always present that "total activity" of the executioner and the "total passivity" of the condemned. The state, acting through its local representatives in the execution chamber, smashes the convicted criminal into oblivion. The one annihilates—reduces to inert lifeless matter—the other. If this is a fair characterization of cruelty, then the death penalty was, is, and always will be a cruel punishment.

What is most compelling about the concept of cruelty understood as a "power-relationship" in the manner described is that it focuses our attention on the salient common factor in all situations where the death penalty is inflicted, however painlessly, and whatever the condemned person has done. For western philosophy, the classic example of capital punishment is provided by the case of Socrates, whose death (if we may believe Plato and Xenophon) was painless and administered by his own hand from the cup of hemlock, which he drank by order of the Athenian court that sentenced him to death. If such a method of execution were revived today we could not easily condemn it as "undignified" and an assault on the "dignity of man," said by the Supreme Court to be the central value protected by the constitutional prohibition of "cruel and unusual punishments."[80] Today, the growing use of lethal injection (and even more "acceptable" modes of execution may be invented and adopted in the future) raises the same difficulty. With death carried out by the state in a manner that does not disfigure the offender's body, apparently causes no pain whatever, and brings about death within a few minutes, it is extremely difficult and maybe even impossible to construct a convincing argument that condemns the practice based on its "indignity." These are awkward facts for those who oppose capital punishment, but they are completely outflanked when cruelty is viewed as a "power-relationship." Cruelty seen in this fashion enables us to recognize that the death penalty is and will remain cruel no matter how or on whom it is inflicted.

The idea of such total obliteration offends our moral imagination, however, only if we grant that using the death penalty destroys something of value. We must still explain what is wrong about cruel punishments and why it matters so much. The only kind of answer worth seeking is one that reveals the worth to us (and not only or even primarily to the person cruelly punished) of what cruelty destroys. But what value is there in a deservedly condemned criminal? Even if true, it does not suffice to say that "there is a nonwaivable, nonforfeitable, nonrelinquishable right—the right to one's status as a moral being, a right that is implied in one's being a possessor of any rights at all."[81] Traditional theories of "natural rights" in the seventeenth and eighteenth centuries fully acknowledged that a person's "natural rights" included a "right to life." But according to these theories this right is "forfeited" by any act of killing another person without excuse or justification. There are, to be sure, difficulties with the idea of forfeiture of natural rights (as I have indicated in earlier chapters). Whether they are any graver than the difficulties in the alternative is not immediately obvious. The alternative holds that there is nothing a person can do or become by virtue of which that person loses status as a moral agent. This is one way to express the underlying conception of the person as shielded by fundamental rights, including the right to life. The essence-relative argument against the death penalty as a "cruel and unusual punishment" turns on it. Without such a conception, we cannot resist the obvious inference: Once a person is fairly found guilty of a ghastly crime (for example, mass, serial, or genocidal murder), then the offender has no moral "worth" or residual "dignity," and deserves no minimal "respect" from society. Only with a conception of fixed rights can we avoid such an inference.

The argument can be advanced from each of three directions. The first draws upon familiar constitutional principles. According to these principles, even the persons convicted of the gravest crimes retain their fundamental rights of "due process of law" and "equal protection of the laws." These rights cannot be forfeited or waived. If government officials violate them, that is sufficient to nullify whatever legal burdens were placed on the person arising out of the violation and quite apart from whatever consequences may ensue. What this shows is that our society already has in place, and fully acknowledges, the principle that the individual *cannot* do anything that utterly nullifies his or her "moral worth" and standing as a person. The essence-relative argument against the death penalty thus does not aim to invent an unfamiliar type of reasoning or appeal to a novel and unprecedented type of principle, and then inject it into constitutional thinking. It would merely extend into the area of the substantive constitutional law of punishments something that has long been recognized as appropriate to the use of procedures and practices in criminal law.

The second line of reasoning draws upon quotidian experience. This assures us that those persons actually condemned by law to die for their crimes are not merely living members of *homo sapiens*, but that they are also persons capable of the full range of moral action and passion unique to moral creatures. However dangerous, irrational, self-centered, stupid, or beyond improvement convicted felons may in fact be, these deficiencies do not overwhelm their capacity for moral agency—for responsible action, thought, and judgment, in solitude and in relationship with other persons. In particular, none of these capacities vanishes as a result of the person's being at fault for causing willful, deliberate homicide. Anyone who doubts this will put doubt aside after reading recent accounts of men on America's death rows, such as Robert Johnson's *Condemned to Die: Life Under Sentence of Death*. The act of murder itself does not cause the varying moral capacities of murderers that experience amply reveals.[82] No plausible empirical argument can support an alleged loss of moral agency in a convicted murderer as a result of the act of murder. Even more to the point, so far as moral agency is concerned, there is no evidence to show that convicted murderers are different from other convicts.[83] So the doctrine that criminals forfeit or relinquish all their basic human rights by their criminal acts, and thereby cease to be moral persons, receives no support from experience.

The third direction in which to look for support is more obscure and controversial; it concerns moral theory and the nature of the person. Despite recent remarks from the federal bench expressing hostility to all such theories,[84] they cannot be ignored. We human beings are not merely biological specimens of the species *homo sapiens*, nor merely self-motivating, information-processing creatures; we are moral beings. The meaning of this proposition cannot be intuitively grasped or read off from any value-neutral set of descriptions about our behavioral capacities;[85] it can be understood only as the product of reflective thought about our capacities, and any remotely adequate account will embody or rely upon moral theory. As a consequence, the nature of the person (as well as any account of that nature) itself changes over time as a result of changes in our self-perceptions. History assures us that we are permanently engaged in our own progressive self-understanding as individuals and as societies. For several centuries—and in particular, since the Age of Enlightenment—philosophers have struggled to enunciate a conception of the person as fundamentally social, rational, and autonomous, and as immune to change in these respects by virtue of any contingencies of history or circumstance. Such personal traits and capacities are no guarantee against immorality in private or public conduct. Nor do they protect us from mortality; these traits may decay with senescence and can vanish prior to biological death. In particular cases it is also true that illness, abnormality, and other misfortunes can prevent the normal development of these traits in otherwise "normal" persons. Yet these capacities are not, and cannot be thought of as, vulnerable to destruction by the agent's own acts when those acts are deliberate, intentional, responsible—the very qualities properly deemed necessary in a person's conduct before the criminal law subjects a person's harmful conduct to judgment, condemnation, and punishment. On such a theory, even the worst and most dangerous murderer is not a fit subject for annihilation by others. Not even the convicted criminal is a mere object or thing to be disposed of by the decision of others, as though there were no alternative. Society has no authority to create and sustain any institution whose nature and purpose is to destroy some of its own members. Cruelty, which has such a nature and purpose, matters—because our own status as moral creatures matters. Thus deliberate, institutionalized, lethally punitive cruelty matters, too. Bringing it to an end in all human affairs heads the list of desiderata for any society of persons who understand themselves as moral agents.

Why a theory with the consequences sketched above should be accepted in preference to alternative theories of the person is far too large a question to try to answer here. Until that question is answered satisfactorily, however, its conception of the person will not convince the unconverted. Today's handfuls of literate friends of the death penalty are unaware of or unpersuaded by this theory; one can only speculate about what they would offer in its place. Fortunately, during the past decade or so (indeed, coincident with but wholly independent of the Supreme Court's death penalty decisions beginning with *Furman*) several philosophers have begun thorough and systematic work toward developing versions of this theory,[86] including versions that connect it with our constitutional tradition in general and with the concepts employed in the Bill of Rights and fourteenth amendment in particular.[87] It must suffice here to point in this direction and leave for other occasions the detailed characterization and evaluation of this theory.[88]

If the death penalty is an excessively severe punishment, as I believe, then it is in part because the best conception of the person is the one sketched above. According to that conception, given the familiar facts of our society in this century and the unalterable nature of the death penalty itself, this kind of punishment—even when carried out in the most dignified fashion, on the most hardened offenders, for the most heinous crimes—exceeds the severity that society acting through its government may legitimately employ. Translated into the terms of the Constitution's severity-limiting language, the death penalty thus is a "cruel and unusual punishment."

XIII

My investigation has taken us, as philosophical inquiry typically will, from the commonplace to the uncertain, the perplexing, and even the mysterious. To analyze what it is for a punishment to be excessively severe, we must avail ourselves of hypotheses and principles supplied from theories and conceptions having nothing directly to do with punishment at all. A theory of punishment, in the end, is no better than the theory of society, of morality, and of the person out of which it grows (if one thinks organically) or from which it is deduced (if one thinks axiomatically) or into which it is placed (if one thinks contextually). I have tried to show through various lines of inquiry that we can sensibly challenge the death penalty quite apart from attending centrally to the issues as they have been shaped during the past decade or so by the Supreme Court's own pronouncements, rulings, and tergiversations. At present, the Court is hardly more receptive to these theories than is the general public.

Chapter 5

The Death Penalty, Imposed Law, and the Role of Moral Elites

The conclusion is inescapable, we think, that this rare penalty, inflicted upon the smallest handful of murderers, is no part of the regular criminal-law machinery of . . . any . . . State. It is a freakish aberration, a random extreme act of violence, visibly arbitrary and discriminatory—a penalty reserved for unusual application because, if it were usually used, it would affront universally shared standards of public decency. Such a penalty . . . has no place in a democratic government.[1]

[They] have set themselves up as the guardians of evolving standards of decency, and they are asking this Court to set itself up as a super legislature.[2]

In two examples drawn from the recent history of capital punishment in Oregon, we have models of two different kinds of laws. The first we might call imposed law; the second might be considered its opposite—self-imposed, or autonomously accepted, law.

Imposed Law In the mid-1950s, the governor of Oregon, Robert D. Holmes, announced that henceforth he would commute any death sentence that reached his desk in a clemency proceeding. On conscientious grounds he was completely opposed to capital punishment, and he said he intended to use his commutation authority in accordance with his convictions. During

129

Holmes's one term as chief executive, he did commute all three death sentences that came before him; no legal executions occurred in Oregon while he was in office. As he knew, however, there was no public clamor to end executions, nor was there a long history of abolition only recently reversed by a maverick legislature. No commission on criminal-law reform in Oregon had called upon the governor to end the death penalty summarily by exercise of his clemency power. Nor could the governor defend his initiative as a reasonable anticipation of imminent repeal of capital statutes by the Oregon legislature or of their invalidation by the Oregon appellate judiciary. Capital indictments may have been infrequent, but so was murder. Jury nullification—a refusal to convict the guilty—was unknown in capital cases.[3] In short, Governor Holmes's policy of commutation amounted to a virtual edict, and came as close to the imposition of law as is possible in a constitutional democracy—in this instance, the abrupt suspension of the constitutionally authorized death penalty in favor of a substitute punishment of life imprisonment.

Self-imposed Law   A decade later, in the mid-1960s, the people of Oregon voted to revise the state constitution so as to abolish the death penalty for all crimes and to substitute a punishment of life imprisonment. This was done, following extensive public discussion in all the media, after enactment by the Oregon legislature of statutes that were contingent on the relevant referendum passing. And pass it did, by an impressive 455,654 to 302,105. It was carried in all but four of Oregon's three dozen counties; and in the most populous, Multnomah, where the abolition campaign was concentrated, the referendum was endorsed by a ratio of almost two to one. Throughout the months prior to the election, no organization or spokesman emerged to defend the death penalty. (I discuss this campaign in detail in Chapter 6.) The success of the referendum owed more to the skillful management of the abolition campaign by a moral minority, as we might call it, or moral elite, than to any irresistible upsurge of public revulsion at the spectacle of further executions. Nevertheless, unless we are to treat all law duly enacted and enforced as imposed law—surely an absurd idea—the repeal of capital punishment in Oregon in the 1964 referendum qualifies as a clear case of self-imposed law.

We may now formulate the main question to which the rest of this chapter is addressed: Which of these two models most nearly fits the recent status of the death penalty in the United States?

I

As recently as the end of World War II, executions, death sentences, and capital statutes were commonplace throughout the United States. All but two of the fifty competent jurisdictions (forty-eight states, the District of Columbia, and the federal government) had at least one capital statute; several authorized the death penalty for any of a dozen crimes. Some of these statutes called for a mandatory death penalty; most were in a form that left the choice of sentence between life imprisonment and death to the discretion of the trial court. Death sentences were frequent. Although most were meted out to offenders convicted of murder, in the southern states as many as 20 percent each year were for rape. Executions occurred nationally at the rate of ten each month. Public opinion, insofar as it was measured at all, was in favor of the death penalty by a ratio of two to one. Opposition to the death penalty was scattered and relatively uninformed; active concern was found mainly among the thousand or so members of the American League to Abolish Capital Punishment (founded in 1925).

The death penalty seemed securely fixed in the law. No legislature, state or federal, had abolished the death penalty for murder since Missouri had done so in 1917 (it was reinstated there two years later). Bills to abolish the death penalty were not uncommon; occasionally one would be scheduled for a public hearing, but rarely did the legislative leadership allow such bills to be brought to the floor for a vote. Not until four decades after 1917 did any legislature repeal any capital statute anywhere in the United States. In the executive branch, State House or White House, where the power ranged from the decision on indicting for a capital offense to the decision on signing a death warrant, there was no particular reluctance to enforce the death penalty. Although commutations of death sentences to life imprisonment were not unknown, they were infrequent; probably no more than 5 percent of death sentences were nullified in this way.

In the trial and appellate courts—state and federal—the death penalty was also a fixture. Forty years ago, all but a few jurisdictions gave the trial courts statutory authority to sentence to life imprisonment after conviction of a capital crime, and the courts did so in most cases. The choice between the death penalty and life imprisonment was based on a variety of factors, ranging from sympathy through vengeance to racial or ethnic prejudice. Judges at trial rarely plea-bargained a murder defendant into prison in order to secure his conviction or the conviction of his codefendants. At the appellate-court level, death-sentence convictions were occasionally reversed.

The grounds for appeal were narrow, and review of state death-sentence convictions in federal courts was difficult to obtain. The constitutionality of capital punishment—despite the express requirements of "equal protection of the laws" (fourteenth amendment), "due process of law" (fifth and fourteenth amendments), and the prohibition against "cruel and unusual punishments" (eighth amendment)—seemed secure. No capital statute and no mode of inflicting the death penalty had ever been declared unconstitutional. No class of offenders, such as juveniles, had ever been declared constitutionally exempt from the application of a death penalty statute. No death sentence had ever been voided by any appellate court on any ground except that the conviction on which it was based was in error.

The national history of racism powerfully distorted the use of capital punishment. This was nowhere more evident than in the sordid facts about lynching—capital punishment in the streets, the most violent symbol of black helplessness and white brutality. Not until the mid-1950s did the annual rate of lynchings decline to a level where the Bureau of Census ceased to collect and publish data on them. Until about 1935, they occurred at the rate of more than one per month; 90 percent of the victims were black.[4] As for legal executions in the South during the late 1940s, six blacks were put to death for each white. Every empirical study of the death penalty and race in the United States confirmed the judgment of Gunnar Myrdal: "the South makes the widest application of the death penalty and Negro criminals come in for much more than their share of the executions."[5]

All things considered, then, the status of the death penalty forty or so years ago in the United States hardly provides us with an instance of imposed law. Death sentences and executions were too frequent and too widely favored; commutation of death sentences and repeal of capital statutes were too rare. The whole issue of capital punishment itself hardly caused a ripple of public controversy.

II

Today, after a decade of significant change in the 1970s, the national scene is very different in several respects. Capital statutes, it is true, continue in force in thirty-seven jurisdictions. By the end of 1986, however, virtually none authorized a mandatory death sentence, and for reasons explained elsewhere (see Chapter 7), it is doubtful whether any death sentence imposed under a mandatory death statute could be carried out. Only criminal homicide in its various forms (premeditated murder, felony-murder, etc.) was subject to the death penalty. Of the thirteen abolitionist jurisdictions at the beginning of 1986, perhaps half a dozen could be regarded as unlikely to reinstate any capital statutes.

Capital sentencing, however, has by no means come to an end, nor has it even dramatically diminished. At the beginning of 1986, there were more than 1,600 people under death sentence in thirty-two states. Since the mid-1960s, upwards of 3,000 death sentences have been handed down by the trial courts in forty-two jurisdictions (including Washington, D.C., and the federal government). Since the watershed year of 1972, 90 percent of the nation's death sentences have issued from eleven jurisdictions, eight of them in the South. Predictably, sex continues to be the strongest correlate of a death sentence, followed by race. No more than 1 percent of those sentenced to death are female, although about 23 percent of criminal homicides are committed by women. As for race, about 55 percent of all those sentenced to death are nonwhite, slightly more than the proportion of all criminal homicides committed by nonwhites.[6]

Executions began their historic decline during World War II; they dropped noticeably again a decade later, especially in the South, where two thirds of all executions in the United States have taken place since 1930. The greatest decline, amounting to de facto abolition, did not occur until a concerted legal campaign was launched in 1967 to secure review of all death sentences by the federal courts and nullification on constitutional grounds of all capital statutes. In fact, between July 1967 and December 1976—a few months less than ten years—this campaign stalled all execu tions. In July 1976, when the Supreme Court ratified death penalty statutes in Florida, Georgia, and Texas, it became clear that it would be only a matter of time before executions resumed. They did, slowly at first—one in 1977, none in 1978, two in 1979, none in 1980—and then with increasing frequency: five in 1983, twenty-one in 1984, eighteen in 1985, and eighteen by the end of 1986. During the rest of this century, more executions seem certain; so is an increasing rate of executions.

Looked at institutionally and politically over the past several decades, the most interesting change has been in the behavior of the federal appellate courts. During a period of five years, between 1972 and 1977, the Supreme Court forged a series of major holdings that modified the status of the death penalty across the nation. Although these rulings boosted the campaign to secure judicial abolition of the death penalty, they fell short of a ruling that capital punishment per se was unconstitutional. In *Gregg v. Georgia* and its companion cases, in 1976, the Supreme Court upheld several different capital statutes, all of which imposed the death penalty for murder under procedures that required the trial courts to weigh mitigating as well as aggravating factors relevant to the determination of sentence (as I shall explain in greater detail in Chapter 7). Thus the United States began the final decades of this century with the death penalty still permissible under law in most jurisdictions, still sought by prosecutors and meted out by trial courts, and still given nominal approval by the bulk of society.

III

Can the present status of the death penalty in the United States usefully be viewed as an instance of imposed law? Does the model of imposed law proposed earlier give us a way of understanding it? The argument for the affirmative, reduced to its basic elements, is as follows:

1. The decade-long national moratorium on executions (1967–1976) and the relative infrequency of executions during recent years are entirely owing to the initiatives undertaken by the self-appointed guardians of civil rights and civil liberties in the United States, notably the NAACP Legal Defense and Educational Fund (LDF) and the American Civil Liberties Union (ACLU). Since the mid-1960s these non-governmental organizations have devoted a significant fraction of their total resources to the fight for abolition and, in so doing, have contributed funds and talent in unprecedented quantity to this cause. Without their efforts, the status of the death penalty today would not be very different from what it was a generation ago.

2. The initiatives of this moral minority have been effective in altering the status of persons under death sentence and the status of capital statutes because they were addressed directly to a counterpart elite in government itself, the life-appointees of the federal appellate bench, including in particular the nine members of the Supreme Court. It is these judges, and virtually these judges alone, who have ruled progressively against the death penalty in case after case, secure in their immunity from the political process that, had they been directly vulnerable to it, probably would have expelled them from office for ruling as they did from *Furman* to *Coker*. Their immunity freed them to consider the appeal to moral principles advanced by the LDF attorneys and their allies in a manner that could be expected of no other branch of government.

3. These moral and judicial elites have had continuing support from the highly educated academic and professional elites (social scientists, physicians, lawyers, humanists) from whom they are drawn. Though not unanimously opposing the death penalty, members of this third elite have put their resources at the disposal of the LDF and the ACLU in a variety of ways, not least of which have been the public interpretation, justification, and rationalization of the abolitionist cause and of the tactics used by the LDF and the ACLU to implement it.

4. Most of the multi-issue groups and organizations on record against the death penalty, including even the LDF and the ACLU, know that their rank-and-file members have been slow to join this particular campaign. The lay members of the churches, as well as many of the clergy, have not supported the increasingly firm policy favoring abolition expressed by their national religious organizations and by spokesmen for social justice. Although the National Coalition against the Death Penalty (NCADP, founded in 1976) has listed half a hundred national organizations as its members, they represent only a small fraction of the general public—most of which professes to favor restoration of the death penalty for murder and other heinous crimes. Whatever clamor there may be from time to time against a particular execution, or against a particular death sentence, opposition to the death penalty as such is not and never has been *vox populi*.

5. The present status of the death penalty in the United States may not fit exactly the model of imposition of law inspired by reference to the situation in Oregon under Governor Holmes in the mid-1950s. Yet the preceding facts do show that the status of capital punishment during the past two decades far more closely approaches that extreme than it does the other.

That is the argument in its bluntest and briefest form. How sound is it? The position I shall endeavor to establish requires some modifications in this argument—namely, that although it is necessary to acknowledge an indispensable role played by moral elites in bringing the nation so far so quickly toward abolition of the death penalty, it is easy to overestimate their effect and to underestimate the degree of public approval for their efforts and accomplishments. A better, more accurate interpretation of all the facts suggests that the visible and prominent acts of the moral elites opposing the death penalty are the surface phenomena of deeper social forces moving slowly, erratically, and far from implacably in the same direction.

Viewing what has happened as an imposition of the law by the few upon the many is a misleading oversimplification of what in fact is a complex and fundamentally democratic transformation of the law in a whole society.

The Evidence

The Legal Defense Fund If one group has to be identified as chiefly responsible for the progress since the 1960s toward abolition of the death penalty in the United States, it would be the LDF. This group brought the original class-action suits, stopping all executions in 1967 and raising the series of constitutional challenges that kept the issue returning to the federal courts. The LDF planned and financed the national litigational campaign against the death penalty on behalf of its typically indigent clients. Any argument that turns on the decisive role of a moral elite in the death penalty controversy must evaluate carefully the accomplishments of the LDF.

The LDF is without question the nation's oldest and most prominent public-interest law firm. Its crowning achievement is the victory from a unanimous Supreme Court in 1954 in *Brown v. Board of Education,* outlawing legally enforced, racially segregated public education. The former executive director of the LDF, who argued the victory in *Brown,* has for some years himself been a member of the Supreme Court: Justice Thurgood Marshall. As one of the LDF's former litigating attorneys has said, the LDF office law library in New York has often been graced by the "shiny minds from the best law schools . . . so many future professors, senatorial aides, and Supreme Court clerks. . . ."[7]

The chief function of the LDF since its founding in 1939 has been the litigation of major civil-rights issues. In 1975, it had a budget of $3.6 million, about 10 percent of which was used to finance the anti-death-penalty campaign.[8] Although the LDF maintains a staff of twenty-four lawyers, one hundred other employees, several interns and other volunteer support staff, and has a docket of eight hundred to nine hundred cases at any given time, only two of the staff attorneys are available to handle the two hundred or so capital cases.[9] Yet this staff has access to constituencies in every major law school in the nation, as well as several hundred cooperating attorneys across the land, most of whom practice in the South. The annual receptions held by the LDF in New York, Boston, and other major cities for its benefactors and supporters represent every elite in American society: social, financial, political, academic, intellectual, and professional.

Although the LDF is unquestionably part of the nation's moral elite, it is a disinterested one, especially with regard to its opposition to the death penalty. The trustees, staff, and friends of the LDF have little to gain personally from the abolition campaign; neither they nor their families, friends, or associates are likely to suffer from the death penalty or benefit directly from its abolition. Those who would gain are predominantly the lumpenproletariat of America: the poor, the nonwhite, the uneducated, the unemployed, and the sociopathic, the ones most likely to commit the crimes that run a risk of capital punishment. This is not gainsaid by the fact that about half of the LDF's trustees, staff, and employees are black.[10] In social class, the affinity between the LDF and its death penalty clients is no greater than that between those clients and many other groups opposing the death penalty. The motives that led the LDF to undertake its far-reaching, expensive, and controversial litigation campaign grew out of its general desire to defeat racism on constitutional grounds, rather than any other considerations.

What has been said here about the LDF is, to a greater or lesser extent, equally true of the other organizations that make up the NCADP. With a few exceptions, they constitute disinterested moral elites whose opposition to the death penalty grew naturally out of separate prior commitments (prison reform, nonviolent social change, racial reconciliation, pacifism, protection of civil rights and civil liberties). One commentator has suggested that a nation's moral elite is necessarily part of its "strategic elite."[11] This may be true of the LDF and its abolitionist allies, but it cannot be claimed that these groups are part of what C. Wright Mills called the nation's "power elite." The political and economic power at the disposal of these groups is far less than their ability to symbolize a widespread moral unity in opposition to the death penalty. The likelihood that such an elite by itself is capable of imposing its views through the law is not very great.

The Bar   Support for an abolitionist position among members of the bar in general is difficult to document. Although several legal organizations belong to the NCADP (for example, the National Bar Association, the National Lawyers Guild, the National Legal Aid and Defender Association), it is also true that two of the few national organizations to favor the death penalty are the National District Attorneys Association and the National Association of Attorneys General. (Two others are police organizations.) In the 1960s the nation's most prestigious legal organization, the American

Law Institute, completed its influential Model Penal Code project with a compromise on the issue of capital punishment. Stopping short of recommending abolition, the Institute did go so far as to say that if the death penalty is to be permitted under law, then it should be imposed only after conviction at a separate trial, at which "aggravating" and "mitigating" circumstances relevant to the choice of sentence are reviewed; this is precisely what happened under the Supreme Court's rulings in *Gregg* and allied cases in 1976. The American Bar Association has never taken a position against the death penalty. In 1976 the leadership prevented a resolution on abolition from reaching the membership for a vote,[12] and in 1978 the House of Delegates, by a vote of 168 to 69, defeated a resolution from its Section on Individual Rights and Responsibilities urging state legislatures to repeal all death penalty statutes.[13] In 1983 the House of Delegates approved with no debate and by voice vote a resolution opposing the execution of anyone who committed a capital offense while under the age of eighteen.[14] In 1984 the Board of Governors voted to recruit 1,000 volunteer attorneys to handle post-conviction appeals of death-row inmates. Two years later, however, the recruiting effort had yet to get off the ground.[15] During this period, a poll conducted for the ABA reported that 68 percent of the nation's lawyers favored carrying out the death sentences already imposed by the courts.[16]

The Judiciary Evidence for a pattern of abolitionist sentiment in appellate courts is hard to trace. Strongly abolitionist rulings by state appellate courts in capital cases are very rare. (I discuss this issue in detail in Chapter 8.) In the federal courts, there is no record of attitudes or decisions among the district- or circuit-court judges to suggest that a majority favors abolition. On the contrary, what evidence there is shows how reluctant the lower appellate federal courts were to cooperate with abolitionist legal stratagems.[17] Among the federal circuit courts, only one preceded the Supreme Court in ruling against the constitutionality of any capital statute (*Ralph v. Warden* [1970]).

In the Supreme Court itself, all but a few of the major rulings by the court on death penalty questions during the past two decades either evaded the issue or upheld the constitutionality of capital punishment. In its rulings in the major anti-death-penalty cases—*Furman* (1972), *Woodson* (1976), *Coker* (1977), *Harry Roberts* (1977), and *Lockett* (1978)—the Court was badly split. Each anti-death-penalty ruling was sustained by the smallest possible majority, and only two justices—William J. Brennan, Jr., and Thurgood Marshall—have declared, beginning with *Furman*, that in their view the death penalty is per se unconstitutional under the eighth and fourteenth amendments. Of the other justices currently on the Court, all but two— Justice Rehnquist and Justice O'Connor—have voted in at least one case against the constitutionality of the death penalty, and several have indicated their personal moral opposition to a legislative policy of capital punishment. (Justice Antonin Scalia, appointed to the Court late in 1986, as of this writing has yet to vote on his first capital case.) Of the justices who have left the Supreme Court during the past decade, probably three (Arthur J. Goldberg, Abe Fortas, and William O. Douglas) would have translated their personal opposition to the death penalty into a constitutional interpretation against it; it is equally probable that two others (John Marshall Harlan and Hugo L. Black) would not have. Justice Stewart, who retired in 1981, was a crucial member of the slender *Furman* majority. But in *Gregg* he defected to the other side, and wrote the plurality opinion for the Court in upholding the constitutionality of the death penalty. Chief Justice Burger, who retired in mid-1986, was second only to his designated successor, Justice Rehnquist, in refusing to strike down death sentences on federal constitutional grounds.

Beyond question, the Supreme Court has paid an extraordinary amount of attention to death penalty cases during the past several decades.[18] Yet the issue did not enter the agenda of the Court until 1963, when Justices Goldberg, Douglas, and Brennan voted in dissent of the Court's refusal to grant *certiorari* in a death penalty conviction of rape, *Rudolph v. Alabama*. (Under the rules of the Court, any justice may file a written dissent from any action of the Court, but this is rarely done; and no case will be heard unless at least four justices agree that the appellant's case may have merit.) One might argue that over the years the Supreme Court has yielded very little to the pressure from moral elites in favor of abolition, and instead has struggled to discharge its constitutional duty without abusing its own role as an elite, insulated from the political process and ideologically opposed to the apparently prevailing public support of the death penalty. During the 1950s and early 1960s the Court did as little as possible to narrow the scope of the death penalty. In the two chief cases litigated with hopes of severely limiting the death penalty by appeal to the "equal protection" clause of the fourteenth amendment—*Maxwell v. Bishop* (1970) and *McGautha v. California* (1971)—the Court ruled by substantial majorities against abolition. *Furman* (1972) was indeed a victory for all those who wished to see the United States abolish all death penalties forever, and was hailed as such. Yet it quickly proved a narrow and incomplete victory, as the ruling four years later in *Gregg* showed.

Taken together, the evidence so far undermines the original hypothesis that the appellate judiciary, and especially the Supreme Court, has exploited its status as a powerful and virtually invulnerable elite to press for abolition of the death penalty despite the manifest popular will allegedly opposed to abolition. Likewise, this implies that the abolitionist ideology of the non-governmental moral elites does not have at its disposal such political power as the bar and judiciary command.

The Governors A brief look at the role played by state governors in the struggle over the death penalty will serve as a useful supplement to the foregoing account. If the most populist branch of government (the legislature) tends to support death penalties for murder and a few other serious crimes, whereas the least political branch of the government (the appellate judiciary) tends, with a few conspicuous exceptions, to permit the practice of capital punishment as a legitimate exercise of legislative prerogative, the executive branch falls somewhere in between—probably nearer the legislatures than the judiciaries. Wholesale commutation of death sentences is rare; only twice in recent years has it occurred. In 1970 in Arkansas, Governor Winthrop Rockefeller, defeated for re-election, commuted the death sentences of all fifteen men awaiting execution.[19] In 1986 Governor Toney Anaya of New Mexico, barred by the state constitution from running for re-election, commuted the sentences of all five men then on death row in that state. The reason usually given for refusal of commutation, however, is not the political one, which needs no acknowledgment, but rather that, since the mid-1960s, the highest courts have continued to keep the constitutional status of the death penalty under review.

Somewhat more indicative of executive attitudes has been the use of the veto power. Massachusetts and New York are rare in having had governors from each major political party veto death penalty legislation and to have those vetoes sustained as well.[20] Governors in several other states (e.g., Pennsylvania in 1974; Tennessee, California, and Maryland in 1977; and New Jersey in 1978) have also vetoed legislation to restore the death penalty, but such acts are of ambiguous significance. All these governors knew the polls showed that their electorates strongly supported legislative reimposition of the death penalty. They also knew that, at least since 1976, the Supreme Court has ruled the death penalty is not necessarily unconstitutional. Just as they did not wish to offend the moral elites in their states, on whom they rely for support, they were unwilling to risk angering the majority of the electorate. Hence gubernatorial veto messages typically stress that the legislature has enacted bills that are inconsistent with the guidelines implicit in Supreme Court decisions. The most recent veto message by a governor, Mario Cuomo of New York, is a conspicuous exception to this rule because of its forthright embrace of an abolitionist ideology.[21] Events have proved that as more legislatures enacted statutes without obvious constitutional defects, gubernatorial vetoes became harder to secure. In any case, the rarity of such vetoes and the grounds on which many of them have been tendered reinforce the picture of an abolitionist moral minority that finds the levers of political success continually beyond its grasp.

Academics, Intellectuals, and the Foundations   The actual role of academic and professional elites in opposition to the death penalty in the United States is difficult to assess. Even though it is true that some of the most influential members of the relevant scholarly disciplines have publicly opposed the death penalty, many more of their equally distinguished colleagues have been conspicuously silent. The scholarly association most directly concerned with the issue, the American Society of Criminology, has, since its organization in the 1950s, regularly opened its doors to seminars and panels on research related to the death penalty, though without taking a policy position for or against capital punishment. Organizations that have taken a policy position, such as the National Council on Crime and Delinquency (NCCD) in 1963 and the American Correctional Association (ACA) in 1966, are lobbyists on a wide range of issues touching the professional concerns of their members. Neither of these organizations has devoted a large part of its resources to the effort to secure abolition of the death penalty, perhaps in part owing to the absence of strong grass-roots support for such efforts. In any case, the NCCD and the ACA are not scholarly or academic organizations any more than are the ACLU and the LDF.

Among the organizations that are, few have undertaken even to put a scholarly discussion of the death penalty on the official agendas of their meetings, and fewer still have gone so far as to discuss whether to oppose it on principle. An exception is the American Orthopsychiatric Association (AOA), which has sponsored panel discussions and workshops on the death penalty, supported abolition editorially in its *Journal* (1975), and lent its weight to popularizing the empirical—behavioral, clinical, social—evidence against capital punishment.[22] But the AOA is not organized as an elite scholarly or academic organization. Far more typical is the posture of the impeccably elitist National Research Council. In 1976, the Council undertook to re-examine the issue of deterrence, and concluded that "the available studies provide no useful evidence on the deterrent effect of capital punishment."[23] Then in 1981, the NRC undertook to re-examine the issue of racial bias in sentencing, including capital sentencing, and concluded that—except for racial discrimination in the death penalty for rape, now of no more than historic interest—there was little or no convincing evidence that the disproportionate numbers of blacks on death row was owing to racism in sentencing practices.[24] On all policy questions concerning the death penalty, the NRC has been and no doubt will remain silent.

Some further evidence of the role of the academic and intellectual elites in the United States in the death penalty controversy can be found in the series of *amicus curiae* briefs supplied to the Supreme Court during the litigation of the *Furman* case. Twelve such briefs were submitted during 1970/71, all in support of abolition.[25] Of these, one was written by nine former governors, four by church groups (including the National Council of Churches), and two by private parties. The remaining five included two prepared by groups of civil rights and civil liberties organizations, headed by the NAACP and the ACLU, and one by the National Legal Aid and Defender Association. Only two—a brief by an ad hoc group of psychiatrists and another brief from a group of former wardens and corrections officers—could be said to have come from professional groups. But there were no briefs from any established academic organizations, such as the American Sociological Association, the American Psychiatric Association, or the American Philosophical Association. Not that such organizations oppose abolition; rather, their officers and members typically do not regard themselves as having any responsibility to use the organizational resources in a partisan role in public controversies. Part of being an elite organization in the world of scholarship is being free to ignore national policy on questions like that of crime and punishment where the policy is not directly relevant to the professional responsibilities of the members of the profession or academy itself.

In this connection, it is interesting to note by contrast who has spoken out in favor of the death penalty in the United States. Although there is no national coalition to restore the death penalty and carry out death sentences with dispatch, there are several organizations on the political right—Americans for Effective Law Enforcement,[26] as well as the Liberty Lobby,[27] and the John Birch Society[28]—that have taken public positions supporting capital punishment, as well as a few intellectuals and academics who have defended the death penalty against its detractors. Among these latter are the editor of *The National Review*, William F. Buckley, Jr.; the widely syndicated columnist George F. Will (who announced in 1981 his defection from the ranks of abolitionists); and such scholarly authors as Ernest van den Haag (*Punishing Criminals* [1976]), Walter Berns (*For Capital Punishment* [1979]), and Raoul Berger (*Death Penalties* [1982]).

One of the most striking features of the growth of knowledge about capital punishment in the United States since the early 1960s is the relative absence of publicly financed empirical research into disputed areas of fact, and the important role played by private research to fill this void. The first and most impressive of such investigations began in 1965, sponsored by the LDF and supported by grants for this purpose from private sources.[29] From 1973 onward, further studies were undertaken, many of them supported by organizations whose officers were sympathetic to abolition—notably the Russell Sage Foundation.[30] Tax-exempt philanthropic foundations are prohibited by law from engaging in partisan political activities, and no self-respecting social scientist wants to construct his research agenda on the basis of his moral convictions alone. Even so, without the enterprise of social scientists who favor abolition and the support of private foundations, the empirical basis on which the death penalty has been examined during the past decade or so simply would not have existed.

Although there are no polls on the point, it is possible that even in the 1980s a majority of college and university faculty in the United States would favor abolition of the death penalty. A content analysis of all the social-science publications pertinent to the death penalty controversy and published, say, since 1965 has not been undertaken either, but at a guess as many as nine out of every ten of them have the effect of casting doubt on the empirical beliefs that undergird rational support of capital punishment.

If we shift our attention to less-specialized publications, we find a rather different situation. One of the nation's most prestigious journals of criticism, *The New York Review,* despite its interest in the status of human rights abroad and civil liberties and prison reform at home, has never published anything directly critical of capital punishment.* Older liberal journals, such as *The Progressive* and *The Nation,* have opposed the death penalty for decades, though their influence, like their audience, is small in contrast to the millions who daily read the major newspapers. *The New Republic,* as befits its shift to the center, has in the mid-1980s given equal time in its

---

* See, however, Andrei Sakharov's essay (1978), in which he explained his support for the Stockholm conference against the death penalty convened by Amnesty International in December 1977, and the review by Graham Hughes of Walter Bern's book cited earlier.

columns to both sides of the death penalty controversy. The editorial position of several of the nation's leading newspapers—*The New York Times, The Washington Post, The Boston Globe, The Los Angeles Times, The Philadelphia Inquirer,* and *The St. Louis Post-Dispatch*—has unanimously been one of opposition to the death penalty for some time.

Thus the original hypothesis, that the moral elites opposing the death penalty receive sustaining support from the academic and professional elite, is at least in part confirmed by closer examination. This confirmation is sustained, although along a narrower portion of the spectrum, if we consider the degree to which groups concerned to evaluate the entire criminal justice system have favored abolition. The two major national commissions created to study these problems—the President's Commission on Law Enforcement (1967) and the National Commission on Reform of Federal Criminal Laws (1970)—took positions virtually in favor of across-the-board abolition of all death penalties. The President's Commission sidestepped the issue somewhat, implying that the problem of capital punishment was really one for the several states to solve for themselves.[31] The National Commission officially recommended abolition of all federal death penalties, but to accommodate its dissenting members, it also proposed that if capital punishment were to be retained, then the American Law Institute proposals for a two-stage trial should be adopted.[32] The only public groups that have investigated capital punishment and favored retaining it are occasional special commissions established by some of the states, like the New Jersey Commission to Study Capital Punishment (1964). Most of these state commissions, such as the Pennsylvania Governor's Study Commission on Capital Punishment (1973), favored abolition. Among private studies, the final reports of at least five successive national conferences in the 1970s reviewed the criminal justice system and either recommended abolition of the death penalty or conspicuously ignored it: American Friends Service Committee (1971); Annual Chief Justice Earl Warren Conference on Advocacy (1972, 1980); Committee for the Study of Incarceration (1976); Twentieth Century Fund (1976).

The groups represented by the several commissions and conferences cited above form a loosely knit coalition of social activists, correctional professionals (criminologists, penologists), lawyers, and intellectuals. The convergence of their views in opposition to the death penalty suggests that it is the only possible public position serious and informed students of crime and punishment can take on the death penalty controversy in the United States today. To do otherwise—to defend the death penalty in the United

States, urge its retention or expansion, insist that it plays a crucial and indispensable role in social defense, or justify it as a proper retributive response to grave injuries—is to fly in the face of half a century of empirical research and evolving moral principles. It is also to align the nation's continued embrace of the death penalty with the penal policies of other nations—such as the Soviet Union, South Africa, and Iran—with whom we are normally loath to ally ourselves. Hardly any wonder, therefore, that one commentator, when confronted with the claim that the LDF's litigation campaign from 1967 to 1972 deserved most of the credit for the nation's movement toward abolition, objected that throughout this period there have been "significant abolitionist forces at work . . . which had nothing to do with anyone's grand 'strategy.' "[33]

The scope and variety of ideologies and classes that make up the moral elite and its academic/professional supporters in opposition to the death penalty are impressive. Only a small fraction of such groups either have no discernible views on the death penalty or have lent it their support. But as many of these groups tend to merge with the general public and with other organizations and interest groups across the whole spectrum of political and social opinion in the nation, the picture of abolitionists as an isolated moral minority becomes blurred. Likewise, the prior hypothesis—that it is the imposition of their view of the law that accounted for the suspension of the death penalty and the protracted delays in carrying out death sentences—becomes less compelling.

Public Opinion   The conventional wisdom, based mainly on commercial survey-research, is that the American public has moved during the past twenty-five years from being roughly split on the death penalty question to being in favor of it by more than two to one. A 1966 Harris Survey reported that 47 percent of the public opposed capital punishment, 38 percent favored it, and 15 percent had no opinion. A Gallup Poll of the same year reported nearly the same distributions: 47 percent against, 42 percent for, and 11 percent undecided. From that high point in support of abolition, the trend has been steadily the other way. The Harris Survey of June 1973 reported that 59 percent of the public approved of capital punishment, 31 percent opposed it, and 10 percent were unsure. Eighteen months later, the Gallup Poll reported that 63 percent favored the death penalty and 37 percent opposed it. In 1976 the Gallup organization again canvassed public opinion on this question, and reported that the percentage favoring the death penalty had grown to 65 percent, those opposed had declined to 28 percent, and 7 percent were unsure. The Harris organization reported further losses for abolition in 1983: 68 percent favored the death penalty, 27 percent opposed it, and only 5 percent were unsure.

A careful examination of such surveys, however, shows that they reveal very little about the true state of public opinion. The questions typically fail to distinguish between sentencing persons to death and carrying out such sentences; most of the data tending to show that the public approves of capital punishment are ambiguous as to whether they show support for the latter as well as for the former. There is no evidence from any source that the majority of the public clamors for death sentences to be carried out. The hundreds of condemned prisoners not executed during the 1970s owing to the rulings in *Furman* and *Woodson* prompted no mass demonstrations, public outcry, or other unmistakable evidence of general public support for executions. Public support for the death penalty thus seems to be curiously abstract. Perhaps this is because those who profess to support it know little or nothing about its history, actual effects, and probable consequences. As to why the public supports it, researchers are in disagreement. Some believe that an adequately informed public would in fact oppose it, and there is some evidence in favor of such a conclusion.[34] Others have shown that those who favor the death penalty do so because of attitudes that are not easily influenced by the later acquisition of information about the death penalty.[35] Quite apart from other factors, then, the uncertain structure of the public attitudes in support of the death penalty makes it difficult to argue from the premise that only a minority of the public manifestly favors abolition to the conclusion that the failure to execute lawfully imposed death sentences constitutes an imposition of law by a moral elite and a frustration of popular will.

Supply of Executions   Research has shown that the significant decline in executions in the United States precedes by several decades the efforts in the mid-1960s by the LDF to secure the judicial abolition of the death penalty.[36] This fact suggests that the decade of suspended executions was not due solely to the role of moral elites, or at least not solely to their work since the 1960s. Rather, that moratorium was the historic product of a variety of factors that antedated it. These factors—including abolition of mandatory death-sentencing (except for the brief post-*Furman* and pre-*Woodson* movement in the other direction), provisions for automatic appeal of trial-court death sentences (along with the much earlier distinction between degrees of murder), the abolition of public and manifestly cruel methods of execution, the tendency to restrict the death penalty to the crime of murder, and increasing public criticism of capital punishment—are all important in explaining the decline in executions. Even if these factors were originally set in motion and are now sustained by a moral minority, since the middle of this century they have become generally accepted features of the criminal justice system that no popular majority would seriously oppose.

Supply of Death Sentences   The uninterrupted flow of death sentences at the trial court in conjunction with the failure to carry out these sentences does not necessarily imply the power of a moral elite in favor of abolition and at odds with community sentiment. Such an inference fails to take into account two factors revealed by empirical research. First, the law on jury selection in capital cases, which requires that every potential juror be asked whether he has any objection to the death penalty (and that he be disqualified if he does), tends to provide the prosecution with a "hanging jury" in *every* instance.[37] Supposedly, such juries were declared unconstitutional in *Witherspoon v. Illinois* (1968), but the state trial courts have evaded this reading of the decision, and instead have prohibited potential jurors from serving even when their opposition to the death penalty was only nominal, abstract, and based on remote contingencies. The result is that defense counsel enters every capital trial knowing that the accused does not stand to be judged by a true cross-section of the general public, but rather by a carefully winnowed segment of the community from which every opponent of the death penalty has been excluded. Even if the public were overwhelmingly opposed to the death penalty, as long as capital statutes exist and as long as "death qualified" juries are permitted by law, a steady flow of death sentences is all but guaranteed. The Supreme Court's ruling in *Lockhart v. McCree* (1986), refusing to strike down death-qualified juries, also makes it unlikely that the practice will soon change. Second, in the South, where most death sentences are imposed, the racial impact of capital punishment has not disappeared. Although it is true that sometimes convicted white murderers *are* sentenced to death and that many convicted black murderers are not, there is a correlation between race and death sentences as soon as we examine the race of the victim. Published research by several investigators has shown that the death penalty in Florida, Georgia, and Texas is reserved almost exclusively for those (white or black) who kill whites.[38]

147

The Verdict

The foregoing argument, reduced to its barest essentials, runs as follows: Given the original hypothesis that (a) a moral elite has brought about the temporary abolition of the death penalty in the United States and in doing so has imposed its will through law upon the rest of society, there are at least three major subsidiary theses that must be proved before this hypothesis can be accepted. It must be shown that (b) the abolitionists are a moral elite, (c) this moral elite really has succeeded in making its position the dominant one under law, and (d) this constitutes a case of imposition of law. My counterargument has been that (a) is an oversimplification, because although (b) is true, both (c) and (d) are doubtful and in need of significant qualification. Against (c) and (d), I have argued that the abolitionist moral elite is not a prominent part of the nation's power elite, that the decline in executions is a long-term trend, that the moratorium of 1967–1976—with which all branches of government, state and federal, cooperated—was owing to a protracted series of test cases on the constitutionality of death penalty statutes, that the public does not want actual executions so much as it wants the possibility thereof (that is, death penalty statutes), and that the continuing supply of death sentences owes as much to minority community sentiment and subtle racism as to any widespread demand for executions. Finally, as the executions that bracket the moratorium—of Luis Monge (1967) and Gary Gilmore (1977)—show, there is no way that the abolitionist forces can save a condemned man from his fate if he will not attempt to save himself by seeking judicial review, or if the one person in a position to spare him—the chief executive of the jurisdiction—refuses to intervene.

IV

Historically, the death penalty is flanked on all sides by virtually unrestrained use of corporal punishments. Hanging, decapitation, burning at the stake, and other modes of inflicting the death penalty were accompanied in the past by torture of suspects, branding and maiming of thieves and other felons, and flogging of miscreants. In the United States, capital punishment is the only such practice that has not disappeared from the official repertory of legal methods of punishment. How are we to account for the preservation of the death penalty when all punitive practices associated with it have long since fallen into the trash can of history? Nothing is more striking than the fact that those who defend the death penalty—whether on retributive or utilitarian grounds—do not go on to advocate the reintroduction of other methods of corporal punishment. Why this remarkable isolation of the death penalty in the arguments of its advocates? Perhaps what needs explanation is how the death penalty, with so few friends willing to speak for it openly in the United States, nevertheless manages to keep its grip on actual practice to the extent that it has. Some consideration, necessarily brief and inconclusive here, needs to be given to an alternative hypothesis that might explain this.

Crudely put, the failure to abolish the death penalty during the 1960s is due more than anything else to the influence of "law and order" political rhetoric on both the local and the national scene. Beginning with the 1968 presidential campaign, the liberal wing of the Democratic party was vulnerable to criticism in this vein, and this weakness was cynically and effectively exploited by the Republicans and other center and right-wing critics in their efforts to gain and hold public office. The verbal assault on Ramsey Clark, attorney general during the final years of the Johnson Administration and the first person holding that office to speak out forcefully against the death penalty, was a warning of what would happen to anyone who might try to address the American people on this issue. In the early 1960s, public opinion on the death penalty was about equally divided. The "swing vote"— between 10 percent and 20 percent—was moved in the direction of retention by some of the most powerful voices for public education in the land. President Nixon used the leverage of the White House and the solid support of the Department of Justice to defend the death penalty and criticize the Supreme Court from the moment its decision in *Furman* was announced.[39] Trumpeting the constitutionality of the death penalty, the right of the states to determine their own criminal justice system without interference from the federal judiciary, and—above all—the need to combat the rising tide of crimes of personal violence, the death penalty was defended on a national scale in an unprecedented fashion.[40] Thus the possibility of genuine public education and public acceptance of abolition, a political reality for a brief period in the mid-1960s, floundered along with many other social reforms. Since 1980, with the advent of the Reagan Administration to national leadership, all these factors have become more manifest and entrenched. Even if, as I believe, they represent primarily the attitudes of that minority of the far right that professes to be a "Moral Majority," these attitudes have a national platform and spokesman of considerable power. They are epitomized in the political career of Ronald Reagan himself.

In his first campaign for public office, in 1965 in California, Ronald

Reagan was one of those who ran on a "law and order" platform that included support for the death penalty. This was a forecast on the state level of what became a theme in the national Republican party's campaign rhetoric during 1968. (It was not difficult to exploit the rising national crime-rate during the late 1960s to the disadvantage of incumbent Democrats.) As governor, Reagan presided over the last execution in his state, in 1967, refusing to grant clemency to the condemned murderer Aaron Mitchell, who raved that he was "the second coming of Jesus Christ."[41] Reagan had earlier declared that he had no intention of personally participating in any clemency hearing, because "I am not an attorney." When the hearing was being held in Sacramento, he chose instead to attend the Academy Awards ceremony in Los Angeles. At the hour appointed for Mitchell's execution, Reagan was getting ready to board a plane in Sacramento, the state capital, so that he could start a baseball game elsewhere in California.[42]

Two years later, Governor Reagan was asking for a new death penalty law against drug peddling. In 1970, he signed a bill into law providing the death penalty for any bombing that caused grievous bodily harm. In early 1972, when the state supreme court in California ruled in *People v. Anderson* that the death penalty was unconstitutional under the state constitution, Reagan denounced the court for having delivered "an almost lethal blow to society's right to protect law-abiding citizens and their families against violence and crime." Six months later, when the United States Supreme Court handed down its *Furman* ruling, Reagan announced his hope that the California legislature would respond by enacting a mandatory death penalty for murder.[43] No governor of a western state during the 1960s or 1970s had anything approaching a comparable record of support for capital punishment.

As a candidate for the presidency in 1980, Reagan appointed a thirty-two-member task force, under the leadership of Evelle J. Younger, to make recommendations on criminal justice policy. (One of California's most outspoken supporters of the death penalty, Younger had been California's attorney general during Reagan's years as governor. In 1972, he used his office to orchestrate the public initiative that overturned the California state supreme court's ruling against the death penalty in *Anderson*.[44]) Restoration of the federal death penalty was publicly announced as high on the task force's agenda.[45]

Three months after Reagan's inauguration, at the Senate hearings on restoring the federal death penalty, the new Administration was represented on Capitol Hill by testimony from D. Lowell Jensen, a former California district attorney and the newly appointed assistant attorney general of the Criminal Division in the Department of Justice.[46] Since 1972, all federal death penalty statutes, save one for the crime of aircraft hijacking, had become unenforceable because their procedures were unconstitutional under the *Furman* ruling, and death penalty enthusiasts in Congress had been unable to overwhelm or outflank liberal opposition in the House. Jensen reminded the Senate that "Both the President and the Attorney General [William French Smith] have repeatedly indicated in public statements that they support the imposition of the death penalty in carefully circumscribed conditions for the most serious crimes."[47] The Senate heard this testimony only a few days after the attempted assassination of the president (March 1981). Again and again in the following years, Congress would be reminded of this support by the president and his attorney general for a renewed and expanded federal death penalty.[48] Three years later, with the White House presumably looking on in approval, the Senate "continued an election-year anti-crime trend" by voting 63 to 32 to restore the federal death penalty.[49]

But the true measures of Administration and Republican party support for the death penalty were yet to come. In August 1984, meeting in Dallas, the Republican National Convention adopted a platform with a plank on "Crime" that read in part: "We concur with the American people's approval of capital punishment where appropriate and will assure that it is carried out humanely."[50] (Earlier that year the ACLU had reported position statements from three leading Democratic presidential hopefuls—Gary Hart, Jesse Jackson, and Walter Mondale; all expressed unqualified opposition to the death penalty.[51]) Six months later, after his resounding victory at the polls, President Reagan gave his State of the Union address. Following the path broken by Richard Nixon in 1973, the president of the United States used the occasion to advocate the death penalty. Reagan said, "I urge the House to follow the Senate and enact proposals permitting use of all reliable evidence that police officers acquire in good faith. These proposals would also reform the habeas corpus laws and allow, in keeping with the will of the overwhelming majority of Americans, the use of the death penalty where necessary."[52]

Within the year, the president had his first opportunity to act on these words. The issue was peacetime espionage by military personnel. In June 1985, a few months earlier, Secretary of Defense Caspar Weinberger had announced that he favored the death penalty in such cases. The guilty, he said, "should be shot, though I suppose hanging is the preferred method."[53] Seven months later, with surprisingly little fanfare, Reagan signed an executive order amending the Uniform Code of Military Justice to authorize the death penalty for this crime.[54] With this act the president succeeded in posting the threat of the death penalty in one of the many places he professed to believe it was "necessary" and "proportionate."

With the departure of William French Smith from the attorney general's office, it fell to his successor, Edwin Meese 3rd, to be the Administration's chief advocate for restoring and expanding the death penalty. Meese's support for the death penalty went back at least to the days when, as Governor Reagan's clemency secretary, he played a role in the brisk dispatch of Aaron Mitchell in the gas chamber. Meese lost no time in using his new forum to advance the cause. In May 1985 he urged that the death penalty be enacted so that it would have a "deterrent effect" on the killing of police officers by right-wing para-military groups, such as "The Order," a neo-Nazi organization active in the Midwest.[55] A few months later, Meese defended the execution in Texas of a man who had been seventeen at the time he committed murder, on the ground that "you can have very vicious criminals at age 16 or 17." When asked whether he favored any cutoff on grounds of age for liability to the death penalty, Meese commented that he thought "it would depend on the circumstances" whether someone as young as fourteen should be executed. As for other crimes, such as espionage, Meese used the occasion to register his support for treating this crime as capital, though he did not embrace a mandatory death penalty for the crime: "I believe that the death penalty should be reserved for the most serious cases, and I don't think that it would be a good idea to just be asking for the death penalty in every espionage case."[56] A few days later, a Justice Department spokesman went before a congressional subcommittee, where the Senate bill to re-enact capital punishment had been stalled, and urged prompt enactment of the death penalty for spies and presidential assassins: "The Administration regards the passage of this bill as one of its highest priorities in the criminal justice area."[57] In January 1986, the attorney general was back in the news; on NBC's "Meet the Press," Meese stated that the fight against international terrorism would be helped if Congress would make the killing of Americans anywhere in the world a capital crime under American law.[58]

In publicly supporting the death penalty, as he has for twenty years or more, President Reagan has made the death penalty respectable as no public figure before him ever has. Not surprisingly, he has gathered around him others of the same outlook, and they have cultivated American public opinion over the years in its support for capital punishment. They have also helped one of the nation's two major political parties go on record in support of the death penalty, something hitherto unknown in our national politics. Not that there has been little or no support in Congress, regardless of party affiliation, for a restored and expanded federal death penalty. Not that the American public might have opposed entirely abolishing the death penalty, even without leadership from "the bully pulpit" of the White House. Not that there is no legitimate cause for public anxiety about violent crime. Nevertheless, it has been the Republican party at the national level that has chosen for the past two decades to keep up a drumbeat of "law and order" rhetoric, and to reap political benefit from its advocacy of specious remedies and needlessly "get tough" tactics.

Especially noteworthy has been the failure of those politicians who advocate the death penalty to support their position by evidence on deterrence, incapacitation, recidivism, prison management, or criminal behavior that would justify death penalty legislation. Members of the administration, from the president on down, have made no serious attempt to make support for executions appear to be based on the only kind of grounds that could make it reasonable and justifiable. This fact alone tends to make one suspicious of their sincerity and seriousness, and it encourages the view that they have proceeded throughout with little more than partisan political advantage as their aim. The impact of this support, however, has made it all but suicidal for public figures and would-be national officeholders to disagree publicly. A corollary of Gresham's Law in the political arena has been steadily at work. Twenty years of distortions, oversimplifications, appeal to fear of crime, and disregard for the facts have come perilously close to driving the truth on this issue —with its complexity and uncertainty—out of the public forum. The result is anything but a gratifying spectacle to those who think that social justice on matters of life and death in our society ought not to be at the mercy of partisan politics.

What we have, then, is not really a case of imposed law during the 1960s and 1970s, when a moral elite all but swept away the nation's traditional use of the death penalty. Instead we have very nearly the reverse: The preservation of the death penalty (along with many other conservative policies) during the 1970s and 1980s by a different minority, a would-be "Moral Majority," that has obtained powerful political allies and stalled the steady progress toward total abolition of the death penalty.

During the past decade, perceptive criminologists familiar with the American scene have insisted that, from the standpoint of crime control, the death penalty is a matter of "marginal significance" whose importance "could hardly be *under*estimated," and whose abolition or retention is "an issue of singular inconsequence."[59] Only its symbolic significance, therefore—the fact that it is the paradigm of certain powers of government and social attitudes—can account for the continuing controversy over its status under law in the United States. Perhaps the most that can be said in the end, therefore, is that the LDF, the ACLU, and all those groups and individuals in and out of government in the United States who have supported efforts to end the death penalty have succeeded only in channeling a historic development that is subject to forces they can no more accelerate than others can destroy or significantly retard.

Chapter 6

Abolishing the Death Penalty at the Polls

I

In a constitutional democracy the proper role for the public in determining the provisions of the penal code is sometimes a matter of controversy. On most issues, the citizenry seems content to allow crimes and their punishments to be determined by duly elected representatives, in the same manner as the legislature transacts the rest of the public's policy-making business. But when the issue is whether a jurisdiction should adopt, repeal, or modify its laws governing the death penalty, one often hears the claim that the public deserves the right to decide for itself by a direct vote at the polls. Thus, in the general election of November 1972, the voters in California passed Proposition 17, on the ballot by initiative petition. Its purpose was to restore the statutory provision on capital punishment that, ten months previously, had been struck down as unconstitutional by the California Supreme Court. Proposition 17 passed by a wide margin.

Despite the frequency with which a public vote on the death penalty question is discussed, such an event actually occurs relatively rarely. Except in Oregon. There, the voters have faced the issue of capital punishment seven times in this century, the national record by a wide margin. Oregon is also unique in being the only state in the nation in which the people have twice voted to abolish the death penalty, first in 1914 on an initiative measure that carried by the smallest of margins, and again in 1964 on a referendum that passed by a large majority. Of the two, the 1964 referendum is the more important: It has been credited with helping to set in motion a wave of legislation repealing the death penalty in several states across the nation during the mid-1960s.[1]

Today the mood is very different, not least in Oregon. In November 1978, Oregonians voted at the general election to restore the death penalty, thereby bringing to an end a fourteen-year period of abolition. This law was declared unconstitutional in 1981, under the state constitution, by the Oregon Supreme Court (see Chapter 8), but—as in California in 1972— the voters restored the death penalty at the polls in 1984.

Because it may be a long time before a majority of the public anywhere again votes in opposition to the death penalty, and because none of the nation's death penalty initiatives or referenda has been properly chronicled and analyzed, it may be useful to study the 1964 Oregon campaign rather closely. Although that campaign may not be a model for future statutory change, it does present us with a case study of the abolition movement at the summit of its success.

II

The status of capital punishment in Oregon has been unusual because the death penalty has been a matter of *constitutional*—not statutory—authority, as part of the state's Bill of Rights.[2] Other than by constitutional convention, the state's death penalty law could be modified only by public referendum or initiative. This unusual situation began as a triumph of Oregon's most vocal and influential early abolitionist, Governor Oswald West, who sought and obtained constitutional status for the abolition of the death penalty in 1914.[3] Six years later, under another governor, the death penalty was restored by public referendum. Thus, Governor West's legacy was not the constitutional abolition of the death penalty, as he had hoped it would be, but the very reverse—the inspiration for his successors to enshrine the death penalty in the state constitution.

After Governor West, probably no chief executive in Oregon gave firmer public opposition to capital punishment than Robert Holmes, a Democrat, elected in 1956 to complete the two-year unexpired portion of his predecessor's four-year term. For the first time in decades, Oregon abolitionists were hopeful that the state might once again repeal the death penalty. They took their case before the public at the general election in November 1958.

The abolition campaign was not aided by becoming entangled in the gubernatorial struggle between Holmes, the incumbent seeking re-election, and the secretary of state, Mark Hatfield, his young Republican challenger. Throughout his two years in office, Holmes had acted on his avowed scruples against capital punishment by commuting each of the three death sentences to come before him. One of these cases embroiled him in a legal challenge to his exercise of clemency. Although he was vindicated by Oregon's supreme court,[4] Governor Holmes became identified with the abolition movement, so that many of its opponents became his opponents. Hatfield, while reported to favor abolition as a matter of personal conviction, insisted he would uphold the law if elected governor and not use his power of commutation to accomplish what the legislature, trial juries, appellate courts, and electorate refused to do.

On election day in November 1958, Governor Holmes was thoroughly defeated. The anti-capital-punishment referendum lost, too, though by a narrower margin. It was defeated in twenty-five of Oregon's thirty-six counties, with a vote of 278,487 against abolition and 264,434 in favor. In Multnomah County (Portland), where one third of all votes were cast, the measure lost by a mere 8,000 votes. During the next four years, leaders of the effort to repeal the death penalty noted that the abolition referendum would have succeeded if Multnomah County could have been moved into the abolition column.

With Hatfield as governor, three persons were received in Oregon State Prison under death sentence in 1961, and one more in each of the next two years. Despite Hatfield's professed personal scruples, he stuck to his campaign promises. No death sentence was commuted. On August 20, 1962, Leroy Stanford McGahuey was executed in the gas chamber, the first person to be put to death by the state of Oregon since 1953.[5]

III

The earliest suitable occasion for abolitionists to try again was the November 1964 general election. In January 1963, two bills were introduced by state Senator Don S. Willner: Senate Joint Resolution No. 3, a proposed constitutional amendment, would refer the question of abolition to the people at the next general election; Senate Bill No. 10 would punish murder with a minimum prison term of ten years and a maximum of life, a statutory change that would become effective only if the referendum passed. The campaign first became visible to the general public in March of that year, when a public hearing on these and other related bills was held before the Senate Judiciary Committee in the state Capitol. Willner's strategy was to get the death penalty measure onto the ballot as a referendum (rather than as an initiative), with S.B. 10 provisionally enacted, so that the legislature would already be on record in favor of abolishing capital punishment and the public would be put in the position of merely ratifying a sober and thoughtful legislative enactment.

At the hearing, an impressive array of testimony was submitted in favor of abolition, and nothing of any significance was tendered in opposition. A few weeks later, a private meeting was arranged with an influential member of the Judiciary Committee who was known to be skeptical about the advisability of changing the capital punishment law. Apparently the lobbying effort succeeded (if not in capturing his vote, then in neutralizing his influence on the Judiciary Committee), because the Committee favorably reported out both the joint resolution and the abolition bill a month later, and in May both passed the legislature. This was a major step toward eventual victory.

Six months later, during the winter of 1963/64, the nucleus of the campaign organization was consolidated. It consisted of a quartet of liberal young Democrats in Portland, experienced in several recent political campaigns and flushed with success after a struggle in 1962 over another ballot measure. The four were Myron Katz, an economist with the Bonneville Power Administration; Keith Burns, attorney and clerk of the United States District Court; Don S. Willner, the attorney and state senator already mentioned; and Janet McLennan, a citizen active in local politics. These four, aided by half a dozen others, constituted the steering committee of the Oregon Council to Abolish the Death Penalty, the ad hoc organization created to direct the referendum campaign. It is difficult to exaggerate the skill with which this group, and especially its four leading members, did their work. All who served on the council would agree, however, I am sure, in singling out Janet McLennan for special credit. As executive secretary of the council, she undertook the day-to-day guidance of the campaign; its success was owing in no small measure to the energy and intelligence she contributed to its leadership.

From its inception, the steering committee had several strategic and tactical concerns. A state-wide, broad-based council had to be organized to represent as many interest groups and political affiliations as possible. Active support from all the naturally allied civic, social, and religious organizations would have to be mobilized. A hard-hitting mass-media campaign focused on Multnomah County needed to be designed, and a minimum budget of $10,000 raised to finance it. Public speakers, campaign endorsements, favorable publicity—all had to be arranged. During the spring of 1964, each of these requirements was fulfilled precisely as intended. The Council's letterhead eventually carried the names of two dozen well-known Oregonians who had agreed to serve on its executive committee.

There was considerable hand-wringing over the budget. Nowhere in the United States had anyone ever raised $10,000 in a few months for a ballot-measure campaign on capital punishment. In order to reserve space on billboards and buses in Portland—judged to be among the best places to reach the eye of the general public on any local political issue—commitments running to several thousand dollars had to be made well in advance of any funds in hand. A third of the budget, as it turned out, was raised through a quiet but effective nationwide solicitation, arranged with the cooperation of Sara Ehrmann, executive director of the Boston-based American League to Abolish Capital Punishment. In its letter requesting funds the League argued, quite correctly, that the best possible use during 1964 for money aimed at opposing the death penalty was to put it to work in the Oregon campaign. Response to this appeal was forthcoming from almost every state.

IV

By late summer 1964, the campaign had begun to reach the public. Three hundred thousand copies were printed of a brilliantly colored two-sided handbill. In vivid sketches and bold language it presented the case against the death penalty in question-and-answer form. It ended by urging the reader to "Vote YES on Ballot Measure No. 1" (pride of place on the ballot was no accident). At the annual state fair in Eugene, the Council took a small booth and each day handed out these leaflets by the hundreds. During September and October, frequent radio and television discussions were arranged. Every church, business, and fraternal group that the Council's Speakers' Bureau could interest in the death penalty referendum was supplied with a speaker. The official Voter's Pamphlet, which was sent by mail to every registered voter in the state, and the election guide prepared by the League of Women Voters, had statements carefully prepared by the Council, explaining its position in simple, unqualified language.

Throughout the summer and fall, considerable effort was devoted by the Council to preparing a series of staff research papers examining every aspect of capital punishment in Oregon. Fourteen such texts, each three or four pages long, were published. Week by week, as they were completed, they were sent out to every major news medium in the state.[6] The Portland newspapers vied with each other in lending their editorial weight to the campaign, and several of the research papers were reprinted and singled out for praise. Along with a carefully staged series of press releases, and a rebuttal to every pro-death-penalty letter-to-the-editor published in any Oregon newspaper, the steady flow of research papers helped the Council to keep its views on the issues before the public throughout the campaign. These cogent and succinct statements were in part responsible for the editorial support for abolition in all but one of the state's twenty-one daily newspapers; they were frequently quoted and paraphrased in editorials. A series of articles on the death penalty, written by reporter James Long, was published in Portland's *Oregon Journal* and was widely circulated and reprinted elsewhere in the state.

On a mid-October weekend, the campaign peaked at several different venues. At Lewis and Clark College, on the outskirts of Portland, the Council cosponsored with Portland's four major institutions of higher education a national conference on capital punishment, the first such undertaking anywhere in the nation. For two days local audiences heard symposia and panel discussions, as well as nationally prominent figures in the abolition movement; heading the list were Donal E. J. MacNamara, President of the American League to Abolish Capital Punishment; and Clinton T. Duffy, former warden of San Quentin Prison and author of *88 Men and 2 Women*. Concurrently, in downtown Portland, the Portland City Club's report on Ballot Measure No. 1 was presented to the club at its regular monthly luncheon meeting. The twenty-page document, prepared by one of the club's research committees, thoroughly reviewed all the issues; it ended with a unanimous recommendation for "Yes" on No. 1.[7] The assembled members of the City Club, crowded into the largest ballroom in the Benson Hotel, endorsed the report overwhelmingly. The following Sunday, the Oregon Council of Churches arranged for the day's sermon in most parishes to be devoted to an examination of the death penalty from a biblical, religious, and moral perspective.

During the last month before the election, full-sized billboards in black, white, and Day-Glo orange were to be seen in many parts of Portland, emblazoned with the imperative: "You are the Executioner! End the Death Penalty! Vote YES on No. 1!" Three figures, each hanging from a gallows, were starkly portrayed in a corner of the sign, hinting at a famous execution on Golgotha long ago.

Throughout the campaign, full support had been obtained from almost every public figure. Republican Governor Hatfield cautiously declared his personal support. So, in much more vigorous language, did Oregon's two Democratic senators and other top state officials, including the secretary of state, both Republican and Democratic candidates for that office, and the state treasurer and his successful challenger (both of whom went on to serve as governors during the period of abolition). Among the most effective spokesmen for abolition were Multnomah County's two most important elected law-enforcement officials, Sheriff Donald Clark and District Attorney George Van Hoomissen. Probably at no other time and place in this century has there been so much organized, outspoken support on behalf of ending the death penalty as there was in Oregon in the fall of 1964.

Public opposition to Ballot Measure No. 1 was infrequent and unorganized. Responsible law-enforcement representatives who might have opposed it with some force (as have their colleagues in other states, often with grim determination) did not do so with any enthusiasm. Two personal anecdotes may be cited to illustrate the point. Late in the campaign, during the discussion after a debate with an FBI special agent attached to the Portland office, the agent surprised everyone present by declaring that he, too, was personally in favor of ending the death penalty and had argued for it publicly only to air the case for the other side. A week or so later, during a round-table discussion on television, firm and unqualified support for the death penalty was provided by a panelist who had recently served as district attorney in a down-state county. Afterwards she confided to me, somewhat bitterly, that her outspoken defense of capital punishment would be used against her in future political campaigns. As for members of the Oregon legislature and other elected officials, who were by no means unanimously in support of abolition, whatever misgivings or objections they may have had were not publicized to the electorate during the campaign. Since no one of any standing or influence in the state came forward to defend the death penalty, one might even argue that there was, in fact, no true public debate over its merits. Instead, there was an uncontested effort to educate and persuade the public to oppose unnecessary executions, unfair death sentences, and cruel and unusual punishments; and to favor safe incarceration, the possibility of rehabilitation, and the right to life.

During the last three weeks before the election, taped spot announcements by Hollywood celebrities urging a "Yes" vote on No. 1 were played frequently. Obtaining these endorsements was one of the many ways the state affiliate of the American Civil Liberties Union aided the campaign. When a poll demonstrated some confusion over whether a "Yes" or a "No" vote was required for abolition, additional spots (financed at virtually the last moment) were broadcast on the eve of the election, emphasizing that a vote against the death penalty required a " 'Yes' on No. 1 Vote."

V

When the polls closed on election day, and the early returns began to come in, it was clear that the death penalty was on its way to a smashing defeat. The final tally showed that Ballot Measure No. 1 carried by 455,654 to 302,105. This majority represented a bit more than 60 percent of the votes cast on the issue and 49 percent of all eligible registered voters. Of Oregon's three dozen counties, No. 1 carried all but four. In Multnomah County, where the campaign had been concentrated, the victory was an overwhelming 151,833 to 83,265.

How is this triumph to be explained? Those experienced in other ballot-measure campaigns in Oregon could say, with some claim to truth, that the death penalty was abolished by concentrating $10,000 worth of political effort in the state's single most populous county. No doubt the referendum effort was helped also by the general interest surrounding the presidential contest between Lyndon Johnson and Barry Goldwater. With a light vote in an off-year election, the death penalty referendum might have failed even after a campaign like the one mounted in 1964. Victory at the polls may also have been helped by other factors, such as the growing number of young voters (who in the 1950s and 1960s tended, more than their elders, to oppose the death penalty). Probably the great majority of those who became eligible to vote between 1958 and 1964 favored passage of Ballot Measure No. 1. All these are only speculations, however. What is beyond dispute is that on November 3, 1964, the voters in Oregon looked with favor and by a wide margin on the repeal of the death penalty. Of all the public measures in the United States decided at the polls on that day, few were so uncontroversial.

The next day Governor Hatfield proclaimed the death penalty abolished and the state constitution amended as of the end of the month. He also promptly commuted the death sentences of the two men and one woman then awaiting execution. Throughout the early 1960s in Oregon, the controversy over capital punishment had been symbolized for many by Jeannace June Freeman, twenty, awaiting execution for the murder of another woman's children. During 1963, Tom Gaddis, a Portland resident and author of the famed *Birdman of Alcatraz,* had argued and cajoled in a series of articles in a Portland newspaper against the execution of Freeman. Even among those who favored retaining capital punishment, few must have truly regretted that she was spared the gas chamber.

For anyone who worked in the Oregon abolition campaign in 1964 and who had tasted defeat on the issue in earlier years, the referendum victory was the perfect reward. Yet even then sober reflection suggested that the death penalty could be abolished at the polls only by an unusual combination of factors, including shrewd reliance on methods familiar to professional politicians—not exactly gratifying to those of us who prefer a more cognitive approach (or who have little taste for politics). One also suspects the circumstances present in Oregon during the early 1960s that aided the abolition campaign may not soon reappear elsewhere.

VI

In the years since 1964, public referenda on the death penalty have been used exclusively to restore, not abolish, the death penalty. Successful ventures of this sort in California in 1972 and in Oregon in both 1978 and 1984 have already been mentioned. The explanation is to be found in part in the willingness of the appellate courts, especially the United States Supreme Court beginning in the late 1960s, to nullify the death penalty by reference to constitutional standards that had hitherto been assumed, without serious challenge, to be consistent with executions however imposed and administered. These recent referenda are thus in part a populist response to the role of the appellate judiciary in the continuing national debate over the death penalty—a fascinating story that has been told in part in the preceding chapter and need not be reviewed here.

When the Supreme Court in *Gregg v. Georgia* (1976) announced that the death penalty was not necessarily a "cruel and unusual punishment," in violation of the eighth amendment, that marked a major setback for the abolition movement. It is now clear that our society is willing to tolerate occasional executions, and that abolition will not come by dramatic, large-scale public campaigns. When the death penalty is finally abolished in the United States, it is unlikely that historians will be able to point to many events like Oregon's referendum in 1964. That campaign may well be destined to occupy a unique place in the annals of our political history.

Chapter 7

The "New" Death Penalty Laws

Even the most superficial observation of the national scene tells us that the death penalty is alive and well and that it gives every evidence of remaining so for years to come. No legislature has abolished any death penalty statute since the 1960s. On the contrary, since 1972, thirty-six states have enacted one or more capital statutes, and in 1984 the Senate voted to restore the federal death penalty.[1] Executions, which resumed in 1977 after a de jure moratorium of a decade, have increased in frequency, and the tempo may well accelerate. During 1986 nearly two thousand persons awaited execution, far and away the largest number in our history.

The current status of the death penalty is owing to several factors, two of which are paramount. One of them is the focus of this chapter. Foremost is the apparent popularity of the death penalty with the American public. For over a decade, pollsters have reported that the general public approves of the death penalty by a wide margin, varying from two or three to one (with relatively few undecided). What causes this support and what role it should play in determining legislation are, of course, controversial matters. What is not controversial is the way this support helps to explain not only legislative enactment of capital statutes and gubernatorial reluctance to veto proposed death penalty laws or to commute death sentences, but even the unwillingness of appellate courts to invalidate capital statutes and to delay or nullify very many individual death penalties.

Those of us who oppose the death penalty and would destroy it root and branch if we could are, and may well remain for the rest of this century, in a distinct minority. We have to face the fact that we have so far failed to persuade the general public of the error of its ways, even if "informed opinion" continues to agree with us, and even if we have scored great successes in limiting the death penalty and putting it on the defensive.

The other factor, to the discussion of which the rest of this chapter is devoted, is the series of decisions, beginning in 1976, in which the United States Supreme Court has upheld the basic proposition that if a legislature wants to enact a capital statute, it may do so in the confidence that nothing in the federal constitution is thereby necessarily violated. Without such ratification of the death penalty from our highest court, we would not have capital statutes, death sentences, and executions in the form in which they presently exist. With this ratification, given public support of the death penalty, no other situation is imaginable. A sober and critical evaluation of the death penalty at present, therefore, must focus on the decisions of the Supreme Court during the past decade; they are the *sine qua non* underlying the present state of the law.

I

Popular struggle against the death penalty has a history as old as the nation itself. In this century, beginning in the 1950s, the death penalty came under steadily mounting criticism when the examples of abolition in Canada and Great Britain inspired similar efforts to be launched here. Although some encouraging successes were scored (for example, in 1958 the Delaware legislature abolished the death penalty for all crimes, in 1964 the Oregon constitution was amended by referendum to the same effect, and in 1970 the governor of Arkansas commuted all death sentences), it was clear that a national policy of abolition could be achieved only by the federal government, and that the best route to this end was favorable constitutional rulings by the Supreme Court. In the mid-1960s efforts were launched to that end. After frustration in cases where the distinctive provisions of the eighth amendment (barring "cruel and unusual punishments") were *not* the issue—*Maxwell v. Bishop* (1968) and *Witherspoon v. Illinois* (1968)—abolitionists scored their greatest victory in 1972 when the Court ruled in *Furman v. Georgia* that the death penalty was unconstitutional under the eighth and fourteenth amendments.

The *Furman* ruling was precarious, vague, and temporizing. Precarious, in that the majority consisted of the minimum of five justices who were held together by no single express rationale, each of the five preferring to write his own opinion. Vague, in that it was not clear exactly what the Court had forbidden and what it would permit. To be sure, it was clear that all then-current (nonmandatory) capital statutes, at least for such crimes as murder and rape, were no longer enforceable. At fault principally was their maladministration, which permitted "freakish" and "arbitrary" (as well as racially discriminatory) factors to play a decisive role in sentencing. But precisely why this freakish pattern of death sentencing was in violation of the eighth amendment, rather than merely an offense to extraconstitutional moral sensibilities, remained unclear, especially since virtually the same freakish pattern had been held not unconstitutional a year earlier in *McGautha v. California* (1971). And the ruling was temporizing, in that the death penalty was not abolished outright (only Justices Brennan and Marshall were willing to go so far). Given the public mood, hostile in the 1970s to any policies that appeared to be "soft" on criminals, it was certain that some (perhaps most) legislatures would rapidly re-enact capital statutes to test just how sweeping and rigid the Court's opposition to the death penalty had become.

Legislative response to *Furman* was immediate, and it took two main forms. One, a throwback to earlier decades, was the enactment of mandatory death statutes in the presumed hope that by preventing any choice in sentence after conviction of a capital crime, the faulty administrative outcomes against which *Furman* seemed to be primarily aimed would be avoided. The other response was a legislative tightening of procedures governing the sentencing process in capital cases and the appellate review of death sentences.

The attempt to restore the death penalty by the route of mandatory capital statutes had two obvious strikes against it. For one, it flew directly in the face of an unswerving historical development against tying the trial court's hands in capital sentencing. Sentencing discretion in capital cases has long been practiced in this nation, in sharp deviation from English common and statutory criminal law and procedure. By the late 1960s, there were no mandatory capital statutes anywhere in this country except for very unusual and infrequent crimes. (I discuss in detail an important statute of this sort in Chapter 9.) For another, the practice of "individualizing" sentences of all sorts seemed to be something that advocates of otherwise incompatible (retributive, deterrent, reformative) punitive philosophies could readily accept. It is hardly surprising, therefore, that the Supreme Court, beginning in 1976 with its rulings in *Woodson v. North Carolina* and *Roberts v. Louisiana,* has found reasons to nullify *every* mandatory capital statute brought before it.

Not so where the new discretionary capital statutes were concerned. At the very time that the Court ruled in *Woodson* and *Roberts* against reviving and extending mandatory death penalties, it upheld capital punishment systems that were built around statutes designed to control sentencing discretion in a very different fashion. It is these schemes, involving "guided discretion," that characterize our current (and probably our future) death penalty jurisprudence. Before turning to look at these statutes, let us examine the basic constitutional arguments by the Supreme Court that underlie their defense. For that argument, we must turn to the plurality opinion of the Court in *Gregg v. Georgia.**

II

The argument of the plurality in *Gregg* is constructed in three unequal parts. The first part is in effect addressed to answering the question: What can we learn about the standards implicit in the constitutional ban against "cruel and unusual punishments" from the intent of the framers of the Constitution and from the precedent cases? The plurality takes the view that however unclear the intention of the framers may be, the prior decisions of the Court are reasonably clear. First, there are "objective indicia" as well as "standards of decency" on which the Court may rely in deciding whether a statutory penalty is or is not unconstitutionally cruel and unusual (p. 173). The Court need not rest its decision on merely "subjective judgment," whether of the members of the Court or of anyone else. Second, the standards that emerge are these: Any punishment is cruel and unusual if it is "excessive," and it is excessive if it "involve[s] the unnecessary and wanton infliction of pain," or if it is "grossly out of proportion to the severity of the crime" (p. 173). (It seems best to formulate these criteria with "if" rather than with "if and only if" because the stronger formulation would over-determine what the Court seems to have been saying. Thus there is a certain unavoidable incompleteness in the criteria as they stand.)

Some critics have objected that there is no basis in history for imputing any such implicit proportionality test to the eighth amendment.[2] I am un-

---

*428 U.S. 153 (1976), at pp. 158–207. (Page references in the text of this chapter are to this opinion.)

persuaded by such criticism; in any case, it cannot be argued that the Court in deciding both capital and noncapital cases prior to *Gregg* has never relied on any proportionality test; it obviously has. More to the point, if proportionality is the essence of the ban against cruel and unusual punishments, then only some (possibly quite few) criminal homicides are disproportionately punished by death—in which case there is no bar in principle on this ground to capital punishment—or the Court would have to repudiate the conventional view that the gravity of the crime of murder is roughly equivalent to the severity of the penalty of death. Some critics of the death penalty have done precisely that (see the passage quoted from Albert Camus at the end of Chapter 1).

Defenders of the death penalty would no doubt regard such a position as a sentimental exaggeration; whether for that or some other reason, it is a view not likely to be embraced by sober judges on the Supreme Court. (I, too, have doubts about arguments directed against the death penalty on the ground that "waiting for it" introduces a disproportionate and hence "cruel and unusual" feature to our current death penalty system.) Thus the Court's readiness to confine the standards implicit in the eighth amendment to a prohibition against "excessiveness," which in turn is to be understood in terms of disproportionality, plainly forecasts a holding that there is no principled inconsistency between the eighth amendment and the death penalty. That the Court need not have confined itself to such a stress on proportionality—a theme to which I will return below—is amply borne out by the dissenting opinions in *Gregg* by Justices Brennan and Marshall.

The second part of the plurality's argument consists largely of genuflections before the principle of judicial restraint. The essential claim here is that, given this principle, the Court "may not require the legislature to select the least severe penalty possible so long as the penalty selected is not cruelly inhumane or disproportionate to the crime involved" (p. 175). The Court's comment is too tendentious to be passed over in acquiescence. Even if one grants that the Court may not require of legislatures that they impose the *least* severe penalty, it does not follow that the Court may not reasonably require a *less* severe penalty if there is no evidence to support the claim that a valid social purpose is achieved and is achievable only by the *more* severe penalty, where the more severe penalty is death. After all, the *Gregg* plurality itself, later in its opinion, is prepared to grant the chief premise on which my criticism here relies—namely, that "death is different" (p. 188). Surely one of the germane differences is that a heavier burden rests on a legislature that permits the death penalty in preference to well-established alternative punishments of imprisonment. Judicial intervention here does not entail judicial meddling with every other legislative choice in the penal code. The question was never one of requiring states to impose the "least severe penalty"; it was always only that of requiring them to impose the alternative, very severe penalty of long-term imprisonment, a penalty long used as the punishment for murder and other crimes against persons in the vast majority of the cases.

Even the critic, however, must admit to a certain sympathy with the Court's predicament. The Court having failed to rule conclusively against the death penalty in *Furman,* state legislatures moved quickly to re-enact capital statutes. By 1974 over two dozen had passed new death penalties, thereby confronting the Court with a potentially severe challenge to its political authority. This was all the more evident when, late in 1972, Californians voted to amend their state constitution in order to guarantee its consistency with the death penalty—an important political event. The majority of the Supreme Court might well have reasoned that it was better to invoke the principle of judicial restraint than to invite nationwide attempts to amend the federal constitution; the *Gregg* plurality even went so far as to allude (on p. 176) to this very possibility. The other major alternative open to the *Gregg* Court—overruling *Furman* entirely, on the ground that it was utterly aberrant—was an option probably never seriously entertained. The Court's own prestige, not to mention public policy, would have been needlessly harmed by such a self-inflicted wound. The appeal to judicial restraint thus became the fig leaf with which the Court endeavored to hide its desperate defense of compromise once again, this time between outright abolition on the one hand and abandonment of any attempt to curb legislative excess and popular folly in support of death penalties on the other.

The *Gregg* plurality points out next that the death penalty for murder "has a long history of acceptance both in the United States and in England." (The opinion failed to note that England had abolished the death penalty for murder, although not as a violation of its constitution, in 1969.) We can grant the point and grant as well that for those of an unreflectively conservative cast of mind, or who believe no evidence casts doubt on the justice or necessity of a given penalty, there is a certain limited wisdom in retaining the death penalty. But the presumption in favor of it—gained by its long history—is surely rebuttable in principle, with respect to both its legislative advisability and its consistency with a proper interpretation of the eighth amendment, as *Furman* itself proved. Little support for a constitutional ruling that would preserve death penalty statutes can be derived from any such argument, as the Court no doubt recognized. The Court's task was the narrower and more difficult one of fashioning a rationale that would save the death penalty and *Furman* as well. Perforce, the Court had to argue that some relevant factors were then (1976) quite different from what they had been, or had been thought to be, when *Furman* was decided a mere four years earlier.

Accordingly, the Court claimed that "a large proportion of American society continues to regard [the death penalty in general and especially for murder] as an appropriate and necessary criminal sanction" (p. 179). Three different kinds of evidence were cited to support this claim: the widespread legislative re-enactment of capital statutes; the California constitutional referendum that overwhelmingly favored restoring the death penalty; and decisions by nearly five hundred trial juries to use the new capital statutes to mete out death penalties to convicted criminals.

No one can contest these facts, but one can easily contest their relevance to the interpretation of the eighth and fourteenth amendments. We have been told that the justices of the Supreme Court, like the rest of us, read the headlines; but it is rare for the Court to trot them out so blatantly as it did here. I fail to see a single defensible principle of punishment or of constitutional interpretation underlying the *Gregg* plurality's use of the data it cited. (It is easy to think of indefensible principles that might be involved.) No doubt these evidences of popular resistance to the abolition of the death penalty had to be regarded by the Court as storm warnings. That, of course, is another matter entirely. Only a little imagination is required to guess what a comparably cautious, not to say timid, Court would have ruled twenty years earlier in *Brown v. Board of Education*.

III

The heart of the plurality's reasoning in *Gregg* does not lie in the arguments so far reviewed. Rather, it lies in the attempt to show that, despite the undeniable assault upon "human dignity" by a judicially imposed death penalty, in the face of constitutional language in the eighth amendment whose implicit function is to recognize and protect "the concept of human dignity," there is sufficient "penological justification" on behalf of capital punishment to keep it from being a "gratuitous infliction of suffering." That justification is said to be found in the "two principal social purposes" served by the death penalty—"retribution and deterrence" (pp. 182–83). Let us grant, for the sake of argument, that the proper penological grounds on which to debate the constitutional acceptability of the death penalty are (primarily if not exclusively) retribution and deterrence. How far will this take us? Not as far as the Court wants to go.

Retribution   There is an undeniable appeal to the simple equation of "a life for a life." Murderers deserve death, says Mother Wit, and it is easy to embrace these familiar ideas in the higher-sounding language of just retribution. However, any defense of the death penalty on purely retributive grounds faces at least four serious problems. (1) All opportunity to defend death for nonhomicidal crimes is implicitly abandoned. Yet in its appeal to retribution in *Gregg*, the Court neither stated nor implied that a death penalty for nonhomicidal crimes would be unacceptably excessive and thus "cruel and unusual." (2) If the paradigm of the penalty scale is provided by the idea of "a life for a life," then the penalty scale for other crimes will have some very bizarre features, as critics of *lex talionis* since Blackstone in the eighteenth century have pointed out. Retribution, in short, cannot require that punishments *match* or imitate the crime (as "a life for a life" seems to require us to do). If, however, retribution is taken to embody only the idea that severity of punishments must be *proportional* to the gravity of the crime, then no judgment that the death penalty alone is proportional to murder will emerge by this route. (3) Legislatures and trial courts have deemed that the vast majority of convicted killers will not be sentenced to death—the statistics on the point are incontrovertible and the sentencing pattern is of long standing—and so the retributivist must conclude that most murderers do not (and will not) get what they deserve and that society has long accepted this fact. Defending the death penalty by appeals to moral desert in the face of such facts is hopelessly simplistic. (4) Justice in punishment is not exhausted by retribution; other principles have their claims, too. To the extent that one defends the death penalty on the grounds of just retribution, even though only a small fraction of convicted murderers will ever be executed for their crimes, one willingly sacrifices the principle that persons guilty of the same offense should receive the same punishment. (Of course, we do breach this principle in applying many lesser punishments.) At the very least, what needs to be shown is that the death penalty as actually administered does a tolerably good job in weeding out the very worst (the one to two percent actually executed) from among the bad (the rest of the convicted but unexecuted murderers). The *Furman* Court judged that the death penalty prior to the 1970s had failed in this task. The promise of the *Gregg* Court—made explicit in the opinions of Justices Stewart and

White[3]—was that the new death penalties created by post-*Furman* legislation would not.

I conclude from these observations, first, that appeals to the principles
of just retribution in determining the meaning of the "cruel and unusual
punishment" clause are quite appropriate. There is no reason to believe that
the best theories of social and punitive justice dispense entirely with retributive considerations. However, such an appeal in support of the contemporary practice of capital punishment in the United States was and is to
little avail. Although I am not persuaded (as some are[4]) that retribution
properly understood really undermines the moral legitimacy of the death
penalty, I do believe that the only plausible theory of retribution that can
be incorporated into a general theory of punishment is more consistent with
no death penalties than it is with some or with many.

Deterrence   The *Gregg* plurality's appeal to deterrence can be dealt with
more briefly because this prinicple is invoked in a somewhat half-hearted
manner. After conceding (as I would not) that the statistical case against
the unique deterrent effect of the death penalty is not "convincing," the
plurality then alleges that the threat of capital punishment in "many" cases
may nonetheless be "a significant deterrent" (pp. 185–86). What cases are
these, and what evidence supports the claim?

The cases are "carefully contemplated murders," such as "murder for
hire" and "murder by a life prisoner" (p. 186). A little reflection, however,
suggests that the carefully planned murder for hire is most likely to go off
as planned because most of the planning concerns making every effort to
avoid detection and capture. In such cases, the added threat of the death
penalty is entirely discounted by the intending killer. Similarly with murders
by life prisoners: Experience suggests that such crimes arise out of furious
passions or cunning malevolence that no remote deterrent, such as the death
penalty, can curb.[5] As for evidence, none is cited at all, except for the note
that the overall number of murders in the nation rose by ten percent in the
first three years after *Furman*. Even the Court was not so simple-minded as
to imply that this numerical increase could be translated into evidence in
favor of the uniquely deterrent effect of the death penalty for murder in
general, much less for the special types of murders singled out for emphasis.
We are left, then, with the purely conjectural armchair appeals to the myth
of the death penalty's deterrent efficacy.

The fundamental problem with the plurality's reasoning is that the evidence at our disposal (whether in 1972, 1976, or today) regarding the

general deterrent effect of the death penalty simply does not allow us to rest any choice between it and the alternative of long-term imprisonment on the greater efficacy of the former over the latter.[6] No doubt common sense tells us that the death penalty *must* be a better deterrent because it is the more severe sanction.[7] What is this but the same common sense that tells us that patient parents irretrievably "spoil" their children, that teachers who threaten their pupils produce the best scholars, and that nations must have stockpiles of nuclear weapons to protect their interests?

I conclude that whereas punishment as such can be in part justified by its effectiveness in helping to improve compliance with the law, choice among punishments usually cannot turn wholly or largely on differential deterrent effects because the requisite evidence on which to base such choice is unavailable. So the *Gregg* plurality's appeal to the superior deterrent efficacy of the death penalty in certain kinds of cases in the admitted absence of *any* evidence for that efficacy is unwarranted and of no persuasive weight at all.

Proportionality The *Gregg* plurality closes its argument for the constitutionality of the death penalty by returning to the issue of proportionality. So far as the punishment of murder is concerned, the plurality writes, "We cannot say that the punishment of death is invariably disproportionate to the crime" (p. 187). To my earlier comments on this theme I would add here three further thoughts. (1) I agree that the death penalty is not *invariably* disproportionate to the crime of murder, but I have little confidence that public prosecutors, trial judges, and juries of the defendant's peers are capable of distinguishing the cases in which it is proportionate from those in which it is not. The result of their efforts, historically, is there for all to see, and amply impeaches their ability to render such judgments according to any rational criterion of proportionality. (2) Even if we grant that some murders are proportionately punished with death, we must take the further step and face the fact that the methods of carrying out the death penalty are rarely if ever defensible on grounds of proportionality. Given the brutality of some murders, the methods of execution required on grounds of proportionality will be methods clearly prohibited by the eighth amendment on even the narrowest of readings. One can only conclude that proportionality itself has lost most of its authority because it cannot be squared in the context with other related constitutional requirements. (3) As I noted earlier, the *Gregg* plurality did not argue that proportionality exhausts the meaning of the prohibition against cruel and unusual punishments. Thus, it is quite possible in principle to concede that some or even all murders find their deservedly proportional punishment only in death, and at the same time to insist that the death penalty is constitutionally prohibited because it violates the eighth amendment. At stake here is whether non-proportionality considerations derivable from "the concept of human dignity" contradict and outweigh the proportionality considerations. The *Gregg* Court did not explore this question, but the Supreme Court has in several subsequent cases.[8]

I conclude from these reflections that the appeal to proportionality does not settle, or even support very persuasively, the proposition that the death penalty in our society is not in violation of the eighth amendment. I see rather merely one more weak link to add to the prior weak links of retribution and general deterrence that the *Gregg* Court forged in an effort to explain why the nation's Constitution is and must remain silent on the great question of the death penalty.

I am quite aware that my remarks so far give no forthright and constructive argument for a contrary view. My criticisms of the reasoning in *Gregg*, even if correct and persuasive, fall well short of that. Here I can say only that I continue to think that Justice Brennan's concurring opinion in *Furman* lays out the general form of the right kind of argument, and that such revision and supplement as it may need have already been supplied by several others elsewhere.[9] (My own views on this point are most fully set forth in Chapter 4.)

The *Gregg* plurality, of course, was not engaged in writing an essay defending the constitutionality of the death penalty in the abstract. At stake were challenges to the death penalty system fashioned by Georgia and several other states, in which it was argued that the new systems suffered in practice from all the defects of the old ones struck down in *Furman*. On the same day that the Court announced its decision in *Gregg*, it announced decisions in *Jurek v. Texas* and *Proffitt v. Florida*. In each of the three cases, the Court upheld a slightly different death penalty system. Thus, on July 2, 1976 (right on schedule for the nation's Bicentennial!), the Supreme Court in effect offered the legislatures of the nation not one but three different models for constitutionally acceptable death penalty systems. This is the principle legacy of *Gregg*, and to these statutes, their operation, and the subsequent interpretation and modification of them we must now turn.

IV

The Supreme Court deserves commendation for using, in subsequent cases, a proportionality standard implicit in the eighth amendment and anticipated by the reasoning in *Gregg*. This enabled the Court to narrow the substantive range of offenses permissibly punishable by death. Today it is unconstitutional to invoke a death penalty, no matter how scrupulously administered, except for a crime where the life of another is taken. The only possible exceptions may be certain crimes against the state (particularly against the federal government, such as treason and espionage) which are rarely prosecuted and on which the Court has yet to rule and might not for years to come.

The initial application of the proportionality argument accepted by the Court appeared in 1977 in *Coker v. Georgia*. In the crime of rape, that case established that, where the victim's life is neither taken nor threatened, a death penalty is "grossly disproportionate and excessive."[10] *Coker* was quickly followed by a little-noticed decision (*Eberheart v. Georgia*), in which the same reasoning was summarily applied to a death penalty for kidnapping.

Criticism of the Court's rulings in cases such as these has been relatively slight, compared at least with the criticism (on both sides) of its rulings in *Gregg, Jurek,* and *Proffitt*. One line of attack, sketched out by the dissenters in *Coker,* is that even if there is a proportionality requirement in the eighth amendment, the ruling in *Coker* was overbroad and "ranges well beyond what is necessary."[11] Accordingly, the death penalty should not be judged unconstitutionally excessive for nonhomicidal crimes against the person. Rape, after all, is "destructive of the human personality,"[12] even if less so than murder.

No doubt, as I have implied earlier, there must be *some* proportionality requirement hidden in the prohibition against cruel and unusual punishments, or else there is no way to make sense of the implied standard, whatever it may turn out to be. Once this is granted, the next question is where to draw the line between proportional and disproportional severity. One clear line is between those defendants whose crimes involve killing another person and those whose crimes do not. *Coker* incorporates such a line. In addition, although none of the opinions in *Coker* developed the point, everyone who has studied the subject knows that the death penalty for rape was pre-eminently a punishment reserved for black males found guilty of raping white females. By mid-century, the death penalty for rape may not have been the most salient or most pervasive form of racial discrimination, but it was incontestably one of the worst.[13] True, under the ruling in *Coker,* white rapists have benefitted every bit as much as black rapists, and black victims of rape have lost whatever extra protection and retribution for their sufferings has been lost by their white sisters. But these are marginal features on a larger tapestry woven from racist fibers. No one who understands the criminal justice system could reasonably hope to see the racist practices of the death penalty for rape corrected by preserving the death penalty and instead sentencing more whites, as well as more rapists of blacks, to death.

Another application of the disproportionality argument that has found favor with the Court is in modification of the felony-murder rule, through which someone involved in any felony in which a homicide results may be found guilty of murder and sentenced to death, whether or not he was the "trigger-man." In 1982 the Court ruled in *Enmund v. Florida* that the rationale in *Coker* could be extended to this type of case, even though (unlike *Coker*) there was a murder victim. Crucial to the *Enmund* Court's reasoning was that there was no evidence the defendant himself had participated in the felony (armed robbery) with any intent to kill, or had made any attempt to kill, or indeed had killed anyone. This decision is to be applauded because it is one more recognition by the Court that fundamental fairness requires at the very least severely limiting the reach of the death penalty, especially in cases like this. Joint venture and the felony-murder rule in conjunction with plea bargaining could easily—and on occasion did—produce the anomaly that it is not the killer but one of his associates in crime who is sentenced to death.

So far, however, the Supreme Court has not applied the disproportionality argument in yet another tempting direction. Traditionally, one of the most dubious aspects of the practice of capital punishment has been the use of this penalty on youngsters in their teens. As in 1969, in *Boykin v. Alabama,* when the Court sidestepped the then-novel eighth amendment issues against the death penalty raised by the petitioner, so in the 1982 case of *Eddings v. Oklahoma* the Court overturned the death sentence of the sixteen-year-old defendant without ruling against the applicability of capital statutes to one so young. As of 1986, there is still no federal constitutional objection to a state's deciding to sentence a fifteen-year-old to death after having tried and convicted him as an adult on a charge of first-degree murder.[14]

V

The paramount feature of the statutes validated in *Gregg, Jurek,* and *Proffitt,* and crucial to their constitutionality, is the principle that discretion in death sentencing must be controlled, limited, and regularized. There are, in principle, two main ways to do this. One way is to define the crime itself so that only certain forms of homicide count as capital offenses. Efforts of this sort have a long history, beginning nearly two centuries ago when the Pennsylvania legislature invented the concept of "first-degree murder" in order to confine the death penalty to this type of homicide. The other tactic, much more recent, was popularized a generation ago through the American Law Institute's Model Penal Code.[15] The Code proposed that a series of "aggravating" and "mitigating" circumstances be identified and written into a statute so that, in a separate postconviction phase of the trial, the sentencer would receive evidence by both prosecution and defense to establish a factual basis in the defendant's history and criminal conduct to make the choice between life and death less arbitrary and more equitable. Some states, such as Texas, chose to stress the first method, while others, such as Florida, emphasized the second; but virtually every state's capital procedures now exhibit aspects of both.

Beyond this, however, the various statutes differ considerably. When originally enacted in the wake of *Furman,* they typically listed half a dozen or so "mitigating" conditions. Few lists were drawn in identical language; the Court seemed willing to treat them all as equivalent so far as any constitutional requirements of the eighth and fourteenth amendments were concerned. As for the logic of these lists, here again the statutes differed. For example, some required that if any mitigating circumstance were found, then no death sentence could issue; others permitted a death sentence if the aggravating circumstance(s) outweighed the mitigating circumstance(s), either in number or in significance. On neither point has the Supreme Court ruled in favor of any uniformity in our capital jurisprudence. Instead the several states have been left in the condition of hungry diners in a Chinese restaurant, each of whom decides his own meal by ordering one or more items from Column A (the aggravators) and one or more from Column B (the mitigators), according to whatever he fancies at that particular moment.[16]

The first major development after *Gregg* in this area of the law was to widen the range of considerations admissible in mitigation beyond any finite list provided by statute. In 1978 in *Lockett v. Ohio,* the Court insisted that the "sentencer, in all but the rarest kind of capital case, not be precluded from considering as a mitigating factor, any aspect of a defendant's character or record and any of the circumstances of the offense that the defendant proffers as a basis for a sentence less than death." In no other way, the Court argued, could the "individualized decision . . . required . . . in capital cases" be achieved.[17]

In its evaluation of the actual use by trial courts of the statutory aggravating circumstances in death sentencing, the Court seems to have been moved by comparably latitudinarian impulses. From the very start, the notion of an aggravating circumstance was such as to give pause to anyone who might think that the new practice of a bifurcated trial, the second half of which is given over to applying the statutory checklist of aggravating and mitigating factors, would solve or even appreciably alleviate the problems of pre-*Furman* death sentencing. Conspicuous from the start was the provision found in most of the new capital statutes to the effect that it is an aggravating circumstance if the offense was "outrageously or wantonly vile, horrible, or inhuman in that it involved torture, depravity of mind, or an aggravated battery to the victim" (Georgia),[18] or was "especially heinous, atrocious, or cruel" (Florida).[19] Although the image of a savagely brutal murder may readily come to mind when one reads such language, trial courts clearly have been ready to settle for much less. The Supreme Court has been slow to scrutinize and reluctant to reject the varying interpretations given at the trial level to such statutory language.[20]

In 1980 in *Godfrey v. Georgia,* to be sure, the Court did rule that the state had failed to show why the circumstances of the murder, or the facts surrounding the crime, were such as to qualify under a plausible reading of the statutory language quoted above. In concluding its opinions, the Court rightly observed that "there is no principled way to distinguish this case, in which the death penalty was imposed, from the many cases in which it was not."[21] The language of the statute, however, was not objectionable; only its application in this case was deemed to be faulty. Thus the Court expressed more confidence than it should have that this and other statutory aggravating circumstances could and would suffice to enable trial courts to cull the worst from the bad and sentence none but the former to the death they supposedly deserved.

The Court's relative sensitivity in *Godfrey* has been severely blunted by two 1983 rulings, in *Zant v. Stephens* and in *Barclay v. Florida.* In *Zant,* the Court gave its imprimatur to a Georgia death sentence in which the trial judge instructed the jury during the penalty phase to take into account the defendant's previous criminal record, even though this factor is omitted from the statutory list of aggravating factors to be weighed in deciding whether to sentence to death. In *Barclay,* the Court went even further in allowing that one of Florida's nonstatutory aggravating circumstances (again, the defendant's prior criminal record) could be validly cited by a sentencing judge in issuing a death sentence that overrules the jury's recommendations of life imprisonment, even when the prosecution in the case itself did not rely on this factor in its recommendation of death. Both these decisions take us in a retrograde direction, as in the days before *Furman,* when death sentences were issued without even the pretense of being based upon uniform or explicit statutory guidelines.

Despite the manifest preoccupation in *Furman* with controlling discretion, since it is through this wide-open door that most of the offensive results in capital sentencing troop, the Supreme Court has jealously protected, against every onslaught, the discretion exercised by prosecutors in capital cases. Whether to charge and what to charge, whether to try and whether to plea-bargain, what to recommend in verdict and sentence—all these time-honored freedoms for the prosecutor are unlikely to be without effect on the fundamental fairness of capital procedures actually employed by a given jurisdiction. (I examine this in greater detail in Chapter 10.) In a day quite within living memory, when only whites could serve on a trial jury, sit on a judicial bench, or appear before the bar in prosecution of a capital case, the likelihood of racially biased results was not inconsiderable. Today, when the most flagrant versions of these historic practices are behind us, the biases out of which they arose are still with us and not without relevance and subtle effect. The unreviewable reservoir of prosecutorial discretion remains the chief refuge of the older practice and so far has proven immune to every criticism on constitutional grounds.

VI

One of the most troubling features of the new capital-sentencing schemes appears initially in the Texas statutes upheld in *Jurek*. Under its provisions, the defendant convicted of first-degree murder may be sentenced to death only if the trial jury agrees that as a matter of fact and "beyond a reasonable doubt . . . there is a probability that the defendant would commit criminal acts of violence that would constitute a continuing threat to society."[22] The Supreme Court did not appear to be much troubled by the lack of any definition of the key concepts ("criminal acts of violence," "continuing threat to society") nor by the problems—notorious already in 1976—of predicting the future behavior of a convicted killer. Least of all did the Supreme Court show any interest in the worst feature of this law, namely, whether it makes any constitutional or moral sense to authorize a court to *punish* someone on the basis of his predicted *future* conduct. Preventive incapacitation is controversial enough where it involves nothing more than ordinary detention behind bars. But a punishment by death before the fact of the crime(s) it punishes is a doubly offensive idea, and it is obviously open to attack on various grounds. Yet all of those sentenced to death in Texas since 1974 (they number in the hundreds) have been sentenced on precisely this rationale.

Unless, of course, there is reason to doubt whether Texas juries have given a serious or literal interpretation to this statutory requirement. Students of the actual operation of this law in the courtrooms of Texas, as well as other critics, have given ample reason to doubt that prosecutors, juries, trial judges, and expert witnesses do comply with the statutory language.[23] Nevertheless, the Texas Court of Criminal Appeals has found little fault with the conduct of its trial courts in this regard, and the Supreme Court upheld *Jurek* by its 1983 ruling in *Barefoot v. Estelle,* despite considerable evidence to show that the actual practice of the Texas courts thoroughly undermined whatever prima facie merit the statutory practice might have possessed.

The decision in *Barefoot,* in fact, was somewhere between the bizarre and the incredible. After the Court mentioned that psychiatric predictions of future dangerousness, although not always wrong, yet were wrong "only most of the time,"[24] Barefoot's death sentence was upheld even though it was based on the testimony of two psychiatrists who admitted that neither had personally examined the defendant. Even so, they were willing to assure the sentencing court that he would be a "continuing threat to society."[25]

Exactly why Texas decided to incorporate the criterion of future dangerousness into its capital sentencing law, and why so few other states have followed Texas's lead, is unclear. What is not unclear is that no court can reasonably be set the task of making the kind of judgment required by the Texas statute, and that a capital punishment procedure that rests on a legal requirement to make such a judgment cannot reasonably be expected to avoid the problems that led the *Furman* Court to rule out the death sentencing procedures of an earlier day as too "arbitrary" and "capricious" to be constitutionally acceptable. For example, it is within the power of a Texas jury to decide that a convicted capital defendant's previous record of habitual intoxication or drug use might increase the likelihood of future criminal violence. But another Texas jury could decide, on the same facts, that such a defendant's culpability for any future harm he might cause was significantly reduced so as to make unwarranted a death sentence.[26] Yet which way to use the facts in question is left for the jury to decide; it should not be—at least, not if there is a serious intention to remedy the ills that led to *Furman*. Along with several other recent Supreme Court decisions in capital cases, the ruling in *Barefoot* seems to mark a disturbing departure from the Court's own doctrine of the past decade that "death is different," in favor of the view that the capital sentence simply lies along a continuum of possible legal punishments.[27]

VII

Another assumption shared by the majority of the Supreme Court in *Gregg, Jurek,* and *Proffitt* is the importance of adequate state appellate review of death sentences. Appellate review, although it was slow to develop as a statutory or case-law right for capital defendants, was widespread by the time *Furman* was decided. Yet even in 1970 it was not a requirement in every state. It is in fact, however, a feature of every post-*Furman* capital punishment system ratified by the Supreme Court. (It is unclear whether automatic state appellate review is an implicit requirement of *Furman*.)[28] The idea seems to be that, with this right safely in place, the grosser unfairnesses will be caught in state appellate review. This would reduce needless recourse to federal courts and also blunt the gravest complaint against the death penalty as actually administered—namely, that a defendant's life (and not merely his property or freedom) turns on unreviewed decisions made at the trial court level.

Scope, adequacy, and equity in such review, however, were not scrutinized by the Supreme Court in its 1976 decisions, and the actual practice in many states has subsequently come under sharp criticism. For example, the traditionally narrow range of issues subject to review on direct appeal was not appreciably enlarged. Even if "death is different," there is little as a matter of law that is peculiar to the appeal of capital cases, at least in state appellate courts. The one exception is in the requirement (found in most capital jurisdictions) that the state supreme court carry out a "proportionality review." Such a review, highly touted by the *Gregg* Court,[29] is designed to determine whether the several trial courts in the state are imposing the death penalty for roughly the same sort of murder, or whether some courts (in presumed violation of *Furman*) have become execution-prone or otherwise aberrant in their capital-sentencing practices. Recent rulings in federal courts, however, have blunted if not wholly destroyed this requirement. In a 1984 case, *Pulley v. Harris,* the Court argued that no state was required to introduce proportionality review in order to conform to the Constitution. In 1985 in *McClesky v. Kemp* the Court of Appeals for the Eleventh Circuit, confronted with substantial empirical evidence to demonstrate disproportionality, especially in racial outcomes, disallowed it and treated it as inadmissible.

It is obvious on the face of it that there is no federal constitutional requirement that states conduct their capital-sentencing procedures by means of automatic appeals of death sentences or with proportionality review of such cases. Nevertheless, it is equally clear that both such practices were attractive developments for the majority of the *Gregg* Court, when the death penalty was ruled not per se unconstitutional. But a decade of actual practice by state appellate courts in capital cases, as recent studies have shown,[30] gives convincing evidence of a pattern of death-sentencing not very different from what was condemned in *Furman;* there is unfortunately little reason to expect noticeable improvements in the near future.

A distinctive feature of the statutes upheld in *Proffitt* deserves passing notice here. Although Florida's procedure for imposing the death penalty requires the jury to recommend a sentence of life or death, depending on its judgment of the evidence presented at a special postconviction phase of the trial, the trial judge is not required to follow that recommendation in setting the sentence. Thus jury and judge may disagree in their preferred sentences, with one favoring the more severe penalty; but the judge's decision is final.[31] Traditionally, sentencing has been a judicial prerogative, but in the wake of *Furman,* all save a few states chose to bind the hands of the trial judge by awarding finality in capital sentencing to the jury. The legislative history of Florida's unusual response to *Furman* indicates that it was a product of horse-trading in the legislative conference committee appointed to resolve differences in the proposed capital statutes separately voted by the two houses of the Florida legislature.[32]

The Supreme Court in *Proffitt* pointedly denied that jury sentencing in capital cases is constitutionally required, and confidently implied that sentencing by a judge should manifest "even greater consistency" than jury sentencing.[33] Perhaps it should, but the implication has not been borne out in practice; disparities between the jury's recommendations and the trial judge's actual sentences have recently been subjected to empirical scrutiny.[34] This research showed that judges more frequently override a jury recommendation of a prison sentence than of a death sentence. Moreover, they do so without basing the overriding death sentences on any relevant aggravating facts about the crime or the criminal. Given that Florida shares with all post-*Furman* capital statutes upheld by the Court the practice of automatic appellate review, and requires in addition that capital sentences be reviewed for any disparities they may reveal in the practice of the state's several trial courts, it seems more than odd to nullify the jury's sentencing role at the trial court level by deciding the sentence in every capital case, in effect, not once but twice. That this practice is open to abuse was proved as early as 1977, in *Gardner v. Florida*, in which the trial judge's death sentence overrode a jury's recommendation of imprisonment, the judge admitting he had relied on evidence not put before the jury at the trial or at the sentencing hearing.[35]

In a 1984 decision by the Court in *Spaziano v. Florida*, however, the Court declared that the Florida practice did not offend any constitutionally protected right. Even if this is true, the practice is best viewed as one more aberration in the nation's constitutionally permissible capital punishment procedures that are the product of erratic state legislative processes.

I have reviewed the major provisions of the death penalty schemes variously enacted by statute and approved by the Supreme Court as not unconstitutional under the eighth and fourteenth amendments. I have said nothing about many important but relatively technical issues that have become significant in capital punishment litigation. Among other problems too numerous to cite, I refer especially to the problem of effective assistance of counsel, from arrest through the sentencing phase of the trial,[36] and to the problem of "death qualified" juries and the need for individually sequestered *voir dire*.[37] These and many other matters are (and have been for several years) a growing focus for energies in the litigation of capital cases. Nor have I commented on the developments that adversely affect the consideration of federal constitutional issues through "hurry up" procedures recommended by the Supreme Court[38] and the constraints now being pressed against "successor" *habeas corpus* petitions.[39] These, like other important developments I have only mentioned, would take us far afield and leave behind the topics I have reviewed, all of which involve moral questions that are still capable of seizing the imagination of the average person where the death penalty and its constitutionality are concerned.

VIII

Since 1972 the nation has embraced a death penalty system that is the outgrowth of the Supreme Court's judgment in *Furman* that the then-current system was "arbitrary" and "freakish" in its results. So it was. In 1976 the nation was told in *Gregg* that the death penalty as such was not in violation of the Constitution and that the new death penalty systems would in practice remedy the glaring defects of the old system. That promise has not been fulfilled. Recent decisions (the most important of which have been reviewed here) must provoke the earnest spectator to wonder whether the Court itself still cares. Not only has the Court shown no inclination to rule against the death penalty *tout court,* but its rulings suggest it is content with actual practices in the state death penalty systems that are hardly indistinguishable from those that prevailed prior to *Furman.* As Justice Brennan noted in a recent dissent,

> Upon the available evidence, . . . I am convinced that the Court is simply deluding itself, and also the American public, when it insists that those defendants who have already been executed or are today condemned to death have been selected on a basis that is neither arbitrary nor capricious, under any meaningful definition of those terms.[40]

What we have seen the legislatures of the nation enact and the Supreme Court uphold is a death penalty system of enormous complexity, costly and inefficient, a jerrybuilt structure that is a nuisance if not an embarrassment to its defenders. Moreover, and this is the damning irony, it is totally indefensible by reference to those attractive and simple-minded moral intutions on which it purportedly rests, both in the popular mind and in the opinions of the Supreme Court. I refer to that unholy trinity of moral priniciples—retribution, deterrence, and proportionality—made prominent by the Court in *Gregg.* I have no quarrel with incorporating all three ideas into a sound theory of punishment, but, as I have already argued (above and in earlier chapters), they do not by themselves entail or require a death penalty system. And they certainly cannot be cited in defense of the death penalty system that prevails in this nation today. The present system is the product of a Court-wrought compromise between popular forces that would keep and even expand the death penalty and a minority that would abolish it entirely. There is much to be said for compromise in politics, but this one seems to be increasingly unstable.[41]

Chapter 8

State Constitutional Law and the Death Penalty

The provisions of the Bill of Rights (1791) and the fourteenth amendment (1868) are no doubt the most important constitutional protections relevant to the death penalty in the United States. They do not, however, exhaust those protections. Each of the fifty states has its own constitution, and the final authority on the meaning of each state constitution is the highest appellate court in that state. Thus even though in *Gregg v. Georgia* (1976) the death penalty has been held not to violate, per se, any provision of the *federal* Constitution, the possibility exists—it has always existed—that a state supreme court might decide the death penalty violates some provision of a *state* constitution. Indeed, this is more than an abstract possibility. In 1972 the California supreme court in *People v. Anderson* held that the death penalty for murder was a "cruel or unusual punishment," in violation of the state constitution. It thus became the first appellate court in any jurisdiction in the United States to rule that the death penalty was per se unconstitutional.

In the years since that ruling, however, very few other state supreme courts have followed California's lead. Why is not altogether clear. One reason may be that not all state constitutions have provisions like the prohibition against "cruel and unusual punishments" in the eighth amendment of the federal Bill of Rights. Another is that even when a state constitution does contain such a prohibition, the state supreme court might well assume that the meaning of the language in its constitution is identical with the meaning of the equivalent clause of the Bill of Rights, and that it is prudent to wait for the federal courts, in particular the Supreme Court, to take the initiative in interpreting such clauses. Such a view would obviate the need for any independent or contrary interpretation from the state supreme court. Yet another reason is that few state supreme courts are prepared to strike a line of constitutional interpretation that is bolder than the one taken by the nation's Supreme Court. Finally, a state supreme court that summarily rules against the constitutionality of the death penalty may well find itself confronted with a public referendum that rewrites the state constitution. This happened in California nine months after the ruling in *Anderson*; the state constitution now explicitly declares none of its provisions to be inconsistent with capital punishment. For these among other reasons, the contribution to death penalty jurisprudence in the United States from the several state supreme courts has been slight and erratic.

I

Two examples, one from Oregon and the other from Louisiana, illustrate the point. In 1981 the Oregon Supreme Court ruled in *State v. Quinn* that the death penalty statutes adopted by public referendum in 1978 were unconstitutional under the state constitution. The court reasoned that since the statute required the trial judge to decide certain facts regarding the *mens rea* of the defendant as the basis for the choice of sentence, whereas the Oregon constitution guaranteed every defendant "the right to public trial by an impartial jury," the statute clearly violated the intent of the constitutional right.[1] However, although other states (as well as the federal government) have a similar constitutional provision for jury trial, in no other jurisdiction have capital statutes extended the scope of the fact-finding power of the judge in a manner comparable to the Oregon law. As a result, the ruling in *Quinn* has had no effect on the constitutional validity of capital statutes in other states.

In 1984 the Louisiana state supreme court ruled in *Louisiana v. David* that a section of the state's capital statute was unconstitutionally "vague."[2] The crucial statutory language concerned one of the several "aggravating circumstances" that a trial court must evaluate when deciding whether to

sentence the defendant to death or to prison. The clause in question said
that a person convicted of a capital crime could be sentenced to death if
the jury found that the defendant had "a significant prior history of criminal
activity." Whereas other states had also incorporated into their statutes a
recognition that the prior criminal record of the convicted murder defendant
was an "aggravating circumstance" appropriate for the court to consider
in choosing between a death sentence and a prison sentence, no other statute
did so in language so imprecise. The language of the Louisiana statute was
judged by the state supreme court to be in violation of both the federal and
the state constitution because it "provides no standard and leaves the court
and jury free to react to nothing more than their own predilections."[3] The
offending language had been introduced by the legislature in 1979 in order
to broaden the reach of the state's death penalty statute. However, within
a year after the court struck down this clause, the state legislature passed
a new law to replace the vague language ("significant prior history of criminal activity") with more precise wording. The new statute listed four specific
crimes, a prior conviction of any of which constituted an "aggravating
circumstance" against a capital defendant. By this easy maneuver the nullification by the Louisiana supreme court was itself nullified.

II

Rather more significant has been the assault by state supreme courts on
the mandatory death penalty. In its 1972 ruling in *Furman v. Georgia*, the
United States Supreme Court explicitly exempted mandatory capital statutes
from criticism. In theory they were not subject to "arbitrary" or "capricious"
application in the same objectionable manner as were the more typical
statutes, which provided for a discretionary death sentence. Four years later,
however, beginning with *Woodson v. North Carolina* and *Stanislaus
Roberts v. Louisiana*, the Supreme Court evaluated the newly enacted mandatory capital statutes and struck them down. In 1977, in *Harry Roberts
v. Louisiana*, the Court reached the same conclusion against a statute authorizing a mandatory death penalty for the murder of a police officer.
These rulings were both anticipated and subsequently broadened by important decisions from the state supreme courts in Massachusetts, Rhode
Island, and New York.

Among the mandatory capital statutes of some significance in the actual
operation of a state's criminal justice system was the one in Massachusetts,

enacted in 1951, that required the death penalty for anyone convicted of felony-murder-rape. (The administration of criminal justice under this statute is discussed at length in Chapter 9.) In 1975, three years after *Furman* and a year prior to *Woodson*, the Massachusetts Supreme Judicial Court handed down its ruling in *Commonwealth v. O'Neal*. The case involved a death sentence imposed on a black offender for the rape-murder of a white victim. The court ruled that the statute authorizing this penalty was unconstitutional under article 26 of the Massachusetts Declaration of Rights, which prohibits "cruel or unusual punishment." With this decision, the Massachusetts state supreme court became only the second state supreme court to invalidate any state death penalty statute on state constitutional grounds.

Of particular interest is the path-breaking manner in which the Massachusetts court reached its decision. Eschewing any attempt to follow the United States Supreme Court's ruling in *Furman*, the Massachusetts court declared that it would adopt an independent approach. The court argued that the relevant constitutional test is whether the state could show both that the mandatory death penalty for felony-murder-rape "serves a compelling governmental interest" and whether its use is "the least restrictive means" to serve that interest.[4] The court invoked this two-pronged test, holding that the state bears the burden of the argument when it decides to take a life, because "life is a constitutionally protected fundamental right"; such a decision "triggers strict scrutiny," and if a statute is subjected to review under these two tests then it has received the strictest scrutiny possible. The court concluded that

> ... the Commonwealth has not offered an adequate justification for retention of the mandatory death penalty for rape-murder. The Commonwealth has not met its heavy burden of demonstrating that, in pursuing its legitimate objectives, it has chosen means which do not unnecessarily impinge on the fundamental constitutional right to life.[5]

To be sure, this decision was not unanimous (three of the seven justices concurred with Chief Justice Joseph P. Tauro in his opinion, one concurred in the result, and two dissented). What is extraordinary is that the death penalty was judged and found wanting by reference to a test that is both plausible to the lay mind and novel in the jurisprudence of capital punishment. The difficulty, of course, is that under the least-restrictive-means-to-a-compelling-state-interest test, it would appear that virtually *any* penal statute could be put on the defensive. Rarely if ever will the state have adequate empirical evidence to support a claim that the quantum of punitive severity imposed by statute for a given offense is the "least restrictive means" to the various legitimate ends (retribution, deterrence, incapacitation, and so forth) sought by the state. The Massachusetts court anticipated this objection by insisting that the "selection of death as a punishment is a choice entirely different in kind from any other," and so where statutes would impose such an "absolute deprivation," appellate courts have "consistently allowed a closer and more careful scrutiny. . . ."[6]

Within a few months of the Massachusetts court's decision in *O'Neal*, the United States Supreme Court ruled against the mandatory death penalty for murder in *Woodson*, although it also ruled that the death penalty was not per se unconstitutional in *Gregg v. Georgia* and allied cases. (Two years later, with an eye on the *Woodson* ruling, the Washington state supreme court ruled that the state's mandatory death penalty for "aggravated murder in the first degree," even though enacted by a statewide initiative in 1975, was unconstitutional.[7] The Washington ruling, however, did no more than apply the holding in *Woodson* to a state statute, thereby saving litigants the trouble of seeking certain repeal of the state's mandatory death penalty in the federal courts.) Extending the reach of *Woodson* was another matter, and that was done by the state supreme courts in Rhode Island and New York.

III

Another type of mandatory capital statute, untouched by the Supreme Court's series of rulings and more widespread than the unique Massachusetts statute nullified by *O'Neal*, imposed a mandatory death sentence on anyone convicted of murder while in prison. In Rhode Island, for example, the death penalty had been abolished in 1852, with one exception: A prisoner serving a life sentence who was convicted of murder was subject to a mandatory death penalty. In 1973 this law was broadened by the legislature to apply to any adult prisoner guilty of murder. Six years later, the Rhode Island Supreme Court, in a little-noticed decision, *State v. Cline*, ruled that this law was unconstitutional. The court did not rely on its own state constitutional or decisional law, but on the Supreme Court's rulings in *Woodson*, *Roberts*, and especially *Lockett v. Ohio* (1978). The Rhode Island court argued, much as the Supreme Court itself had in *Lockett*, that "a death sentence imposed by a sentencer who is not statutorily authorized to consider mitigating circumstances is a nullity."[8]

Five years later, the New York State Court of Appeals had to decide the constitutionality of a statute that prescribed a mandatory death penalty for a prisoner serving a life sentence for first-degree murder. By a narrow margin the New York court ruled, in *People v. Smith,* that this mandatory death penalty was unconstitutional.[9] As in *Cline,* so in *Smith:* The state's highest court did not appeal primarily to precedent state cases or to provisions of the state constitution, but to the implications of the Supreme Court's rulings in *Woodson* and subsequent cases. The Court of Appeals argued that because the statute failed to provide for "the consideration of individual circumstances" affecting the crime and the criminal, it was unconstitutional.[10] Since the defendant, Smith, was already serving a life sentence for murder and rape-kidnapping, it appears that any attempt to show mitigating circumstances on his behalf to warrant a penalty less than death would be largely pro forma. Consequently, the willingness of the New York court to nullify a statute that made such an attempt impossible reflected a fundamental objection by the court to the death penalty itself. A dissenting judge in the case described it as another instance where an appellate court yields to the "great temptation ... to tinker with statutes to satisfy [its] own likes."[11]

When this ruling reached the Supreme Court on appeal by the State of New York, the Court refused to issue *certiorari.*[12] Although this is not equivalent to a holding by the Court that a mandatory death penalty for the crime in question—much less for other crimes not at issue—is unconstitutional under the federal Constitution, it is the next thing to such a ruling. Thus, federal constitutional law on the death penalty has in effect been made, until further notice, in this New York case.

IV

The state supreme court most persistent by far in acting to nullify capital statutes is the Supreme Judicial Court of Massachusetts. Its most recent such ruling came in 1986, in *Commonwealth v. Colon-Cruz.*[13] In this case, the state court held that death penalty provisions of a 1982 statute to reintroduce the death penalty for murder was in violation of article 12 of the Declaration of Rights of the Massachusetts Constitution. The background and rationale for this ruling deserve a full review.

Nowhere in the United States in this century has the death penalty provoked more public controversy than in Massachusetts. During the past sixty years, beginning with the trial, death sentence, and execution of Sacco and Vanzetti (1921–1927), efforts have been unrelenting to limit, suspend, or abolish capital punishment. The last execution in the state took place in 1947. Four years later the legislature repealed the mandatory death penalty for first-degree murder (except for felony-murder-rape), and made the death penalty discretionary upon recommendation of the trial court. In 1958 a study commission recommended complete abolition of the death penalty. Throughout the middle of this century, bills to abolish the death penalty were filed in every legislative session and hearings at which opponents of executions testified in force were regularly held at the State House in Boston. Gubernatorial commutations of death sentences averted several executions during those years. Then, in 1972, the state's death penalty, along with the death penalty laws in other states, became unconstitutional as a consequence of the Supreme Court's ruling in *Furman*. The two dozen men then under death sentence in Massachusett's Walpole Prison were resentenced to life imprisonment.[14]

Public opinion continued to favor the death penalty, however. In 1968, an advisory public referendum held on election day showed that the voters in Massachusetts favored retaining the death penalty by 1.1 million to 740,000 (nearly half a million voters left their ballots unmarked on this question). As a consequence, the legislature has always been under some pressure to enact new death penalty laws. During 1977, the advocates of a "new model" capital statute in the Massachusetts legislature sought an advisory opinion from the Supreme Judicial Court, to determine whether the bill then pending to reintroduce a discretionary death penalty would be constitutional under the state constitution. In *Opinions of the Justices*, the court replied that the bill if enacted would not be constitutional, and reiterated its argument of two years earlier in *O'Neal:* Unless the State can show that the death penalty "contributes more to the achievement of a legitimate State purpose . . . than the availability in like cases of the penalty of life imprisonment," the death penalty must be in violation of article 26.[15]

In 1979, undeterred by this pronouncement, the legislature enacted a capital statute modeled on those already adopted in many other states and held not unconstitutional under the federal Constitution. The district attorney of Suffolk County (Boston) immediately filed a complaint before the Supreme Judicial Court seeking a determination of the constitutionality of the new statute. The Massachusetts court fulfilled its own prediction and ruled in *District Attorney for Suffolk v. Watson* that this new statute was indeed in violation of article 26 of the state constitution. The court expressly noted that the new statute might well satisfy federal constitutional requirements. Nevertheless, it argued that

> ... the criminal justice system allows chance and caprice to continue to influence sentencing, and we are here dealing with the decisions as to who shall live and who shall die. With regard to the death penalty, such chance and caprice are unconstitutional under art. 26.[16]

The court also insisted that

> ... from our examination of the actual operation of capital punishment provisions in Massachusetts, ... the death penalty, with its full panoply of concomitant physical and mental tortures, is impermissibly cruel under art. 26 when judged by contemporary standards of decency.[17]

In this opinion, written by Chief Justice Edward F. Hennessey, the Supreme Judicial Court completely departed from the theme of its ruling in *O'Neal* (namely, that the death penalty violated article 26 because it was not the least restrictive means to a valid state interest). With the new ruling Massachusetts was in the unique position of being the only jurisdiction in the nation in which the death penalty for any crime, however administered, was determined to be per se an unconstitutionally "cruel and unusual punishment."

Exactly two years later (November 1982), at a public referendum, the voters delivered a stinging rebuke to their highest appellate court when they approved a constitutional amendment to the effect that "No provision of the [state] constitution . . . shall be construed as prohibiting the imposition of the punishment of death."[18] (Similar public referenda in California [1972] and in Oregon [1978 and 1984] had nullified the anti-death-penalty constitutional interpretations by the state supreme courts in those two states.) A month later, Governor Edward J. King eagerly signed into law a new statute authorizing the death penalty in certain cases of first-degree murder, and the stage was set for yet another confrontation between a death penalty statute and the Massachusetts Constitution. This time, however, the state's supreme court would be unable to rule in a manner as sweeping and as principled as it had in *O'Neal* and *District Attorney*.

· When the Massachusetts Great and General Court, the Commonwealth's legislature, enacted the new death penalty law in 1982, the statute provided that if the trial court agreed to accept a defendant's plea of guilty to the charge of first-degree murder, there would be no trial by jury. The statute also provided that the death penalty could be imposed *only* after trial by jury. Consequently, any defendant under indictment for first-degree murder could avoid the death penalty by pleading guilty, thereby being subject to sentence from the bench to a life term in prison. In *Commonwealth v. Colon-Cruz*, the first case testing the new statute, it was this feature of the law the Supreme Judicial Court seized upon. The court argued that the statute violated article 12 of the Declaration of Rights in the state constitution because it "impermissibly burden[s] both the right against self-incrimination and the right to a jury trial,"[19] both of which are guaranteed by the constitution. The court added: "The inevitable consequence is that defendants are discouraged from asserting their right not to plead guilty and their right to demand a trial by jury."[20]

The line of argument developed by the Massachusetts court in *Colon-Cruz* was not original. Its main features had already been laid down by the United States Supreme Court some years earlier in *United States v. Jackson* (1968). In that case, the Supreme Court held unconstitutional the death penalty clause of the Federal Kidnapping Act of 1933, under which a defendant could be sentenced to death only if tried and convicted by a jury. The Supreme Court ruled that the opportunity to choose a trial before a judge in order to avoid the risks of conviction by a jury created an "impermissible burden" on the defendant by forcing him to choose which of two constitutional rights to exercise, namely, the right under the sixth amendment to a trial by jury or the right under the fifth amendment to the presumption of innocence.[21]

The Massachusetts court was careful not to rest its ruling in *Colon-Cruz* on *Jackson;* it cited only the "analogy" between the rulings,[22] thereby avoiding the possibility for subsequent review of its ruling on federal constitutional grounds. The Massachusetts court also pointed out that under the 1983 state death penalty statute, a defendant indicted for a capital crime could reliably avoid the death penalty only by pleading guilty and thus avoiding trial altogether, a far more burdensome situation for the defendant than under the federal statute nullifed in the *Jackson* ruling. The effect of the ruling in *Colon-Cruz* is likely to be much the same as it was in *Jackson*. Neither abolishes the death penalty for any crime, but both require redrafting the capital statute in question so as to avoid the chilling effect on defendant's rights. This can easily be done, albeit at a price, by permitting the trial judge alone to impose a death sentence or by permitting a jury to decide the sentence (life or death) even where the defendant has pleaded guilty to a capital crime. The price, of course, is that under such procedures the prosecution's leverage in plea bargaining is substantially reduced.

Despite this likely development, the Massachusetts court's ruling in *Colon-Cruz* is important for at least three reasons. First, it is further evidence of the readiness of at least one state supreme court to give the closest scrutiny to legislative attempts to create a constitutionally tolerable death penalty. Second, it shows the difficulty in drafting capital statutes that do not run afoul of some constitutionally secured right of the defendant, quite apart from any question whether the death penalty per se is a "cruel and unusual punishment." Third, the extensive briefing the Supreme Judicial Court received from *amici curiae* in *Colon-Cruz* is a testimony to the vigor with which the Massachusetts bar marshaled its resources to challenge the new death penalty legislation despite the substantial apparent popularity of the death penalty as measured by the state's 1982 constitutional referendum.

V

The developments in state constitutional law as they affect the death penalty that have been reviewed here point to the greatest single continuing challenge posed by the death penalty in the United States. This challenge is not new, having been asserted throughout the past twenty years of constitutional litigation over capital punishment at the state and federal level: Do the procedures by means of which the death penalty is actually administered, beginning with the prosecution's decision whether to indict for a capital offense and culminating in the governor's decision whether to extend clemency, constitute a *lawful* process? Or is that process, as critics have insisted, essentially *lawless,* because it continues to be arbitrary, capricious, unnecessary, and occasionally irremediable in its results? The appellate judiciary in both state and federal courts is still struggling to answer these questions.

Chapter 9

Punishing Felony-Murder-Rape with a Mandatory Death Penalty*

I

In 1958, Charles W. Capraro, a member from Boston of the Great and General Court—the Massachusetts legislature—was chairman of the state's Special Commission on Capital Punishment. The report of the commission recommended abolition of the death penalty in the Bay State, but the chairman strongly dissented. He wrote, in part:

> In discussing the retention of capital punishment in connection with a homicide resulting from rape or attempted rape, I should point out at the very outset that present law in Massachusetts makes it mandatory that a person convicted of such a crime be given the death penalty with no recommendations for clemency permitted the jury. It is significant to note that in 1951, when the General Court changed our law to permit the jury in first degree murder cases to make a recommendation for clemency and subsequent life imprisonment, no change was made in the law relative to the crime of murder resulting from rape or attempted rape. The General Court specifically intended that a person convicted of this kind of homicide continue to receive the maximum penalty.
>
> I believe that the General Court exercised great wisdom in insisting that

* I am grateful to the team of undergraduate research assistants at Tufts University (Louis Birnbaum, Ronald Croen, Michael Festa, Diane Gutman, Amy Hershoff, Susan Sherman) who gathered the data for analysis, and especially to Ronald Croen, who assisted me in drafting the initial version of this chapter.

murder resulting from rape or attempted rape be punishable only by death. Rape-murder is, in my opinion, the greatest crime against the laws of nature and the laws of society. When a rape-murder takes place, all society is properly outraged for such a crime strikes at the very core of our family life. It is a heinous crime, abhorrent and detestable to civilized man. It demands, therefore, the greatest punishment which society can inflict for its own protection in order to prevent future occurrences of this type of crime.[1]

At the time Capraro wrote these words, Massachusetts was the only jurisdiction in the nation that singled out felony-murder-rape—the crime of murder in the course of rape or attempted rape—for punishment by a mandatory death penalty. In the language of the statute: "Whoever is guilty of murder in the first degree shall suffer the punishment of death, unless the jury by their verdict . . . recommend that the sentence of death be not imposed, in which case he shall be punished by imprisonment in the state prison for life. No such recommendation shall be made by a jury or recorded by the court if the murder was committed in connection with the commission of rape or an attempt to commit rape."[2] Other jurisdictions in the nation at that time still retained some mandatory capital statutes, although most were confined to crimes of rare occurrences. (For example, statutes in Arizona, California, Colorado, and Idaho provided a mandatory death penalty where perjury resulted in the conviction and execution of an innocent person.) The capital crimes that occurred with greatest incidence—murder and rape, including felony-murder-rape—and for which most death sentences and executions have been inflicted, were governed by statutes that in one way or another provided for discretion of the sort Commissioner Capraro noted had recently been enacted in Massachusetts for all forms of first-degree murder except felony-murder-rape. By early in 1972, when there were more than six hundred persons under death sentence in the United States, only a few were awaiting execution after conviction of a crime for which a mandatory death penalty was decreed by statute. The days of the mandatory death penalty were over. Or so it seemed to most observers.

In its final action of the 1971 term, the United States Supreme Court announced its decision in *Furman v. Georgia* and two consolidated cases. Directly at issue was whether the death penalty for felony-murder and for rape (but not for felony-murder-rape in particular), when imposed by a jury having discretion to mete out either death or imprisonment, was permissible under the federal Constitution. In its *per curiam* opinion, the Court declared that it was not. The majority of the Court was divided into those who insisted that the death penalty per se was unconstitutional and those who did not reach this issue. Among the latter, Justice Potter Stewart pointed out that the Court was not confronted with "the need to decide whether capital punishment is unconstitutional for all crimes and under all circumstances. . . . The constitutionality of capital punishment in the abstract is not . . . before us in these cases."[3] He specifically singled out as untouched by the Court's ruling in *Furman* the "Massachusetts . . . law imposing the death penalty upon anyone convicted of murder in the commission of a forcible rape."[4] Chief Justice Warren Burger, in the course of his lengthy dissent, agreed with Justice Stewart that "today the Court has not ruled that capital punishment is per se violative of the eighth amendment; nor has it ruled that the punishment is barred for any particular class or classes of crimes."[5] He went on to note that one of the ways that legislatures might respond to the ruling in *Furman,* if they wished to preserve some form of capital punishment, would be to enact "mandatory death sentences in such a way as to deny juries the opportunity to bring in a verdict on a lesser charge. . . ." He also indicated his personal preference against such a tactic.[6]

Thus the mandatory death penalty for a crime that occurs with some frequency—a rarity in 1951 and a freakish exception to the usual statutory practice in 1972—suddenly was thrust forward as a possible model for future legislation, because it remained one of the few discernible modes of statutory imposition of the death penalty that was not on its face incompatible with the Court's ruling in *Furman.* Similarly, what had by the 1950s seemed a topic largely of historical interest, with no policy applications for the future—how mandatory death penalties actually "worked" in practice— became overnight a prime candidate for intensive social science inquiry. If it was true that one of the most likely forms in which state and federal legislatures would respond to *Furman v. Georgia* would be by the enactment of mandatory death penalties, then accurate information about how such laws actually functioned could prove crucial, and in any case was highly desirable, for legislative debate and judicial deliberations in appellate courts. Among the few possibilities squarely in point and open for empirical scrutiny, none was a superior candidate to the Massachusetts felony-murder-rape mandatory death penalty statute.

On December 22, 1975, the Supreme Judicial Court of Massachusetts, in the case of *Commonwealth v. O'Neal,* ruled that "the mandatory death penalty for murder committed in the course of rape or attempted rape violates the Massachusetts Declaration of Rights and is unconstitutional."[7]

Although the Massachusetts court had at its disposal considerable social-science information, including much that had been published after *Furman*, none of the research reported here was completed in time to be put before the court. Neither the court itself nor the litigants undertook on their own to obtain comparable information for judicial deliberation. The actual operation of the mandatory death penalty law in Massachusetts is therefore neither relied upon nor illuminated by the opinions in *O'Neal*. However understandable this may be, it is regrettable. The legacy of *Furman* included a tacit encouragement to legislatures to enact mandatory death penalties, and during 1972 and 1973 such statutes were enacted in several states.[8] The circumstances surrounding *O'Neal* presented the Massachusetts courts with a unique opportunity to inform other jurisdictions of the Commonwealth's experience with precisely this kind of statute since 1951. Such information would have been particularly timely, because in 1974 the United States Supreme Court had given notice that it would soon rule on the constitutionality of mandatory capital punishment for murder.[9]

The results of the present research support the Massachusetts Supreme Judicial Court's ruling in *O'Neal*. Although many important empirical questions are not answered by the research presented here, and although no effort has been made to reformulate these research results in the appropriate state (or federal) constitutional language, it does seem reasonable to assert that the actual administration of the mandatory death penalty for felony-murder-rape warrants the condemnation visited on it by the *O'Neal* court. It seems clearly to be in violation of the Massachusetts Declaration of Rights, which requires due process of law and prohibits "cruel and unusual punishments."

II

The data reported and analyzed here are a portion of those obtained from an investigation, initiated during 1973, of criminal homicide in Massachusetts.[10] The data came from a study of all the first-degree murder indictments in the two most populous counties in the Commonwealth—Suffolk and Middlesex. These counties include the bulk of the urban population of Greater Boston as well as the suburban and (then) semi-rural country to the west. The period studied spans a quarter century, beginning in 1946 and terminating in 1970. These years were chosen to avoid pending cases and uncompleted litigation, yet to be close enough to the present so that the analysis would still be relevant to contemporary administrative practice. The initial year was chosen to provide a five-year period prior to the watershed year of 1951, when the statutory law was changed to allow discretionary capital sentencing except for felony-murder-rape. Thus, the study provides a period of twenty-five years for examination of the mandatory death penalty for felony-murder-rape, and concurrently a five-year period of mandatory capital punishment followed by a contiguous twenty-year period of discretionary capital punishment for the study of all forms of first-degree murder other than felony-murder-rape. One of the most important findings from the research, given the overall purpose of the project, is that the year of statutory change (1951) appears to mark no differences of any significance in the administration of criminal justice regarding felony-murder-rape cases.

Data for the study were obtained primarily from four sources. First, persons indicted for first-degree murder were identified from the special-docket records maintained on such offenses by the superior courts in the two counties. (Arrest records in the two counties were not consulted, since there is no central record-collection for arrest data in the Commonwealth or in the two counties.) Other data on offenders were also obtained from the superior-court records. Trial transcripts were examined where they were available (although the files of the prosecution were not made available and no interviews were undertaken with prosecutors, defense counsel, or convicted offenders). Second, the files of the Department of Correction were examined for data on all convicted murderers received by the Department. Third, data from the Bureau of Vital Statistics were obtained on most murder victims. Finally, the newspaper files of *The Boston Globe* were examined in all those crimes where data from the other sources proved insufficient. Data from all of these sources were recorded on a master schedule for each offender. The schedule was developed specifically for this research project and contains entries for over two hundred items of information in a dozen major categories. The categories included a case summary, offender data, offender prior criminal record, victim data, victim prior criminal record, circumstances of the instant offense, pre-trial data, trial court data, state court appeals, federal court appeals, clemency appeals, and execution data.

III

This report is perforce confined to all and only the cases of criminal homicide in which it is conceivable that an indictment, conviction, and death sentence for felony-murder-rape might have issued. Thus, of the four possible offender/victim combinations by sex, only the male/female cases are of interest. In the two counties during the period under study, 128 male offenders were indicted for first-degree murder of a female victim. (In one instance—Case A—the crime charged was second-degree murder. The explanation for inclusion of this case is provided below.) The diverse array of final dispositions (as of December 31, 1970) is shown in Table 1.

TABLE 1   Final Disposition of First-Degree Murder Indictments, Male Offender/Female Victim: Counties of Middlesex and Suffolk, Massachusetts, 1946–1970

Total indictments............................ 128		
Not apprehended................................ 1		
Apprehended and arraigned 127		
Cases pending 1		
Cases disposed of without trial..................... 54		
Died before trial...	1	
Committed to Youth Service Board	1	
Committed to state mental hospital	4	
Pled guilty before trial	48	
To original charge.......................................		0
To lesser charge..		48
Sentenced to term of years...............................		30
Sentenced to life.....................................		17
Sentenced to death		0
Other...		1
Cases tried... 72		
Pled guilty during trial..............................	38	
To original charge..		1
Sentenced to life.....................................		1
To lesser charge	37	
Sentenced to term of years...............................		14[a]
Sentenced to life.....................................		23
Sentenced to death		0
Acquitted...	8	
Not guilty by reason of insanity.......................	5	
Convicted	21	
On original charge	8	
Sentenced to life.....................................		6
Sentenced to death		2
On lesser charge...	13	
Sentenced to term of years...............................		2
Sentenced to life.....................................		11
Sentenced to death		0

[a] Includes one indictment for second-degree murder.

In order to determine which among the 128 offenders are candidates for a felony-murder-rape conviction, it is necessary to examine the cases in terms of the offender/victim relationship. The relationship in each case is shown in Table 2.

As Table 2 shows, the case total increases from 128 to 133, because in 5 of the cases there were 2 victims; thus the 128 offenders were involved in 133 victim relationships. As Table 2 also shows, 33 cases involved legally married spouses and 6 involved common-law spouses. Common law did not permit the prosecution of a male for the rape of his married or common-law wife,[11] and neither did Massachusetts statutory law or case law. Therefore 39, or more than a fourth of all the cases, fail as candidates for felony-murder-rape convictions on purely *legal* grounds. Of the remaining cases, more than three fourths fail on *factual* grounds. In 69 of the cases, the available information indicated that the murder was not rape related. In another 8 cases, insufficient information was available on which to postulate any such relationship. (Given public and media interest in criminal homicide when there is a possibility of felony-murder-rape, it is unlikely that any of these insufficiently documented cases was a felony-murder-rape.) This leaves at most 17 cases where the crime, according to the available evidence, might have given rise to a felony-murder-rape indictment. The remainder of this study is based on an analysis of these 17 cases. They amount to 13.2 percent of all those reported in Table 1, and only about 4 percent of all first-degree murder indictments in Middlesex and Suffolk counties between 1946 and 1970.

TABLE 2   Offender/Victim (O/V) Relation and Possible Felony-Murder-Rape (FMR) Cases: Counties of Middlesex and Suffolk, Massachusetts, 1946–1970

O/V Relation	Definitely Not FMR	Possibly FMR	No Information in re FMR	Total
Son/Mother	7	0	0	7
Father/Daughter	2	0	0	2
Brother/Sister	1	0	0	1
Nephew/Aunt	1	0	0	1
Husband/Wife (married)	33	0	0	33
Husband/Wife (common law)	6	0	0	6
Unrelated	58	16	4	78
Unknown	0	1	4	5
Total	108	17	8	133

IV

Below are summaries of the pertinent facts in each of the 17 potential felony-murder-rape cases,[12] as we identified them, listed chronologically (beginning with Middlesex County cases).

Case A. A white male and a white female were having sexual relations. She insulted him and he strangled her. Middlesex, 1960. (In this case, the indictment was for second-degree murder. The case is included here as a possible felony-murder-rape because the circumstances of the homicide are not significantly different from several other cases in which a first-degree murder indictment did issue. Doubt in this case centered mainly around the degree of the deceased victim's consent to sexual relations with the offender.)

Case B. A white male brutally assaulted a white female in a laundromat. The victim's body was abused beyond recognition, and a coke bottle was found thrust into her vagina. Newspaper reports said the autopsy indicated a sexual assault. Middlesex, 1962.

Case C. A white male and female went together to a yard where they engaged in kissing. He later claimed that she asked him to have sexual intercourse with her, and that when he refused she threatened to tell his wife of the incident. As she started to walk away, he threw her to the ground, beat her over the head and face with a stick, then beat her with a rock and threw the body into a nearby brook. Middlesex, 1965.

Case D. A white male argued with the victim, grabbed her by the throat and threw her out of the car in which they were sitting. He then hit her with a tire iron, tied her to a tree and had sexual intercourse with her. As she was dying, he thrust the tire iron into her vagina and then broke her fingers and arms. Middlesex, 1968. (The description of this case is subject to some controversy. The available evidence reveals considerable dispute and uncertainty over the true scenario of the crime, in a manner quite unlike that to be found in any of the other cases described here.)

Case E. A white male raped and murdered by suffocation a three-year-old girl. The autopsy reported severe internal hemorrhage and a broken hymen. Middlesex, 1969.

Case F. A black male and a white female had sexual intercourse. He attempted to commit sodomy. She objected and he grabbed her by the throat and broke her neck. He then completed the act of sodomy. Suffolk, 1952.

Case G. A white male and a black female met in a café. They went to her apartment where they argued over money. (It was later alleged that she was a prostitute and he a client). He set her apartment on fire and killed her with his hands. She was found nude. Suffolk, 1955.

Case H. A seventy-two-year-old white woman was found dead, naked in bed, murdered by a black male. Suffolk, 1955.

Case I. A black male accosted a white female and attempted to have sexual intercourse with her. She refused. He slashed her throat and chest with his knife. Before she died, he forced her to undergo sodomy. Suffolk, 1955.

Case J. A white male went to the home of a known prostitute. She was not there, but her four-year-old daughter, a black child, was. He raped and killed the child. Suffolk, 1956.

Case K. A white male asked a white female to have sexual relations with him. She refused and he forced himself upon her. Later, he picked up a nearby axe and beat the victim to death. Suffolk, 1956.

Case L. A black male accosted a black female in an alley and strangled her. The autopsy report did not confirm a sexual assault. Suffolk, 1963.

Case M. A white male confessed to the murder of a white female. She was found in bed with severe lacerations, into one of which a broken bottle had been inserted. Suffolk, 1964.

Case N. A white male was found by the police kneeling over a white female who was completely nude. He was nude from the waist down and she was dead, her head bruised. Suffolk, 1966.

Case O. A black male attempted to have sexual intercourse with his lover, a white woman. He failed by reason of impotence. Angered, he thrust a fork into her vagina and later had intercourse with her. The next morning, she died of massive internal hemorrhage. Suffolk, 1967.

Case P. A white male broke into the basement of the home of a white female and went to sleep there. She discovered him and he attacked her with a hammer. Evidence of sexual assault was reported. Suffolk, 1968.

Case Q. A white male entered the store of a white female and robbed the cash register. He hit her with a bottle and she died. Police reported that she had been sexually assaulted. Suffolk, 1969.

The mandatory death penalty was clearly authorized by statute (quoted earlier) not only for murders caused "in the commission of rape," but also for murders caused "in the commission of an attempt to commit rape." Attempted rape is defined in Massachusetts as the crime of "assault with intent to commit rape."[13] Given the brief scenarios above, therefore, it seems hardly to be denied that the crime of felony-murder-rape has occurred in

Massachusetts between 1946 and 1970, and that several (possibly all) of these 17 cases might have involved a prosecution for murder in the course of rape or attempted rape.

Admittedly, in a few of the above cases, the rationale for treating them as potentially felony-murder-rape may not be evident or persuasive. Yet it should be recalled that we have already eliminated 78 male/female cases from further consideration (recall Table 2), even though it is conceivable that the facts in several of these cases, if fully known, might have warranted a felony-murder-rape prosecution. The few dubious cases among the 17, therefore, constitute a very small percentage of all these potentially eligible but excluded cases. Thus, if there is error by overinclusion among the 17 cases treated here as felony-murder-rape, it is probably error in the right direction.

V

Perhaps the most significant single finding in this research is the evident discrepancy between the crimes as they have been described in the case summaries above and the actual indictments, convictions, and sentences obtained in these cases. The divergence, although not occurring in every case, is considerable. In order to illustrate the way in which the prosecution and the courts actually dealt with these offenders, we have arranged the cases by reference to the charges on which each defendant was arraigned, the juncture in the proceedings against each defendant at which his guilt or innocence was established—by plea of guilty before trial, during trial, or after completion of trial—and the sentence, if any, imposed on the convicted offender. This information is presented in Table 3. Each of the cases is entered by the letter assigned to it in the case summaries.

In 10 of the cases, the legal charges actually pressed are not inconsistent with the evidence available to us: Cases A, C, F, G, I, K, M, N, P, Q. In 2 instances—Cases H and L—our information was not sufficient to indicate whether the grave charges against these defendants were warranted. Given the occasional shortcomings in our information, it is as likely that the charges were warranted in these cases as in the previous 10.

However, information obtained in the course of our investigations does seem sufficient to suggest that in 5 cases—B, D, E, J, and O—the circumstances of the crime were such as to constitute a very plausible felony-murder-rape indictment, even though the prosecution made no such charge;

TABLE 3 Charge, Conviction, and Sentence for Felony-Murder-Rape: Counties of Middlesex and Suffolk, Massachusetts, 1946–1970

	Legal Charge in Addition to First-Degree Murder				Sentence					
					Criminal Homicide			Sex Offense		
Type of Conviction	Rape	Assault w/Intent to Rape	Other Sex Offense	No Sex Offense	Life	Term of Years	Other	Life	Term of Years	Other
Guilty plea before trial										
To manslaughter		L				L				L[1]
To murder 2nd				B	B					
To murder 2nd and sex offense	K				K				K	
Guilty plea during trial										
To manslaughter			F[2]	A[a],D,G C,N	C,F,N	A,D,G			F	
To murder 2nd										
To murder 2nd and sex offense		I,Q			I,Q			I,Q		
Found guilty after trial										
Of sex offense only	H						H[3]	H[4]		
Of murder 2nd			J	O E,M	J,O E,M					J[1]
Of murder 1st										
Found not guilty, insane		P					P[5]			P[5]
Total	2	4	2	9	11	4	2	3	2	3

1 Charge dropped
2 Pled guilty to sex offense in separate proceeding
3 Acquitted of charge
4 Convicted of assault with intent to rape
5 Committed to institution for criminally insane

a Indicted for second-degree murder

in none save J was any sex offense charged at all. The helplessness of the victim (in both E and J it was a child), the brutality of the crime, the autopsy evidence of sexual assault—all support this judgment. It seems incredible that none of these cases was treated by the prosecutor and the courts as felony-murder-rape. Yet none was.

The exact theory of the crime on which the prosecution proceeded is not always evident from the charges filed against the defendant. It is not necessary for the prosecutor to file and attempt to prove in court a separate charge of rape or assault with intent to commit rape to obtain a conviction of felony-murder-rape. It is not even necessary to charge the defendant with felony-murder-rape, i.e., to indict under Chapter 265, Section 2 of the Massachusetts General Laws with reference to rape or attempted rape.[14] Nevertheless, it came as a surprise to us to learn that *none* of the 17 felony-murder-rape cases was so indicted. Instead, it was left completely open whether the conviction of the defendant was being sought under the mandatory portion of Chapter 265, Section 2, or under the discretionary portion.[15] The jury could return a verdict of murder in the second degree and, as Table 3 shows, this did happen in 2 cases (J and O). The prosecutor could attempt to prove to the jury's satisfaction either that (1) the defendant committed felony-murder-rape, thereby making him subject to the mandatory death penalty, or that (2) the defendant committed first-degree murder other than felony-murder-rape, with or without involvement in a concurrent sexual assault against the victim, thereby making him subject to the discretionary death penalty. (Of the 6 cases completed by trial, printed transcripts were available in only 2. Examination of the judge's charge to the jury in each case revealed that no instructions were given regarding the possibility of a first-degree murder conviction for felony-murder-rape.) Since nearly two thirds of the 17 cases were settled without completing a trial— a noteworthy fact in itself—we cannot determine precisely whether the prosecution proceeded on theory (1) or on theory (2). The absence of sex-offense charges does not permit the inference that the prosecution was based on theory (2). What does seem clear is that by filing rape or attempted-rape charges against a defendant also charged with first-degree murder, the prosecution put the defendant on notice that his criminal conduct might be viewed by the court as felony-murder-rape and thus as within reach of the mandatory death penalty.

One hypothesis that deserves at least brief consideration is that the kind of conviction and sentence obtained against a possible felony-murder-rape defendant is not a function of whether he is also charged with rape, attempted rape, or any other sex offense. As Table 3 shows, of the 9 felony-murder-rape defendants against whom no sex offense was charged, 6 (or two thirds) were sentenced to life imprisonment anyway. Of the 8 felony-murder-rape defendants against whom some sex offense was charged, 5 (nearly two thirds) were sentenced to life. Although the numbers involved are small and therefore statistically insignificant, they are consistent with the hypothesis. If the hypothesis is true, then it suggests that in all 17 of the cases, the prosecution may have judged that it had little or no realistic chance of obtaining a death sentence (whether mandatory or discretionary), and that little was therefore to be gained in terms of the severity of sentence likely to be imposed on a convicted defendant by charging him in addition with rape or a related offense. The discrepancy, between the analysis of the facts of the 5 cases viewed here as undercharged by the prosecution and the actual charges by the prosecution, may be explained in various ways. Information now available years after these trials may not have been available or usable by the prosecution at the time of trial. Even if the prosecution believed what we believe about Cases B, D, E, J, and O, it does not follow that it could prove it "beyond a reasonable doubt" to a jury. Our purpose in noting the discrepancies between our evaluation of these cases and the indictments and convictions obtained in them is not to criticize the administration of criminal justice in the Commonwealth. It is, rather, to indicate how wide and complex is the gap between what appears to be the crime of felony-murder-rape on the one hand, and the actual application of the mandatory death penalty to such crimes on the other. That gap is visible and it remains, whatever the eventual and complete explanation may be.

VI

Are there significant differences between the overall pattern of disposition received by our 17 cases and the disposition received by all other criminal homicide cases? In our research, we did not have information available on all the criminal homicides in Middlesex and Suffolk counties between 1946 and 1970, or even on all the first-degree-murder indictments in the two counties during those years. We do have, as Table 1 showed, the final disposition of all the male/female cases. To answer the above question here, therefore, it will have to suffice to refer to this base. In order to proceed, we must divide the 128 cases from Table 1 into two groups, one of which comprises our 17 cases and the other the remaining 111 male/female cases.

The contrasts in the stage at which *conviction* is obtained are revealing. Among the felony-murder-rape cases, 3 (or 18 percent) were settled by plea prior to trial; yet more than twice as many of the non–felony-murder-rape cases—46, or 42 percent—never reach trial. Thus where the facts of the situation most nearly approximate felony-murder-rape, the prosecutor appears to be much more reluctant to settle the case without a trial. Moreover, about one half (8 out of 17) of the felony-murder-rape cases are settled by a plea during the course of the trial, whereas only about one quarter (30) of the non–felony-murder-rape cases are. This suggests that, in the cases that most probably involved the crime of felony-murder-rape, the defendant—once a trial is under way—is far more likely to plead guilty and accept a conviction for a lesser offense. Finally, felony-murder-rape cases are more than twice as likely to involve a trial than are non–felony-murder-rape cases: Trials were completed in 6 felony-murder-rape cases, or 35 percent of those studied; on the other hand, only 15 (or 14 percent) of the non–felony-murder-rape cases involved a trial. Again, this confirms the general hypothesis that, in those cases most nearly qualifying as felony-murder-rape (quite apart from the actual charges filed), the prosecutor is much more willing to put the Commonwealth to the time and expense of obtaining a first-degree-murder conviction than in other types of male/female murders. However, comparison of our results with data reported in an earlier study of first-degree-murder indictments for the two counties disconfirms this tentative hypothesis.[16] Our research indicates that in only about one third of the felony-murder-rape cases is it necessary to complete a trial in order to secure a conviction. In the non–felony-murder-rape cases, this proportion drops to one fifth. Earlier research reported results for first-degree-murder indictments essentially identical to ours for felony-murder-rape cases, i.e., in only about one third of the first-degree-murder indictments in the two counties was it necessary to complete a trial in order to dispose of the case. This suggests that the disposition of felony-murder-rape cases, and not the disposition of all male/female cases—at least in the respect under discussion—is more typical of the disposition of all first-degree-murder cases. Whether this is what one would expect depends on the extent to which male/female criminal homicide constitutes a representative sample of all first-degree-murder indictments. This result suggests that the felony-murder-rape cases in general are not handled with any greater reluctance to dispose of the case through a negotiated plea than are other types of first-degree-murder cases. To this extent, it also appears that neither prosecutors nor judges regard felony-murder-rape cases as an especially serious or aggravated form of first-degree murder.

The data regarding *sentencing* provide some reinforcement for the view that prosecutorial and judicial treatment of the felony-murder-rape and the non–felony-murder-rape cases have not been as different as it might seem they should have been. Among the 17 felony-murder-rape offenders, the proportion sentenced to life imprisonment (11, or 65 percent) is only half again larger than the proportion sentenced to life among the non–felony-murder-rape offenders (47, or 42 percent). One might also expect that a life sentence without the possibility of parole would be meted out to felony-murder-rape offenders with greater frequency than to non–felony-murder-rape offenders. This is not borne out by the data. Among non–felony-murder-rape cases, the vast proportion (42, or 89 percent) of the life sentences were for conviction of second-degree murder, which allows for parole eligibility after fifteen years.[17] Among the 11 felony-murder-rape offenders sentenced to life, the proportion (9, or 82 percent) is nearly the same. Moreover, nearly one third (35, or 32 percent) of the non–felony-murder-rape offenders were sentenced to a term of years, whereas only one fourth (4, or 24 percent) of the felony-murder-rape offenders were. Finally, in none of the felony-murder-rape cases was anyone sentenced to death, whereas in two of the non–felony-murder-rape cases, death sentences (although not executions) did result.

Two tentative conclusions emerge from these data and interpretations. First, although there are indications that felony-murder-rape offenders are treated by the courts with greater rigor than the non–felony-murder-rape cases, from the perspective of the severity of sentences received, the felony-murder-rape offenders as a group are less distinguishable from other men convicted of killing women than might be expected. Second, it appears that it is the discretionary death penalty, and not the mandatory death penalty, that constitutes the greater threat to male offenders whose victims are female, because felony-murder-rape offenders are treated much like all other persons indicted for first-degree murder. Superimposed upon both the discretionary death penalty and life imprisonment, the threat of the mandatory death penalty plays an elusive and obscure role.

VII

Assuming that the offenses charged give an indication of the kind of conviction the prosecution thinks it can obtain, a clear difference emerges in the prosecutorial practices between Suffolk and Middlesex counties. (As will be recalled from the case summaries, 5 of the felony-murder-rape cases originated in Middlesex County, while 12 originated in Suffolk County.)

In 8 of the 17 cases, a rape-related charge in addition to the charge of murder was brought against the offender. In 6 of these 8 cases, the charge of rape or of assault with intent to rape put the defendant on notice that his criminal conduct was explicitly being brought within the reach of the felony-murder-rape mandatory death penalty statute. All of these cases occurred in Suffolk. Yet rape-related criminal homicides were not unknown in Middlesex. In our analysis of the felony-murder-rape cases, there were 5 cases where a felony-murder-rape prosecution seemed highly plausible, although there were no indictments for rape-related offenses to reflect this fact. Of these 5, 3 originated in Middlesex (Cases B, D, and E). This pattern of indictments suggests that the Suffolk County district attorney's office was far more inclined to use the possibility of a felony-murder-rape conviction as a threat hanging over the defendant than was the neighboring office in Middlesex County. The search for a deeper significance in the way in which charging patterns in the two counties affect convictions and sentencing outcomes is frustrated by the small number of cases involved. For example, it is plausible to seek differences of significance in comparisons between the Suffolk cases in which rape-related offenses were charged, the Suffolk cases in which no such charges were filed, and the Middlesex cases in which no such charges were filed. Such comparisons would reveal the tendencies, if any, to handle those cases in which rape-related offenses were charged in a more severe manner. However, the distribution of cases is too small to yield any statistically significant patterns of this sort.

Small as the number of cases is, it nevertheless confirms two hypotheses of interest. First, during the same period of years, there is a significant difference between adjacent jurisdictions in the Commonwealth in the charging practices for murder involving rape-related offenses. Second, it appears that the mandatory death penalty for felony-murder-rape, if it is fitted together with the right pattern of charges against a defendant, may play a role in accelerating disposition of a case by obtaining a guilty plea to a lesser charge.

The findings reported here permit some comparisons with those reported in two earlier Massachusetts studies, one by Herbert B. Ehrmann involving 212 criminal-homicide indictments in Suffolk and Middlesex counties between 1925 and 1941,[18] and the other by Francis J. Carney and Ann L. Fuller involving the same number (212) of murder indictments in the same two counties between 1956 and 1965.[19] Unfortunately, those two studies and ours are not fully comparable in the data they report, because the present one concerns only felony-murder-rape cases that involved indictments for first-degree murder (except for Case A); Ehrmann's study concerned all criminal-homicide indictments, and Carney and Fuller's study omitted manslaughter indictments. However, the results of these two other studies are worth comment here because they do not confirm the hypothesis that there are significant differences in the prosecutorial practices concerning criminal homicide in the two counties.

First, an examination of the ratio of first-degree-murder convictions to second-degree-murder and manslaughter convictions as reported for 1925–1941 indicates that it is 1:5:8 in Suffolk and 3:4:5 in Middlesex. Our research for 1946–1970 on felony-murder-rape convictions shows that they are distributed in the ratios 1:7:2 (Suffolk) and 1:2:2 (Middlesex). Thus, the ratio for first- and second-degree murder remains approximately the same within each of the two counties but is sharply divergent between the two counties, throughout the past half-century.[20] A discrepancy between the earlier and the later data emerges only when the proportion of manslaughter convictions is examined. In recent years in Suffolk County, the felony-murder-rape offender was far less likely to end up with a manslaughter conviction than he was in Middlesex, and far less likely than in earlier years in Suffolk. However, much of this discrepancy is undoubtedly due to the neglect in the present study of all but the felony-murder-rape cases, which guarantees the exclusion of all indictments (though not all convictions) for manslaughter. Second, with respect to the disposition of first-degree-murder indictments, the two counties seem essentially indistinguishable in one respect: the proportion of first-degree-murder indictments disposed of without a completed trial on the merits of the case. Between 1956 and 1965, the proportion of first-degree-murder indictments disposed of without a trial in Suffolk and Middlesex counties was quite similar.[21] This research yields the same result. In only one case in three in each county is it necessary to complete a trial of a felony-murder-rape defendant in order to secure his conviction.

However, apart from this one respect in which the two counties are similar, on balance it remains true that, although Suffolk and Middlesex are contiguous counties, the "respective records of the two counties for disposing of murder cases are strangely different."[22]

VIII

One's first reaction upon learning that Chapter 265, Section 2, of the Massachusetts General Laws (1970) includes *attempted* rape as a crime in the course of which any murder will constitute felony-murder-rape (and thus be punishable by the mandatory death penalty) is that this language is a green light from the legislature encouraging a prosecutor to seek a conviction whenever the murder victim is female and the offender male, provided only that there is a colorable showing of attempted rape by the offender charged with the murder.

If this was the legislature's intent, it appears that prosecutors have ignored it. For purposes of examining the evidence, those cases that involved a rape indictment (viz., H and K) can be dismissed. Table 3 shows that only 4 offenders were charged with assault with intent to rape (Cases I, L, P, and Q). These 4 are only a small fraction of all the cases identified in which sexual assault occurred or might have occurred, and in which it might have been charged and proved. Furthermore, of these 4, only in 1 (L) is there any possibility, in our opinion, of prosecutorial overcharge. By contrast, there appears to be much more reason to allege prosecutorial undercharge: in the 5 cases (viz., B, D, E, J, and O) where, if our evidence is correct, rape itself occurred; and in the remaining 6 cases, where sexual assault short of rape either occurred or might have occurred.

Whatever may have been the legislative intent in including attempted rape within the scope of the felony-murder-rape mandatory death penalty, our data provide no evidence that prosecutors have seized on this opportunity to indict, and thus try to convict, male criminal homicide offenders of this crime. Since so many of our cases involved a strong possibility of rape or attempted rape, one can only speculate on the conduct of prosecutors who apparently ignored the legislature's invitation to bring upon such offenders the heaviest possible penalty.

IX

During 1974 and 1975 one of the few death sentences for felony-murder-rape in the history of the Commonwealth was on appeal in the case of *Commonwealth v. O'Neal.* The defendant was a black male, the victim a white female. Because of the documented history in the South of rape prosecutions where the death sentence was involved, which has shown that black males were most likely to be sentenced to death when the rape victim was white, whereas white male rapists were almost never sentenced to death regardless of the race of their victim,[23] one might hypothesize that even in Massachusetts, the felony-murder-rape mandatory death penalty would fall mainly and perhaps solely on black males who raped and killed white female victims. Our evidence does not confirm this hypothesis. During the period under study, there were 4 cases meeting this description, and in none was a conviction obtained for felony-murder-rape. (Of the other 13 cases studied, 1 involved a black offender and a black victim, 2 involved a white offender and a black victim, and 10 involved a white offender and a white victim.) In all 4 cases (F, H, J, and O) it appears that there were ample grounds to inspire a zealous prosecutor to seek a felony-murder-rape conviction in order to secure a mandatory death penalty. But no such conviction ensued. In fact, not even the discretionary death penalty fell upon any of these defendants, although all did receive sentences of life imprisonment. Moreover, in all but 1 (F) of these 4, the sentence was received not by plea bargaining but by jury verdict. Thus, the risk of either a discretionary death sentence or the severest alternative sentencing outcome was much greater for this racial combination of offender/victim than for any or all of the other three combinations. It is also true that in 2 of the 4 black/white cases, there is a possible undercharge by the prosecutor, whereas in the other 2 there may have been an overcharge. These conjectures apart, the pattern of our data clearly shows that the most outrageous racist hypothesis one could contemplate—that the mandatory death penalty has been reserved by prosecutors and juries for black male offenders who sexually assault and kill white female victims—is false, at least in Middlesex and Suffolk counties in Massachusetts during the period in question.

Victim precipitation? Offender's use of weapons? Previous history of crimes of personal violence by the offender? Age of offender, and age of victim? Use of drugs or alcohol? Location of the initial encounter, and of the homicidal and sexual offense? These and other personal and situational variables familiar from previous research on homicide and rape, so far as we have examined them, play no discernible role in characterizing the group of 17 cases where felony-murder-rape may have occurred. Consequently, it is not possible to confirm or disconfirm any of the hypotheses that are generated by other investigators and involve these variables. Indeed, partly because the sample of cases is so small and partly because the patterns in the case studied are so elusive or nonexistent, there is disappointingly little of a conventional criminological nature that can be hypothesized with regard either to description or explanation of the disposition of felony-murder-rape cases in Massachusetts.

X

Let us imagine that we knew none of the data reported in this study, except the fact that between 1946 and 1970 no one was executed for felony-murder-rape in Massachusetts. In an ideal world, the preferred explanation for this datum would be that there have been no death *sentences* to execute for this crime, because no one was *convicted* of it, no one *prosecuted* for it, no one *indicted* for it, and all this because no one *committed* the crime in the first place. In an ideal world, given our initial datum, all this would be true, and it would be the correct explanation of the datum in question. Consider now, instead of that datum, two other data that also emerge from this research: Between 1946 and 1970 offenses describable as felony-murder-rape have actually occurred in Massachusetts, and felony-murder-rape is punishable by a "mandatory" death penalty. If any attempt is made to construct an ideal world to accommodate these two data then it might be argued that all felony-murder-rape offenders would have been promptly arrested, and indicted, prosecuted, and convicted of felony-murder-rape, and duly sentenced to death and (legal and moral objections to the death penalty aside) executed.

The research reported above shows precisely what our knowledge of the real world would lead us to expect, however. In Massachusetts we have not lived in either of these two ideal worlds. Instead, we live in a real world built around all three of our data cited above, with the result that the legislative intent and statutory purpose embodied in the felony-murder-rape death penalty statute is blurred and perhaps entirely defeated. A study of felony-murder-rape in Massachusetts, despite the *mandatory* penalty for this crime, thus turns out to be a study in *discretionary* justice.

In this and other fundamental respects, our research shows that the felony-murder-rape death penalty statute in Massachusetts was a demonstrable failure. First, it failed to rid the Commonwealth of the crime it was designed to punish. Felony-murder-rape has occurred throughout the period studied in this research, despite the severity of the supposed deterrent embodied in a "mandatory" death penalty. Second, this "mandatory" death penalty failed to send anyone to death during the period under study, despite several occurrences of the crime. Every kind of judicial disposition other than a conviction for first-degree murder in the course of rape or attempted rape and every type of sentence other than death was found in the felony-murder-rape cases we examined. Third, the "mandatory" death penalty did not secure even-handed justice in felony-murder-rape cases, unless one views no death sentences for any felony-murder-rape offenders as even-handed justice. By other measures, there is considerable difference both within and between adjacent county jurisdictions in their disposition of felony-murder-rape cases. The "mandatory" death penalty statute, it appears, was a threat

214

with variable and unpredictable effect upon the plea-bargaining process in two different counties. Finally, the disposition of felony-murder-rape cases is not measurably so different, overall, from what is to be found in the disposition of all other types of murder or even all murders where the victim is female and the offender male. Murder aggravated by sexual brutality, violence, and abuse inflicted by men upon women against their will has not been uniformly singled out by the courts for notably harsher treatment than have other kinds of murder. The presumably greater gravity of felony-murder-rape over every other type of murder, to be inferred from the uniquely severe penalty provided for it by statute, is simply not borne out by comparably greater severity in the actual punishments meted out to offenders who have committed this crime. No one should look to the "mandatory" death penalty for felony-murder-rape to vindicate the special sanctity of female life and virtue. Furthermore, there is no reason to believe that the legislature would have it any different if it could. The absence of any conspicuous outcry from the Great and General Court in protest over the justice dispensed in Suffolk and Middlesex counties during the quarter century studied in this research surely suggests that it does not care about the judicial outcome of felony-murder-rape cases. If that is true, then the sharp legislative purpose so easily attributed to the "mandatory" death penalty for felony-murder-rape may be more an artifact of wishful retrospective thinking than a legitimate inference to be drawn from the fact that this statute was part of our law.

If the Commonwealth, in response to the decision in *Commonwealth v. O'Neal*,[24] were free from constitutional constraints and so could choose penalties for felony-murder-rape (or other crimes), there is no reason to believe that such new legislation would succeed where the old legislation failed.[25] The problem, by its very nature, is not one that can be solved merely by enacting a "mandatory" penal statute. The record of a quarter century of criminal justice under a "mandatory" death penalty indicates that such statutes contribute little or nothing toward uniform, even-handed, nonarbitrary, and predictable justice. This is not an indictment of Massachusetts law, its judiciary, district attorneys, or police. There is no reason to believe one would find a better record in other jurisdictions. Even so, the experience reported here should cast severe doubts on future attempts, in Massachusetts or elsewhere, to secure due process, equal protection, and the avoidance of cruel and unusual punishment, by the mere expedient of enacting "mandatory" death penalties. Such statutes are neither self-executing nor self-administering. No matter what their purpose as conceived by the legislature, no matter how heinous the crimes they are intended to punish, these laws cannot affect the actual administration of criminal justice apart from the intentions, decisions, and purposes of courts and prosecutors. The fact, therefore, that "mandatory" death penalty statutes eliminate any possible sentencing discretion by the judge or the jury means next to nothing when such statutes leave intact the vast reservoir of discretion that remains with prosecutors and trial courts.

Charles L. Black, Jr., an astute observer of the criminal justice system and the death penalty controversy in this country, has observed:

> If strictly mandatory death-penalty statutes are enacted, the law will give somewhere; one of the places where it *can* give is at the stage of *charging*, and I would expect to see many cases of prosecutors' charging less than they might have proved, to avoid the danger of this most drastic of sentences. But those decisions are not subject to any rule, and cannot ... practicably be made subject to any rule. ... Just as with the "charging" process, reduction to rule of the "plea-bargaining" process would require the impossible—an *adjudication* of the exact degree of guilt of the defendant, in advance of trial, or, as a rather inefficient and quite problematic alternative, forcing the prosecutor to go to trial in every case on the maximum charge barely suggested by the known evidence, without regard to his own estimate of the probabilities of conviction. ...
>
> So, within any foreseeable future, one of the absolutely crucial decisions for life or death—the decision whether to offer the defendant a chance to plead guilty to a noncapital offense—will be made administratively, on the basis of administrative discretion, without clear standards in law.[26]

This unsettling picture, projected in 1974 as a possible future in which "mandatory" death penalties had become widespread because they were the preferred legislative response to *Furman,* could have served as well as a sketch of the actual history of the experience in Massachusetts with the "mandatory" death penalty for felony-murder-rape.

Chapter 10

Witness to a Persecution

The discretionary power . . . in determining whether a prosecution shall be commenced or maintained may well depend upon matters of policy wholly apart from any question of probable cause.[1]

Petitioner's argument that prosecutors behave in a standardless fashion in deciding which cases to try as capital felonies is unsupported by any facts.[2]

I

When the definitive history of capital punishment in the United States is written, the full story about capital trials, death sentences, and executions in the State of Georgia deserves to play a prominent role.[3] Preliminary tallies of all executions in this country since the seventeenth century place Georgia third in the nation behind New York and Pennsylvania. Between 1930 and 1985, Georgia legally put to death 371 persons; in this period no other jurisdiction executed so many. In no other state in the nation have so many blacks—298[4]—been executed nor in any other state have blacks been so large a percentage of the total. Twenty-five years ago, Georgia led all other jurisdictions in the nation in the variety of statutory offenses for which the

217

death penalty could be imposed.[5] Among classic miscarriages of justice, Georgia also has made its contribution with the death in 1915 of Leo Frank, lynched near Marietta after a commutation of his death sentence for a murder it is now generally conceded he did not commit.[6] Perhaps it is hardly surprising, therefore, that another Georgia death penalty case during 1977, involving the "Dawson Five," added one more chapter to the annals of injustice. This chapter, largely in the form of a personal reminiscence, narrates one of the central series of events in that complex and disturbing case.

The case of the Dawson Five had all the ingredients of a classic southern death penalty scandal: the robbery-murder of a white victim in a remote rural setting; only one eyewitness, another white; the prompt arrest of an illiterate black teen-ager by an all-white police force; a confession implicating four other black youths; no circumstantial evidence against the accused; denial of bail; a charge of coerced confessions; and looming over it all, the threat of the death penalty and execution in Georgia's electric chair.

The case burst on the national scene within days of the inauguration of President Jimmy Carter in January of 1977. The Southern Poverty Law Center (SPLC) undertook to supply legal counsel for the defendants, and in order to raise funds, sent a letter over the signature of Julian Bond (then President of the SPLC) in a nationwide appeal. A copy of this letter arrived in my mail on January 23, 1977.[7] Since Dawson, where the crime occurred, is only twenty miles south of Carter's hometown of Plains, the national media quickly seized on the case to point up the paradoxes of the "new South." Here was the first president from the Deep South since before the Civil War, supported by southern black leadership from the civil rights movement and eager to show the nation that Georgia was ready to share the national consensus on racial equality. Here was also a president who was going to make the government's protection of human rights, abroad and presumably at home as well, something more than a rhetorical flag flapping in the political breeze. Yet in Dawson, on his very doorstep, a wretched story was unfolding that hearkened back to the very worst days of Georgia's ugly past, a land bloody with five hundred blacks lynched since Reconstruction.[8] To make matters even worse, the death penalty statute under which the Dawson Five were to be tried had been signed into law on March 28, 1973, by none other than then-Governor Carter.[9]

The case began exactly a year before Carter's inauguration. On January 22, 1976, in mid-morning, a male customer in a small roadside general store on the outskirts of Dawson was shot and killed (so the store owner later testified) during an armed robbery. The next day (or two days later—

reports differ) the store owner told Dawson police that he recognized one of the youths who had allegedly committed the holdup-murder. He was Roosevelt Watson, 18, who lived at home nearby with his parents. Young Watson was promptly taken into custody by the sheriff's department and an agent of the Georgia Bureau of Investigation (GBI). Under interrogation thirty miles away at police headquarters in Americus, Watson allegedly confessed to the shooting and implicated four others—his older brother, Henderson, 21; a cousin, J. D. Davenport, 18; and two friends: James ("Junior") Jackson, 17; and his brother, Johnny, 18.

The threat of the death penalty entered the case right from the start. Once Roosevelt Watson was out on $100,000 bail, after serving nine months in jail, he told reporters that the police "told me they gonna put me in the electric chair. . . . They had these two things hooked up to my fingers. Had a thing on my arm, real tight. Said they gonna electrocute me if I didn't tell 'em."[10] It was only later, apparently, that Watson learned he was merely undergoing the usual polygraph testing. The GBI investigator conceded to reporters that during Watson's interrogation "there was talk of electrocution."[11] According to a *New York Times* report, all five defendants were "indicted on charges of armed robbery and first degree murder, with the recommendation that they be given the death penalty if convicted."[12] In its fund-raising appeals, the SPLC stressed the threat of electrocution; the media understandably emphasized the grim prospect of execution as well.

The talk about the death sentence from the accused and from the police was all the more alarming because of serious doubts about the guilt of the five defendants. Claims that they were innocent were heard virtually from the moment Roosevelt Watson was taken off the polygraph in Americus and returned to Dawson. At the preliminary hearing, he repudiated his confession, claiming that it was coerced. Neither he nor any of his codefendants was willing to sign a confession. All the police had were alleged statements from Watson implicating the others, and similar statements by the others implicating each other. No physical evidence, such as the murder weapon (a "Saturday night special," according to the eyewitness), fingerprints, or stolen money ($100) linked any of the defendants to the crime. None of the defendants had any prior criminal record. Alibi witnesses (all blacks) alleged that the five young men were two miles away from the scene of the crime that morning. According to these informants, the defendants were drawing water from a neighbor's well to haul to the Watsons' home, an unpainted wooden farmhouse, not quite a shanty, by the side of a country road northeast of Dawson.

Guilty or innocent, the Dawson Five desperately needed legal counsel. After the preliminary hearing, during which they were represented by a local attorney, efforts were made to interest the SPLC in taking over the defense of these five dirt-poor prisoners. The SPLC, with its headquarters some distance away in Montgomery, Alabama, agreed to accept the case and turned over the task to its (then) affiliate, Team Defense, based in Atlanta. Organized during 1976, and already active in providing defense counsel in capital cases, Team Defense consisted of a "group of lawyers and social scientists who plan[ned] to use relatively new trial techniques in an effort to avoid executions, even in support of hopeless cases."[13] These techniques were reported to include: "Appealing to logic rather than compassion in arguments against the death penalty; prolonging trials to allow jurors to become well acquainted with defendants; using a proliferation of motions to 'capture the atmosphere of the trial' for appeal, if necessary; using social scientists to assist in challenging the composition of jury pools and evaluating the character of prospective jurors."[14]

Heading Team Defense was Millard Farmer, 42, white, an attorney whose Atlanta-based practice had been largely confined to typical small-office civil and criminal matters. Not any more. By 1977, Farmer was more appropriately described by *New York Times* editor Tom Wicker, who saw in Farmer "a passionate south Georgian possessed of a voice like a bullfrog with laryngitis."[15] In one of the local Georgia newspapers, he was described succinctly as "the most controversial lawyer in Georgia"[16] as a result of the novel trial tactics he pioneered in capital cases. Farmer's collaborator in working out trial strategy was a social psychologist, Courtney Mullin, 37, white, from Raleigh, North Carolina, "a hippy-looking girl without the hippy mind,"[17] as one unfriendly but respectful observer had put it. She had turned her talents to forensic psychology and was well known for her work on jury selection during the notorious Joan Little case in 1975.[18] Completing the Team Defense staff in the Dawson Five case were a couple of social activists and several students on leave or vacation from their studies in college or law school.

By the summer of 1977, a year and a half after the crime and the arrest of the defendants, Team Defense had been working on the case for many months, trying first to get the defendants out on bail (which entailed helping to raise the bail money), challenging the racial composition of the jury lists (which delayed inception of the trial), and helping to get publicity for the case far and wide (which included cooperating with a film crew from Boston's WGBH that was making a documentary for television on the case).[19]

Throughout its involvement in the Dawson Five case, Team Defense made its headquarters in Albany, twenty three miles southeast of Dawson. Those with a memory of the struggles of the civil rights movement in the early 1960s would recall the Dawson-Albany region. It had made national head-lines for months with its protracted boycotts, sit-ins, night-riding white racists, KKK rallies, and sporadic shootings and bombings that killed and wounded civil rights workers and their sympathizers. Just as Scottsboro, Alabama—another obscure southern town—had forty years earlier become a household word because of a death penalty case tried there, Dawson was on the threshold of notoriety because of the arrest and impending capital trial of the Dawson Five.

A sleepy country town of about six thousand people, situated deep in the heart of southwest Georgia's peanut and cotton farmland, Dawson is also the county seat of Terrell County. Known as "Terrible Terrell" during the civil rights movement, it had been more recently described by Millard Farmer as "the buckle on the Death Belt."[20] It was from Terrell County and other rural districts like it in the Deep South that small-town juries (usually all white) tried and convicted men (usually black) of first-degree murder and (especially if the victim was white) sentenced them to death. Such results were virtually guaranteed by the exclusion of blacks from the jury pool. In Terrell in 1976, when the population was about 60 percent black, the jury pool was 74 percent white.[21] This racial imbalance was the target for the first of the many pre-trial motions on behalf of the Dawson Five, and in April 1977 the courts ordered a new jury pool with equal black and white members.[22]

On July 26, 1977, Farmer filed seven further pre-trial motions, covering a wide variety of issues. One motion sought to dismiss the indictment on grounds of state misconduct. Another attacked the scrupled juror qualifi-cations in the Georgia death penalty statute. The boldest sought to strike down the entire death penalty statute as unconstitutional. It was this motion that served as the basis for my involvement in the case.

II

The hearing on these pre-trial motions was scheduled to begin at 9:30 on Monday morning, the first of August, in the Terrell County Courthouse in Dawson. Along with more than a dozen other witnesses scheduled to testify on these motions, I had flown into Albany on the Friday before the hearing. I spent the weekend getting to know the other witnesses, the Team

Defense staff, the two defendants then out on bail, their families, and the countryside. Three days later, my contribution was over and I was on the plane back to Boston. Within those seventy-two hours was sandwiched one of the more remarkable episodes provoked by the death penalty, and for those of us who witnessed it, an unforgettable drama and sobering lesson.

On the face of it, a pre-trial motion in 1977 to throw out Georgia's death penalty statute as unconstitutional would have struck most informed observers as implausible and farfetched, even frivolous and dilatory. Exactly one year earlier, in *Gregg v. Georgia,* the United States Supreme Court had sustained the Georgia Supreme Court in turning back a challenge to the constitutionality of this very statute. No doubt, as subsequent litigation and commentary were to prove,[23] the statute was vulnerable to criticism. But the likelihood that any Georgia court, trial or appellate, in the summer of 1977 would look favorably on a frontal challenge to the constitutionality of the death penalty seemed not merely slight—it seemed zero.

The defense motion in question, styled "Motion to Strike and Quash As Unconstitutional the Georgia Statutes Providing for the Imposition of the Death Penalty and Their Application to This Case," consisted of eight legal pages in which eleven points were argued. The point given the most extensive development was devoted to the contention that the racist practices imposed by the white minority on the black majority made Terrell County "simply a modern version of the plantation system," with a criminal justice system that employed the threat of capital punishment as its ultimate tool of repression. The motion argued that this racist factor was crucial to the state's declared intention to seek the death penalty for the defendants:

> Differential treatment of minorities in the application of criminal sanctions is an inherent product of such an environment. This is particularly so with regard to the death penalty, with its historic over-imposition on minorities. The quality of justice which the defendants will receive is a product of such a system and thus cannot be untainted by this pervasive and blatant discrimination. The above acts have perpetuated a system where a black person's life has never been as highly esteemed as that of a white person, a system in which the State's most racist tool—the death penalty and its threat—has historically been racist as applied and is now racist as applied in this county. In this case, death as punishment is only being used as the white man's "boogie man" to instill fear in these young black kids and the entire black community. It is an ever-present threat to the poor, the black and the oppressed. Therefore, the State should be prevented from seeking the ultimate punishment against these defendants.

Whether the Georgia death penalty was functionally racist and whether this was a sufficient ground for a court to rule on the unconstitutionality of the statute as the motion implied, and as I was ready to believe, did not especially concern me. I knew I was not qualified by my own empirical research as an expert on the racial aspects of the death penalty, although I had gathered and analyzed some data in northern jurisdictions relevant to this issue,[24] and I was familiar with the important research on the subject published by other investigators. Besides, it was not primarily in this connection that Team Defense sought my testimony; others in the group of expert witnesses (notably William Bowers[25] and Marc Riedel[26]) could speak on this theme with authority.

A memorandum prepared by Team Defense and distributed to all the witnesses outlined the general themes that the expert testimony was expected to cover: (a) the demography of capital punishment, including the arbitrariness and discrimination to be found in its administration; (b) the unreliability of the process of selecting capital offenders, which defeats any rational legislative purpose underlying the adoption and enforcement of capital statutes; (c) the cruelty of executions and of death-row confinement; (d) the cruelty of the death penalty as judged by contemporary social-science and moral theory; (e) problems with selecting jurors in capital trials; (f) the evidence against the deterrent efficacy of the death penalty; and (g) the economic costs of capital punishment. In a briefing session the day before the pre-trial motions were to be argued, Farmer and Mullin explained to me that my testimony was needed on the general history and trends of the death penalty nationally and worldwide, in order to provide the setting into which the more detailed testimony from the other witnesses could be fitted.

Team Defense wanted, in effect, to put capital punishment on trial right from the start in this case to show that this was what the case was all about. The court, the prosecution, and the media needed to be made to understand this as unambiguously and persuasively as possible. Farmer decided that I should be his opening witness at the hearing. In thinking over how matters would go in court the next day, I was not anxious about my ability to answer direct questions from Farmer or to respond to cross-examination, insofar as my responses would turn on knowledge of the relevant facts. By the summer of 1977, I had already spent a good fraction of twenty years reading, writing, and talking about the death penalty, and I was confident that I could summon ad lib an appropriate range of things to say that would inform the court. But one thing about my forthcoming testimony did give me pause. This was not the first time I had been invited by the defense in a murder trial to appear as an expert witness on capital punishment.

The previous occasion had been in the summer of 1965 in Seattle, Washington, in a case that also involved black defendants and a white victim. Defense counsel in that case believed there was little room for maneuver on the question of guilt; it was solely on the issue of sentence that they thought I might be helpful. They knew of my book, *The Death Penalty in America*, then recently published, and telephoned to ask whether I would agree to testify for their clients. Since I lived at that time in Portland, Oregon, it was not difficult for me to arrange to comply. In fact, I was eager to testify. The whole idea of putting my scholarly knowledge to practical use in a courtroom appealed to me. I arrived as planned and was placed on the stand, the judge having temporarily excused the jury prior to ruling on the admissibility of my testimony. As soon as defense counsel began to qualify me as an expert, however, the prosecution interrupted and moved to have me dismissed, on the grounds that any testimony I might give would be irrelevant and inappropriate. The trial judge immediately sustained the objection. I had been warned that this might happen, since I had no "expert" knowledge about any facts concerning this particular case. Even so, I was subdued and frustrated; I even felt a bit of a fool. I was soon on the train back to Portland, convinced that my days as an expert witness in capital trials were over before they had even begun. True, that 1965 case was very different from the situation in the Dawson Five case; in Seattle my testimony had not been sought in support of a pre-trial motion on the constitutionality of the statute itself, but directly before the jury on the issue of sentence. And during the subsequent decade, the death penalty controversy had undergone enormous legal transformations. Still, my experience in futility in that Seattle courtroom was an unwelcome precedent not far from my mind.

To my surprise, Farmer and Mullin did not share my worry. They explained they were counting on the trial judge's willingness to allow my testimony. He would go some distance, they thought, perhaps even bend over backward, to show that the accusations of racism in Terrell County's system of criminal justice that were then being broadcast nationwide by the media were false, or at least much exaggerated, and certainly would not corrupt his handling of the trial of the Dawson Five. They also believed that if the judge were to rule out my testimony as irrelevant, or deem me to be unqualified as an expert on the motion, such rulings could be exploited in the courtroom of the streets, where television cameramen and newspaper reporters ruled. Excluding my testimony would be viewed in that forum as simply further evidence of the refusal of the State of Georgia to hear the truth in open court about the death penalty system that was propelling five black teen-agers toward the electric chair. Either way, Farmer and Mullin were convinced, the defendants stood to gain some benefit from my testimony.

Farmer also explained that he would try to construct questions for me to answer in such a way that in the course of establishing my qualifications as an expert, I would already be offering the general substance of my testimony. Thus there would never be a precise point when his questions and my answers shifted from the technical issue of my credentials as an expert to the substantive issues of my views on the death penalty. Farmer hoped that the prosecution would defer interruptions to challenge my status as an expert or the relevance of my testimony, or that the court would defer ruling in favor of any such prosecution challenges, until a great deal of what he wanted from me was already on the record. Farmer's strategy seemed a plausible way to get around the problem that had had me expelled summarily from that Seattle courtroom years earlier. Even if I were not allowed to testify, I might be able to serve the defense's purpose by helping to turn the case around from one in which five black teen-agers were on trial for their lives in a backwater Georgia courtroom into a case in which the town of Dawson and Terrell County (with their long history of manifest racism), and Georgia's newly minted death penalty statutes, were on trial in every household of the nation that could be reached by newspaper and television.

III

August 1, 1977—the opening day of the hearing—dawned bright and hazy, with the promise of damp, sweltering heat within a few hours. In a car with other witnesses, I was driven from Albany across the flat drought-ridden farmland that stretched west and north to Dawson. The streets of Dawson were nearly empty when we arrived shortly after 9:00 A.M. at the courthouse parking lot. The century-old Terrell County Courthouse was in its own way an imposing edifice of brick and stone. On the sidewalk in front, a few bystanders watched as television crews were setting up their equipment. On the portico and front steps of the courthouse, uniformed state troopers flanked the entrance. One by one we entered and climbed the staircase to the courtroom on the second floor.

The courtroom was larger than I had expected, roughly square, high ceilinged, with a bar railing that stretched across the entire front of the room. The room had been modernized recently, so that it was comfortably air-conditioned and brightly lit by the indirect fluorescent lighting typical of lecture halls. The spectators were provided with rows of comfortable seats arranged, not as in most courtrooms, but in the semicircular fashion of an amphitheater. Sitting in the top row in the back, one would be just below eye level with the judge. The witness stand, where I would soon be sitting, was immediately to the left of the bench and directly in front of the table reserved for the prosecution. As we filed down the aisle to our seats near the defense table, other spectators, reporters, and court officers also entered and the room slowly began to fill. In the corner to the judge's right, eight or nine men lounged in the jury box. Most of the men were heavyset and casually dressed. We were told they were detectives, town police, and GBI officers in plainclothes there to keep the peace. The side arms of several were in plain view.

Murder trials were not an everyday occurrence in the Terrell County Courthouse, and local observers assured us that nothing remotely like the Dawson Five case had ever transpired in this courtroom before. Presiding over the case was Judge Walter I. Geer, white, and said to be "highly respected on the seven-county Pautula Circuit."[27] He was not in the best of health, as was soon to be evident; he suffered from emphysema as well as other inconveniences of advancing age. Within a few weeks he would retire from the case (only temporarily, as it turned out) on the grounds that he was simply "not physically able" to continue.[28] Representing the prosecution was another elderly white man, District Attorney John R. Irwin. He looked ashen and frail; he was ill from cancer and the side effects of radiation therapy.[29] He did not look strong enough to direct an effective prosecution in a case such as this. At his side was a much younger man, Michael Stoddard, an assistant attorney general sent down from Atlanta as a special prosecutor and assistant to the district attorney. Unlike Geer and Irwin, whose age, dress, and manner seemed more suitable to an earlier era far from the limelight of national attention, Stoddard looked alert, businesslike, and dapper in a well-cut dark suit. Before the morning was over, he was to become a central figure.

As soon as Judge Geer was seated at the bench, he recognized the attorney for the defendants.[30] Farmer immediately sought to establish the mood he wanted in the courtroom that morning by a series of sparring maneuvers. He insisted, firmly but politely, that the prosecution leave ample room at the table for the defense to spread out its papers and its persons. Judge Geer assured him there would be no territorial encroachments by the prosecution.

In answer to the judge's query about a small boxlike apparatus on the defense table, Farmer explained that it was a tape recorder, that it was running, and that the defense intended to use it to record all the proceedings in order to assist it in reviewing each day's testimony and rulings. That way, Farmer said, the defense would not have to depend on the efficiency of the court reporter in preparing the daily transcript. No objection. Judge Geer's attention was distracted by a young man who was distributing a folder of papers to each of several persons throughout the courtroom; Farmer explained that this was one of his assistants, who was providing members of the press with a packet of materials on the motions and on the experts who were soon to begin their testimony. Again no objection. Then, starting with Courtney Mullin, he turned to his companions around the defense table and introduced them one by one. As he introduced the five defendants, he made an emphatic point of saying that, although when he spoke to them he would use their first names, because he knew them personally, he expected the court and the prosecution always to address the defendants with "Mister"—Mr. Watson, Mr. Jackson, etc.[31] Finally, he presented to the court his young assistants, four men and eight women; of these twelve, seven were blacks.

With these preliminaries behind him, Farmer announced to the court that he was withdrawing several defense motions as no longer germane, including the motion for a speedy trial and the motion to recompose the (grand and trial) jury pools. That brought him to the centerpiece of his morning's work, the motion to throw out the Georgia death penalty statute and the expert testimony he had arranged to present. Farmer addressed the court:

> Your Honor, I think maybe if I just made one short statement to the court before I started, the court might understand where we are going with these motions. As the court knows, in July of 1976 the U.S. Supreme Court in the decision of Gregg versus the State of Georgia said that on its face the Georgia statute asking for death, to allow death as punishment, was constitutional. We are now in the era of what in the slang of the profession we would say is the "constitutionality-as-applied-to-the-statute" attacks. Is the death penalty constitutional as applied? And we are ready to proceed on that with our first witness, Dr. Hugo Bedau.

IV

I walked across the courtroom to the witness stand next to the bench, sat down, and found myself perched on an armchair looking down on everyone in the room except for the judge. Staring back at me were perhaps a hundred and fifty people: the press, the guards and court officers, the two prosecutors and the defense team, the five defendants, and the spectators. Most of the spectators were local residents, black men and women along with their children, whole families dressed plainly but neatly in their best Sunday clothes. Conspicuous by contrast with everyone else in the room were the other expert witnesses waiting their turn and seated here and there in groups of three or four. At a glance they were obviously outsiders; each had a briefcase, several of the men had beards, and their attire was more suitable to a less humid and more urban environment. All were white.

Farmer began by asking me to tell the court some of my qualifications and publications, and I did. I mentioned in particular *The Death Penalty in America,* the book I had edited in the 1960s. I described it as the first book to gather the resources from every viewpoint—religious, legal, historical, and sociological. It was, I said, "designed to be a kind of encyclopedia" on all aspects of the death penalty. At that point I handed a copy of the book to Judge Geer for his inspection. He reached over to take it from me, put on his glasses, and looked down at the cover for a few seconds. Then he put the book down on the desk before him and leaned back, implying I should go on. I did:

> Most of the book is devoted to trying to look at whether the death penalty does provide a special protection to society, whether it prevents and deters crime, and also whether the death penalty has, in its history, been applied fairly and equitably so that it doesn't violate the canons of justice but conforms to them. These are the two most controversial issues in the discussion of the death penalty throughout its history. Is the death penalty really a protection for society or isn't it? Is it a better protection than imprisonment or isn't it? And, secondly, is it really fair in its applications? I think the evidence of thirteen years ago, as included in that book, confirmed by subsequent publications by me and others, is that the death penalty has not proved an effective social defense; has not proved to be a better deterrent and preventer of crimes of murder, rape, and other crimes against a person or property; and also, it has not proved to be a punishment that society wants to use fairly. . . . The death penalty has not been fairly applied and the death penalty has not been effective, uniquely effective, particularly effective, as a social deterrent to crime.

Farmer then asked me about the status of the death penalty in other countries. I explained that Great Britain, whose laws were historically most akin to our own, had already abolished capital punishment, and that Canada had also done so just a year before. I added:

228

And on Friday of this past week, the French government received a 700-page report recommending that the guillotine in France be abolished.[32] Now Canada, Great Britain, and France are not inconsequential nations to compare ourselves with. They are indeed the source of considerable cultural influence on us, so that the retention of the death penalty in the United States today is in marked contrast to what we find in the practice of other nations most like us.

So far, so good; there were no interruptions from the prosecution or the judge. I continued with my testimony to comment on the death penalty in Georgia, pointing out that until very recently Georgia statutes had retained the death penalty for some very remarkable crimes, the most peculiar being desecration of a grave with the intent to commit robbery.[33] The repeal of that statute, I argued, was an example of what had been happening across the nation throughout this century in reducing the variety of capital crimes. The overall pattern and direction, I insisted, was quite clear: "It's toward the reduction and abolition of all capital statutes."

As I was speaking, four black women got up from their seats in the courtroom, squeezed past other spectators toward the aisle, and headed for the exit. Judge Geer watched them until the courtroom doors closed behind them. I continued:

> It's a hundred and thirty years since the first United States jurisdiction abolished the death penalty: Michigan, 1847. Now in that hundred and thirty years, every single state in the country has moved in that direction, some more rapidly than others. Georgia, eleven years ago,[34] eliminated half its death penalty statutes, a very striking move in this direction, and typical of what's happening in the United States.

All the while, Farmer was standing diagonally across from me on the other side of the bench, smiling and encouraging me to go on. As no one seemed to object—a deputy yawned, a bailiff looked down at his hands in his lap, John Irwin leaned forward onto the table, Michael Stoddard leaned back with his hands behind his head—I went on:

> Historically, capital punishment, as we know it from the Bible, is part and parcel of a system of punishment that involves maiming people, castration, cutting off the hands of thieves, branding people, flogging people. Killing people is historically among methods of punishment that involve other corporal punishments: flogging, maiming, branding. I think the most striking historical fact about capital punishment is that it survives and the others have been banished. The moral attitudes of our society throughout the country

229

prohibit the use of these other punishments. It would not be possible for a legislature to undertake to introduce maiming or branding or flogging as a punishment, even if people felt that retribution required it, and many people do, and even if somebody thought that it would be a good deterrent, and maybe it would be. But our moral attitudes and our interpretation of the Constitution have developed to the point that unquestionably prohibits the use of those other methods.

A hundred years ago, nobody could have said what I just said. Two hundred years ago, anybody who said this would have been laughed out of the court. Today, if we think about it, we realize that we all know this, and that we accept it without any hesitation. So, the surprising thing is that capital punishment survives the condemnation that has been visited on all the similar punishments that once were widespread in our society.

Why does it survive? When we sit in a courtroom such as this with a capital case about to unfold, we might tend to take for granted that capital punishment is, of course, a part of contemporary penology and jurisprudence. The truth of the matter is that it's an anachronism. It is part of a past that hardly survives into the present, and which certainly will not survive into the future. That's what the full historical record discloses. And to answer the question "Why capital punishment survives?" we have to look again at some of its peculiarities.

There is a deep-seated belief that it does protect; there is a deep-seated belief that it does provide retributive justice; there is a deep-seated belief that people can be put to death in a humane and painless way. And the old maxim "out of sight, out of mind" still applies as far as the death penalty is concerned. ... People who are put to death are forgotten. Whereas if we saw people walking around in society with their hands lopped off, or "T" for "thief" branded in their forehead, we would be vividly reminded of the barbarities that we practiced, and we wouldn't stomach it.

So, capital punishment is an anachronistic survivor from a primitive past, all of its common modes or related punishments long since abolished, and it survives, I believe the record shows, for the reasons that I've indicated.

Perhaps as much as twenty minutes had gone by since I had taken the stand. Almost everyone in the room by now appeared to be paying attention to the mini-lecture they were hearing from the witness stand. I fleetingly wondered whether the things I was saying that morning had ever been heard before in a rural Georgia courtroom. Having completed my answer to Farmer's question, I was in need of another query from him to get me started off in a new direction. Instead, he indicated to the court that my testimony was at an end. I could tell by the way he looked at the judge that he was enormously pleased with how things had gone. He had managed to get all of my testimony before Judge Geer without a single pause or interruption. The tactic of having me provide the court with a seamless self-qualification-cum-substantive-testimony apparently had worked. Whether or not the judge would eventually rule against my testimony, he had at least allowed me to have my say, and that was more than half the battle.

V

As soon as Farmer ended direct examination, I expected Judge Geer to turn the prosecution loose on me. Instead, audibly struggling for breath, Judge Geer wheezed, "We're gonna take a twenty-minute break." Then speaking to a black spectator near the front row, a young girl whose even younger companions had apparently fallen asleep, he said kindly, "Little lady, wake your colleagues up." I wondered whether the judge's preoccupation with children dozing in his courtroom had interfered with his attention to what I had been saying for the previous few minutes.

During the recess I spoke with several of the defense staff and my colleagues, the other visiting expert witnesses, and we shared our amazement that it had all been so uneventful so far. We speculated over how the prosecution might react. Would they perhaps choose not to cross-examine me at all, thereby quickly getting rid at last of a witness who seemed articulate, self-confident, and competent? Farmer thought that might happen even though he was quite content (and so was I) to have me parry thrusts with Irwin and Stoddard as long as they wanted to joust.

As the recess neared its end, I resumed my seat on the stand. Judge Geer called the court to order and immediately asked the prosecution whether they were ready to cross-examine me. Irwin remained seated. Stoddard stood up and addressed the court. Because he was standing directly in front of me, no more than a couple of steps away, I could hear him quite easily. But Farmer, standing fifteen or twenty feet from him on the other side of the bench, had to strain to catch every word. The spectators, who could see only Stoddard's well-tailored back, could hear almost nothing of what he said. What he said, not loudly but in a normal speaking voice, was this: "Your Honor, at this point we would like to have this witness' testimony struck as the defense does not have any standing, we contend, to contest the constitutionality of the death penalty." So, I thought, it's going to be like Seattle after all. Farmer immediately started to interrupt, but changed his mind. The young prosecutor continued, audibly enough to me and to Judge Geer, but barely so to others in the room:

The State has never given the defense any notice of aggravating circumstances that is required by Code Section Twenty-seven-twenty-five-oh-three.[35] We don't think that the death penalty has been invoked in this case; we do not concede that it is unconstitutional; we contend that the defense has no standing to challenge it in this case since we have not given notice in this case . . .

Judge Geer interrupted, somewhat incredulously, it appeared. The following colloquy ensued:

COURT: Let me stop you right there, Mr. Stoddard. We are trying to come to some conclusion on a pre-trial motion.

STODDARD: Yessir.

COURT: Now, I don't know if the State anticipated asking for the death penalty or not. But if you're not, I think Mr. Farmer is entitled to know at this stage of the proceedings whether you are or are not since you made your objection. If you're not, then we'll stop this motion right where we are now.

STODDARD: Your Honor, we do not intend to ask for the death penalty.

I was thunderstruck. *Not ask for the death penalty!* I couldn't believe my ears. My mind raced. The death penalty was what this case was all about. How could the prosecution *not* ask for the death penalty, just like that, after a year and a half of allowing the police, the defendants, and the reporters to think the contrary? While these thoughts tumbled through my mind, I could see that Farmer was not quite sure he had heard Stoddard correctly. Others seated at the defense table could tell that something important had just happened, but exactly what they were not sure. The courtroom buzzed as the spectators filled each other in, as well as they could, on what Stoddard had been saying. After a moment's hesitation, Judge Geer spoke to the special prosecutor, saying, "All right, sir, let's let this witness go down." By now, most of those in the courtroom had been able to piece together what had transpired, and the spectators burst out with applause and some cheers. Judge Geer immediately gaveled the room back to order, turned to me and said, "All right, you may go down."

I thanked him, and as I walked toward the defense table, Farmer was on his feet and approached the bench. Even now, he seemed not fully to believe what he understood he had heard from the prosecution and the judge. He knew he had won a major victory at a phase in the proceedings where he least expected it, and his delight momentarily took the wind out of his sails. He spoke to Judge Geer:

FARMER: Your Honor, may we have, uh, that's, that's, uh, that's very much a surprise to us. The district attorney told us last week he *was,*

definitely would seek the death penalty. We need just a *short* recess
to get our other witnesses together and we'll be ready to go on, just
a five-minute recess.

COURT: I would assume that the district attorney, like all other lawyers,
reserves the right to change his mind, Mr. Farmer.

Smiling broadly, Farmer answered, "I certainly don't mind his changing his
mind about that, Your Honor." As Farmer addressed the court, the black
spectators and Team Defense staff again audibly showed their pleasure at
the way things had gone. The police, court officers, and a few local whites
in the courtroom sat still and silent. Judge Geer raised his voice above the
chatter and said, "All right, just one minute."

After this short recess, the courtroom was quiet again, and the judge
recognized Michael Stoddard:

STODDARD: We'd like to, uh, Your Honor, we, uh, did not tell Mr. Farmer
last week that we were going to ask for the death penalty. He asked
us if we would waive it, and we inquired, uh, in terms of negotiations,
why we should waive it.

We had never given him notice under these indictments; uh, the
only notice given was to a different attorney under different indictments.[36] So, Mr. Farmer never asked us about the aggravating circumstances or anything else, so . . .

Judge Geer shut him off, and sounded slightly sarcastic and more than
a little impatient when he said, "Well, thank you Mr. Stoddard, let's leave
that and move on to something else."

Judge Geer turned to Farmer and asked how much time he would need.
Farmer again asked for four or five minutes. The judge then inquired what
this development did to the other motions. Farmer fumbled for words, then
admitted, "To be honest with you, it's a surprise to us and we just need a
little time to regroup and see . . .

COURT: Get your sense back?
FARMER: Sir?
COURT: To get your senses back?

Judge Geer grinned slightly and the crowd chuckled, giggled and mur-
mured happily. Farmer responded, "That's right. To get our feet on the
ground. And to see what exactly we want to hear, because we had approximately three days and probably fifteen witnesses on this motion." Geer
questioned Farmer further, Farmer finally responding: "What I'm telling

the court is that it leaves me where I need to think about it a little bit. . . . We had three days planned out and it just went down and we'll be ready in just a little bit." Judge Geer agreed: "Anything that saves this court three days, disposing of anything, take your five minutes."

By now, the mood in the courtroom had completely changed, and outright laughter seconded Judge Geer's agreement to recess. Nevertheless, Farmer went on, no doubt exhilarated by the events of the past few minutes: "Yessir. Now I'll tell you the next motion is to dismiss the indictment and if they're willing to waive that one, we can save the court a whole lot more time!"

The courtroom erupted again and Judge Geer gaveled for order before repeating to Farmer that he could have his five minutes. But Stoddard then rose, and said, "The court doesn't want to hear me on that one?" Judge Geer, surprised, looked at him and said, "What?" Was it possible that Stoddard would equally abruptly propose to withdraw the indictments and drop the case altogether? It was not to be. Stoddard said, bluntly, "We aren't prepared to dismiss the indictment." Judge Geer, apparently somewhat bewildered, even annoyed, merely responded, "All right, thank you." With that, the court recessed.

There is much more to the story of the Dawson Five, and someone should tell it before it is forgotten; but it is anticlimactic for the present purpose. Suffice it to state here that nearly five months later, on December 19, 1977, District Attorney John Irwin announced that he was dropping all charges against the five defendants. He had no other choice, he said, after a ruling by Judge Geer a week earlier that ordered suppression of the statement to the police given by Roosevelt Watson.[37] After two years less a month, the ordeal for the Dawson Five was over.

VI

When special prosecutor Stoddard announced to Judge Geer that the State had no intention of seeking the death penalty for the Dawson Five, the seemingly spontaneous character of his announcement, coming immediately on the heels of my testimony as it did, naturally tempted several of us to think that something in what I had said or in the way that Judge Geer had allowed Farmer to lead me by the hand caused the prosecution during the short recess to re-evaluate its professed sentencing goal. Yet I instinctively hesitated to yield to any such temptation lest I commit the fallacy of reasoning noted in every elementary logic textbook, *post hoc ergo propter hoc* ("after this, therefore because of this"). Elated by the unanticipated success of the morning, which obviated the need for any further expert testimony on general aspects of the death penalty (though not on the question of jury selection or on other particular issues in the case),[38] one of my fellow witnesses (Brian Forst,[39] as I recall) quipped:

> Well, it's obvious how Team Defense should defend capital cases from now on. All they have to do is to bring Bedau in to testify on this kind of pre-trial motion, and instead of bothering with any of the rest of us experts, they should hire some local actors to sit together in a row in the courtroom, dressed in three-piece suits and with briefcases on their laps. That'll help create the proper, intimidating atmosphere, but they'll never be needed.

We all laughed at the idea of such an outrageous ploy, knowing that factors quite apart from my testimony must have been at work. But what were they? When asked later by the local newspaper reporters, District Attorney Irwin was quoted as saying simply that the prosecution decided to drop the death penalty because of "the ages of the boys, they were all young, . . . and because of the lack of any prior records."[40]

Even now, several years later, the full story is still not clear. There are two supplementary though somewhat overlapping versions, neither of which fully supports John Irwin's explanation. Both these subsequent stories are supplied by Roy Herron, who was then a member of Team Defense and among the staff present in the Dawson courtroom that morning. The first version is from Morris Dees, who was the chief trial counsel for the SPLC at the time. While in Albany on a visit to his in-laws the day before the pre-trial hearing, Dees explained in an interview with Herron, he succeeded in persuading the prosecutor to drop the death penalty.

> I told John [Irwin] that I thought that for the benefit of Georgia and with [President] Carter being from there, they ought to drop going for the death sentence. And I just convinced him that he couldn't get the death penalty, because he was gonna get virtually an all-black jury. . . . He said he would drop it at the first open-court hearing.[41]

In a subsequent interview with Herron, Michael Stoddard gave a somewhat different explanation:

> I think Morris Dees' conversation helped John [Irwin] to see it in a different light. But John did not really decide whether to go for the death penalty or not. I felt it was John's decision. I was to assist the local district attorney. He's the one who takes the heat and gets the credit. But one of the things we

knew was it'd be an all-black jury if we got to the jury. A lot of the whites we talked with didn't want to be on juries because of their racial feelings. They didn't want to serve and have to be with blacks. The chances of conviction we thought would be lessened if jurors were worried about having to vote on a death sentence. It would be difficult enough to get a conviction, was what I told John, but easier if they did not have to face the death penalty.

Still, the decision not to go for the death penalty was not made until I stood up and waived it. There'd been a witness on the stand and it was my turn to cross-examine and we had to either fish or cut bait. John had been indecisive. I told John, "We've gotta decide." Finally, I told him, "Well, John, we've got to decide *now*. Unless you tell me not to, I'm going to waive it." It was time to fish or cut bait. So I stood up and waived it.[42]

It does not matter much which of these two versions, or perhaps some other version altogether, is more accurate, because from each the same point emerges. It is the chief point of this essay, one that has been made before by others,[43] though not, to my knowledge, ever in the harsh light cast by a case like that of the Dawson Five; nonetheless, the point deserves to be repeated, and can be succinctly expressed in two propositions.

First, in capital cases as the law currently stands[44] the prosecution has complete, untrammeled, and unreviewable discretion to decide whether to use its death penalty card, to leave it in the deck, or—as in the unusual case of the Dawson Five—to let it be put into play in the early stages of the game and then abruptly revoke it as the trial opens. Second, whatever might be said for the role of bargaining chips in the game of criminal justice, it is difficult to make out a rational case for the death penalty as such a chip. Its utterly discretionary employment by the prosecution is surely inconsistent with the spirit, if not the letter, of the standards that govern capital cases. These standards are expressed in the epigram "death is different," a notion that has increasingly found recognition among appellate courts[45] and commentators.[46] So long as the prosecution in a murder case can do what was done to the Dawson Five, the death penalty is treated as being in principle no different from any other criminal sanction. It is viewed as simply one among many possible punitive outcomes in the case, albeit more severe than others. This view, of course, flies in the face of reality. A possible death sentence and a possible life term in prison do not differ in the way that a suspended sentence and probation, or probation and short-term confinement, differ—much less in the way that a ten-year and a twenty-year prison sentence differ.

The power and the freedom of the prosecution to act as it did in the

Dawson Five case is not unique to Georgia law, nor is the danger of the misuse and abuse of this freedom and power confined to the Deep South. It is characteristic of the death penalty system in the United States as it operates in the present legal environment, and it is difficult to imagine any possible remedy for it short of abolishing the death penalty itself. Quite apart from any other aspect of the current death penalty system, the very existence of capital punishment as a statutory option for a crime such as murder will in practice impose unwarranted burdens, provoke needless fears, increase economic costs, and make justice bend to expediency.

Conclusion

Insofar as fundamental moral questions are raised by the death penalty, their resolution does not turn on what a majority of the Supreme Court says the Constitution permits or forbids. Nor does it rest on what the tea leaves of public-opinion polls can be construed to mean. Morally speaking, what are at stake are the *reasons* that can be brought forward to support or to criticize this punishment. These reasons—familiar from public debates, letters to the editor, and radio and television talk shows—have not significantly altered over the past generation, and perhaps not even during the past century.

In order of increasing importance, the main reasons for support seem to me to be these six: (1) the death penalty is a far less expensive method of punishment than the alternative of life imprisonment; the death penalty is more effective in preventing crime than the alternative because (2) it is a more effective deterrent, and because (3) it more effectively incapacitates; (4) the death penalty is required by justice; (5) in many cases there is no feasible alternative punishment; and (6) the death penalty vindicates the moral order and thus is an indispensable symbol of public authority. In bringing this volume to a close, I want to evaluate each of these reasons and elaborate especially on those of salient current importance.

The Taxpayer's Argument Is the death penalty really so much less expensive than long-term imprisonment? The answer depends on how one allocates the costs imposed under the two alternatives. The few attempts that have been made to do this in a manner comparable to the way economists try to answer other questions about the cost of alternative social policies are in agreement. In the words of the most recent study, "A criminal justice system that includes the death penalty costs more than a system that chooses life imprisonment."[1] Why this is true is easily understood. It is mainly a consequence of the commendable desire to afford every protection to a defendant whose life is at stake, and virtually every such defendant avails himself of all these protections. If the defendant is indigent, as are most of those accused of crimes that put them in jeopardy of the death penalty, then society has to foot the bill for the defendant's attorney as well as for the costs involved in the prosecution, jury selection, trial, and appeals. Although in theory these costs would need to be paid even if the defendant were not on trial for his life, in practice the evidence shows that non-death-penalty trials and appeals are generally less protracted and therefore less expensive. So the taxpayer's argument, as I have called it, is simply wrong on the facts.

But, of course, even if it were sound, no decent citizen or responsible legislator would support the death penalty by relying on this argument alone. Those who seriously advance it do so only because they also believe that the criminals in question ought to be executed whatever the cost to society and however galling the expenditure may be. As a consequence, the taxpayer's argument is really no more than a side issue, since defenders and critics of the death penalty agree that economic costs should take a back seat to justice and social defense where human life is concerned.

Uniquely Effective Deterrent No one has ever offered any scientific evidence that the death penalty is an effective deterrent, or more effective than the alternative of long-term imprisonment, to any such crime as rape, arson, burglary, kidnapping, aircraft hijacking, treason, espionage, or terrorism (which itself typically involves one or more of these other crimes). All arguments for the death penalty that rest on belief in its superior deterrent capacity to prevent or reduce the incidence of these crimes depend entirely on guesswork, common sense, or analogy to its allegedly superior deterrent effects on the crime of murder.

What, then, is the evidence that the death penalty is an effective deterrent to murder? There is little or none. Murder comes in many different forms (gangland killings, murder among family members, murder during armed robbery or burglary, murder in jail or prison, murder for hire, murder to escape custody or avoid arrest), but very little of the research on deterrence has concentrated exclusively on one of these types to the exclusion of all the rest. The threat of executions is conceivably a much better deterrent to some types of murder than to others; but no research currently exists to confirm such a hypothesis.

It doesn't really matter. Deterrence is increasingly a make-weight in the argument for the death penalty. Public opinion surveys indicate that most of those who profess support for the death penalty would support it even if they were convinced—contrary to what they believe—that it is not a better deterrent than life imprisonment.[2] I find this plausible. Although from time to time there is sporadic evidence in favor of the deterrent power of executions (hardly anyone who thinks about it attaches much differential deterrent efficacy to the death penalty *statutes,* all by themselves), none of it survives careful scrutiny very long.[3] If anything, there is a steadily accumulating body of evidence to suggest that on balance the death penalty may cause (or encourage, or set the example for) more homicides than it prevents, because its "brutalizing" effect out-performs its deterrent effect.[4]

Furthermore, and quite apart from the status of the evidence on the issue of deterrence vs. brutalization, one would expect that the rationale for deterrence in our society is of slowly declining importance. In previous centuries and up to a generation ago, when our society punished many *non*-homicidal crimes with death, deterrence was the most plausible reason for hanging a counterfeiter or a horse thief or a claim jumper. Today, however, with the death penalty applied exclusively to murder, nondeterrent considerations naturally play an increasingly prominent role all the time. Indeed, social science research, public opinion, and Supreme Court rulings all neatly converge at this point. Despite more than a decade of effort to obtain convincing support for rational belief in the superior deterrent power of the death penalty, the evidence points the other way. During the same period, advocates of capital punishment—both those who are and those who are not aware of this lack of evidence—shifted the basis of their support for executions from deterrence to other reasons. Meanwhile, the Supreme Court has said in effect that the death penalty is unconstitutional except where it is not disproportionate to the crime and regardless of its deterrent effects.

From a public-policy perspective, one can say this: During the past fifteen years, the legislative re-enactment of death penalty statutes has been no more than a series of stabs in the dark, insofar as these laws have been predicated on their supposed superior deterrence. A legislature ought to have better reasons than this for trying to protect the life of its citizens by imposing the threat of the death penalty. On moral grounds, as I have explained in earlier chapters of this book, general deterrence is certainly a legitimate function of the criminal law and therefore a justifiable basis on which to construct a system of punishments under law. Nevertheless, the choice of more rather than less severity in punishment for particular crimes on grounds of better deterrence alone encounters two different objections. One is that we violate moral principles if we are willing to use punitive methods, regardless of their savagery, in order to secure slight improvements in deterrence; the other is that there simply is no adequate evidence in favor of the superior deterrent efficacy of the death penalty.

Incapacitation and Prevention   No one can dispute that capital punishment, when carried out, does effectively incapacitate each offender who is executed. (This has nothing to do with deterrence, however, because deterrence operates by threat and intimidation, not by destroying the capacity to break the law.) Does this incapacitation make a significant dent in the crime rate? The Department of Justice has reported that as of the end of 1984 "approximately 2 of every 3 offenders under sentence of death had a prior felony conviction; nearly 1 out of 10 had previously been convicted of homicide."[5] These data indicate that more than a hundred of those currently under sentence of death may be some of the worst offenders in the nation— and that several hundred more served a prison term for robbery, assault, or some other crime, and then, after their release, went on to commit the even graver crime of murder. (Of course, these data simultaneously show that the vast majority of condemned prisoners are *not* recidivist murderers.) But do these data also show that society needs the incapacitating power of death to prevent more crimes from being committed by convicted capital offenders?

If parole boards and release authorities knew in advance which inmates would murder after their release, the inmates in question would obviously be prevented from committing these offenses by being kept in some form of custody. Yet we have no reliable methods for predicting future dangerousness, and especially not for the propensity of a convicted murderer to murder again.[6] Consequently, the only effective general-policy alternatives to the present one are a system of mandatory death penalties and a system of mandatory prison terms for life. Even then, if the Bureau's own statistics are reliable, this would prevent only a tiny fraction of the twenty thousand or so murders committed in this nation each year. The truth is, as all release statistics agree, very few of the persons convicted of homicide and sent to prison are ever convicted of homicide again. Either to kill all those convicted of murder or to keep them all in prison forever, because of a few exceptions that cannot be identified in advance, would be an expensive and unjustified policy that very few of us, on reflection, would want to support.

Opponents of the death penalty encounter their stiffest objections when they try to explain why even the multiple or serial or recidivist murderer should not be executed. Few would disagree that "the thirst for revenge is keenest in the case of mass murder, . . . especially when it includes elements of sadism and brutality against innocent victims."[7] Revenge apart, incapacitation probably has its most convincing application in such cases. It is hardly surprising that many who generally oppose the death penalty would be willing to make an exception for such killers.

Let us note first that if the death penalty were confined to such cases, abolitionists would have scored a major victory. The immediate consequence of such a policy would be an unprecedented reduction in the annual number of death sentences—a drop from more than two hundred per year to fewer than twenty, if we can rely on the Bureau of Justice Statistics report quoted above. Any policy change that reduced death sentences by more than 90 percent should be welcomed by opponents of the death penalty as a giant step in the right direction.

More controversial is whether abolitionists could accommodate such an exception on moral grounds. The best way to do so, it seems to me, is to argue much as George Bernard Shaw did earlier in this century in his little book *The Crime of Imprisonment* that the execution of such murderers is society's only alternative—we have no nonlethal methods of sedation or restraint that suffice to make certain that such offenders will not and cannot kill yet again. However, this is a factual question, and I (unlike Shaw) think that once the offender is in our custody, we are never in the position where our only recourse is to lethal methods. Others who have studied the problem more carefully agree;[8] there are reasonably humane methods at our disposal for coping with the most difficult and dangerous prisoners.

In the end, however, I think one must admit that the refusal to execute a murderer who has repeated his crime—not to mention those who embody murderous evil on a gigantic scale, such as an Adolph Eichmann or a Lavrenti Beria—is evidence of a position on the death penalty that owes something to fanatic devotion as well as to cool reason. Dedicated pacifists and devoutly religious opponents of the death penalty may well be able to embrace such categorical opposition to executions without fear of rebuke from reason. Conscientious liberals, however, cannot so easily refuse to compromise. Do they not already compromise on other life-and-death is-sues—often tolerating suicide, euthanasia, abortion, the use of lethal force in social and self-defense—thereby showing that they refuse to accept any moral principle that categorically condemns all killing? If so, what is so peculiarly objectionable, from the moral point of view as they see it, in an occasional state-authorized killing of that rare criminal, the murderer who has murdered more than once? I cannot point to any clear and defensible moral principle of general acceptability that is violated by such a compro-mise, a principle that *absolutely forbids* such executions. If one nonetheless opposes all executions, as I do, then it must be on other grounds.

Retributive and Vindictive Justice   Today there is substantial agreement that retribution is an essential aspect of the criminal justice system, and that a general policy of punishment for convicted criminals is the best means to this end. Less agreement exists on whether retribution alone justifies the practice of punishment; and there is no consensus on how to construct a penalty schedule on retributive grounds, matching the severity of punish-ments to the gravity of crimes. Regrettable confusion of the dangerous (though normal) emotion of anger and the desire for revenge it spawns—neither of which has any reliable connection to justice—with moral indig-nation at victimization—which does—often clouds the thinking of those who defend the "morality" of capital punishment.[9] There is also disagree-ment on whether other considerations of justice—such as equality, fairness of administration, and respect for the rights of the accused—should yield or prevail when they conflict with the demands of retribution.

These issues are inescapably philosophical, and I have my own views on them, which I have explained in this book and elsewhere.[10] In a word, the most that principles of retribution can do for the death penalty is to *permit* it for murder; principles of retribution are strained beyond their capacity if they are invoked to justify the death penalty for any other crime. Thus if retribution is the moral principle on which defenders of the death penalty want to rest their case, then morality requires that nonhomicidal crimes must be punished in some less severe manner. However, the principles of retribution do not *require* us to punish murder by death; what they require is the severest punishment for the gravest crime consistent with our other moral convictions. Consequently, the appeal to retribution in the present climate of discussion—and it is a widespread appeal—fails to justify the death penalty.

In fact I think there is considerable self-deception among those who think they rest their defense of the death penalty on the moral principles of just retribution. Those principles cannot explain why society actually executes those few whom it does, and why it sentences to death no more than a small percentage of the murderers it convicts. Retribution is another fig leaf to cover our nakedness, I am afraid, even if it appears to be a respectable line of moral reasoning when taken in the abstract.

In recent years, neo-conservative writers of various sorts—such as columnist George F. Will, New York's Mayor Edward Koch, and academicians Walter Berns and Ernest van den Haag—have made much of the vindictive powers of the death penalty and of the civilizing and moralizing influence it thus wields. Van den Haag writes, "The [death] penalty is meant to vindicate the social order."[11] Berns elaborates the point: "The criminal law must be made awful, by which I mean, awe-inspiring. . . . It must remind us of the moral order by which alone we can live as *human* beings, and in our day the only punishment that can do this is capital punishment."[12] The language is resonant, but the claim is unconvincing.

One purpose of *any* system of punishment is to vindicate the moral order established by the criminal law—and properly so, because that order protects the rights of the law-abiding and because in a liberal society those rights are the basis for self-esteem and mutual respect. To go further, however, and insist that lethal punishment is the "only" appropriate response by society to the gravest crimes is wrong on two counts. The claim itself relies on naked moral intuitions about how to fit punishments to crimes, and such intuitions—with their deceptive clarity and superficial rationale—are treacherous. The least bit of historical sophistication would tell us that our forebears used the same kind of intuitive claims on behalf of maiming and other savageries that we would be ashamed to preach today. Furthermore, the claim makes sense only against the background of a conception of the state as a mystical entity of semi-divine authority, a conception that is hardly consistent with our pluralistic, liberal, nontheocratic traditions.

The Alternative   Imprisonment as it is currently practiced in this country is anything but an ideal alternative to the death penalty. Life imprisonment without the possibility of parole has been opposed by all experienced prison administrators as a virtually unmanageable option. The more one knows about most American prisons the more one judges long-term imprisonment to be a terrible curse for all concerned.[13] Defenders of the death penalty rightly point out that persons in prison can and sometimes do murder other inmates, guards, or visitors—although such crimes occur much less frequently than some of those defenders imply. (Nor do they occur with greater frequency in the prisons of states that do not punish these crimes with death than in the prisons of states that do.[14]) So imprisonment for ten or twenty years, not to mention for life, is vulnerable to many objections. Indeed, a cynic might even go so far to say that one of the best reasons for the death penalty is the alternative to it. Nevertheless, I think this alternative is still superior to execution—and will have to suffice until something better is proposed—for at least three important reasons.

First, society avoids the unsolvable problem of picking and choosing among the bad to try to find the worst, in order to execute them. Experience ought long ago to have taught us that it is an illusion to expect prosecutors, juries, and courts to perform this task in a fashion that survives criticism. Deciding not to kill any among the murderers we convict enables us to punish them all more equitably, just as it relieves us of the illusion that we can choose the worst among the bad, the irredeemable from the others, those who "deserve to die" from those who really do not.

Second, we avoid the risk and costly error of executing the innocent, in favor of the equally risky but far less costly error of imprisoning the innocent. Arresting, trying, convicting, and punishing the innocent is an unavoidable problem, whose full extent in our history is only now beginning to be understood. Recent research on persons erroneously convicted of capital crimes in this century in the United States has identified some 350 such cases.[15] Scores of these convictions occurred in states where there was no death penalty; dozens of these errors were corrected and in some instances the wrongly convicted defendant was indemnified. Not so in all cases in the death penalty states. Where is the necessity—moral or empirical—to run the risk of executing the innocent?[16]

Third, there is a crucial symbolic significance in drawing the line at punishments that deprive the offender of his liberty. Just as we no longer permit the authorities to use torture to secure confessions or to attack the body of the convicted offender with whips, branding irons, or other instruments that maim and stigmatize, nor to carry out the death penalty by the cruelest means our fevered imaginations can devise—even though some still cry out that social defense and just retribution require it—so we should repudiate the death penalty. It belongs alongside these other barbaric practices, which our society has rejected in principle.

For at least these reasons, the alternative of imprisonment is preferable to death as punishment in all cases.[17]

The Symbolism: Death or Life?   During earlier centuries, the death penalty played a plausible, perhaps even justifiable, role in society's efforts to control crime and mete out just deserts to convicted offenders. After all, the alternative of imprisonment—the modern form of banishment—had yet to be systematically developed. Consequently, society in an earlier age could tolerate the death penalty with a clearer conscience than we can today. For us, however, the true dimension in which to assess this mode of punishment is neither its crime-fighting effectiveness nor its moral necessity, but its symbolism. Mistaken faith in deterrent efficacy, confusion over the requirements of justice, indifference to unfair administration, ignorance of nonlethal methods of social control—all these can explain only so much about the current support for the death penalty. The rest of the explanation lies elsewhere, in what executions symbolize, consciously or unconsciously, for those who favor them.

This symbolism deserves a closer look.[18] The death penalty, today as in the past, symbolizes the ultimate power of the state, and of the government of society, over the individual citizen. Understandably, the public wants visible evidence that the authority of its political leaders is intact, their powers competent to deal with every social problem, and their courage resolute in the face of any danger. Anxiety about war, fear of crime, indignation at being victimized provoke the authorities to use the power of life and death as a public gesture of strength, self-confidence, and reassurance. Not surprisingly, many are unwilling to abandon the one symbol a society under law in peacetime has at its disposal that, above all others, expresses this power with awe-inspiring finality: the death penalty.

This is precisely why, in the end, we should oppose the death penalty in principle and without exception. As long as capital punishment is available under law for any crime, it is a temptation to excess. Tyrannical governments, from Idi Amin's Uganda to the Ayatollah's Iran, teach this lesson. At best the use of the death penalty here and elsewhere has been and continues to be capricious and arbitrary. The long history of several of our own states, notably Michigan and Wisconsin, quite apart from the experience of other nations, proves that the government of a civilized society does not *need* the death penalty. The citizenry should not clamor for it. Their political leaders should know better—as, of course, the best of them do—than to cultivate public approval for capital statutes, death sentences, and executions. Instead a civilized government should explain why such practices are ill-advised, and why they are ineffective in reducing crime, removing its causes, and responding to victimization.

Notes

Introduction

1. Robert L. Kidder, in Sandra B. Burman and Barbara E. Harrell-Bond, eds., *The Imposition of Law* (1979), p. 300.

2. Gilbert Geis, in Duncan Chappell, Robley Geis, and Gilbert Geis, eds., *Forcible Rape: The Crime, the Victim, and the Offender* (1977), p. 37.

Chapter 1

1. The best recent discussions of moral rights by philosophers—Ronald Dworkin, *Taking Rights Seriously* (1977); J. Roland Pennock and John W. Chapman, eds., *Human Rights: Nomos XXIII* (1981); Theodore M. Benditt, *Rights* (1982); Alan Gewirth, *Human Rights* (1982)—ignore the death penalty. An exception is A. I. Melden, *Rights and Persons* (1977), pp. 233–35.

2. W. D. Ross, *The Right and the Good* (1930), pp. 60–61.

3. John Locke, *Two Treatises of Government* (1690), Second Treatise, §§23, 172.

4. Ibid., §12.

5. Such a right is made a central feature of one important recent theory of punishment; see Herbert Morris, "Persons and Punishment," *The Monist* 52 (1968):475–501, and "A Paternalistic Theory of Punishment," *American Philosophical Quarterly* 18 (1981):263–71.

6. Immanuel Kant, *The Metaphysical Elements of Justice* (1797), trans. John Ladd (1965), p. 102. See generally Don E. Scheid, "Kant's Retributivism," *Ethics* 93 (1983):262–82.

7. Kant, *The Metaphysical Elements of Justice,* p. 100.

8. Ibid., p. 101.

9. See, e.g., Bruce L. Danto, John Bruhns, and Austin H. Kutscher, eds., *The Human Side of Homicide* (1982), and I. L. Kutash, S. B. Kutash, and L. S. Schlesinger, eds., *Violence: Perspectives on Murder and Aggression* (1978).

10. John Stuart Mill, *Utilitarianism* (1861), ch. 2, penultimate paragraph.

11. See Bedau, ed., *The Death Penalty in America,* 3d ed. (1982), pp. 17–18, 33–34; and Scott Christianson, "Corrections Law Developments: Execution by Lethal Injection," *Criminal Law Bulletin* 15 (1979):69–78.

12. See, e.g., Bedau, ed., *The Death Penalty in America,* rev. ed. (1967), pp. 402–4.

13. Cesare Beccaria, *On Crimes and Punishments* (1764), trans. Henry Paolucci (1963), p. 50.

14. See George Bishop, *Witness to Evil* (1971).

15. For a recent argument that attempts to meet such objections, see Graeme Newman, *Just and Painful: A Case for the Corporal Punishment of Criminals* (1983).

17. For a thoughtful historical and critical discussion, see George P. Fletcher, *Rethinking Criminal Law* (1978), pp. 237, 352–53, 856–75.

18. The best theoretical discussion of deterrence and related issues is Jack P. Gibbs, *Crime, Punishment, and Deterrence* (1975).

19. See Bernard L. Diamond, "Murder and the Death Penalty," and George F. Solomon, "Capital Punishment as Suicide and as Murder," reprinted in Bedau and Pierce, eds., *Capital Punishment in the United States* (1976).

20. See Bedau and Radelet, "Miscarriages of Justice in Potentially Capital Cases," *Stanford Law Review* 39 (1987).

21. See Comment, "The Cost of Taking a Life: Dollars and Sense of the Death Penalty," *U. C. Davis Law Review* 18 (1985):1221–74; New York State Defenders Association, Inc., *Capital Losses: The Price of the Death Penalty for New York State* (1982); and Barry Nakell, "The Cost of the Death Penalty" (1978), reprinted in Bedau, *The Death Penalty in America,* 3d ed. (1982).

22. The relevant biblical texts and ancient Jewish law are discussed in Haim Cohen, "Capital Punishment," *Encyclopedia Judaica* (1971) 5:142–45. See also Edna Erez, "Thou Shalt Not Execute: Hebrew Law Perspective on Capital Punishment," *Criminology* 19 (1981):25–43; and Thorsten Sellin, *The Penalty of Death* (1980), pp. 9–15.

23. See United States, Department of Justice, Bureau of Justice Statistics, *Capital Punishment 1982* (1984), p. 14 (Table 1).

24. Code of Georgia Annotated, §26–8117 (repealed 1963).

25. Kant, *The Metaphysical Elements of Justice,* p. 101.

26. Edwin R. Keedy, "History of the Pennsylvania Statute Creating Degrees of Murder," *University of Pennsylvania Law Review* 97 (1949):759–77.

27. Kant, *The Metaphysical Elements of Justice,* p. 106.

28. McGautha v. California, 402 U.S. 183 (1971), at 204 (Harlan, J.).

29. Albert Camus, *Resistance, Rebellion, and Death* (1961), p. 199.

30. See especially Charles L. Black, Jr., *Capital Punishment: The Inevitability of Caprice and Mistake,* 2d ed. (1981).

31. Furman v. Georgia, 408 U.S. 238 (1972), at 251–52 (Douglas, J., concurring).

32. Marvin E. Wolfgang and Marc Riedel, "Race, Judicial Discretion, and the Death Penalty," *The Annals* 407 (May 1973):119–33.

33. Samuel R. Gross and Robert Mauro, "Patterns of Death: An Analysis of Racial Disparities in Capital Sentencing and Homicide Victimization," *Stanford Law Review* 37 (1984):27–153.

34. NAACP Legal Defense and Educational Fund, Inc., Brief for Petitioner, Aikens v. California, reprinted in part in Philip English Mackey, ed., *Voices Against Death* (1976), p. 288.

35. These figures are estimates based on execution data reported in the United States Department of Justice bulletin, *Capital Punishment,* and on data reported annually since 1930 by the F.B.I. in *Uniform Crime Reports* on the volume of murder and nonnegligent manslaughter and the clearance (arrest) rates for those crimes.

Chapter 2

1. Viewing the duty of the state and the justification of punishment this way goes, I believe, very naturally with a general theory of social justice such as that advanced by John Rawls, *A Theory of Justice* (1971).

2. I have discussed this point at greater length in another paper, a preliminary version of which was published as "Punishment in a Just Society: Could It Be Eliminated?" in Robert E. Cleary, ed., *The Role of Government in the United States: Practice and Theory* (1985), pp. 168–79.

3. See Bedau, "The Right to Life," *The Monist* 52 (1968):550–72. For a more general discussion of this and related problems, see my essay "International Human Rights" in Tom Regan and Donald VanDeVeer, eds., *And Justice For All* (1982), pp. 287–308.

4. All these examples and more can be found in B. G. Ramcharan, ed., *The Right to Life in International Law* (1985).

5. Whether the right to life really is inalienable, as Locke and others have insisted, may be doubted. If it is inalienable, then no one could have the right to take his or her own life, no one could have the right to enlist others to that end, and no one could have the right to agree to provide such assistance.

6. According to the bulletin *Capital Punishment,* published annually by the Bureau of Justice Statistics, United States Department of Justice, only forty-three commutations of death sentences were granted in the United States between 1973 and 1985.

7. According to *Capital Punishment* (supra), during the years 1973–1983, state prisons received from the courts 2,266 persons under death sentence.

8. A thorough history of capital punishment in the United States, showing the details state by state, crime by crime, of efforts to impose and to repeal mandatory death penalties, has yet to be written. See, however, Philip English Mackey, "The Inutility of Mandatory Capital Punishment: An Historical Note," reprinted in Bedau and Pierce, eds., *Capital Punishment in the United States* (1976), pp. 49–53; and the sketch of the nation's experience with mandatory death penalties in the plurality opinion for the Supreme Court, by Justice Stewart, in Woodson v. North Carolina (1976).

9. In 1983, a Harris Survey reported that "no more than 27 percent of the people nationwide feel that all who are found guilty [of the crime of first-degree murder] should be put to death." When the crime is killing a policeman or prison guard, still only 31 percent favor a mandatory death penalty. Louis Harris, "Sizable Majorities Against Mandatory Death Penalty," *Harris Survey,* 10 February 1983, p. 1. Earlier data are reported in Bedau, ed., *The Death Penalty in America,* 3d ed. (1982),

p. 89. Supporters of the death penalty looking for guidance on this point from serious scholarly treatises written in its defense—Ernest van den Haag's *Punishing Criminals* (1975), Walter Berns's *For Capital Punishment* (1979), and Raoul Berger's *Death Penalties* (1982)—will find neither a defense of mandatory death penalties nor an explanation of why nonmandatory death penalties are to be preferred.

10. I am indebted to Stephen Nathanson's excellent discussion of this point in his essay, "Does It Matter if the Death Penalty is Arbitrarily Administered?" *Philosophy & Public Affairs* 14 (1985):149–64.

11. Based on national data for the years 1971–75, concerning parole outcome during the first (but not any subsequent) year after release from conviction of willful homicide; see Bedau, ed., *The Death Penalty in America*, 3d ed. (1982), pp. 173–80.

12. I have discussed the "new" retributivism more fully in "Retribution and the Theory of Punishment," *Journal of Philosophy* 75 (1978):601–20. For different views, see Roger Wertheimer, "Understanding Retribution," *Criminal Justice Ethics* 2 (Summer/Fall 1983):19–38; and Jeffrie G. Murphy, "Retributivism, Moral Education, and the Liberal State," *Criminal Justice Ethics* 4 (Winter/Spring 1985):3–11. An interesting popular discussion may be found in Susan Jacoby, *Wild Justice: The Evolution of Revenge* (1983).

13. The now-classic research on this point is by Marvin E. Wolfgang and Marc Riedel, "Race, Judicial Discretion, and the Death Penalty," *The Annals* 407 (May 1973):119–33.

14. On the racial aspects of the death penalty, the most recent data are discussed in the articles by Samuel R. Gross, by Arnold Barnett, and by David C. Baldus, George Woodworth, and Charles A. Pulaski, Jr., in *U. C. Davis Law Review* 18 (1985). On the arbitrariness of the decisions by trial courts to impose the death sentence, see Michael L. Radelet's article in the same volume; also Radelet and Glenn L. Pierce, "Race and Prosecutorial Discretion in Homicide Cases," *Law & Society Review* 19 (1985):587–621.

Chapter 3

1. Étienne Dumont, the editor of Bentham's works in French, is quoted as having said that "the manuscripts from which I have extracted *La Théorie des Peines,* were written in 1775." Jeremy Bentham, *The Rationale of Punishment* (1830), p. 4. (Hereinafter cited as *Rationale.*) H. L. A. Hart, however, implies that Bentham was still working on this text in 1777. Jeremy Bentham, *An Introduction to the Principles of Morals and Legislation*, J. H. Burns and H. L. A. Hart, eds. (1970), p. xxxviii. (Hereinafter cited as *Introduction.*)

Not published until 1811, and then only in French, Bentham's *Rationale* did not appear in English until 1830. This text was edited and translated from Dumont's French version by Richard Smith. See *Introduction*, p. 158 note 1. The French and English texts are not identical; Smith observed, "I have freely used the rights of an Editor— . . . I have translated, commented, abridged, or supplied . . . [text in order to] present . . . as faithfully as the nature of things will permit, the work of Mr. Bentham." *Rationale*, p. 5.

Today this book is more readily available in the John Bowring edition of Bentham's works, in which the *Rationale* is reprinted in its entirety; see *The Works of Jeremy Bentham*, ed. J. Bowring (1843), 1:388–525 (hereinafter cited as *Works*). Future page references to the *Rationale* in the text and notes, infra, are to this version of the text. Bowring reprinted the *Rationale* not as a separate book but as though it were merely a part (namely, Part II) of a larger work of Bentham's titled *Principles of Penal Law*. See *Works*, 1:365–580.

2. "Jeremy Bentham To His Fellow Citizens of France, On Death Punishment" (1831). In an opening footnote to his essay (*Works*, 1:525), Bentham mentions the date of December 17, 1830; but the context suggests that this date is probably prior to the date of composition. At the end of the essay he appends a reprint of an article on the death penalty from a London newspaper, *The Spectator*, dated 28 May 1831; the article appeared, he says, "[w]hile these pages [were] under revision." *Works*, 1:532. This article may well be identical to the item from *The Spectator* on the death penalty cited by Bentham in his memorandum book, *Dicenda*, entry for 21 June 1831; see *Works*, 1:69. If so, one may infer that the essay itself could not have been published before mid-1831 at the earliest.

3. *Works*, 1:525–32. Henceforth, I shall cite the text of this 1831 essay in this version, with page and column references in the Bowring edition indicated in the same manner that I use for citations to his 1775 essay. (See the note at the foot of page 64.) Except in punctuation style, I detect no differences between this reprint and the text of the original pamphlet.

4. In his posthumous biography of Bentham, Bowring reports that in late 1830, Bentham undertook to address a series of letters to the French people, but "[o]nly one, however, was written." *Works*, 11:56. Bowring seems to have overlooked the pamphlet "On Death Punishment," which was in effect another of these "letters." It even opens with the words, "Hear me speak a second time!" *Works*, 1:525. Bentham styled himself in these communications to the French as a "fellow citizen" because he had in fact been made a French citizen in 1792. Charles Atkinson, *Jeremy Bentham: His Life and Work* (1905), p. 100.

5. A recent commentator notes that "[p]oisoning by means of hemlock juice (conium) seems to have been a common method of execution at Athens. Death was apparently painless but rather slow." Plato, *The Last Days of Socrates*, trans. Hugh Tredennick (1959), p. 196.

6. Jeremy Bentham, *Theory of Legislation*, 2d ed. (1874), pp. 353–54, cited in Hart, *Essays on Bentham*, p. 41.

7. Cesare Beccaria, *On Crimes and Punishments* (1764), trans. Henry Paolucci (1963), pp. 45–52. How much Bentham's argument in his 1775 essay can be said to have relied upon, or been anticipated by, this treatise I have not attempted to ascertain. For a general discussion of Beccaria's influence on Bentham, see Hart, *Essays on Bentham*, pp. 40–52. On the influence of other thinkers upon Bentham, see Leon Radzinowicz, *A History of English Criminal Law and Its Administration from 1750* (1948), 1:301–54.

8. Immanuel Kant, *The Metaphysical Elements of Justice* (1797), trans. John Ladd (1965), pp. 102–7.

9. John Stuart Mill, "Parliamentary Debate on Capital Punishment Within Prisons Bill," *Hansard's Parliamentary Debates*, 3d Series, 192 (21 April 1868), cols. 1047–55; reprinted in Ezorsky, ed., *Philosophical Perspectives on Punishment* (1972). See also L. W. Sumner, "Mill and the Death Penalty," *The Mill News Letter* 11:1 (Winter 1976):2–7, and "Mill and the Death Penalty: Some Addenda," *The Mill News Letter* 13:2 (Summer 1978):13–19.

10. See, e.g., J. J. C. Smart and Bernard Williams, *Utilitarianism For and Against* (1973), pp. 4, 9, 73.

11. *Works* 1:402–6; cf. *Introduction*, pp. 175–86.

12. In his *Rationale*, pp. 405–6, Bentham added another property, "Simplicity of Description," omitted from the list he offers in his *Introduction*.

13. *Works* 1:399–402.

14. No thorough study of Bentham's views on punishment is available, and the topic is neglected in most scholarly discussions of his life and works, despite the obvious importance he attached to his labors in this area. However, see Radzinowicz, *A History of English Criminal Law*, 1:355–96. The general continuity of Bentham's views and the relative severity of the alternatives to the death penalty he favored are discussed in Michael Ignatieff, *A Just Measure of Pain: The Penitentiary in the Industrial Revolution, 1750–1850* (1978).

15. John Austin, *The Province of Jurisprudence Determined* (1832).

16. He explicitly links the two concepts in his *Introduction* (p. 178) and in the *Rationale* (p. 404). In the latter work he discusses the "Analogy Between Crimes and Punishments" in some detail (pp. 407–9).

17. See Radzinowicz, *A History of English Criminal Law*, 1:3–79, 611–59.

18. Furman v. Georgia, 408 U.S. 238 (1972), at 362–63. For a discussion of the "Marshall hypothesis," see Bedau, ed., *The Death Penalty in America*, 3d ed. (1982), p. 66, and the works cited there.

19. *Works*, 1:396; cf. *Introduction*, p. 158, where Bentham adds in a note: "The immediate principal end of punishment is to control action . . . , that of the offender, or of others."

20. Beccaria, *On Crimes and Punishments*, pp. 46–47.

21. It is true that bills before American legislatures that would abolish the death penalty for murder by substituting a punishment of "life" imprisonment frequently prohibit parole eligibility. However, among opponents of the death penalty it is generally (though not universally) agreed that this is only a concession to political expediency and is neither necessary for public safety nor desirable on other grounds. For a more detailed discussion of alternatives to the death penalty, see Bedau, *The Death Penalty in America*, 3d ed. (1982), pp. 228–31.

22. See Thomas Perry Thornton, "Terrorism and the Death Penalty" (1976), reprinted in Bedau, *The Death Penalty in America*, 3d ed. (1982), pp. 181–85.

23. Elsewhere Bentham introduces a conception of "extraordinary punishment" and a general argument for it on utilitarian grounds. See Jeremy Bentham, *Of Laws in General*, ed. H. L. A. Hart (1970), p. 212. His argument in this passage can be seen as a forerunner of the contemporary policy in the United States to the effect that "life" imprisonment will be the normal punishment for murder except where a court finds certain "aggravating" factors to be present—for example, the offender's previous conviction of murder. Bentham's reluctance to embrace total abolition in 1775 and Mill's opposition to it a century later reflect the notion that there may be utilitarian grounds for an occasional exception to the policy of complete abolition of the death penalty.

24. See Ignatieff, *A Just Measure of Pain*, pp. 109–11.

25. It has been calculated that the cost in New York State during the 1980s of a death penalty trial alone ($1.4 million) would be more than double the cost of lifetime imprisonment in the penitentiary ($600,000). See the report prepared by the New York State Defenders Association, Inc., *Capital Losses: The Price of the Death Penalty for New York State* (1982).

26. *Works*, 1:402–3; cf. *Introduction*, p. 175.

27. *Works,* 1:403; cf. *Introduction,* pp. 175–76. One might well wonder whether there is *any* punishment such that when different people experience it they undergo exactly the same discomfort and deprivation.

28. Beccaria remarks on the importance of "certainty in punishment" as a factor in effective deterrence. Beccaria, *On Crimes and Punishments,* p. 58.

29. See Charles L. Black, Jr., *Capital Punishment: The Inevitability of Caprice and Mistake,* 2d ed. (1981).

30. See David Bien, *The Calas Affair: Persecution, Toleration, and Heresy in Eighteenth-Century Toulouse* (1960), and Edna Nixon, *Voltaire and the Calas Case* (1961). For other such cases in the eighteenth century, see John McManners, *Death and the Enlightenment: Changing Attitudes to Death Among Christians and Unbelievers in Eighteenth Century France* (1981), p. 397.

31. James Avery Joyce, *Capital Punishment: A World View* (1961), p. 75.

32. NAACP Legal Defense and Educational Fund, Inc., "Death Row, U.S.A." (1 May 1986), p. 4.

33. See Bedau, *The Courts, the Constitution, and Capital Punishment* (1977), pp. xvi–xvii, 67–68; also Bedau, *The Death Penalty in America,* 3d ed. (1982), pp. 234–41. With Michael L. Radelet, I have now completed a lengthy research project, under the title "Miscarriages of Justice in Potentially Capital Cases," a study of wrongful convictions in homicide and rape cases in the United States since 1900. A preliminary version was presented to the American Society of Criminology in 1985; the final version is published in *Stanford Law Review* 39 (1987).

34. Amnesty International, *The Death Penalty* (1979), p. 1.

35. As Justice Douglas observed, "One searches our chronicles in vain for the execution of any member of the affluent strata of this society." Furman v. Georgia, 408 U.S. 238 (1972), at 251–52. This echoes the judgment of Clarence Darrow half a century earlier: "[I]t . . . is the poor who fill prisons and who go to the scaffold." Philip English Mackey, ed., *Voices Against Death* (1976), p. 178.

36. Cf. Radzinowicz, *A History of English Criminal Law* 1:83–106, 138–64, 727–32.

37. Cf. Philip English Mackey, "The Inutility of Mandatory Capital Punishment: An Historical Note," *Boston University Law Review* 54 (1974):32–35.

38. See Edwin R. Keedy, "History of the Pennsylvania Statute Creating Degrees of Murder," *University of Pennsylvania Law Review* 97 (1949):759–77, at 772–77.

39. See Bedau, *The Death Penalty in America,* 3d ed. (1982), pp. 9–12. An adequate history of the origin and development of discretionary death sentencing in the United States has yet to be written.

40. Karl Marx, "Capital Punishment" (1853), reprinted in Lewis S. Feuer, ed., *Basic Writings on Politics and Philosophy: Karl Marx and Friedrich Engels* (1959). For a full discussion of the history of this idea, as well as for the most recent research on the "brutalization hypothesis," see William J. Bowers and Glenn L. Pierce, "Deterrence or Brutalization: What Is the Effect of Executions?" *Crime & Delinquency* 26 (1980):453–84.

41. See, e.g., Thorsten Sellin, *The Death Penalty* (1959), pp. 65–69.

42. Radzinowicz, *A History of English Criminal Law,* 1:107–37, 158–64, 555–57.

43. J. J. C. Smart and Bernard Williams, *Utilitarianism For and Against* (1973), p. 10.

44. Elsewhere, Bentham explains that a punishment is "needless" whenever "less

expensive [i.e., less painful] means" would have sufficed to achieve the same benefits; thus a punishment's "needlessness" is tantamount to what he discussed earlier under the category of "frugality." See *Works*, 1:397; cf. *Introduction*, p. 164.

45. On Howard and Bentham, see Ignatieff, *A Just Measure of Pain*, pp. 47–71. On Lucas, see André Normandeau, "Pioneers in Criminology: Charles Lucas—Opponent of Capital Punishment," *Journal of Criminal Law, Criminology and Police Science* 61 (1970):218–28.

46. As Bentham must have known from reading Beccaria, the death penalty had been abolished in Russia even prior to its abolition in Tuscany. See Beccaria, *On Crimes and Punishments*, p. 46. Apparently, however, no data were then (or are now) available concerning the volume of crime before, during, and after this Russian experiment. For a general account, see Will Adams, "Capital Punishment in Imperial and Soviet Criminal Law," *American Journal of Comparative Law* 18 (1970): 575–94.

47. Karl F. Schuessler, "The Deterrent Influence of the Death Penalty," *The Annals* 284 (November 1952):54–62.

48. Sellin, *The Death Penalty* (1959).

49. Isaac Ehrlich, "The Deterrent Effect of Capital Punishment: A Question of Life and Death," *American Economic Review* 65 (1975):397–417. For an evaluation of the methods of Ehrlich and Sellin, supra, see David C. Baldus and James W. L. Cole, "A Comparison of the Work of Thorsten Sellin and Isaac Ehrlich on the Deterrent Effect of Capital Punishment," *Yale Law Journal* 85 (December 1975):170–86.

50. See *Works* 1:403; cf. *Introduction*, p. 177.

51. See *Works* 1:405; cf. *Introduction*, p. 192.

52. See Dan W. Brock, "Recent Work in Utilitarianism," *American Philosophical Quarterly* 10 (1973):241–76.

53. Smart and Williams, *Utilitarianism For and Against*, pp. 32, 38.

54. Usually, social scientists who investigate the issues relating to the death penalty do not avow a utilitarian outlook, even though they often seem tacitly to accept it (or some neighboring form of consequentialism). One observer of the contemporary American debate over capital punishment has complained that it "has been framed largely in utilitarian terms." James Q. Wilson, *Thinking About Crime* (1977), p. 208.

55. As an instructive example, consider the argument by H. L. A. Hart in his essay, "Murder and the Principles of Punishment: England and the United States" (1957), reprinted in his *Punishment and Responsibility: Essays in the Philosophy of Law* (1968), pp. 54–89. Hart carefully lays out an ostensibly utilitarian view of the death penalty controversy (with virtually no reference, however, to Bentham's views). Yet he does not rest his own opposition to the death penalty exclusively on such grounds, as his appeals to "civilized moral thought" and the constraints it places on an unqualified "pursuit of the utilitarian goal" (which he seemingly has identified, wrongly, with reductions in the crime rate) indicate (p. 80). The result, as he rightly points out, is that his argument is only a "qualified utilitarian" criticism of the death penalty (p. 88).

56. Walter Berns, in *For Capital Punishment: Crime and the Morality of the Death Penalty* (1979), presents a strongly antiutilitarian defense of the death penalty. For antiutilitarian arguments against the death penalty, see especially Jeffrey H. Reiman, "Justice, Civilization, and the Death Penalty: Answering van den Haag," *Philosophy & Public Affairs* 14 (1985):115–48; also Robert A. Pugsley, "A Retri-

butivist Argument Against Capital Punishment," *Hofstra Law Review* 9 (1981):1501–23.

57. A conspicuous exception may be Ernest van den Haag, who has recently written, "I now find a pure deterrence theory sufficient to justify threats, punishments and their distribution." Van den Haag, "Comments on 'Challenging Just Deserts: Punishing White-Collar Criminals,' " *Journal of Criminal Law and Criminology* 73 (1982):764–68, at 764. This expresses an extreme form of consequentialism, much narrower than Benthamite utilitarianism. As is obvious from Bentham's own writings discussed in this chapter, no utilitarian would try to "justify threats, punishments and their distribution" by appeal to *nothing* but "pure deterrence." As van den Haag also notes, his adoption of a "pure deterrence" theory represents a shift in his views from those expressed a few years earlier in his book, *Punishing Criminals: Concerning a Very Old and Painful Question* (1975). There he manifestly disavowed pure utilitarianism because he wanted to defend a theory of punishment that would accommodate the claims of both "justice" and "utility" (pp. 24–25). In a yet earlier essay, van den Haag defended the death penalty on what he claimed were purely utilitarian grounds (without implying that he was such a utilitarian), but he wrongly took a utilitarian evaluation of the death penalty to be equivalent to evaluating the death penalty as a deterrent. See van den Haag, "On Deterrence and the Death Penalty," *Journal of Criminal Law, Criminology and Police Science* 60 (1969): 141–47. Elsewhere, I have pointed out in specific criticism of van den Haag that a utilitarian must consider more than deterrence; see Bedau, *The Courts, the Constitution, and Capital Punishment* (1977), pp. 46–48.

Chapter 4

1. The five justices constituting the majority wrote separate and non-concurring opinions. For discussion, see Welsh S. White, *Life in the Balance: Procedural Safeguards in Capital Cases* (1984), pp. 21–31; and Michael Meltsner, *Cruel and Unusual: The Supreme Court and Capital Punishment* (1973), pp. 289–309.

2. See Bedau, *The Courts, the Constitution, and Capital Punishment* (1977), pp. 91–93, 103–4, 111; and Meltsner, *Cruel and Unusual*, pp. 305–16.

3. Justices Brennan and Marshall are the only members of the Court who, beginning with their separate, concurring opinions in *Furman*, have continued to hold that the death penalty is per se a "cruel and unusual punishment." See Furman v. Georgia, 428 U.S. 238 (1972), at 257–306, 314–74, respectively; and their separate, dissenting opinions in Gregg v. Georgia, 428 U.S. 153 (1976), at 227–31 and 231–41, respectively.

4. See, e.g., Margaret Jane Radin, "Cruel Punishment and Respect for Persons: Super Due Process for Death," *Southern California Law Review* 53 (1980):1143–85; Radin, "The Jurisprudence of Death: Evolving Standards for the Cruel and Unusual Punishment Clause," *University of Pennsylvania Law Review* 126 (1978):989–1064.

5. See, e.g., David Bruck, "Decisions of Death," *New Republic*, 12 December 1983, pp. 18–25, and the essays by Anthony Amsterdam, Charles L. Black, Jr., Henry Schwarzschild, and John Howard Yoder, reprinted in Bedau, ed., *The Death Penalty in America*, 3d ed. (1982).

6. This includes the recent attack, on the Supreme Court's reasoning in *Furman* and subsequent anti-death-penalty rulings, by Raoul Berger, *Death Penalties: The*

Supreme Court's Obstacle Course (1982). Several commentators have criticized Berger's analysis, including Stephen Gillers, in *Yale Law Journal* 92 (1983):731–48; Margaret Jane Radin, in *Journal of Criminal Law and Criminology* 74 (1983):1115–22; David A. J. Richards, in *California Law Review* 71 (1983):1372–98. So have I in my review of Berger's book, "Berger's Defense of the Death Penalty: How Not to Read the Constitution," *Michigan Law Review* 81 (1983):1152–65. Berger's arguments do not deepen our grasp of the basic issue because, as his reviewers have made abundantly clear, he is fundamentally uninterested in all the substantive moral issues concerning the death penalty as well as the theoretical issues concerning cruel and unusual punishments. His preoccupation is with the authority and scope of federal judicial review. Accordingly, he declares that the sole issue is "the preservation of constitutional limits on power," and "not whether death penalties are socially and morally wrong." Berger, "Death Penalties and Hugo Bedau: A Crusading Philosopher Goes Overboard," *Ohio State Law Journal* 45 (1984):863–81, at 880.

7. See Larry Charles Berkson, *The Concept of Cruel and Unusual Punishment* (1975); and Malcolm E. Wheeler, "Toward a Theory of Limited Punishment: An Examination of the Eighth Amendment," *Stanford Law Review* 24 (1972):838–73.

8. Anthony F. Grannuci, " 'Nor Cruel and Unusual Punishments Inflicted': The Original Meaning," *California Law Review* 57 (1969):839–65; Richard L. Perry and John C. Cooper, eds., *The Sources of Our Liberties: Documentary Origins of Individual Liberties in the United States Constitution and Bill of Rights* (1959), pp. 222–50. For a discussion of the history surrounding the enactment of the English Bill of Rights, see Berger, *Death Penalties*, pp. 36–39, and Grannuci, supra, at 852–60.

9. But see now Jeffrie G. Murphy and Jules L. Coleman, *The Philosophy of Law* (1984), pp. 138–57; Jeffrie G. Murphy, "Cruel and Unusual Punishments," in Murphy, *Retribution, Justice, and Therapy* (1979), pp. 223–49; Burton M. Leiser, *Liberty, Justice, and Morals*, 2d ed. (1979), pp. 236–57; David A. J. Richards, *The Moral Criticism of Law* (1977), pp. 249–59; Robert Gerstein, "Capital Punishment—'Cruel and Unusual'? A Retributivist Response," *Ethics* 84 (1974):75–79; Thomas Long, "Capital Punishment—'Cruel and Unusual'?" *Ethics* 83 (1973): 214–23.

10. John Locke, *Two Treatises of Government* (1690), ed. Peter Laslett, 2d ed. (1963). Laslett argues that Locke wrote most of his Second Treatise in 1679–1680 (p. 65) and that the two treatises were published as one volume in 1689 (p. 121), even though the publication date of the first printing was listed as 1690 (p. 3).

11. The general subject of punishment has received no more than intermittent attention from Anglo-American philosophers, and there is no adequate history of the philosophy of punishment among English-speaking thinkers. See, however, James Heath, *Eighteenth Century Penal Theory* (1963); Michael Ignatieff, *A Just Measure of Pain: The Penitentiary in the Industrial Revolution, 1750–1850* (1978); Edmund L. Pincoffs, *The Rationale of Legal Punishment* (1966); Leon Radzinowicz, *A History of English Criminal Law and Its Administration from 1750* (1948). For representative discussions during the past century, see H. B. Acton, ed., *The Philosophy of Punishment: A Collection of Papers* (1969), and Gertrude Ezorsky, ed., *Philosophical Perspectives on Punishment* (1972).

12. See, e.g., Michel Foucault, *Discipline and Punish: The Birth of the Prison* (1977), pp. 1–69.

13. See, e.g., Karl Menninger, *The Crime of Punishment* (1968); cf. George Bernard Shaw, *The Crime of Imprisonment* (1946).

14. The point has been discussed often and by many courts; see, e.g., Commonwealth v. O'Neal, 369 Mass. 242 (1975), at 293–94 (Wilkins, J., concurring).

15. Note, however, that the phrases, "excessively cruel" and "unnecessary cruelty," do appear in opinions from the Supreme Court, e.g., in *Furman*, 408 U.S., at 391–93 (Burger, C. J., dissenting). It is not clear how such language avoids the criticism levied against it in the text.

16. See, however, ibid., at 378–79 (Burger, C. J., dissenting).

17. Thus the most charitable view to take of the recent proposal to adopt corporal punishment in the form of electric shock as punishment for offenders guilty of crimes against persons or property is that it is offered in this spirit. See Graeme Newman, *Just and Painful: A Case for the Corporal Punishment of Prisoners* (1983).

18. This is essentially the argument that Justice Douglas used in his concurring opinion in *Furman*, 408 U.S., at 242–45, 249.

19. Ibid., at 249–55 (Douglas, J., concurring); ibid., at 274–77, 291–306 (Brennan, J., concurring); ibid., at 309–10 (Stewart, J., concurring); ibid., at 313–14 (White, J., concurring); ibid., at 363–66 (Marshall, J., concurring).

20. Ibid., at 378–79 (Burger, C. J., dissenting and joined by Blackmun, Powell, Rehnquist, JJ.).

21. On the extent to which the usual concept of murder has built into it the idea of moral unjustifiability and inexcusability, see G. E. M. Anscombe, *The Collected Philosophical Papers of G. E. M. Anscombe* (1981), 1:3–9; and Joel Feinberg, *Doing and Deserving: Essays in the Theory of Responsibility* (1970), pp. 38–54.

22. Writing a generation ago, the leading constitutional commentator Edward S. Corwin observed, "What this clause appears to require today is that . . . there shall be *no* distinction made on the sole basis of race or alienage as to certain rights." Edward S. Corwin, *The Constitution and What It Means Today*, 12th ed. (1958), p. 268. While the example in the text is useful, it is also improbable, because no state legislature since the Civil War would have been so foolish as to enact a statute with such transparent racial bias. A more interesting and relevant question, however, is whether discretionary death penalties were enacted to supersede mandatory death penalties in the aftermath of the Civil War in the erstwhile Confederate states in order to permit all-white courts to practice racial discrimination in capital sentencing, or whether existing racial bias merely exploited sentencing discretion in capital cases that had been introduced on other grounds. I have speculated on this issue before; Bedau, "Berger's Defense of the Death Penalty," p. 1157. No historical research, to my knowledge, has yet addressed this issue. The major equal-protection attack on the death penalty for rape antedated the ruling in *Furman* by several years; see Maxwell v. Bishop, 398 F.2d 138 (8th Cir., 1968), *remanded and vacated on other grounds*, 398 U.S. 262 (1970). In *Maxwell*, the issue was not the intention of the Arkansas legislature or of the trial court to discriminate on grounds of race, but the functional equivalent thereof in outcome. The statute punishing rape with death or life at the unfettered discretion of the trial court was not, of course, racially biased on its face.

23. When Klaus Barbie (former Gestapo commandant in Lyon) was arrested and extradited from the United States to France, one observer commented, "The crimes of this man are such that there is no penalty equal to them." *The New York Times*, 8 February 1983, p. A8, col. 3. Many would surely agree that the punishment actually meted out to some such criminals (e.g., the hanging of Adolf Eichmann)

was insufficient; see Hannah Arendt, *Eichmann in Jerusalem: A Report on the Banality of Evil* (1964), pp. 248–52.

24. Niccolò Machiavelli, *The Prince* (1513), ed. Jean-Pierre Barricelli (1975), pp. 96, 101, 105.

25. A century ago, Nietzsche wrote that "pain did not hurt as much [in earlier centuries] as it does today." Friedrich Nietzsche, *On the Genealogy of Morals* (1887), trans. Walter Kaufmann and R. J. Hollingdale (1967), p. 68. Whether this claim in its context really disagrees with my claim in the text (viz., that although pain does not change, cruelty does) is unclear, since Nietzsche's epigrammatic style and conscious effort to achieve striking effects often require him to exaggerate and distort.

26. Georg Rusche and Otto Kirchheimer, *Punishment and Social Structure* (1939), p. 23. In general, see Erich Fromm, *The Anatomy of Human Destructiveness* (1973), pp. 129–81, 218–68; Barrington Moore, Jr., *Reflections on the Causes of Human Misery and Upon Certain Proposals to Eliminate Them* (1972), pp. 1–77; and Susan Jacoby, *Wild Justice: The Evolution of Revenge* (1983).

27. The distinction between a conception and a concept is explained by John Rawls, *A Theory of Justice* (1971), pp. 5 and 10, and by Ronald Dworkin, *Taking Rights Seriously* (1977), pp. 128, 134–36, 147, 226. This distinction was employed by Margaret Jane Radin in the controversy over determining "the original intention" of the framers of the "cruel and unusual punishments" clause; see Radin, review of Berger, *Journal of Criminal Law and Criminology*, at 1118.

28. Weems v. United States, 217 U.S. 349 (1910), at 378.

29. Trop v. Dulles, 356 U.S. 86 (1958), at 101.

30. See *Weems*, 217 U.S., at 368; O'Neil v. Vermont, 144 U.S. 323 (1892), at 339 (Field, J., dissenting); *In re* Kemmler, 136 U.S. 436 (1890), at 446 (burning at the stake, crucifixion, breaking on the wheel); and Wilkerson v. Utah, 99 U.S. 130 (1878), at 136.

31. On the semantics of rigid designators, see Saul Kripke, *Naming and Necessity* (1980).

32. See Berger, *Death Penalties,* pp. 43–58; also Walter Berns, *For Capital Punishment: Crime and the Morality of the Death Penalty* (1979), pp. 31–40; Ernest van den Haag, *Punishing Criminals: Concerning a Very Old and Painful Question* (1975), pp. 225–28; van den Haag, "In Defense of the Death Penalty: A Legal—Practical—Moral Analysis," *Criminal Law Bulletin* 14 (1978):51–68. Berger in particular rests his entire argument on what can be found in "the minds of the Founders" (supra, p. 44). He concludes that "the Framers did not intend 'cruel and unusual' to exclude death penalties" (p. 47). The idea of the original intention of the founders and framers can be and has been used, of course, by those who have no intention of relying on it to settle the meaning of the clause, as, e.g., in the examination of "the Framers' intent" by Justice Brennan in *Furman*, 408 U.S., at 258–69.

33. David A. J. Richards best expresses this critical interpretation; see Richards, "Constitutional Interpretation, History, and the Death Penalty: A Book Review," *California Law Review* 71 (1983):1372–98, at 1378–80.

34. Berger, *Death Penalties,* p. 47; Ernest van den Haag, in van den Haag and John Conrad, *The Death Penalty: A Debate* (1983), p. 157. Berger and van den Haag also argue that it was *not* part of the original intention that the Supreme Court, under the pretense of interpreting the clause, should be the arbiter of punishments duly enacted by state legislatures; see Berger, supra, p. 9; and van den Haag, "In Defense of the Death Penalty," p. 52.

35. See the fifth amendment (1791) and the fourteenth (1868), both of which allude to the deprivation of a person's "life" under "due process of law."

36. Act of April 30, 1790, ch. 9, 1 Stat. 115, authorizing the death penalty for murder, forgery of public securities, robbery, and rape, cited in Berger, *Death Penalties,* p. 31.

37. The first execution under federal law took place on June 25, 1790, in Portsmouth, Maine, for the crime of murder. *Cumberland Gazette,* 28 June 1790 (no page available). Three years later, four sailors were hanged on Oracoke Island, North Carolina, under federal law for the crime of mutiny. *Coastland Times* (no date or page available). I am grateful to Watt Espy for these references.

38. In my review of Berger's book, I show how an argument can be constructed that makes a ruling in the 1970s against the death penalty as per se a "cruel and unusual punishment" fully within the scope of the original intention of the framers. Bedau, "Berger's Defense," pp. 1162–64. An elaborate historical analysis of the general problem of establishing the original intention may be found in H. Jefferson Powell, "The Original Understanding of Original Intent," *Harvard Law Review* 98 (1985):885–948.

39. The best attempt to do this is still the concurring opinion in *Furman* by Justice Brennan; see *Furman,* 408 U.S., at 270–81.

40. This general approach to constitutional interpretation has been argued during the past decade or so most influentially by Ronald Dworkin; see his *Taking Rights Seriously* and his subsequent book, *A Matter of Principle* (1985).

41. See, generally, Foucault, *Discipline and Punish;* Ignatieff, *A Just Measure of Pain;* and John McManners, *Death and the Enlightenment: Changing Attitudes to Death Among Christians and Unbelievers in Eighteenth Century France* (1981), pp. 368–408.

42. See Deborah A. Schwartz and Jay Wishingrad, "The Eighth Amendment, Beccaria, and the Enlightenment: An Historical Justification for the *Weems v. United States* Excessive Punishment Doctrine," *Buffalo Law Review* 24 (1975):783–838, at 806–30.

43. There may be such a semantic connection, however, if the concept of a cruel and unusual punishment is identified with the concept of an excessively severe punishment. In this case, "excessively severe" may well be taken to mean "more severe than another available punishment." Excessive severity, however, need not be understood in this fashion.

44. In addition to the role played by alternative feasible punishments from a purely logical point of view, such punishments could play, and in a few instances already have played, an even more central role in appellate litigation. During the past decade at least one appellate court has explicitly argued that the death penalty is a "cruel and unusual punishment" today because it is not the least restrictive mode of punitive constraint available to government in pursuit of valid state objectives. See Opinions of the Justices; 372 Mass., at 912, 917 (1977), citing Commonwealth v. O'Neal, 369 Mass. 242, 251–63 (1975). This test was already applied in *Furman* by Justice Brennan, 408 U.S., at 342, 359 n.141 (Brennan, J., concurring). However, Justice Brennan did not rely upon the test to the extent that the Supreme Judicial Court of Massachusetts did. The New York State Defenders Association also relied in part on this test in its brief *amicus curiae* in People v. Smith, Amicus Curiae Brief of the N.Y. State Defenders Association at 112–30, People v. Smith, 63 N.Y.2d 41 (1984), although it did not show why this was an appropriate (much less a pre-emptive) test.

The test is also popular among philosophers quite apart from discussions of punishment and without explicit reliance on exclusively utilitarian assumptions. See, e.g., Joel Feinberg and Hyman Gross, eds., *Philosophy of Law* 2d ed. (1980), pp. 239, 596. For an application of this principle to punishment generally, see Martin R. Gardner, "The Renaissance of Retribution—An Examination of Doing Justice," *Wisconsin Law Review* (1976):781–815, at 787; Jeffrie G. Murphy, "Retributivism and the State's Interest in Doing Justice," in J. Roland Pennock and John W. Chapman, eds., *Criminal Justice: Nomos XXVII* (1985), pp. 157–58. For an application to the death penalty controversy, see Murphy and Coleman, *Philosophy of Law*, pp. 142–43; Thomas Hurka, "Rights and Capital Punishment," *Dialogue* 21 (1982):647–60.

Commentators have questioned the appropriateness of the least-restrictive-means-to-a-valid-state-interest test, chiefly because it could lead to endless judicial re-examination of the legislative judgments that traditionally establish a jurisdiction's penal policy. See, e.g., *Furman*, 408 U.S., at 395–96 (Burger, C.J., dissenting); *O'Neal*, 369 Mass., at 288–93 (Reardon, J., dissenting). For further discussion, see John E. Nowak, Ronald D. Rotunda, and J. Nelson Young, *Constitutional Law*, 2d. ed. (1983), pp. 590–99.

45. This is Ernest van den Haag's preferred rebuttal when challenged by the evidence supporting the claim of racial discrimination in the administration of the death penalty. See van den Haag, *Punishing Criminals*, p. 221; and van den Haag and Conrad, *The Death Penalty*, pp. 223–25.

46. It is, of course, possible to finesse the challenge to propose alternative standards by arguing that, according to the Constitution, it is not the Supreme Court's business to intervene in state criminal practices except in the clearest possible cases. This maneuver is exploited by many commentators, chief among whom is Berger; see Berger, *Death Penalties*, pp. 77–111. Even so, the best-known recent defenders of the death penalty have not rested with this consideration. Insofar as they address the question directly at all, they evidently believe that whatever standards are implicit in the constitutional clause barring "cruel and unusual punishments," these standards are not and have not been violated by the death penalty in the United States, either prior to *Furman* or subsequently, for any crime for which it has been lawfully imposed in this century, whether under a mandatory or discretionary statute. See Berger, *Death Penalties*, pp. 29–58, 112–52; Berns, *For Capital Punishment*, pp. 31–35, 124–27, 177–89; van den Haag, *Punishing Criminals*, pp. 157–62, 180–83, 213–15.

47. A useful if elementary exercise, and one not undertaken here, would be to use this taxonomy to reconstruct the arguments presented since 1970 to the Supreme Court as well as those used in the opinions of the Court itself, beginning with *Furman*, to show that the death penalty is (or is not) a "cruel and unusual punishment."

48. See Victor L. Streib, "Death Penalty for Children: The American Experience With Capital Punishment for Crimes Committed While Under Age Eighteen," *Oklahoma Law Review*, 36 (1983):613–41, at 613, n.6; David Bruck, "Executing Juveniles For Crimes," *New York Times*, 16 June 1984, p. 23, col. 1. In 1983 the American Bar Association voted to oppose in principle the imposition of capital punishment upon any person for any offense committed while under the age of eighteen. See ABA Juvenile Justice Letter No. 9, 11 August 1983.

49. See Eddings v. Oklahoma, 455 U.S. 104 (1982); Trimble v. Maryland, 300 Md. 387 (1984). For discussion, see Streib, "Death Penalty for Children"; and

Comment, "Capital Punishment for Minors: An Eighth Amendment Analysis," *Journal of Criminal Law and Criminology* 73 (1983):1471–1517.

50. See, e.g., Roberts (Harry) v. Louisiana, 431 U.S. 633 (1977).

51. Woodson v. North Carolina, 428 U.S. 280 (1976), at 304 (Stewart, Powell, Stevens, JJ., plurality opinion).

52. Ibid., at 302–5.

53. The exact number of death sentences overturned under the ruling in *Woodson* is unclear. One source reports that "between July 1976 and October 1979, *Gregg* and *Woodson* resulted in the vacating of approximately 414 capital sentences." Jack Greenberg, "Capital Punishment as a System," *Yale Law Journal* 91 (1982):908–36, at 916.

54. *Furman*, 408 U.S., at 249–56 (Douglas, J., concurring); ibid., at 291–95 (Brennan, J., concurring); ibid., at 309–10 (Stewart, J., concurring); ibid., at 313 (White, J., concurring); ibid., at 363–66 (Marshall, J. concurring).

55. Ibid., at 386–90, 398–99 (Burger, C.J., dissenting); see also works cited in n.2 and n.4 supra.

56. Coker v. Georgia, 433 U.S. 584 (1977).

57. Eberheart v. Georgia, 433 U.S. 917 (1977).

58. See James G. Wilson, "Chaining the Leviathan: The Unconstitutionality of Executing Those Convicted of Treason," *University of Pittsburgh Law Review* 45 (1983):99–179.

59. The idea of a canonical list of the "purposes" of punishment, or of the intentions with which a sentencer must sentence the guilty, is an illusion. A century ago, Nietzsche identified a dozen "meanings" (*Sinnen*) of punishment; see Nietzsche, *On the Genealogy of Morals*, pp. 80–81. A typical modern treatise on the criminal law identifies six "theories" of punishment; see Hyman Gross, *A Theory of Criminal Justice* (1979), pp. 385–400. Yesterday's "meanings" of punishment and today's "theories" of punishment are essentially indistinguishable from each other, as are the general "reasons" or "justifications" of punishment. Thus, Justice Marshall identifies "six purposes conceivably served by capital punishment: retribution, deterrence, prevention, . . . encouragement of guilty pleas and confessions, eugenics, and economy." *Furman*, 408 U.S., at 342 (Marshall, J., concurring). All of these "purposes" can be readily grouped under the pair of categories proposed in the text; all but the first are forward-looking or consequentialist in nature.

60. See Herbert Morris, "A Paternalistic Theory of Punishment," *American Philosophical Quarterly* 18 (1981):263–71.

61. Several independent defenses of retribution in punishment have been provided during the past decade or so; none defends *lex talionis*. See Jacoby, *Wild Justice;* Robert Nozick, *Philosophical Explanations* (1981), pp. 363–97; Richard G. Singer, *Just Deserts: Sentencing Based on Equality and Desert* (1979); Andrew von Hirsch, *Doing Justice: The Choice of Punishments* (1976); Claudia Card, "Retributive Penal Liability," *American Philosophical Quarterly Monographs*, no.7 (1973):17–35; J. P. Day, "Retributive Punishment," *Mind* 87 (1978):498–516; John Finnis, "The Restoration of Retribution," *Analysis* 32 (1972):131–35; Sidney Gendin, "A Plausible Theory of Retribution," *Journal of Value Inquiry* 1 (1970):1–16; Robert A. Pugsley, "Retributivism: A Just Basis for Criminal Sentences," *Hofstra Law Review* 7 (1979):379–405; James P. Sterba, "Retributive Justice," *Political Theory* 5 (1977):349–62; Roger Wertheimer, "Understanding Retribution," *Criminal Justice Ethics* 2 (Summer/Fall 1983):19–38; and Donald Wittman, "Punishment as Retribution," *Theory and Decision* 4 (1974):209–37. A version of *lex talionis*

is defended in Michael Davis, "How to Make the Punishment Fit the Crime," *Ethics* 93 (1983):726–52; Igor Primorac, "Life for Life: Arguments Against Capital Punishment," *Philosophical Studies* [Dublin] 29 (1982):186–201; and Primorac, "On Capital Punishment," *Israel Law Review* 17 (1982):133–50. I do not find persuasive the reasoning of Davis and Primorac insofar as it claims that retributive principles *require* the death penalty.

62. "Nothing works" is the antirehabilitative slogan bruited about by cynics and neo-conservatives alike during the past decade. It derives from the influential work of Robert Martinson, "What Works?—Questions and Answers About Penal Reform," *The Public Interest* 10 (Spring 1974):22–54. Usually overlooked is Martinson's later protest of this characterization of his views; see Martinson, "New Findings, New Views: A Note of Caution Regarding Sentencing Reform," *Hofstra Law Review* 7 (1979):243–58, at 254. For criticism, see Francis T. Cullen and Karen E. Gilbert, *Reaffirming Rehabilitation* (1982), pp. 111–12, 170–73; also Lee Seechrest, Susan O. White, and Elizabeth D. Brown, eds., *The Rehabilitation of Criminal Offenders: Problems and Prospects* (1979).

63. This conventional view of Kant is disputed in Don E. Scheid, "Kant's Retributivism," *Ethics* 93 (1983):262–82.

64. I believe that the best way to start to fit the two together is to follow the lead of H. L. A. Hart, *Punishment and Responsibility: Essays in the Philosophy of Law* (1968), pp. 8–13. On this view, the "general justifying aim" of a system or practice of punishment is broadly utilitarian (reducing the incidence of crime within a framework of a putatively just system of law), and its "distribution" or allocation is broadly retributive (those with the authority to punish do so—based on a fair procedure—with the aim of visiting it on all those and only those found guilty of a crime). Utilitarian considerations thus answer the question, "Why have a system of punishment at all?" (rather than, say, a system of forgiveness or of reward for the law-abiding). Retributive considerations answer a quite different question, "Why is this person being punished?" (rather than, say, someone else). Both answers, however, must rely on some prior or more inclusive theory of social justice that justifies the threat and use of force for noncompliance with the law. The best such theory so far is the one developed by Rawls in *A Theory of Justice.*

65. Retributivists who ignore or repudiate the death penalty, including all those cited earlier in n.61 supra, do not make it clear whether this is owing to some feature *internal* to their retributive theory, or to something else. Recently, some have even argued that retributivism can preclude the death penalty, e.g., John Conrad, in van den Haag and Conrad, *The Death Penalty,* pp. 17–28; Gerstein, "Capital Punishment—'Cruel and Unusual'?," pp. 78–79; Robert A. Pugsley, "A Retributivist Argument Against Capital Punishment," *Hofstra Law Review* 9 (1981): 1501–23; Jeffrey H. Reiman, "Justice, Civilization, and the Death Penalty: Answering van den Haag," *Philosophy & Public Affairs* 14 (1985):115–48, at 131–32. Retributivist theorists who address the death penalty typically defend it, e.g., Walter Berns, *For Capital Punishment.* Berns's vindictive-retributive argument in general is unconvincing if only because it rests on nothing more than intuitive grounds as it picks and chooses among penalties for crimes, rather than generating the fit between the two by means of something more systematic. See my review of Berns's book, *Ethics* 90 (1980):450–52, and Graham Hughes, "License to Kill," *New York Review of Books,* 28 June 1979, pp. 22–25.

66. See the brief from the attorneys for the NAACP Legal Defense and Educational Fund, Inc., in Aikens v. California, O.T. 1971, reprinted in part in Philip

English Mackey, ed., *Voices Against Death: American Opposition to Capital Punishment, 1787–1975* (1976), pp. 264–88.

67. *Furman*, 408 U.S., at 257–306.

68. Ibid., at 314–74; see also the subsequent dissenting opinions of Justice Brennan and of Justice Marshall in *Gregg*, 428 U.S., at 227–31 (Brennan, J., dissenting) and 231–41 (Marshall, J., dissenting).

69. See, e.g., Arthur J. Goldberg and Alan M. Dershowitz, "Declaring the Death Penalty Unconstitutional," *Harvard Law Review* 83 (1970):1773–1819; Gerald H. Gottlieb, "Testing the Death Penalty," *Southern California Law Review* 34 (1961):268–81.

70. See, e.g., Radin, "Cruel Punishment and Respect for Persons."

71. Judith N. Shklar, "Putting Cruelty First," in her book *Ordinary Vices* (1984), pp. 7–44.

72. Ibid., p. 8. Shklar mentions the death penalty (pp. 23–24) but does not discuss whether its use was or is cruel.

73. Martin R. Gardner, "Illicit Legislative Motivation as a Sufficient Condition for Unconstitutionality Under the Establishment Clause—A Case for Consideration: The Utah Firing Squad," *Washington University Law Quarterly* (1979):435–99; and Gardner, "Executions and Indignities—An Eighth Amendment Assessment of Methods of Inflicting Capital Punishment," *Ohio State Law Journal* 39 (1978): 96–130.

74. *New York Times*, 13 December 1984, p. A18. On electrocution generally, see the dissent by Justice Brennan to the denial of *certiorari* in Glass v. Louisiana, 53 L.W. 3773 (1985).

75. Thus, Walter Berns concedes that carrying out the death penalty by "drawing and quartering and disemboweling" would be a "cruel and unusual punishment"; Berns, *For Capital Punishment*, p. 32. Raoul Berger allows that carrying out the death penalty by means of "crucifixion or boiling in oil" was, in 1689, a "cruel and unusual punishment" and so would be today; Berger, *Death Penalties*, p. 41. Ernest van den Haag, so far as I can see, nowhere has conceded that any mode of inflicting the death penalty that a duly elected legislature has enacted is a "cruel and unusual punishment," but he seems to imply that this would be the proper judgment regarding "the death penalty for pick-pockets or car thieves"; van den Haag, in van den Haag and Conrad, *The Death Penalty*, p. 203. Elsewhere he observes that "death being the ultimate penalty, it should be inflicted only for the gravest crimes, in their most aggravated form, e.g., not for rape, but for rape-murder"; van den Haag, *Punishing Criminals*, p. 227.

76. Philip P. Hallie, *Cruelty* (1982). Hallie mentions the death penalty once (p. 97), but only in passing; he makes no attempt to decide whether the death penalty was or is a cruel punishment.

77. Ibid., p. 90.

78. Ibid., p. 34.

79. Ibid.

80. *Trop*, 356 U.S., at 100, quoted in *Furman*, 408 U.S., at 270 (Brennan, J., concurring). While my argument does not rely on the concept of human dignity, I see no reason to encourage those who, it appears, would like to see it discarded with contempt; see, e.g., Berger, *Death Penalties*, p. 118 ("empty rhetoric") and p. 118, n.30 ("arrant nonsense"). Nor would I repeat the pusillanimities others display over this idea; see, e.g., Ernest van den Haag, in van den Haag and Conrad,

The Death Penalty, pp. 262, 276, 297–98. Among defenders of the death penalty, much the most serious treatment of the concept is given by Walter Berns; see Berns, *For Capital Punishment*, pp. 24–28, 162–63. However, Berns balks at the idea that even "the vilest criminal" retains *some* "human dignity" (p. 189).

81. Herbert Morris, "A Paternalistic Theory of Punishment," p. 270.

82. See, e.g., Bruce L. Danto, John Bruhns, and Austin H. Kutscher, eds., *The Human Side of Homicide* (1982), pp. 3–20, and the extensive literature cited therein. No doubt "murderers have defective super egos, that is, they have defective consciences" (p. 7), incontestably proved by their criminal acts. But no evidence in the research surveyed in this book contradicts my claims.

83. Whether the issue has ever been tested directly is not clear, but it is clear that some of those who have studied convicted murderers agree with the statement in the text. See, e.g., Albert Morris, *Homicide: An Approach to the Problem of Crime* (1955), who writes that "the murderer's mental processes are those common to us all" (pp. 18–19). Other research has shown that the murderer is typically male, young, and in other ways like those who commit nonhomicidal crimes of violence against the person; see, e.g., Marvin E. Wolfgang, ed., *Studies in Homicide* (1967), pp. 3–4. Thus murderers as a class may well be like other violent offenders and unlike most nonviolent offenders.

84. Judge Robert J. Bork of the U.S. Circuit Court of Appeals has declared that "contractarian . . . philosophy" (along with other philosophies) is unsuitable as a "constitutional ideolog[y]" because it is "abstract," lacks "democratic legitimacy," and because "[o]ur constitutional liberties . . . do not rest on any general theory." *New York Times*, 4 January 1985, p. A16, col. 5. "Contractarian philosophy" is a generic term whose best specific instance is the moral philosophy of John Rawls; see Rawls, *A Theory of Justice*. Judge Bork also condemned what he described as the attempt to "substitute" the "abstractions of moral philosophy" for "our constitutional freedoms." Rawls and other contractarian philosophers, however, have never argued for any such "substitution." They do argue that the best theory of these "freedoms" is to be found in the "abstractions" of their "moral philosophy"— a very different matter. To dispute that thesis is, of course, to rely on some alternative way to make sense of "our constitutional freedoms," and to do that is to engage in explanation and justification of these freedoms—which, of course, is impossible without use of the "abstractions of moral philosophy," whatever they may be called.

85. It has become standard practice to distinguish several concepts of the person, the most primitive of which is that of a biological member of our species (*homo sapiens*), and the most complex of which is that of an autonomous rational claimer of rights. A useful introductory discussion will be found in Jay Rosenberg, *Thinking Clearly About Death* (1984), pp. 108–23. Various commentators have argued persuasively that a moral dimension to personhood is necessary to any adequate account of human persons; see, e.g., Daniel Dennett, "Conditions of Personhood," in Amelie Oksenberg Rorty, ed., *The Identities of Persons* (1976), pp. 175–96; also Stuart Hampshire, *Thought and Action* (1959).

86. Bruce A. Ackerman, *Social Justice and the Liberal State* (1980); Alan Gewirth, *Reason and Morality* (1978); A. I. Melden, *Rights and Persons* (1977); David A. J. Richards, *A Theory of Reasons For Actions* (1971); Rawls, *A Theory of Justice*.

87. Hyman Gross, *A Theory of Criminal Justice;* Dworkin, *Taking Rights Seriously;* Richards, *The Moral Criticism of Law;* Richards, *Sex, Drugs, Death, and the Law: An Essay on Human Rights and Overcriminalization* (1982). See also O.

H. Green, ed., "Respect for Persons," *Tulane Studies in Philosophy*, 31 (1982): 1–217.

88. The central moral philosophy around which these reflections focus is that of John Rawls. His work has received extensive and varied criticism, e.g., H. Gene Blocker and Elizabeth H. Smith, eds., *John Rawls' Theory of Social Justice: An Introduction* (1980). However, little or none of this criticism is aimed at or touches the conception of the person central to Rawls's (and allied) moral theory. For an exploration of some of these issues, see Norman Daniels, "Moral Theory and the Plasticity of Persons," *The Monist* 62 (1979):265–87.

Chapter 5

1. Attorneys for the NAACP Legal Defense Fund, Inc., brief for the petitioner, Aikens v. California, Supreme Court of the United States, O.T. 1971; reprinted in Philip English Mackey, ed., *Voices Against Death: American Opposition to Capital Punishment, 1787–1975* (1976), p. 288.

2. Ronald M. George, Deputy Attorney General of California, during the oral argument before the Supreme Court on 6 January 1972 in Aikens v. California, quoted in Michael Meltsner, *Cruel and Unusual: The Supreme Court and Capital Punishment* (1973), p. 272.

3. See Bedau, "Capital Punishment in Oregon, 1903–64," *Oregon Law Review* 45 (1965):1–39.

4. Jessie Parkhurst Guzman, "Lynching" (1952), reprinted in Allen D. Grimshaw, ed., *Racial Violence in the United States* (1969), pp. 56–59.

5. Gunnar Myrdal, *An American Dilemma: The Negro Problem and Modern Democracy* (1944), 1:554.

6. See the quarterly bulletin "Death Row, U.S.A.," published by the NAACP Legal Defense and Educational Fund, Inc., and the annual bulletin, *Capital Punishment*, published by the Bureau of Justice Statistics, United States Department of Justice.

7. Meltsner, *Cruel and Unusual*, p. 111.

8. Robert B. McKay, *Nine For Equality Under Law: Civil Rights Litigation* (1977).

9. Jack Greenberg, "Someone Has to Translate Rights Into Realities," *Civil Liberties Review* 2 (Fall 1975):104–28, at 107, 112.

10. McKay, *Nine For Equality*, p. 12.

11. Suzanne Keller, "Elites," *Encyclopedia of Social Science* (1968), 5:26–59, at 26.

12. Zachary Sklar, "Trial by Ennui," *Juris Doctor*, October 1976, pp. 16–18.

13. *New York Times*, 15 February 1977, sec. II, p. 6.

14. American Bar Association, Juvenile Justice Letter No. 9, 11 August 1983.

15. *New York Law Journal*, 10 March 1986, p. 1. The creation of the ABA's Post-Conviction Death Row Representation Project was reported in *Litigation News* 10 (Spring 1985):1.

16. Lauren Rubenstein Reskin, "Law Poll: Majority of Lawyers Support Capital Punishment," *American Bar Association Journal* 71 (April 1985):44.

17. See Meltsner, *Cruel and Unusual*, pp. 126–48.

18. See Barrett Prettyman, Jr., *Death and the Supreme Court* (1961).

19. Meltsner, *Cruel and Unusual*, pp. 233–36. See also Winthrop Rockefeller,

"Executive Clemency and the Death Penalty," *Catholic University Law Review* 21 (1971):94–102.

20. See Bedau, "*Furman*'s Wake in the Land of Bean and Cod," *Prison Journal* 53 (Spring—Summer 1973):4–18.

21. The latest such veto occurred on March 17, 1986; see *New York Times*, 18 March 1986, p. B20.

22. Chester M. Pierce, "Capital Punishment: Effects of the Death Penalty: Data and Deliberations from the Social Sciences," *American Journal of Orthopsychiatry* 45 (1975):580.

23. Alfred Blumstein, Jacqueline Cohen, and Daniel Nagin, eds., *Deterrence and Incapacitation: Estimating the Effects of Criminal Sanctions on Crime Rates* (1978), p. 9

24. Alfred Blumstein, Jacqueline Cohen, Susan E. Martin, and Michael H. Tonry, eds., *Research on Sentencing: The Search for Reform* (1983), 1:13–16, 88–110.

25. Meltsner, *Cruel and Unusual*, pp. 254–57.

26. See Frank G. Carrington, *Neither Cruel Nor Unusual* (1978).

27. Liberty Lobby, "Capital Punishment," *Georgia Journal of Corrections* 3 (August 1974):29–30.

28. John Birch Society, "Capital Punishment," *Georgia Journal of Corrections* 3 (August 1974):32–37.

29. Marvin E. Wolfgang, "The Death Penalty: Social Philosophy and Social Science Research," *Criminal Law Bulletin* 14 (1978):18–33, at 23–29; see also Meltsner, *Cruel and Unusual*, pp. 76–78, 86–89; McKay, *Nine For Equality*, pp. 11–12.

30. For an account of the origins of the Russell Sage Foundation's contributions to research in this area, see Bedau, *The Courts, the Constitution, and Capital Punishment* (1977), pp. 93, 96–97.

31. President's Commission on Law Enforcement and Administration of Justice, *The Challenge of Crime in a Free Society* (1967), p. 143.

32. National Commission on Reform of Federal Criminal Laws, *Final Report* (1970), 310–15; see also National Commission on Reform of Federal Criminal Laws, *Working Papers* (1970), 2:1347–76.

33. Laughlin McDonald, book review of Michael Meltsner, *Cruel and Unusual*, *Civil Liberties*, no. 300 (January 1974):15.

34. See Austin D. Sarat and Neil Vidmar, "Public Opinion, the Death Penalty, and the Eighth Amendment: Testing the Marshall Hypothesis," *Wisconsin Law Review* (1976):171–206.

35. Tom R. Tyler and Renee Weber, "Support for the Death Penalty: Instrumental Response to Crime, or Symbolic Attitude?" *Law & Society Review* 17 (1982):21–45; and Charles W. Thomas, "Eighth Amendment Challenges to the Death Penalty: The Relevance of Informed Public Opinion," *Vanderbilt Law Review* 30 (1977):1005–30.

36. William J. Bowers, *Executions in America* (1974). pp. 21–29.

37. See Craig Haney, ed., "Special Issue: Death Qualification," *Law and Human Behavior* 8 (1984):1–195; for a discussion of the earliest research on this issue see Bedau, *The Death Penalty in America*, 3d ed. (1982), pp. 15–21.

38. See William J. Bowers, *Legal Homicide: Death as Punishment in America, 1864–1982* (1984), pp. 193–269, 337–75; and the research reviewed by Samuel R. Gross, "Race and Death: The Judicial Evaluation of Evidence of Discrimination

in Capital Sentencing," *U.C. Davis Law Review* 18 (1985):1275–1326; also David C. Baldus, George Woodworth, and Charles A. Pulaski, Jr., "Monitoring and Evaluating Contemporary Death Sentencing Systems: Lessons from Georgia," *U.C. Davis Law Review* 18 (1985):1375–1408; and Michael L. Radelet, "Rejecting the Jury: The Imposition of the Death Penalty in Florida," *U.C. Davis Law Review* 18 (1985):1409–32.

39. See Bedau, "The Nixon Administration and the Deterrent Effect of the Death Penalty," *University of Pittsburgh Law Review* 34 (1973):557–66; Zachary Sklar, "Carter v. Ford on the Legal Issues," *Juris Doctor,* October 1976, pp. 47–50.

40. The best example so far of these forces at work is the California Death Penalty Initiative of 1972. It is briefly described in Bertram H. Wolfe, *Pileup on Death Row* (1973), p. 409; also John H. Culver, "The Politics of Capital Punishment in California," in Stuart Nagel, Erika Fairchild, and Anthony Champagne, eds., *The Political Science of Criminal Justice* (1983), pp. 14–26.

41. Meltsner, *Cruel and Unusual,* pp. 127, 136.

42. Wolfe, *Pileup on Death Row,* pp. 31–33.

43. Ibid., pp. 300, 320, 385, 408; also Meltsner, *Cruel and Unusual,* p. 284.

44. Wolfe, *Pileup on Death Row,* p. 358.

45. *Los Angeles Herald Examiner,* 9 December 1980, p. A-8.

46. *Boston Globe,* 23 February 1984, p. 35.

47. United States Congress, "Capital Punishment," *Hearings on S. 114,* Committee on the Judiciary, U.S. Senate, 97th Congress, First Session, April-May 1981, p. 34.

48. United States Congress, "Federal Criminal Law Revision," *Hearings on H.R. 1647 [etc.],* Subcommittee on Criminal Justice, Committee on the Judiciary, U.S. House of Representatives, 97th Congress, First and Second Sessions, October 1981-December 1982, Part 3, p. 2032.

49. *Boston Globe,* 23 February 1984, p. 35.

50. *Boston Globe,* 21 August 1984, p. 12.

51. *Civil Liberties,* Spring 1984, p. 5.

52. *New York Times,* 7 February 1985, p. B8.

53. *New York Times,* 13 June 1985, p. 1.

54. *Boston Globe,* 20 February 1986, p. 3.

55. *Boston Globe,* 6 May 1985, p. 3.

56. *Boston Globe,* 17 September 1985, p. 10.

57. *New York Times,* 26 September 1985, p. A19.

58. *New York Times,* 13 January 1986, p. A8.

59. Norval Morris and Gordon Hawkins, *Letter to the President on Crime Control* (1977), pp. 79, 81, 82.

Chapter 6

1. See "Oregon Abolishes Death Penalty," *Federal Probation,* December 1964, p. 81; *The Nation,* 23 November 1964, p. 367; *The New Republic,* 30 January 1965, p. 11; and *The Economist,* 13 February 1965, p. 671.

2. See Robert H. Dann, "Capital Punishment in Oregon," *The Annals* 284 (November 1952):110–14.

3. For a popular historical sketch, see Dick Pintarich and Ray Stout, "Execution Oregon Style," *Oregon Times Magazine,* June 1977, pp. 25–32.

4. Eacret et ux. v. Holmes, 215 Or. 121, 333 P.2d 741 (1958).

5. See Bedau, "Capital Punishment in Oregon, 1903–64," *Oregon Law Review* 45 (1965):1–39.

6. A copy of the full set of research papers prepared by the Oregon Council to Abolish the Death Penalty, entitled "The Case against Capital Punishment in Oregon," was deposited with the Oregon State Library in Salem, Oregon.

7. See "Capital Punishment Bill," *Portland City Club Bulletin*, 16 October 1964, pp. 52–72.

Chapter 7

1. *New York Times*, 23 February 1984, p. A18. For the debate on S. 1765, see *Congressional Record*, 8 February 1984, pp. S1129–S1163, S1189.

2. See Raoul Berger, *Death Penalties: The Supreme Court's Obstacle Course* (1982), pp. 114–15. For a different view, see the review of Berger's book by Stephen Gillers, "Berger Redux," *Yale Law Journal* 92 (1983):731–48, at 734–40.

3. Gregg v. Georgia, 428 U.S. 153 (1976), at 198–207 (Stewart, Powell, and Stevens, JJ.) and 221–26 (White, J., concurring).

4. See Jeffrey H. Reiman, "Justice, Civilization, and the Death Penalty: Answering van den Haag," *Philosophy & Public Affairs* 14 (1985):115–48; and Robert A. Pugsley, "A Retributivist Argument Against Capital Punishment," *Hofstra Law Review* 9 (1981):1501–23.

5. See especially Wendy Phillips Wolfson, "The Deterrent Effect of the Death Penalty upon Prison Murder," in Bedau, ed., *The Death Penalty in America*, 3d ed. (1982). On prison violence generally, see Robert Johnson and Hans Toch, eds., *The Pains of Imprisonment* (1982).

6. For the period up to *Furman*, see Bedau, "Deterrence and the Death Penalty: A Reconsideration" (1971), reprinted in Bedau, *The Courts, the Constitution, and Capital Punishment* (1977). For the period up to *Gregg*, see David C. Baldus and James W. L. Cole, "A Comparison of the Work of Thorsten Sellin and Isaac Ehrlich on the Deterrent Effect of the Death Penalty," *Yale Law Journal* 85 (December 1975):170–86. For the most recent evaluation, see Richard Lempert, "The Effect of Executions on Homicides: A New Look in an Old Light," *Crime & Delinquency* 29 (1983):88–115.

7. See Michael Davis, "Death, Deterrence, and the Method of Common Sense," *Social Theory and Practice* 7 (1981):145–78. Davis's essential claim has been nicely refuted by Reiman, "Justice, Civilization, and the Death Penalty," p. 144 n. 36.

8. One defender of the death penalty has been provoked by my argument here to defend the retributivist by saying, "It is enough that we extend our retributive judgments, like our moral imaginations, to the limits of what civilization permits." Jeremy Rabkin, "Justice and Judicial Hand-Wringing: The Death Penalty Since *Gregg*," *Criminal Justice Ethics* 4 (Summer/Fall 1985):18–29, at 20. Unless the moral principles that define "the limits of what civilization permits" are specified— and Rabkin leaves the reader to guess what they are—we have no way of judging whether this riposte is consistent with retributivism or relies to some extent on nonretributive principles, or whether it is mere bluff.

9. See in particular Margaret Jane Radin, "The Jurisprudence of Death: Evolving Standards for the Cruel and Unusual Punishment Clause," *University of Pennsylvania Law Review* 126 (1978):989–1064, and "Cruel Punishment and Respect for

Persons: Super Due Process for Death," *Southern California Law Review* 53 (1980):1143–85.

10. Coker v. Georgia, 433 U.S. 584 (1977), at 593 (White, J.).

11. Ibid., at 601 (Powell, J.).

12. Ibid., at 612 (Burger, C.J., dissenting).

13. See Marvin E. Wolfgang and Marc Riedel, "Race, Judicial Discretion, and the Death Penalty," *The Annals* 407 (May 1973):119–33.

14. See Trimble v. Maryland, 300 Md. 387 (1984). For a general discussion, see Victor L. Streib, "Death Penalty for Children: The American Experience With Capital Punishment for Crimes Committed While Under Age Eighteen," *Oklahoma Law Review* 36 (1983):613–41.

15. American Law Institute, *Model Penal Code and Commentaries*, pt. 2:1 (1980), §210.6.

16. See the thorough review of capital statutes in Stephen Gillers, "Deciding Who Dies," *University of Pennsylvania Law Review* 129 (1980):1–124, at 101–19.

17. Lockett v. Ohio, 438 U.S. 586 (1978), at 606 (Burger, C.J.).

18. Georgia Code Annotated. §27–25341 (b) (7) (Supp. 1975).

19. Florida Statutes Annotated, §921.141 (5) (b) (Supp. 1976–77).

20. See, for discussion, George E. Dix, "Appellate Review of the Decision to Impose Death," *Georgetown Law Journal* 68 (1979):97–161, at 112–15.

21. Godfrey v. Georgia, 446 U.S. 420 (1980), at 433 (Stewart, J.). For discussion, see John J. Donohue III, "*Godfrey v. Georgia:* Creative Federalism, the Eighth Amendment, and the Evolving Law of Death," *Catholic University Law Review* 30 (1980):13–64.

22. Texas Code of Criminal Procedure, Article 37.071 (b) (2) (Supp. 1975–76).

23. See Charles P. Ewing, " 'Dr. Death' and the Case for an Ethical Ban on Psychiatric and Psychological Predictions of Dangerousness in Capital Sentencing Proceedings," *American Journal of Law and Medicine* 8 (1983):407–28; Charles L. Black, Jr., "Due Process for Death: *Jurek v. Texas* and Companion Cases" (1976), reprinted in Black, *Capital Punishment: The Inevitability of Caprice and Mistake*, 2d ed. (1981).

24. Barefoot v. Estelle, 463 U.S. 880 (1982), at 901 (White, J.).

25. Ibid., at 917 (Blackmun, Brennan, Marshall, JJ., dissenting).

26. See David C. Baldus, Charles A. Pulaski, Jr., George Woodworth, and Frederick D. Kyle, "Identifying Comparatively Excessive Sentences of Death: A Quantitative Approach," *Stanford Law Review* 33 (1980):1–74, at 19 n. 65.

27. Note, "The Supreme Court, 1982 Term," *Harvard Law Review* 97 (1983):118–35.

28. See Gillers, "Deciding Who Dies," at 13–19; also Peggy C. Davis, "The Death Penalty and the Current State of the Law," *Criminal Law Bulletin* 14 (1978):7–17.

29. *Gregg*, 428 U.S. at 198, 204–6 (Stewart, Powell, and Stevens, JJ.) and 222–24 (White, J., concurring).

30. See David C. Baldus, Charles Pulaski, and George Woodworth, "Comparative Review of Death Sentences: An Empirical Study of the Georgia Experience," *Journal of Criminal Law and Criminology* 74 (1983):661–753; and Michael L. Radelet and Margaret Vandiver, "The Florida Supreme Court and Death Penalty Appeals," *Journal of Criminal Law and Criminology* 74 (1983):913–26.

31. Florida Statutes Annotated, §921.141 (3) (1983).

32. See Charles W. Ehrhardt and L. Harold Levinson, "Florida's Legislative Response to *Furman:* An Exercise in Futility?" *Journal of Criminal Law and Criminology* 64 (1973):10–21, at 15.

33. Profitt v. Florida, 428 U.S. 242, at 252 (Stewart, Powell, and Stevens, JJ.).

34. See Michael L. Radelet, "Rejecting the Jury: The Imposition of the Death Penalty in Florida," *U.C. Davis Law Review* 18 (1985):1409–32.

35. Gardner v. Florida, 430 U.S. 349 (1977), at 352–53.

36. This problem was addressed in Strickland v. Washington, 104 S.Ct. 2052 (1984); see also the remarks delivered by Justice Marshall at N.Y.U. Law School on 9 April 1984; and Gary Goodpaster, "The Trial for Life: Effective Assistance of Counsel in Death Penalty Cases," *New York University Law Review* 58 (1983):299–362.

37. See Craig Haney, ed., "Special Issue: Death Qualification," *Law and Human Behavior* 8 (1984):1–195; and Welsh S. White, *Life in the Balance: Procedural Safeguards in Capital Cases* (1984), pp. 33–54, 97–154. In Lockhart v. McCree, 106 S.Ct. 1758 (1986), the Supreme Court rejected attacks on "conviction-prone" capital juries that result from "death-qualification" as modified and upheld in Witherspoon v. Illinois, 391 U.S. 510 (1968).

38. See the comments of Justice Powell at the 11th Circuit Conference on 9 May 1984, as reported in *Wall Street Journal,* 10 May 1984, p. 1, col. 1.

39. See the comments of the 11th Circuit Court of Appeals on 19 June 1984, in denial of a stay of execution to Carl Shriner, as reported in *Boston Globe,* 2 September 1984, p. 16, col. 6.

40. Pulley v. Harris, 104 S.Ct. 871 (1984), *cert. denied,* at 885 (Brennan, J., dissenting).

41. For a subtle and elaborate critique of the post-*Gregg* death penalty system, which came to my attention only well after my own remarks were written, see Robert Weisberg, "Deregulating Death," *The Supreme Court Review 1983* (1984):305–395.

Chapter 8

1. State v. Quinn, 290 Or. 383 (1981), at 407. Cf. Oregon Constitution, art. I, §11.

2. Louisiana v. David, 468 So.2d 1126 (1984).

3. Ibid., at 1130.

4. Commonwealth v. O'Neal, 369 Mass. 242 (1975), at 251.

5. Ibid., at 263.

6. Ibid., at 246 n. 2.

7. State v. Green, 91 Wash.2d 431 (1979).

8. State v. Cline, 121 R.I. 299 (1979); see case comment in *Suffolk University Law Review* 14 (1980):578–600. *Cline* was cited in Shuman v. Wolf, 571 F.Supp. 213 (1983), in which a similar statute enacted in Nevada in 1977 was declared unconstitutional by the federal district court.

9. People v. Smith, 63 N.Y.2d 41 (1984). For discussion see *Albany Law Review* 49 (1985):926–66.

10. Ibid., at 78.

11. Ibid., at 91.

12. New York v. Smith, 105 S.Ct. 1226 (1985), *cert. denied;* 105 S.Ct. 2042 (1985), *reh'g denied.*

13. See in general David A. Kaplan, "State Courts Mount New Attack on Executions," *The National Law Journal,* 19 November 1984, p. 5.

14. For a fuller discussion, see Bedau, *"Furman's* Wake in the Land of Bean and Cod," *Prison Journal* 53 (Spring—Summer 1973):4–18; also Edwin Powers, "The Legal History of Capital Punishment in Massachusetts," *Federal Probation* 45 (September 1981):15–20.

15. Opinions of the Justices to the House of Representatives, 372 Mass. 912 (1977), at 917.

16. District Attorney for the Suffolk District v. Watson et al., 381 Mass. 648 (1980), at 668.

17. Ibid., at 665.

18. Commonwealth v. Colon-Cruz, 393 Mass. 150 (1984), at 161, quoting article 116, amendment to the Massachusetts constitution (1979).

19. Ibid., at 163.

20. Ibid.

21. United States v. Jackson, 390 U.S. 570 (1968), at 572, 583.

22. *Colon-Cruz,* 393 Mass., at 170. Cf. State v. Frampton, 95 Wash.2d 469 (1981), in which the Washington state supreme court ruled that the state's death penalty statute was unconstitutional under *Jackson.* A month later, the legislature replaced the unconstitutional law with one that remedied the defect; for discussion see Comment, "Refinement of Washington's Death Penalty Act," *Gonzaga Law Review* 17 (1982):715–34.

Chapter 9

1. Massachusetts Special Commission Established for the Purpose of Investigating and Studying the Abolition of the Death Penalty in Capital Cases, *Report and Recommendations* (1959), pp. 53–54.

2. Massachusetts General Laws Annotated, ch. 265, §2 (1970).

3. Furman v. Georgia, 408 U.S. 238 (1972), at 307, 308 (Stewart, J., concurring).

4. Ibid.

5. Ibid., at 396 (Burger, C.J., dissenting).

6. Ibid., at 401 (Burger, C.J., dissenting).

7. Commonwealth v. O'Neal, 369 Mass. 242 (1975), at 243.

8. For an examination of state statutes providing a mandatory death sentence, see James R. Browning, "The New Death Penalty Statutes: Perpetuating a Costly Myth," *Gonzaga Law Review* 9 (1974):651–705.

9. Fowler v. North Carolina, 285 N.C. 90 (1974), 419 U.S. 963 (1974), *restored for reargument,* 428 U.S. 904 (1976).

10. The research was part of a larger project involving three jurisdictions (District of Columbia, Massachusetts, and New York), to establish the significance for death sentencing of the statutory shift from mandatory to discretionary death sentences. See Marvin E. Wolfgang and Marc Riedel, *Race, Discretion and the Death Penalty: Final Report,* submitted to the Ford Foundation and to NILECJ in 1979. That report includes a version of the present chapter.

11. See Rollin M. Perkins, *Cases on Criminal Law and Procedure,* 3d ed. (1966), p. 88.

12. Massachusetts General Laws Annotated, ch. 6, §173 (Supp. 1975), provides

that those who have access to criminal-record information for the purposes of research shall preserve "the anonymity of the individual to whom such information relates, shall . . . [complete] . . . nondisclosure agreements . . . and shall [be subject to] such additional requirements and conditions . . . [as are] necessary to assure the protection of privacy and security interests." Consequently, the cases as described here lack any offender identification information.

13. Massachusetts General Laws Annotated, ch. 265, §24 (Supp. 1975).

14. See Commonwealth v. DiStasio, 298 Mass. 562 (1938), at 564, which held that an indictment is sufficient if it simply specifies the crime as murder and leaves the degree to be determined by the jury.

15. See Commonwealth v. McLaughlin, 352 Mass. 218 (1967), at 222 and 224, which held that the Commonwealth need not disclose the type of murder it intends to prove.

16. See Francis J. Carney and Ann L. Fuller, "A Study of Plea Bargaining in Murder Cases in Massachusetts," *Suffolk University Law Review* 3 (1969):292–307, at 305 (Table VII).

17. Massachusetts General Laws Annotated, ch. 127, §133A (1973).

18. Herbert B. Ehrmann, "The Death Penalty and the Administration of Justice," *The Annals* 284 (November 1952):73–84, at 78 (Table 2).

19. Carney and Fuller, "A Study of Plea Bargaining," pp. 297–305.

20. From the data reported by Carney and Fuller, supra, pp. 301 and 305, it is possible to construct a ratio regarding murder indictments in the two counties comparable to the ratios constructed above for convictions. Of the 212 murder indictments Carney and Fuller report for Middlesex and Suffolk counties between 1956 and 1965, 151 are in Suffolk; 71 involved a first-degree murder indictment and 80 a second-degree murder indictment. The remainder were in Middlesex, of which 20 involved a first-degree murder indictment and 41 a second-degree murder indictment. Thus the ratio of murder indictments for the two degrees of murder was 7:8 in Suffolk and 1:2 in Middlesex. This is consistent with the claim in the text that the two counties differ significantly in their treatment of criminal homicide. The evidence reported here, however, reverses their relative rigor; it is Suffolk rather than Middlesex where a murder defendant is more likely to be confronted with a first-degree indictment.

21. Carney and Fuller, supra, p. 305 (Table VII), report that in Suffolk County, 69 percent of all first-degree murder indictments are disposed of without trial; in Middlesex, it is 65 percent.

22. Ehrmann, "The Death Penalty and the Administration of Justice," p. 78.

23. Marvin E. Wolfgang and Marc Riedel, "Race, Judicial Discretion, and the Death Penalty," *The Annals* 407 (May 1973):119–33, at 125–33.

24. Commonwealth v. O'Neal, 369 Mass. 242 (1975).

25. Several bills were filed in the Massachusetts legislature during the 1976 legislative session in an attempt to provide mandatory death penalties for certain forms of murder: House No. 518 (all forms of first-degree murder); House No. 1339 (felony-murder-rape only); House No. 1341 (felony–murder–breaking-and-entering only); House No. 1343 (all forms of first-degree murder); House No. 264 (all forms of first-degree murder). None of these bills ever reached a vote in the House.

26. Charles L. Black, Jr., *Capital Punishment: The Inevitability of Caprice and Mistake,* 1st ed. (1974), pp. 40–42 (emphasis in original).

Chapter 10

1. United States v. Cox, 342 F.2d 167, at 171 (5th Cir.), *cert. denied*, 381 U.S. 935 (1965); for comment, see Charles L. Black, Jr., *Capital Punishment: The Inevitability of Caprice and Mistake*, 2d ed. (1981), p. 38.

2. Gregg v. Georgia, 428 U.S. 153 (1976), at 225 (White, J., concurring).

3. The death penalty has been subjected to more empirical and legal research in Georgia than in any other jurisdiction in the nation; see, e.g., Ursula Bentele, "The Death Penalty in Georgia: Still Arbitrary," *Washington University Law Quarterly* 6 (1985):573–646; Marvin E. Wolfgang and Marc Riedel, "Rape, Race, and the Death Penalty in Georgia," *American Journal of Orthopsychiatry* 45 (1975):658–68; Stephanie Auerbach, "Common Myths About Capital Criminals and Their Victims," *Georgia Journal of Corrections* 3 (August 1974):41–54; and sources cited infra, nn. 6, 9, 23.

4. As of 1982, Georgia had executed 851 persons, Pennsylvania 1,052, and New York 1,081; memorandum from Watt Espy, 23 August 1982, p. 1. Execution data since 1930 may be found in United States Department of Justice, Bureau of Justice Statistics, *Capital Punishment 1982* (1984), p. 15 (Table 2).

5. According to the inventory of capital statutes published by the Library of Congress in 1962, seven homicidal and twelve nonhomicidal offenses were punishable by death in Georgia. *Congressional Record* 108 (1 March 1962), p. S3301. According to the same source, Alabama was in second place with four homicidal and eight nonhomicidal capital offenses (p. S3300). An earlier inventory placed Alabama first with thirteen capital offenses, followed by Georgia with seven. Leonard D. Savitz, "Capital Crimes as Defined in American Statutory Law," *Journal of Criminal Law, Criminology and Police Science* 46 (1955):355–63, at 361 (Table II).

6. On March 11, 1986, the Georgia Board of Pardons and Paroles granted Leo Frank a posthumous pardon for the crime for which in 1913 he had been sentenced to death. See in general Leonard Dinnerstein, *The Leo Frank Case* (1968).

7. On the same day, the case apparently received its first national publicity, in the *Chicago Tribune*, 23 January 1977, p. 8, col. 1.

8. The exact number is unknown. According to one source, 491 blacks were lynched in Georgia between 1882 and 1951. See Jessie Parkhurst Guzman, "Lynching" (1952), reprinted in Allan D. Grimshaw, ed., *Racial Violence in the United States* (1969), pp. 56–59, at 57 (Table 1). Another source gives the total as 510 between 1882 and 1927; Walter White, *Rope and Faggot* (1969), p. 255 (Table VII).

9. *New York Times*, 2 August 1977, p. 12, col. 3. For discussion, see Comment, "Constitutional Law—Capital Punishment—*Furman v. Georgia* and Georgia's Statutory Response," *Mercer Law Review* 24 (1973):891–937, at 930.

10. *New York Times*, 21 April 1977, p. A18, col. 5.

11. Ibid.

12. Ibid. See also *Chicago Tribune*, 23 January 1977, p. 8, col. 1. *Newsweek*, 23 May 1977, p. 26, wrote that the defendants "could be sentenced to death if convicted." *Progressive*, May 1977, p. 40, reported that they "face the death penalty."

13. *New York Times*, 5 December 1976, p. 60, col. 1.

14. Ibid. For a slightly different account of Team Defense's strategy, see Mark Pinsky, "Legal Aid in the 'Death Belt,'" *Nation*, 26 March 1977, pp. 367–68.

15. *New York Times,* 14 August 1977, p. E17.

16. *Albany Sunday Herald,* 31 July 1977, p. A6, col. 1.

17. Quoted from an unidentified source in James L. Reston, Jr., *The Innocence of Joan Little: A Southern Mystery* (1977), p. 177.

18. Ibid., ch. 9 ("Courtney Mullin and Judge Henry McKinnon"). See also Courtney Mullin, "The Jury System in Death Penalty Cases: A Symbolic Gesture," *Law and Contemporary Problems* 43 (Autumn 1980):137–54.

19. "Life and Death: Dawson, Georgia," was broadcast in Boston on WGBH the evening of 2 August 1977; see *Boston Globe,* 2 August 1977, p. 41.

20. Quoted in Pinsky, "Legal Aid in the 'Death Belt,' " p. 367.

21. *Chicago Tribune,* 23 January 1977, sect. 1, p. 8, col. 3.

22. *New York Times,* 21 April 1977, p. A18, col. 2.

23. See Davis v. Georgia, 429 U.S. 122 (1976); Coker v. Georgia, 433 U.S. 584 (1977); Presnell v. Georgia, 439 U.S. 14 (1978); Green v. Georgia, 442 U.S. 951 (1979); Godfrey v. Georgia, 446 U.S. 420 (1980); Zant v. Stephens, 456 U.S. 410 (1982). For general criticism, see John J. Donohue III, "*Godfrey v. Georgia:* Creative Federalism, the Eighth Amendment, and the Evolving Law of Death," *Catholic University Law Review* 30 (1980):13–64. As of mid-1986, however, the statute had survived all the constitutional challenges brought against it.

24. See Bedau, "Death Sentences in New Jersey, 1907–1960," *Rutgers Law Review* 19 (1964):1–64; and Bedau, "Capital Punishment in Oregon, 1903–64," *Oregon Law Review* 45 (1965):1–39; and also Chapter 9 of this book.

25. See William J. Bowers, *Executions in America* (1974).

26. See Marc Riedel, "Discrimination in the Imposition of the Death Penalty: A Comparison of the Characteristics of Offenders Sentenced Pre-*Furman* and Post-*Furman,*" *Temple Law Quarterly* 49 (1976):261–87; Wolfgang and Riedel, "Rape, Race, and the Death Penalty in Georgia."

27. *New York Times,* 16 August 1977, p. 35, col. 5.

28. *New York Times,* 27 August 1977, p. 12, col. 4.

29. *Boston Globe,* 10 August 1977, p. 15.

30. The account of events in the courtroom that follows in the text is derived in part from personal recollection, but mostly from an unpublished transcript of the hearing and an accompanying commentary (also unpublished) prepared by Mr. Roy Brasfield Herron, now an attorney in Dresden, Tennessee. Mr. Herron kindly provided me with a draft in typescript of this material and gave me his permission to extract and paraphrase from it here, and I have done so extensively. He is, of course, in no way to be held responsible for any use or misuse of his material in the account that follows. All quotations in the text not otherwise attributed are taken from the Herron transcript of the hearing and the subsequent interviews included in his typescript.

31. In another Georgia trial court less than two years later, this same admonition was to cause Farmer no small inconvenience. In April 1979, in Blackshear, Georgia, he made the same request of the court; when he refused to withdraw it, the judge held him in contempt and he was briefly jailed.

32. In saying this, I was relying on my memory of an item that had been published a few days earlier in the *Boston Globe,* 29 July 1977, p. 38. Apparently, however, this news was in error, as no such "report" could be located. I later learned from Dr. Jan Stepan, chief librarian, Swiss Institute of Comparative Law, that there had been published a two-volume document, *Réponses à la violence: Rapport du comité d'études sur la violence, la criminalité et la délinquance,* presented on behalf of the

committee to the French government by Alain Peyrefitte, in which recommendation 103 (pp. 217–38) was the abolition of the death penalty. Four years later, on 30 September 1981, the French Senate voted to abolish the death penalty effective "probably next week." *New York Times,* 1 October 1981, p. A4.

33. Georgia Code Annotated, §26–8117, repealed in 1963.

34. "Eleven years" was in error; in a general revision of the criminal code nine years earlier (1968), the Georgia legislature abolished many capital statutes. See *Congressional Record* 108 (1 March 1962), p. S3301. See also Georgia Laws 1968 Session (adopting the Criminal Code of Georgia, effective 1 July 1969), pp. 1249–1351, especially at 1337–51 (Sec. 2, Specific Repealer).

35. The reference was to Georgia Code Annotated §27–2503 (1975 Supp.), which provides that "only such evidence in aggravation as the State has made known to the defendant prior to his trial shall be admissible [at the postconviction hearing prior to sentencing in a capital case]."

36. Neither the news sources available to me, cited in the notes supra, nor Herron, supra n. 30, mention the name of this attorney.

37. Later developments in the case during the rest of 1977 can be followed through references in the *New York Times Index.* See also *Afro-American* (Baltimore, Md.), 31 December 1977, p. 1.

38. Testifying in the afternoon of 1 August 1977 was Dr. Faye Goldberg Girsh, an expert on the effects of juror attitudes toward conviction-proneness and severity in sentencing; see Faye Goldberg, "Toward Expansion of *Witherspoon:* Capital Scruples, Jury Bias, and Use of Psychological Data to Raise Presumptions of Law," *Harvard Civil Rights–Civil Liberties Law Review* 5 (1970):53–69.

39. Mr. Forst had been expected to testify on the issue of deterrence; see Brian E. Forst, "The Deterrent Effect of Capital Punishment: A Cross-State Analysis of the 1960's," *Minnesota Law Review* 61 (1977):743–67.

40. *New York Times,* 2 August 1977, p. 12, col. 5.

41. Herron, supra n. 30, at p. 16.11. Four weeks later, Farmer was quoted as saying that "the first 60 to 70 prospective jurors from which the trial jury is to be selected is about 70 percent black, a figure that closely reflects the county proportion." *New York Times,* 29 August 1977, p. 18, col. 1. On challenging the racial composition of capital trial juries, see Millard C. Farmer, "Jury Composition Challenges," *Law and Psychology Review* 2 (1976):43–74; and Mullin, "The Jury System in Death Penalty Cases."

42. Herron, supra n. 30, at pp. 16.12–16.13.

43. See Black, *Capital Punishment,* 2d ed., pp. 15, 37–44. Black concentrates on the prosecutor's use of the death penalty as leverage in plea bargaining; this was never a factor in the Dawson Five case, however. Black does not address the more complex and elusive issues raised by the availability of the death penalty in a case such as this, concerning the propriety of the prosecutor's apparent willingness to allow the defendants, their counsel, and the public to believe that the death sentence was the preferred outcome, when in fact the prosecution either had made no such decision or was willing to reconsider it quite apart from plea-bargaining initiatives by the defense. In the original version of this chapter, I speculate on the point; see Bedau, "Witness to a Persecution: The Death Penalty and the Dawson Five," *Black Law Journal* 8 (1983):7–28, at 26–28.

44. Discussion of prosecutorial discretion by the Supreme Court in capital cases is rare. The confidence expressed by Justice White in Gregg v. Georgia (1976) and

quoted in the epigraph to this chapter is perhaps representative of the views of a majority of the current Court.

45. Gregg v. Georgia, 428 U.S. 153 (1976), at 188 ("the penalty of death is different in kind from any other punishment imposed under our system of criminal justice) (Stewart, J.); also Woodson v. North Carolina, 428 U.S. 280 (1976), at 303–4 ("death is a punishment different from all other sanctions in kind rather than degree") (Stewart, J.). The phrase "death is different" was singled out for shudder quotes by Justice Rehnquist in his dissenting opinion in *Woodson;* see 428 U.S. at 322.

46. See, e.g., Black, *Capital Punishment,* 2d ed., p. 21 ("the thesis [is] that death is different"). Cf. the remark by Camus: "capital punishment is not merely death. It is different . . ."; Albert Camus, *Reflections on the Guillotine* (1959), p. 25.

Conclusion

1. Comment, "The Cost of Taking a Life: Dollars and Sense of the Death Penalty," *U. C. Davis Law Review* 18 (1985):1221–74, at 1270.

2. See *The Gallup Report,* January-February 1986, nos. 244–45, pp. 10–16; and Phoebe C. Ellsworth and Lee Ross, "Public Opinion and Capital Punishment: A Closer Examination of the Views of Abolitionists and Retentionists," *Crime & Delinquency* 29 (1983):116–69, at 147.

3. The findings reported by Isaac Ehrlich, "The Deterrent Effect of Capital Punishment: A Question of Life and Death," *American Economic Review* 65 (1975):397–417 ("[each] additional execution . . . may have resulted . . . in 7 or 8 fewer murders") have been extensively criticized; see, e.g., Lawrence R. Klein, Brian Forst, and Victor Filatov, "The Deterrent Effect of Capital Punishment: An Assessment of the Estimates," in Alfred Blumstein, Jacqueline Cohen, and Daniel Nagin, eds., *Deterrence and Incapacitation: Estimating the Effects of Criminal Sanctions on Crime Rates* (1978), pp. 336–60. The findings reported by James A. Yunker, "Is the Death Penalty a Deterrent to Homicide? Some Time Series Evidence," *Journal of Behavioral Economics* 5 (1976).45–81 ("one execution will deter 156 murders") have been evaluated and found wanting by James Alan Fox, "The Identification and Estimation of Deterrence: An Evaluation of Yunker's Model," *Journal of Behavioral Economics* 6 (1977):225–42. The findings reported by David P. Phillips, "The Deterrent Effect of Capital Punishment: New Evidence on an Old Controversy," *American Journal of Sociology* 86 (1980):139–48 (". . . in the two weeks following a public execution the frequency of homicide drops by 35.7%") has been refuted by William J. Bowers, "Deterrence or Brutalization: What is the Truth About Highly Publicized Executions?" (unpublished). The latest claims in this vein are by Stephen K. Layson, "Homicide and Deterrence: A Reexamination of the United States Time-Series Evidence," *Southern Economic Journal* 52 (1985):68–89 ("the tradeoff of executions for murders is approximately − 18.5," i.e., each execution results in a net decrease of 18.5 murders); for criticism see James Alan Fox, "Persistent Flaws in Econometric Studies of the Death Penalty: A Discussion of Layson's Findings," testimony submitted to the Subcommittee on Criminal Justice, House of Representatives, U.S. Congress, 7 May 1986.

4. See Bowers, "Deterrence or Brutalization."

5. United States, Department of Justice, Bureau of Justice Statistics, *Capital Punishment 1984* (1985), p. 1.

6. Mark H. Moore et al., *Dangerous Offenders: The Elusive Target of Justice* (1984), and Ted Honderich et al., "Symposium: Predicting Dangerousness," *Criminal Justice Ethics* 2 (Winter/Spring 1983):3–17.

7. Jack Levin and James Alan Fox, *Mass Murder: America's Growing Menace* (1985), p. 222. The authors do not support the death penalty for serial, mass, or recidivist murderers.

8. See especially Norval Morris, *The Future of Imprisonment* (1974), pp. 85–121.

9. This is especially true of Walter Berns, *For Capital Punishment: Crime and the Morality of the Death Penalty* (1979), pp. 153ff. The arousal of "anger" is not evidence that anything morally wrong is its cause. There is no reason to believe that the punitive policies adopted by a society "angry" at criminals will be fair or effective in reducing crime. The revenge that "anger" can motivate has no claim as such to the title of just retribution. Moral indignation is another matter. As a feeling, it may be indistinguishable from anger, but its claim for a different status rests on its essential connection to a moral principle; one's indignation is aroused only if an important moral principle has been violated. Even when this happens, the policies inspired by moral indignation are not thereby guaranteed to be just or effective; and the capacity for self-deception about the legitimacy of one's indignation is legendary.

10. See Bedau, "Classification-Based Sentencing: Some Conceptual and Ethical Problems," *New England Journal of Criminal and Civil Confinement* 10 (1984):1–26; Bedau, "Prisoners' Rights," *Criminal Justice Ethics* 1 (Winter/Spring 1982):26–41; Bedau, "Retribution and the Theory of Punishment," *Journal of Philosophy* 75 (1978):601–20; Bedau, "Penal Theory and Prison Reality Today," *Juris Doctor* 2 (December 1972):40–43.

11. Ernest van den Haag, "The death penalty vindicates the law," *American Bar Association Journal* 71 (April 1985):38–42, at 42; cf. van den Haag, "Refuting Reiman and Nathanson," *Philosophy & Public Affairs* 14 (1985):165–76 ("punishment must vindicate the disrupted public order").

12. Berns, *For Capital Punishment*, p. 173.

13. See, e.g., Robert Johnson and Hans Toch, eds., *The Pains of Imprisonment* (1982).

14. See Wendy Phillips Wolfson, "The Deterrent Effect of the Death Penalty upon Prison Murder," in Bedau, ed., *The Death Penalty in America*, 3d ed. (1982), pp. 159–73.

15. Hugo Adam Bedau and Michael L. Radelet, "Miscarriages of Justice in Potentially Capital Cases," presented at the annual meeting of the American Society of Criminology, November 1985.

16. Ernest van den Haag argues, with evident complacency, that the death penalty does "lead to the unintended death of some innocents in the long run"; he goes on to add that this leaves the death penalty precisely where other things of the same sort are: "in the long run nearly all human activities are likely to lead to the unintended deaths of innocents." Van den Haag, "The death penalty vindicates the law," p. 42. This tends to obscure three important points. First, lawful activities that take "statistical lives" (e.g., coal mining) are not designed to kill anyone, whereas every death by capital punishment (whether of a guilty or of an innocent person) is intentional. Second, society permits dangerous commercial and recreational activities on various grounds—it would be wrongly paternalistic to interfere with what people choose to do at their own risk (e.g., scaling dangerous cliffs), and society

can better afford the cost of the risky activity than the cost of its complete prevention or stricter regulation (e.g., public highways crowded with long truck-trailer rigs rather than separate highways for cars and trucks). But these reasons have no bearing on the choice between the death penalty and imprisonment, unless the combined deterrent/incapacitative effects of executions are demonstrably superior to those of the alternative. Since no defender of the death penalty has sustained the burden of the proof on this point—see the papers cited in n. 3 supra—van den Haag's argument is undermined. Van den Haag's position would be less vulnerable to objection if the only executions he favored were of persons convicted of several—serial, multiple, or recidivist—murders. But he does not confine his support for the death penalty to such cases.

17. Michael Davis has recently argued that the death penalty is no more "irrevocable," in any important sense of that term, than many other punishments, including life in prison. See Davis, "Is the Death Penalty Irrevocable?" *Social Theory and Practice* 10 (1984):143–56. Insofar as he addresses the arguments I put forward in Chapter 1, to explain why death is a "more severe" punishment than imprisonment, he does not seem to disagree. On his interpretation, however, the issue of revocability has nothing to do with severity (see p. 147). Basic to his argument that the punishments of death and of life in prison are equally (ir)revocable is the idea that (a) an irrevocable punishment is such that if it is erroneously imposed on someone, then there is no way to compensate the person for the injustice he suffers, and (b) anyone has interests that are not extinguished with the end of natural life (see p. 146). But as compensating a person is not always identical with conferring a benefit on something he is interested in—rather, it is sometimes a matter of benefiting *him*, directly and in his own person—the truth of (a) and (b) do not entail that there is no difference, relative to irrevocability, that distinguishes the punishment of death from a life behind bars.

18. See Barbara Ann Stolz, "Congress and Capital Punishment: An Exercise in Symbolic Politics," *Law & Policy Quarterly* 5 (1983):157–80; and Tom R. Tyler and Renee Weber, "Support for the Death Penalty: Instrumental Response to Crime, or Symbolic Attitude?" *Law & Society Review* 17 (1982):21–45. Tyler and Weber bifurcate all defenses of the death penalty into the "instrumental" and the "symbolic." Thus a retributive defense of the death penalty is, for them, merely "symbolic." Nor do they make it clear whether the "symbolic" role of this punishment is a conscious and intentional one. Stolz is concerned with the conscious symbolism of enacting national (more precisely, federal) criminal penalties; how much of what she reports could be transferred without loss to the reasons for enactment of state death penalty laws or to the reasons the public supports executions (state or federal) is not clear.

Bibliography
of Works Cited

Ackerman, Bruce A. *Social Justice and the Liberal State*. New Haven, Conn.: Yale University Press, 1980.

Acton, H. B., ed. *The Philosophy of Punishment: A Collection of Papers*. London: Macmillan Press, 1969.

Adams, Will. "Capital Punishment in Imperial and Soviet Criminal Law." *American Journal of Comparative Law* 18 (1970):575–94.

American Friends Service Committee. *Struggle for Justice: A Report on Crime and Punishment in America*. New York: Hill and Wang, 1971.

American Law Institute. *Model Penal Code and Commentaries* (Official Draft and Revised Comments). Part 2. 3 vols. Philadelphia: American Law Institute, 1980.

Amnesty International. *The Death Penalty*. London: Amnesty International Publications, 1979.

Amsterdam, Anthony G. "Capital Punisment," *The Stanford Magazine*, Fall/Winter 1977, pp. 42–47. Reprinted in Bedau, ed., *The Death Penalty in America*, 3d ed., pp. 346–58.

Annual Chief Justice Earl Warren Conference on Advocacy in the United States. *The Death Penalty: Final Report*. Washington, D.C.: The Roscoe Pound–American Trial Lawyers Foundation, 1980.

Annual Chief Justice Earl Warren Conference on Advocacy in the United States. *A Program for Prison Reform: The Final Report*. Cambridge, Mass.: The Roscoe Pound–American Trial Lawyers Foundation, 1972.

Anscombe, G. E. M. *The Collected Philosophical Papers of G. E. M. Anscombe.* 3 vols. Minneapolis: University of Minnesota Press, 1981.

Arendt, Hannah. *Eichmann in Jerusalem: A Report on the Banality of Evil.* New York: Viking Press, 1964.

Atkinson, Charles Milner. *Jeremy Bentham: His Life and Works.* London: Methuen, 1905.

Auerbach, Stephanie. "Common Myths About Capital Criminals and Their Victims." *Georgia Journal of Corrections* 3 (August 1974):41–54.

Austin, John. *The Province of Jurisprudence Determined* (1832). London: Weidenfeld and Nicholson, 1954.

Baldus, David C., and Cole, James W. L. "A Comparison of the Work of Thorsten Sellin and Isaac Ehrlich on the Deterrent Effect of Capital Punishment." *Yale Law Journal* 85 (December 1975):170–86.

Baldus, David C.; Pulaski, Charles; and Woodworth, George. "Comparative Review of Death Sentences: An Empirical Study of the Georgia Experience." *Journal of Criminal Law and Criminology* 74 (1983):661–753.

Baldus, David C.; Pulaski, Charles A., Jr.; Woodworth, George; and Kyle, Frederick D. "Identifying Comparatively Excessive Sentences of Death: A Quantitative Approach." *Stanford Law Review* 33 (1980):1–74.

Baldus, David C.; Woodworth, George; and Pulaski, Charles A., Jr. "Monitoring and Evaluating Contemporary Death Sentencing Systems: Lessons from Georgia." *U.C. Davis Law Review* 18 (1985):1375–1408.

Barnett, Arnold. "Some Distribution Patterns for the Georgia Death Sentences." *U.C. Davis Law Review* 18 (1985):1327–74.

Beccaria, Cesare. *On Crimes and Punishments* (1764). Translated by Henry Paolucci. Indianapolis: Bobbs-Merrill, 1963.

Bedau, Hugo Adam. "Berger's Defense of the Death Penalty: How Not to Read the Constitution." *Michigan Law Review* 81 (1983):1152–65.

Bedau, Hugo Adam. Book review of Walter Berns, *For Capital Punishment. Ethics* 90 (1980):450–52.

Bedau, Hugo Adam. "Capital Punishment in Oregon, 1903–64." *Oregon Law Review* 45 (1965):1–39.

Bedau, Hugo Adam. "Classification-Based Sentencing: Some Conceptual and Ethical Problems." *New England Journal of Criminal and Civil Confinement* 10 (1984):1–26.

Bedau, Hugo Adam. *The Courts, the Constitution, and Capital Punishment.* Lexington, Mass.: D. C. Heath, 1977.

Bedau, Hugo Adam. "Death Sentences in New Jersey: 1907–1960." *Rutgers Law Review* 19 (1964):1–64.

Bedau, Hugo Adam. "Deterrence and the Death Penalty: A Reconsideration." *Journal of Criminal Law, Criminology and Police Science* 61 (1971):539–48.

Bedau, Hugo Adam. "*Furman's* Wake in the Land of Bean and Cod." *Prison Journal* 53 (Spring—Summer 1973):4–18.

Bedau, Hugo Adam. "International Human Rights." In *And Justice for All: New Introductory Essays in Ethics and Public Policy,* edited by Tom Regan and

Donald VanDeVeer, pp. 287–308. Totowa, N.J.: Rowman and Littlefield, 1982.

Bedau, Hugo Adam. "The Nixon Administration and the Deterrent Effect of the Death Penalty." *University of Pittsburgh Law Review* 34 (1973):557–66.

Bedau, Hugo Adam. "Penal Theory and Prison Reality Today." *Juris Doctor* 2 (December 1972):40–43.

Bedau, Hugo Adam. "Prisoners' Rights." *Criminal Justice Ethics* 1 (Winter/Spring 1982):26–41.

Bedau, Hugo Adam. "Punishment in a Just Society: Could It Be Eliminated?" In *The Role of Government in the United States: Practice and Theory,* edited by Robert E. Cleary, pp. 168–79. Lanham, Md.: University Press of America, 1985.

Bedau, Hugo Adam. "Retribution and the Theory of Punishment." *Journal of Philosophy* 75 (1978):601–20.

Bedau, Hugo Adam. "The Right to Life." *The Monist* 52 (1968):550–72.

Bedau, Hugo Adam. "Witness to a Persecution: The Death Penalty and the Dawson Five." *Black Law Journal* 8 (1983):7–28.

Bedau, Hugo Adam, ed. *The Death Penalty in America: An Anthology.* New York: Doubleday Anchor, 1964; rev. ed., 1967.

Bedau, Hugo Adam, ed. *The Death Penalty in America.* 3d ed. New York: Oxford University Press, 1982.

Bedau, Hugo Adam, and Pierce, Chester M., eds. *Capital Punishment in the United States.* New York: AMS Press, 1976.

Bedau, Hugo Adam, and Radelet, Michael L. "Miscarriages of Justice in Potentially Capital Cases." *Stanford Law Review* 39 (1987).

Benditt, Theodore M. *Rights.* Totowa, N.J.: Roman and Littlefield, 1982.

Bentele, Ursula. "The Death Penalty in Georgia: Still Arbitrary." *Washington University Law Quarterly* 6 (1985):573–646.

Bentham, Jeremy. *An Introduction to the Principles of Morals and Legislation* (1789). Edited by J. H. Burns and H. L. A. Hart. London: Athlone Press, 1970.

Bentham, Jeremy. *Of Laws in General* (1782). Edited by H. L. A. Hart. London: Athlone Press, 1970.

Bentham, Jeremy. *On Death Punishment.* London: Robert Heward, 1831. Reprinted in Bentham, *Works,* ed. Bowring, 1:525–32.

Bentham, Jeremy. *The Rationale of Punishment.* Translated by Richard Smith. London: Robert Heward, 1830. Reprinted in Bentham, *Works,* ed. Bowring, 1:388–525.

Bentham, Jeremy. *The Works of Jeremy Bentham.* Edited by John Bowring. 11 vols. Edinburgh: William Tait, 1838–43.

Berger, Raoul. *Death Penalties: The Supreme Court's Obstacle Course.* Cambridge, Mass.: Harvard University Press, 1982.

Berger, Raoul. "Death Penalties and Hugo Bedau: A Crusading Philosopher Goes Overboard." *Ohio State Law Journal* 45 (1984):863–81.

Berkson, Larry Charles. *The Concept of Cruel and Unusual Punishment.* Lexington, Mass.: D. C. Heath, 1975.

Berns, Walter. *For Capital Punishment: Crime and the Morality of the Death Penalty.* New York: Basic Books, 1979.

Bien, David D. *The Calas Affair: Persecution, Toleration, and Heresy in Eighteenth-Century Toulouse.* Princeton, N.J.: Princeton University Press, 1960.

Bishop, George. *Witness to Evil.* New York: Dell Publishing, 1971.

Black, Charles L., Jr. *Capital Punishment: The Inevitability of Caprice and Mistake.* New York: W. W. Norton, 1974 (1st ed.), 1981 (2d ed.).

Black, Charles L., Jr. "Reflections on Opposing the Penalty of Death." *St. Mary's Law Journal* 10 (1978):1–12. Reprinted in Bedau, ed., *The Death Penalty in America,* 3d ed., pp. 359–64.

Blocker, H. Gene, and Smith, Elizabeth H., eds. *John Rawls' Theory of Social Justice: An Introduction.* Athens: Ohio University Press, 1980.

Blumstein, Alfred; Cohen, Jacqueline; Martin, Susan E.; and Tonry, Michael H., eds. *Research on Sentencing.* 2 vols. Washington, D.C.: National Academy Press, 1983.

Blumstein, Alfred; Cohen, Jacqueline; and Nagin, Daniel, eds. *Deterrence and Incapacitation: Estimating the Effects of Criminal Sanctions on Crime Rates.* Washington, D.C.: National Academy of Science, 1978.

Bowers, William J. "Deterrence or Brutalization: What is the Truth About Highly Publicized Executions?" Unpublished.

Bowers, William J. *Executions in America.* Lexington, Mass.: D. C. Heath, 1974.

Bowers, William J. *Legal Homicide: Death As Punishment in America, 1864–1982.* Boston: Northeastern University Press, 1984.

Bowers, William J., and Pierce, Glenn L. "Deterrence or Brutalization: What is the Effect of Executions?" *Crime & Delinquency* 26 (1980):453–84. Reprinted in William J. Bowers, *Legal Homicide,* pp. 271–302.

Brock, Dan W. "Recent Work in Utilitarianism." *American Philosophical Quarterly* 10 (1973):241–76.

Browning, James R. "The New Death Penalty Statutes: Perpetuating a Costly Myth." *Gonzaga Law Review* 9 (1974):651–705.

Bruck, David. "Decisions of Death." *New Republic,* 12 December 1983, pp. 18–25.

Bruck, David. "Executing Juveniles For Crimes." *New York Times,* 16 June 1984, p. 23.

Camus, Albert. *Reflections on the Guillotine.* Michigan City, Ind.: Fridtjof-Karla Publications, 1959.

Camus, Albert. *Resistence, Rebellion, and Death.* New York: Alfred Knopf, 1961.

Card, Claudia. "Retributive Penal Liability." *American Philosophical Quarterly Monographs,* no.7 (1973):17–35.

Carney, Francis J., and Fuller, Ann L. "A Study of Plea Bargaining in Murder Cases in Massachusetts." *Suffolk University Law Review* 3 (1969):292–307.

Carrington, Frank G. *Neither Cruel Nor Unusual.* New Rochelle, N.Y.: Arlington House, 1978.

Christianson, Scott. "Corrections Law Developments: Execution by Lethal Injection." *Criminal Law Bulletin* 15 (1979):69–78.

Cohen, Haim. "Capital Punishment." *Encyclopedia Judaica* (1971 ed.), 5:142–45.

Comité d'études sur la violence, la criminalité et la délinquance. *Réponses à la violence*. 2 vols. Paris: Presses Pocket, 1977.

Comment. "Capital Punishment for Minors: An Eighth Amendment Analysis." *Journal of Criminal Law and Criminology* 73 (1983):1471–1517.

Comment. "Constitutional Law—Capital Punishment—*Furman v. Georgia* and Georgia's Statutory Response." *Mercer Law Review* 24 (1973):891–937.

Comment. "Constitutional Law—Mandatory Death Penalty Declared Unconstitutional for Failure to Permit Consideration of Any Mitigating Circumstances." *Suffolk University Law Review* 14 (1980):578–600.

Comment. "The Cost of Taking a Life: Dollars and Sense of the Death Penalty." *U. C. Davis Law Review* 18 (1985):1221–74.

Comment. "Flanagan v. Watkins et al.: Massachusetts State Death Penalty Statute Held Unconstitutional—Legal Decision or Moral Choice of the Justices?" *New England Journal of Prison Law* 7 (1981):429–70.

Comment. "Refinement of Washington's Death Penalty Act." *Gonzaga Law Review* 17 (1982):715–34.

Corwin, Edward S. *The Constitution and What It Means Today*. 12th ed. Princeton, N.J.: Princeton University Press, 1958.

Cullen, Francis T., and Gilbert, Karen E. *Reaffirming Rehabilitation*. Cincinnati, Ohio: Anderson Publishing, 1982.

Culver, John H. "The Politics of Capital Punishment in California." In *The Political Science of Criminal Justice*, edited by Stuart Nagel, Erika Fairchild, and Anthony Champagne, pp. 14–26. Springfield, Ill.: Charles Thomas Publisher, 1983.

Daniels, Norman. "Moral Theory and the Plasticity of Persons." *The Monist* 62 (1979):265–87.

Dann, Robert H. "Capital Punishment in Oregon." *The Annals* 284 (November 1952):110–14.

Danto, Bruce L.; Bruhns, John; and Kutscher, Austin H., eds. *The Human Side of Homicide*. New York: Columbia University Press, 1982.

Davis, Michael. "Death, Deterrence, and the Method of Common Sense." *Social Theory and Practice* 7 (1981):145–78.

Davis, Michael. "How to Make the Punishment Fit the Crime." *Ethics* 93 (1983):726–52.

Davis, Michael. "Is The Death Penalty Irrevocable?" *Social Theory and Practice* 10 (1984):143–56.

Davis, Peggy C. "The Death Penalty and the Current State of the Law." *Criminal Law Bulletin* 14 (1978):7–17.

Day, J. P. "Retributive Punishment." *Mind* 87 (1978):498–516.

Dennett, Daniel. "Conditions of Personhood." In *The Identities of Persons,* edited by Amelie Oksenberg Rorty, pp. 175–96. Berkeley and Los Angeles: University of California Press, 1976.

Diamond, Bernard L. "Murder and the Death Penalty: A Case Report." *American Journal of Orthopsychiatry* 45 (1975):712–22. Reprinted in Bedau and Pierce, eds., *Capital Punishment in the United States*, pp. 445–60.

Dinnerstein, Leonard. *The Leo Frank Case*. New York: Columbia University Press, 1968.

Dix, George E. "Appellate Review of the Decision to Impose Death." *Georgetown Law Journal* 68 (1979):97–161.

Donohue, John J., III. "*Godfrey v. Georgia:* Creative Federalism, the Eighth Amendment, and the Evolving Law of Death." *Catholic University Law Review* 30 (1980):13–64.

Dworkin, Ronald. *A Matter of Principle*. Cambridge, Mass.: Harvard University Press, 1985.

Dworkin, Ronald. *Taking Rights Seriously*. Cambridge, Mass.: Harvard University Press, 1977.

Ehrhardt, Charles W., and Levinson, L. Harold. "Florida's Legislative Response to *Furman:* An Exercise in Futility?" *Journal of Criminal Law and Criminology* 64 (1973):10–21.

Ehrlich, Issac. "The Deterrent Effect of Capital Punishment: A Question of Life and Death." *American Economic Review* 65 (1975):397–417.

Ehrmann, Herbert B. "The Death Penalty and the Administration of Justice." *The Annals* 284 (November 1952):73–84.

Ellsworth, Phoebe C., and Ross, Lee. "Public Opinion and Capital Punishment: A Closer Examination of the Views of Abolitionists and Retentionists." *Crime & Delinquency* 29 (1983):116–69.

Erez, Edna. "Thou Shalt Not Execute: Hebrew Law Perspective on Capital Punishment." *Criminology* 19 (1981):25–43.

Ewing, Charles P. " 'Dr. Death' and the Case for an Ethical Ban on Psychiatric and Psychological Predictions of Dangerousness in Capital Sentencing Proceedings." *American Journal of Law and Medicine* 8 (1983):407–28.

Ezorsky, Gertrude, ed. *Philosophical Perspectives on Punishment*. Albany, N.Y.: State University of New York Press, 1972.

Farmer, Millard C. "Jury Composition Challenges." *Law and Psychology Review* 2 (1976):43–74.

Feinberg, Joel. *Doing and Deserving: Essays in the Theory of Responsibility*. Princeton, N.J.: Princeton University Press, 1970.

Feinberg, Joel, and Gross, Hyman, eds. *Philosophy of Law*. 2d ed. Belmont, Calif.: Dickenson Publishing, 1980.

Finnis, John. "The Restoration of Retribution." *Analysis* 32 (1972):131–35.

Fletcher, George P. *Rethinking Criminal Law*. Boston: Little, Brown, 1978.

Forst, Brian E. "The Deterrent Effect of Capital Punishment: A Cross-State Analysis of the 1960's." *Minnesota Law Review* 61 (1977):743–67.

Foucault, Michel. *Discipline and Punish: The Birth of the Prison*. New York: Pantheon Books, 1977.

Fox, James Alan. "The Identification and Estimation of Deterrence: An Evaluation of Yunker's Model." *Journal of Behavioral Economics* 6 (1977):225–42.

Fox, James Alan. "Persistent Flaws in Econometric Studies of the Death Penalty: A

Discussion of Layson's Findings." Testimony submitted to the Subcommittee on Criminal Justice, Committee on the Judiciary, House of Representatives, 7 May 1986.

Fromm, Erich. *The Anatomy of Human Destructiveness*. New York: Holt, Rinehart and Winston, 1973.

Gaddis, Thomas E. *Birdman of Alcatraz: The Story of Robert Stroud*. New York: New American Library, 1958.

Gallup Poll. "The Death Penalty." *The Gallup Report*, nos. 244–245, January–February 1986, pp. 10–16.

Gardner, Martin R. "Executions and Indignities—An Eighth Amendment Assessment of Methods of Inflicting Capital Punishment." *Ohio State Law Journal* 39 (1978):96–130.

Gardner, Martin R. "Illicit Legislative Motivation as a Sufficient Condition for Unconstitutionality Under the Establishment Clause—A Case for Consideration: The Utah Firing Squad." *Washington University Law Quarterly* (1979):435–99.

Gardner, Martin R. "The Renaissance of Retribution—An Examination of Doing Justice." *Wisconsin Law Review* (1976):781–815.

Geis, Gilbert. "Forcible Rape: An Introduction." In *Forcible Rape: The Crime, the Victim, and the Offender*, edited by Duncan Chappell, Robley Geis, and Gilbert Geis, pp. 1–44. New York: Columbia University Press, 1977.

Gendin, Sidney. "A Plausible Theory of Retribution." *Journal of Value Inquiry* 1 (1970):1–16.

Gerstein, Robert. "Capital Punishment—'Cruel and Unusual'? A Retributivist Response." *Ethics* 84 (1974):75–79.

Gewirth, Alan. *Human Rights: Essays on Justification and Applications*. Chicago: University of Chicago Press, 1982.

Gewirth, Alan. *Reason and Morality*. Chicago: University of Chicago Press, 1978.

Gibbs, Jack P. *Crime, Punishment, and Deterrence*. New York: Elsevier, 1975.

Gillers, Stephen. "Berger Redux." *Yale Law Journal* 92 (1983):731–48.

Gillers, Stephen. "Deciding Who Dies." *University of Pennsylvania Law Review* 129 (1980):1–124.

Goldberg, Arthur J., and Dershowitz, Alan M. "Declaring the Death Penalty Unconstitutional." *Harvard Law Review* 83 (1970):1773–1819.

Goldberg, Faye. "Toward Expansion of *Witherspoon*: Capital Scruples, Jury Bias, and Use of Psychological Data to Raise Presumptions of Law." *Harvard Civil Rights–Civil Liberties Law Review* 5 (1970):53–69.

Goodpaster, Gary. "The Trial for Life: Effective Assistance of Counsel in Death Penalty Cases." *New York University Law Review* 58 (1983):299–362.

Gottlieb, Gerald H. "Testing the Death Penalty." *Southern California Law Review* 34 (1961):268–81.

Grannuci, Anthony F. " 'Nor Cruel and Unusual Punishments Inflicted': The Original Meaning." *California Law Review* 57 (1969):839–65.

Green, O. H., ed. "Respect for Persons." *Tulane Studies in Philosophy* 31 (1982):1–217.

Greenberg, Jack. "Capital Punishment as a System." *Yale Law Journal* 91 (1982):908–36.

Greenberg, Jack. "Someone Has to Translate Rights Into Realities." *Civil Liberties Review* 2 (Fall 1975):104–28.

Gross, Hyman. *A Theory of Criminal Justice*. New York: Oxford University Press, 1979.

Gross, Samuel R. "Race and Death: The Judicial Evaluation of Evidence of Discrimination in Capital Sentencing." *U. C. Davis Law Review* 18 (1985):1275–1326.

Gross, Samuel R., and Mauro, Robert. "Patterns of Death: An Analysis of Racial Disparities in Capital Sentencing and Homicide Victimization." *Stanford Law Review* 37 (1984):27–153.

Guzman, Jessie Parkhurst. "Lynching" (1952). Reprinted in *Racial Violence in the United States*. Edited by Allan D. Grimshaw, pp. 56–59. Chicago: Aldine Publishing, 1969.

Hallie, Philip P. *Cruelty*. Middletown, Conn.: Wesleyan University Press, 1982.

Hampshire, Stuart. *Thought and Action*. London: Chatto and Windus, 1959.

Haney, Craig, ed. "Special Issue: Death Qualification." *Law and Human Behavior* 8 (1984):1–195.

Harris, Louis. "Sizable Majorities Against Mandatory Death Penalty." *Harris Survey*, 10 February 1983.

Hart, H. L. A. *Essays on Bentham: Jurisprudence and Political Theory*. Oxford: Clarendon Press, 1982.

Hart, H. L. A. "Murder and the Principles of Punishment: England and the United States." *Northwestern University Law Review* 52 (1957):433–61. Reprinted in Hart, *Punishment and Responsibility*, pp. 54–89.

Hart, H. L. A. *Punishment and Responsibility: Essays in the Philosophy of Law*. New York: Oxford University Press, 1968.

Heath, James. *Eighteenth Century Penal Theory*. Oxford: Oxford University Press, 1963.

Honderich, Ted, et al. "Symposium: Predicting Dangerousness." *Criminal Justice Ethics* 2 (Winter/Spring 1983):3–17.

Hughes, Graham. "License to Kill." *New York Review of Books*, 28 June 1979, pp. 22–25.

Hurka, Thomas. "Rights and Capital Punishment." *Dialogue* 21 (1982):647–60.

Ignatieff, Michael. *A Just Measure of Pain: The Penitentiary in the Industrial Revolution, 1750–1850*. London: Macmillan Press, 1978.

Jacoby, Susan. *Wild Justice: The Evolution of Revenge*. New York: Harper and Row, 1983.

John Birch Society. "Capital Punishment." *Georgia Journal of Corrections* 3 (August 1974):32–37.

Johnson, Robert. *Condemned to Die: Life Under Sentence of Death*. New York: Elsevier, 1981.

Johnson, Robert, and Toch, Hans, eds., *The Pains of Imprisonment*. Beverly Hills, Calif.: Sage Publications, 1982.

Joyce, James Avery. *Capital Punishment: A World View.* New York: Thomas Nelson and Sons, 1961.

Kant, Immanuel. *The Metaphysical Elements of Justice* (1797). Translated by John Ladd. Indianapolis, Ind.: Bobbs-Merrill, 1965.

Kaplan, David A. "State Courts Mount New Attacks on Executions." *The National Law Journal,* 19 November 1984, p. 5.

Keedy, Edwin R. "History of the Pennsylvania Statute Creating Degrees of Murder." *University of Pennsylvania Law Review* 97 (1949):759–77.

Keller, Susan. "Elites." *Encyclopedia of Social Science* (1968), 5:26–59.

Kidder, Robert L. "Toward an Integrated Theory of Imposed Law." In *The Imposition of Law,* edited by Sandra B. Burman and Barbara E. Harrell-Bond, pp. 289–306. New York: Academic Press, 1979.

Klein, Lawrence R.; Forst, Brian; and Filatov, Victor. "The Deterrent Effect of Capital Punishment: An Assessment of the Estimates." In Blumstein, Cohen, and Nagin, eds., *Deterrence and Incapacitation,* pp. 336–60.

Kripke, Saul. *Naming and Necessity.* Cambridge, Mass.: Harvard University Press, 1980.

Kutash, I. L.; Kutash, S. B.; and Schlesinger, L. S., eds. *Violence: Perspectives on Murder and Aggression.* San Francisco: Jossey-Bass Publishers, 1978.

Layson, Stephen K. "Homicide and Deterrence: A Reexamination of the United States Time-Series Evidence." *Southern Economic Journal* 52 (1985):68–89.

Leiser, Burton M. *Liberty, Justice, and Morals: Contemporary Value Conflicts.* 2d ed. New York: Macmillan Publishing, 1979.

Lempert, Richard. "The Effect of Executions on Homicides: A New Look in an Old Light." *Crime & Delinquency* 29 (1983):88–115.

Levin, Jack, and Fox, James Alan. *Mass Murder: America's Growing Menace.* New York: Plenum Press, 1985.

Liberty Lobby. "Capital Punishment." *Georgia Journal of Corrections* 3 (August 1974):29–30.

Locke, John. *Two Treatises of Government* (1690). Edited by Peter Laslett. 2d ed. Cambridge: Cambridge University Press, 1963.

Long, Thomas A. "Capital Punishment—'Cruel and Unusual'?" *Ethics* 83 (1973):214–23.

Machiavelli, Niccolò. *The Prince* (1513). Edited by Jean-Pierre Barricelli. Woodbury, N.Y.: Barron's Educational Series, 1975.

Mackey, Philip English. "The Inutility of Mandatory Capital Punishment: An Historical Note." *Boston University Law Review* 54 (1974):32–35. Reprinted in Bedau and Pierce, eds., *Capital Punishment in the United States,* pp. 49–53.

Mackey, Philip English, ed. *Voices Against Death: American Opposition to Capital Punishment, 1787–1975.* New York: Burt Franklin & Co., 1976.

Martinson, Robert. "New Findings, New Views: A Note of Caution Regarding Sentencing Reform." *Hofstra Law Review* 7 (1979):243–58.

Martinson, Robert. "What Works?—Questions and Answers About Penal Reform." *The Public Interest* 10 (Spring 1974):22–54.

Marx, Karl. "Capital Punishment" (1853). Reprinted in *Basic Writings on Politics and Philosophy: Karl Marx and Friedrich Engels,* edited by Lewis S. Feuer, pp. 485–86. New York: Doubleday Anchor Books, 1959.

Massachusetts. Special Commission Established for the Purpose of Investigating and Studying the Abolition of the Death Penalty in Capital Cases. *Report and Recommendations.* Boston: Wright and Potter, 1959.

McDonald, Laughlin. Book review of Michael Meltsner, *Cruel and Unusual. Civil Liberties,* no. 300 (January 1974):15.

McKay, Robert B. *Nine For Equality Under Law: Civil Rights Litigation.* New York: Ford Foundation, 1977.

McManners, John. *Death and the Enlightenment: Changing Attitudes to Death Among Christians and Unbelievers in Eighteenth Century France.* Oxford: Clarendon Press, 1981.

Melden, A. I. *Rights and Persons.* Berkeley and Los Angeles: University of California Press, 1977.

Meltsner, Michael. *Cruel and Unusual: The Supreme Court and Capital Punishment.* New York: Random House, 1973.

Menninger, Karl. *The Crime of Punishment.* New York: Viking Press, 1968.

Mill, John Stuart. "Parliamentary Debate on Capital Punishment Within Prisons Bill." *Hansard's Parliamentary Debates,* 3d Series. 192 (21 April 1868), cols. 1047–55. Reprinted in Ezorsky, ed., *Philosophical Perspectives on Punishment* (1972), pp. 271–78.

Mill, John Stuart. *Utilitarianism* (1861). Indianapolis, Ind.: Hackett Publishing, 1979.

Moore, Barrington, Jr. *Reflections on the Causes of Human Misery and Upon Certain Proposals to Eliminate Them.* Boston: Beacon Press, 1972.

Moore, Mark H.; Estrich, Susan; McGillis, Daniel; and Spelman, William. *Dangerous Offenders: The Elusive Target of Justice.* Cambridge, Mass.: Harvard University Press, 1984.

Morris, Albert. *Homicide: An Approach to the Problem of Crime.* Boston: Boston University Press, 1955.

Morris, Herbert. "A Paternalistic Theory of Punishment." *American Philosophical Quarterly* 18 (1981):263–71.

Morris, Herbert. "Persons and Punishment." *The Monist* 52 (1968):475–501. Reprinted in Morris, *On Guilt and Innocence: Essays in Legal Philosophy and Moral Psychology.* Berkeley and Los Angeles: University of California Press, 1976.

Morris, Norval. *The Future of Imprisonment.* Chicago: University of Chicago Press, 1974.

Morris, Norval, and Hawkins, Gordon. *Letter to the President on Crime Control.* Chicago: University of Chicago Press, 1977.

Mullin, Courtney. "The Jury System in Death Penalty Cases: A Symbolic Gesture." *Law and Contemporary Problems* 43 (Autumn 1980):137–54.

Murphy, Jeffrie G. "Cruel and Unusual Punishments." In Murphy, *Retribution, Justice, and Therapy,* pp. 223–49. Dordrecht: D. Reidel Publishing, 1979.

Murphy, Jeffrie G. "Retributivism and the State's Interest in Doing Justice." In

Criminal Justice: Nomos XXVII, edited by J. Roland Pennock and John C. Chapman, pp. 156–64. New York: New York University Press, 1985.

Murphy, Jeffrie G. "Retributivism, Moral Education, and the Liberal State." *Criminal Justice Ethics* 4 (Winter/Spring 1985):3–11.

Murphy, Jeffrie G., and Coleman, Jules L. *The Philosophy of Law*. Totowa, N.J.: Rowman and Allanheld, 1984.

Myrdal, Gunnar. *An American Dilemma: The Negro Problem and Modern Democracy*. 2 vols. New York: Harper & Bros., 1944.

NAACP Legal Defense and Educational Fund, Inc. "Death Row, U.S.A." New York: published quarterly.

NAACP Legal Defense and Educational Fund, Inc. Brief for Petitioner, *Aikens v. California*, No. 68–5027, O.T. 1971. Reprinted in part in Mackey, ed., *Voices Against Death*, pp. 265–88.

Nakell, Barry. "The Cost of the Death Penalty." *Criminal Law Bulletin* 14 (1978):68–80. Reprinted in Bedau, ed., *The Death Penalty in America*, 3d ed., pp. 241–46.

Nathanson, Stephen. "Does It Matter if the Death Penalty is Arbitrarily Administered?" *Philosophy & Public Affairs* 14 (1985):149–64.

New Jersey. Commission to Study Capital Punishment. *Report*. Trenton, N.J. [n.p.], 1964.

Newman, Graeme. *Just and Painful: A Case for the Corporal Punishment of Criminals*. New York: Macmillan Publishing, 1983. .

New York State Defenders Association, Inc. *Capital Losses: The Price of the Death Penalty for New York State*. Albany, N.Y.: N.Y. Defenders Association, 1982.

Nietzsche, Friedrich. *On the Genealogy of Morals* (1887). Translated by Walter Kaufmann and R. J. Hollingdale. New York: Vintage Books, 1967.

Nixon, Edna. *Voltaire and the Calas Case*. New York: Vantage Press, 1961.

Normandeau, André. "Pioneers in Criminology: Charles Lucas—Opponent of Capital Punishment." *Journal of Criminal Law, Criminology and Police Science* 61 (1970):218–28.

Note. "*People v. Smith:* Mandatory Death Laid to Rest." *Albany Law Review* 49 (1985):926–66.

Note. "The Supreme Court. 1982 Term." *Harvard Law Review* 97 (1983): 118–35.

Nowak, John E.; Rotunda, Ronald D.; and Young, J. Nelson. *Constitutional Law*. 2d ed. St. Paul: West Publishing Co., 1983.

Nozick, Robert. *Philosophical Explanations*. Cambridge, Mass.: Harvard University Press, 1981.

Pennock, J. Roland, and Chapman, John W., eds. *Human Rights: Nomos XXIII*. New York: New York University Press, 1981.

Pennsylvania. Governor's Study Commission on Capital Punishment. *Report*. [n.p.], 1973.

Perkins, Rollin M. *Cases on Criminal Law and Procedure*. 3d ed. Mineola, N.Y.: Foundation Press, 1966.

Perry, Richard L., and Cooper, John C., eds. *The Sources of Our Liberties: Documentary Origins of Individual Liberties in the United States Constitution and Bill of Rights.* New York: American Bar Foundation, 1959.

Phillips, David P. "The Deterrent Effect of Capital Punishment: New Evidence on an Old Controversy." *American Journal of Sociology* 86 (1980):139–48.

Pierce, Chester M. "Capital Punishment: Effects of the Death Penalty: Data and Deliberations from the Social Sciences." *American Journal of Orthopsychiatry* 45 (1975):580.

Pincoffs, Edmund L. *The Rationale of Legal Punishment.* New York: Humanities Press, 1966.

Pinsky, Mark. "Legal Aid in the 'Death Belt,'" *Nation,* 26 March 1977, pp. 367–68.

Pintarich, Dick, and Stout, Ray. "Execution Oregon Style." *Oregon Times Magazine,* June 1977, pp. 25–32.

Plato. *The Last Days of Socrates.* Translated by Hugh Tredennick. Baltimore: Penguin Books, 1959.

Portland City Club. "Capital Punishment Bill." *Portland City Club Bulletin,* 16 October 1964, pp. 52–72.

Powell, H. Jefferson. "The Original Understanding of Original Intent." *Harvard Law Review* 98 (1985):885–948.

Powers, Edwin. "The Legal History of Capital Punishment in Massachusetts." *Federal Probation* 45 (September 1981):15–20.

Prettyman, Barrett, Jr. *Death and the Supreme Court.* New York: Harcourt, Brace & World, 1961.

Primorac, Igor. "Life for Life: Arguments Against Capital Punishment." *Philosophical Studies* [Dublin] 29 (1982):186–201.

Primorac, Igor. "On Capital Punishment." *Israel Law Review* 17 (1982):133–50.

Pugsley, Robert A. "Retributivism: A Just Basis for Criminal Sentences." *Hofstra Law Review* 7 (1979):379–405.

Pugsley, Robert A. "A Retributivist Argument Against Capital Punishment." *Hofstra Law Review* 9 (1981):1501–23.

Rabkin, Jeremy. "Justice and Judicial Hand-Wringing: The Death Penalty Since *Gregg.*" *Criminal Justice Ethics* 4 (Summer/Fall 1985):18–29.

Radelet, Michael L. "Rejecting the Jury: The Imposition of the Death Penalty in Florida." *U. C. Davis Law Review* 18 (1985):1409–32.

Radelet, Michael L., and Pierce, Glenn L. "Race and Prosecutorial Discretion in Homicide Cases." *Law & Society Review* 19 (1985):587–621.

Radelet, Michael L., and Vandiver, Margaret. "The Florida Supreme Court and Death Penalty Appeals." *Journal of Criminal Law and Criminology* 74 (1983):913–26.

Radin, Margaret Jane. Book review of Raoul Berger, *Death Penalties. Journal of Criminal Law and Criminology* 74 (1983):1115–22.

Radin, Margaret Jane. "Cruel Punishment and Respect for Persons: Super Due Process for Death." *Southern California Law Review* 53 (1980):1143–85.

Radin, Margaret Jane. "The Jurisprudence of Death: Evolving Standards for the Cruel and Unusual Punishment Clause." *University of Pennsylvania Law Review* 126 (1978):989–1064.

Radzinowicz, Leon. *A History of English Criminal Law and Its Administration from 1750.* vol. 1, *The Movement for Reform.* London: Stevens, 1948.

Ramcharan, B. G., ed. *The Right to Life in International Law.* Dordrecht: Martinus Nijhoff Publisher, 1985.

Rawls, John. *A Theory of Justice.* Cambridge, Mass.: Harvard University Press, 1971.

Reiman, Jeffrey H. "Justice, Civilization, and the Death Penalty: Answering van den Haag." *Philosophy & Public Affairs* 14 (1985):115–48.

Reskin, Lauren Rubenstein. "Law Poll: Majority of Lawyers Support Capital Punishment." *American Bar Association Journal* 71 (April 1985):44.

Reston, James L., Jr. *The Innocence of Joan Little: A Southern Mystery.* New York: New York Times Books, 1977.

Richards, David A. J. "Constitutional Interpretation, History, and the Death Penalty: A Book Review." *California Law Review* 71 (1983):1372–98.

Richards, David A. J. *The Moral Criticism of Law.* Belmont, Calif.: Dickenson Publishing, 1977.

Richards, David A. J. *Sex, Drugs, Death, and the Law: An Essay on Human Rights and Overcriminalization.* Totowa, N.J.: Rowman and Littlefield, 1982.

Richards, David A. J. *A Theory of Reasons for Actions.* Oxford: Clarendon Press, 1971.

Riedel, Marc. "Discrimination in the Imposition of the Death Penalty: A Comparison of the Characteristics of Offenders Sentenced Pre-*Furman* and Post-*Furman.*" *Temple Law Quarterly* 49 (1976):261–87.

Rockefeller, Winthrop. "Executive Clemency and the Death Penalty." *Catholic University Law Review* 21 (1971):94–102.

Rosenberg, Jay. *Thinking Clearly About Death.* Englewood Cliffs, N.J.: Prentice-Hall, 1984.

Ross, W. D. *The Right and the Good.* Oxford: Clarendon Press, 1930.

Rusche, Georg, and Kirchheimer, Otto. *Punishment and Social Structure.* New York: Columbia University Press, 1939.

Sarat, Austin D., and Vidmar, Neil. "Public Opinion, the Death Penalty, and the Eighth Amendment: Testing the Marshall Hypothesis." *Wisconsin Law Review* (1976):171–206. Reprinted in Bedau and Pierce, eds., *Capital Punishment in the United States,* pp. 190–223.

Savitz, Leonard D. "Capital Crimes as Defined in American Statutory Law." *Journal of Criminal Law, Criminology and Police Science* 46 (1956):355–63.

Scheid, Don E. "Kant's Retributivism." *Ethics* 93 (1983):262–82.

Schuessler, Karl F. "The Deterrent Influence of the Death Penalty." *The Annals* 284 (November 1952):54–62.

Schwartz, Deborah A., and Wishingrad, Jay. "The Eighth Amendment, Beccaria, and the Enlightenment: An Historical Justification for the *Weems v. United States* Excessive Punishment Doctrine." *Buffalo Law Review* 24 (1975):783–838.

Schwarzschild, Henry. "In Opposition to Death Penalty Legislation." In Bedau, ed., *The Death Penalty in America,* 3d ed., pp. 364–70.

Sechrest, Lee; White, Susan O.; and Brown, Elizabeth D., eds. *The Rehabilitation of Criminal Offenders: Problems and Prospects.* Washington, D.C.: National Academy of Sciences, 1979.

Sellin, Thorsten. *The Death Penalty.* Philadelphia: American Law Institute, 1959.

Sellin, Thorsten. *The Penalty of Death.* Beverly Hills, Calif.: Sage Publications, 1980.

Shaw, George Bernard. *The Crime of Imprisonment.* New York: Philosophical Library, 1946.

Shklar, Judith N. *Ordinary Vices.* Cambridge, Mass.: Harvard University Press, 1984.

Singer, Richard G. *Just Deserts: Sentencing Based on Equality and Desert.* Cambridge, Mass.: Ballinger Publishing, 1979.

Sklar, Zachary. "Carter v. Ford on the Legal Issues." *Juris Doctor,* October 1976, pp. 47–50.

Sklar, Zachary. "Trial by Ennui." *Juris Doctor,* October 1976, pp. 16–18.

Smart, J. J. C., and Williams, Bernard. *Utilitarianism For and Against.* Cambridge: Cambridge University Press, 1973.

Solomon, George F. "Capital Punishment as Suicide and as Murder." *American Journal of Orthopsychiatry* 45 (1975):701–11. Reprinted in Bedau and Pierce, eds., *Capital Punishment in the United States,* pp. 432–44.

Sterba, James P. "Retributive Justice." *Political Theory* 5 (1977):349–62.

Stolz, Barbara Ann. "Congress and Capital Punishment: An Exercise in Symbolic Politics." *Law & Policy Quarterly* 5 (1983):157–80.

Streib, Victor L. "Death Penalty for Children: The American Experience With Capital Punishment for Crimes Committed While Under Age Eighteen." *Oklahoma Law Review* 36 (1983):613–41.

Sumner, L. W. "Mill and the Death Penalty." *The Mill News Letter* 11:1 (Winter 1976):2–7.

Sumner, L. W. "Mill and the Death Penalty: Some Addenda." *The Mill News Letter* 13:2 (Summer 1976):13–19.

Thomas, Charles W. "Eighth Amendment Challenges to the Death Penalty: The Relevance of Informed Public Opinion." *Vanderbilt Law Review* 30 (1977):1005–30.

Thornton, Thomas Perry. "Terrorism and the Death Penalty." *America,* 11 December 1976, pp. 410–12. Reprinted in Bedau, ed., *The Death Penalty in America,* 3d ed., pp. 181–85.

Twentieth Century Fund Task Force on Criminal Sentencing. *Fair and Certain Punishment.* New York: McGraw-Hill, 1976.

Tyler, Tom R., and Weber, Renee. "Support for the Death Penalty: Instrumental Response to Crime, or Symbolic Attitude?" *Law & Society Review* 17 (1982):21–45.

United States. Congress. "Capital Punishment." *Hearings on S. 114.* Committee on the Judiciary, U. S. Senate, 97th Congress, First Session, April–May 1981. Washington, D.C.: Government Printing Office, 1981.

United States. Congress. "Federal Criminal Law Revision." *Hearings on H.R. 1647* [etc.]. Subcommittee on Criminal Justice, Committee on the Judiciary, House of Representatives, 97th Congress. Washington, D.C.: Government Printing Office, 1982.

United States. Department of Justice. Bureau of Justice Statistics. *Bulletin: Capital Punishment*. Washington, D.C.: published annually.

United States. Department of Justice. Federal Bureau of Investigation. *Uniform Crime Reports*. Washington, D.C.: published annually.

United States. National Commission on Reform of Federal Criminal Laws. *Final Report*. Washington, D.C.: Government Printing Office, 1970.

United States. National Commission on Reform of Federal Criminal Laws. *Working Papers*. 2 vols. Washington, D.C.: Government Printing Office, 1970.

United States. President's Commission on Law Enforcement and Administration of Justice. *The Challenge of Crime in a Free Society*. Washington, D.C.: Government Printing Office, 1967.

van den Haag, Ernest. "Comments on 'Challenging Just Deserts: Punishing White-Collar Criminals.' " *Journal of Criminal Law and Criminology* 73 (1982): 764–68.

van den Haag, Ernest. "The death penalty vindicates the law." *American Bar Association Journal* 71 (April 1985):38–42.

van den Haag, Ernest. "In Defense of the Death Penalty: A Legal—Practical—Moral Analysis." *Criminal Law Bulletin* 14 (1978):51–68.

van den Haag, Ernest. "On Deterrence and the Death Penalty." *Journal of Criminal Law, Criminology and Police Science* 60 (1969):141–47.

van den Haag, Ernest. *Punishing Criminals: Concerning a Very Old and Painful Question*. New York: Basic Books, 1975.

van den Haag, Ernest. "Refuting Reiman and Nathanson." *Philosophy & Public Affairs* 14 (1985):165–76.

van den Haag, Ernest, and Conrad, John. *The Death Penalty: A Debate*. New York: Plenum Press, 1983.

von Hirsch, Andrew. *Doing Justice: The Choice of Punishments*. New York: Hill and Wang, 1976.

Weisberg, Robert. "Deregulating Death." *The Supreme Court Review 1983* (1984):305–395.

Wertheimer, Roger. "Understanding Retribution." *Criminal Justice Ethics* 2 (Summer/Fall 1983):19–38.

Wheeler, Malcolm E. "Toward a Theory of Limited Punishment: An Examination of the Eighth Amendment." *Stanford Law Review* 24 (1972):838–73.

White, Walter. *Rope and Faggot: A Biography of Judge Lynch*. New York: Arno Press, 1969.

White, Welsh S. *Life in the Balance: Procedural Safeguards in Capital Cases*. Ann Arbor: University of Michigan Press, 1984.

Wilson, James G. "Chaining the Leviathan: The Unconstitutionality of Executing Those Convicted of Treason." *University of Pittsburgh Law Review* 45 (1983):99–179.

Wilson, James Q. *Thinking About Crime*. New York: Vintage Books, 1977.

Wittman, Donald. "Punishment as Retribution." *Theory and Decision* 4 (1974):209–37.

Wolfe, Bertram H. *Pileup on Death Row*. Garden City: Doubleday, 1973.

Wolfgang, Marvin E. "The Death Penalty: Social Philosophy and Social Science Research." *Criminal Law Bulletin* 14 (1978):18–33.

Wolfgang, Marvin E., ed. *Studies in Homicide*. New York: Harper & Row, 1967.

Wolfgang, Marvin E., and Riedel, Marc. *Race, Discretion and the Death Penalty: Final Report*. Submitted to the Ford Foundation and to NILECJ, 1979.

Wolfgang, Marvin E., and Riedel, Marc. "Race, Judicial Discretion, and the Death Penalty." *The Annals* 407 (May 1973):119–33.

Wolfgang, Marvin E., and Riedel, Marc. "Rape, Race, and the Death Penalty in Georgia." *American Journal of Orthopsychiatry* 45 (1975):658–68. Reprinted in Bedau and Pierce, eds., *Capital Punishment in the United States*, pp. 99–121.

Wolfson, Wendy Phillips. "The Deterrent Effect of the Death Penalty upon Prison Murder." In Bedau, ed., *The Death Penalty in America*, 3d ed., pp. 159–73.

Yoder, John Howard. "A Christian Perspective." In *The Interpreter*, January 1979, pp. 3–6. Reprinted in Bedau, ed., *The Death Penalty in America*, 3d ed., pp. 370–75.

Yunker, James A. "Is the Death Penalty a Deterrent to Homicide? Some Time Series Evidence." *Journal of Behavioral Economics* 5 (1976):45–81.

Table of Cases

Index

299

Index

Lucas, C., 86
Lynching, 50, 132, 220

McClesky v. Kemp, 182
McGahuey, L. S., 157
McGautha v. California, 40, 139, 166
Machiavelli, N., 102
McLennan, J., 158
MacNamara, D. E. J., 160
Maiming, 29, 109
Mandatory death penalty: administration of, 13–14; attempts to enact, 150; constitutionality of, 57, 187–90; for crimes by prisoners, 189, 190, 241; desirability of, 57; as discretionary justice, 214; for felony-murder-rape, 195–216; history of, 57, 84; public opinion on, 57
Manslaughter, 40
Manson, C., 28, 74
Marshall, T., 72, 122, 136, 138, 166
Marx, K., 84
Maryland, 140
Massachusetts, 7, 93, 187–89, 190–94, 195–216
Maxwell v. Bishop, 139, 165
Meese, E., III, 152
Mengele, J., 101
Mercy, 56, 57
Michigan, 112, 231, 246
Mill, J. S., 19, 20, 66–67, 93
Mills, C. W., 137
Miscarriage of justice, 80–81, 245
Missouri, 131
Mitchell, A., 150, 152
Mitigating circumstances, 177–78, 189
Model Penal Code, 138, 177
Mondale, W., 151
Monge, L., 148
Montesquieu, 66, 109
Moral Majority, 49, 153
Mullin, C., 220, 223, 224–25
Murder, *see also* Manslaughter; definition of, 99, 258; degrees of, 40, 84, 177; as deserving death, 39; deterrence of, 34, 239–41; vs. execution as cruel, 41–42; felony-, 176; for hire, 172; by life-term prisoners, 172, 189, 190; risk of, 33; suicide by, 84; types of, 239–40
Murderers: as deserving death, 12, 16–17, 39–42; as forfeiting life, 12–15, 63;

genocidal, 11; moral status of, 126–27, 265; motivations of, 17; parole of, 59, 241; recidivism among, 32–33, 59, 75, 241–42
Myrdal, G., 132

NAACP Legal Defense and Educational Fund, Inc. (LDF), 134–35, 136–37, 145, 153
Nation, 143
National Association for the Advancement of Colored People, 142
National Association of Attorneys General, 137
National Bar Association, 137
National Coalition Against the Death Penalty, 135, 137
National Commission on Reform of Federal Criminal Laws, 144
National Council of Churches, 142
National Council on Crime and Delinquency, 141
National District Attorneys Association, 137
National Lawyers Guild, 137
National Legal Aid and Defender Association, 137, 142
National Research Council, 141–42
National Review, 142
Natural rights, *see* Rights
Nazis, 13
New Jersey, 140, 144
New Mexico, 140
New Republic, 143–44
New York, 7, 140, 187, 189, 190, 219
New York Times, 144, 219
New York v. Smith, 271
Nixon, R. M., 149, 151

O'Connor, S. D., 139
Offenses, capital and noncapital, *see specific crimes*
O'Neil v. Vermont, 259
Opinion polls, *see* Public opinion
Opinions of the Justices to the House of Representatives, 191
Oregon, 13, 129–30, 135, 155–63, 186, 226
Oregon Council of Churches, 160

304